Shojo Beat

Stepping on Roses

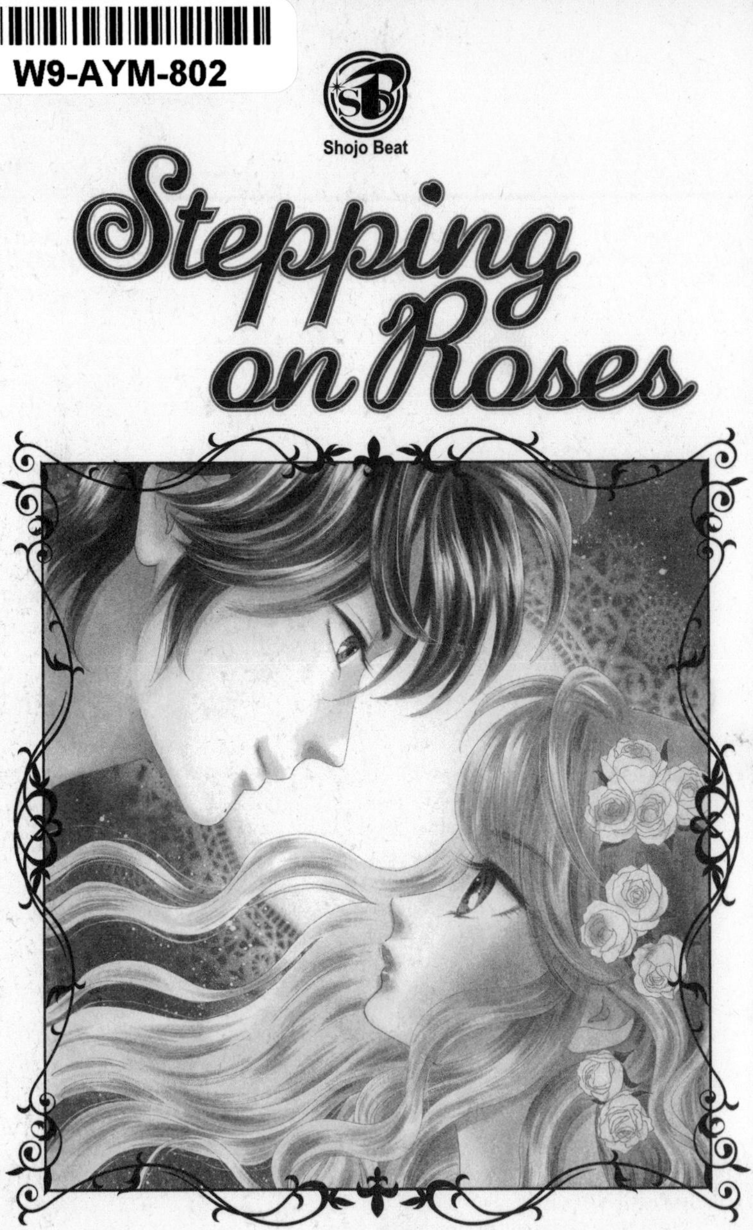

Vol. 3

Story & Art by

Rinko Ueda

Stepping on Roses

Volume 3
CONTENTS

Chapter 13 3

Chapter 14 29

Chapter 15 57

Chapter 16 83

Chapter 17 119

Chapter 18 145

Chapter 19 171

Glossary........198

Story Thus Far

Sumi Kitamura was living a life of poverty and taking care of the young orphans that her elder brother Eisuke would bring home from the streets. Then, in order to pay off Eisuke's debts, she marries Soichiro Ashida, the heir to a wealthy conglomerate. Even though Sumi has feelings for Soichiro's friend Nozomu Ijuin, she does not respond to Nozomu's advances because she is committed to being Soichiro's wife.

After making a successful debut at a party, Sumi goes to the seaside with Komai, the Ashida household butler. There, she runs into Nozomu, who persuades her to elope with him. Sumi then learns about Soichiro's painful childhood as well as the reason behind his fear of fire. She tries to go back to Soichiro's place, but Nozomu stops her...!

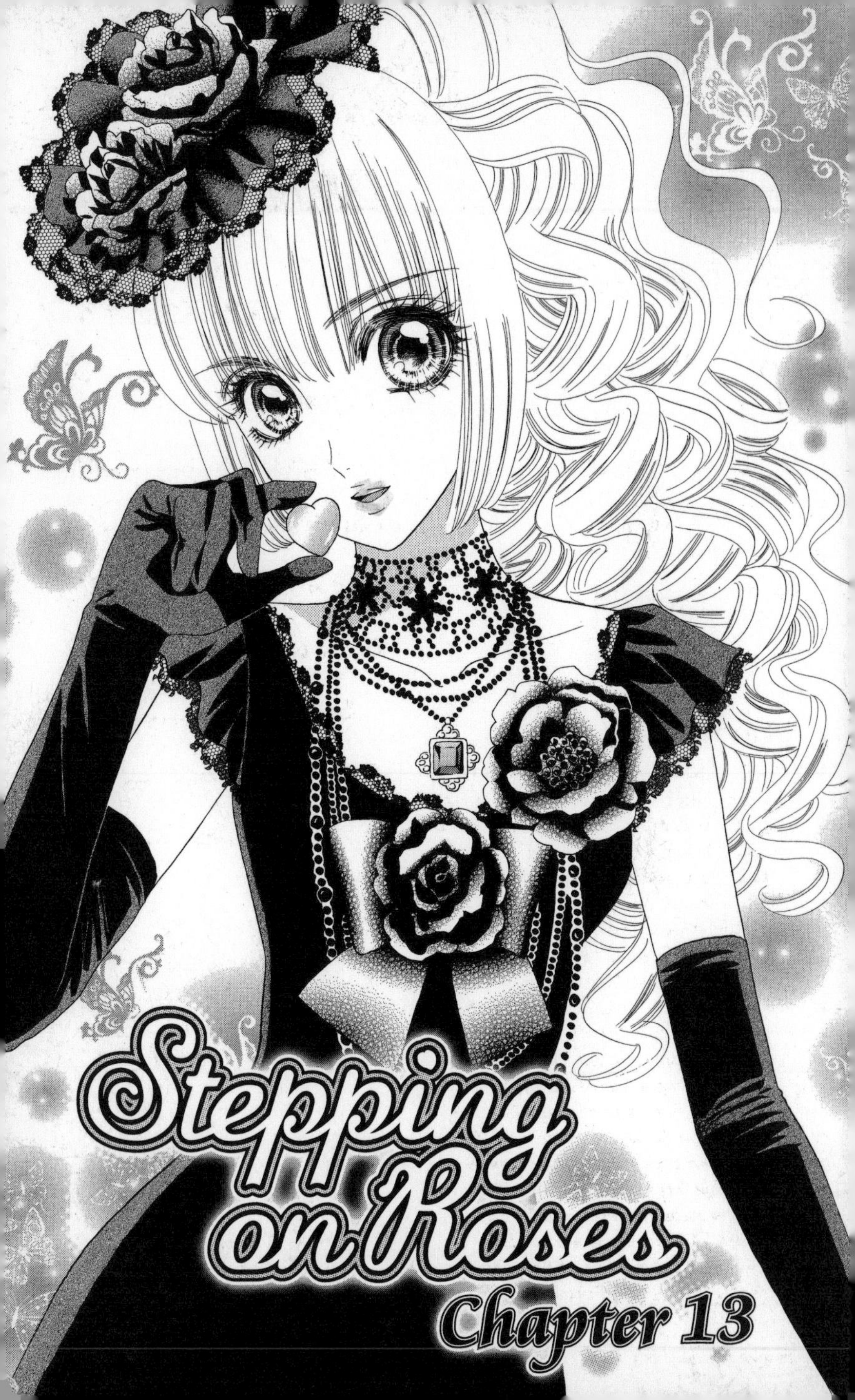
Stepping on Roses
Chapter 13

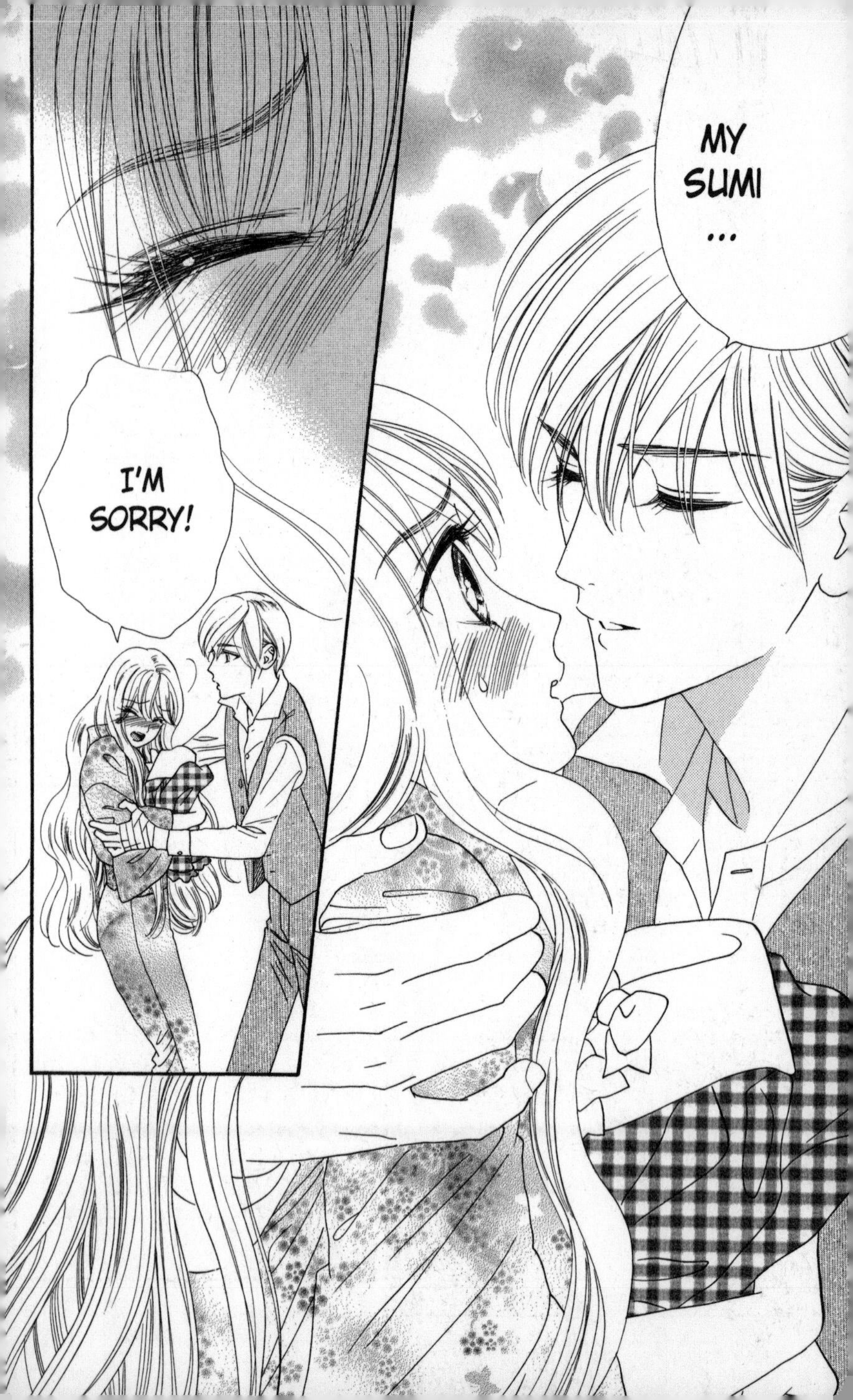
MY SUMI ...
I'M SORRY!

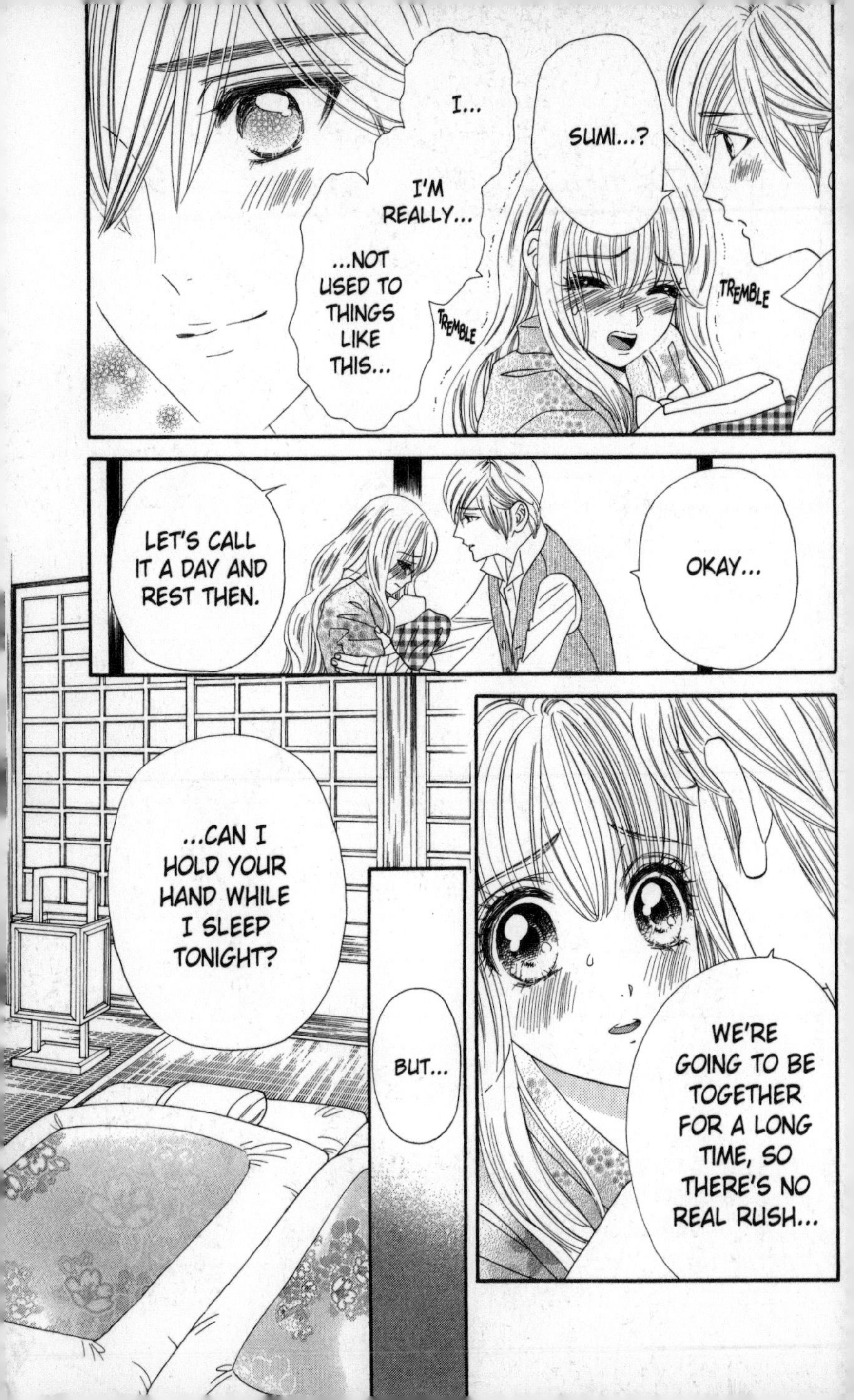
SUMI...?
I...
I'M REALLY...
...NOT USED TO THINGS LIKE THIS...
TREMBLE
TREMBLE
OKAY...
LET'S CALL IT A DAY AND REST THEN.
WE'RE GOING TO BE TOGETHER FOR A LONG TIME, SO THERE'S NO REAL RUSH...
BUT...
...CAN I HOLD YOUR HAND WHILE I SLEEP TONIGHT?

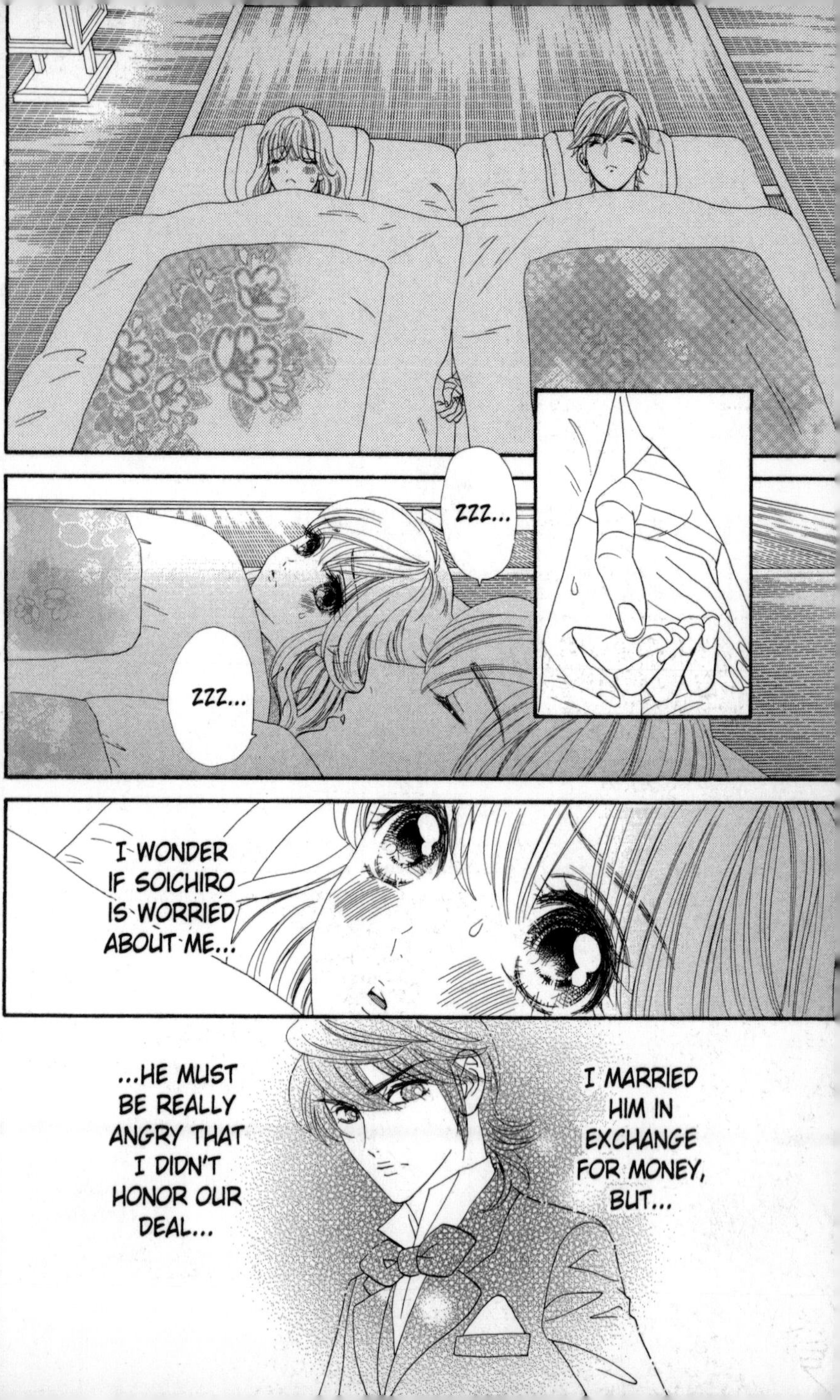
ZZZ...
ZZZ...
I WONDER IF SOICHIRO IS WORRIED ABOUT ME...
I MARRIED HIM IN EXCHANGE FOR MONEY, BUT...
...HE MUST BE REALLY ANGRY THAT I DIDN'T HONOR OUR DEAL...

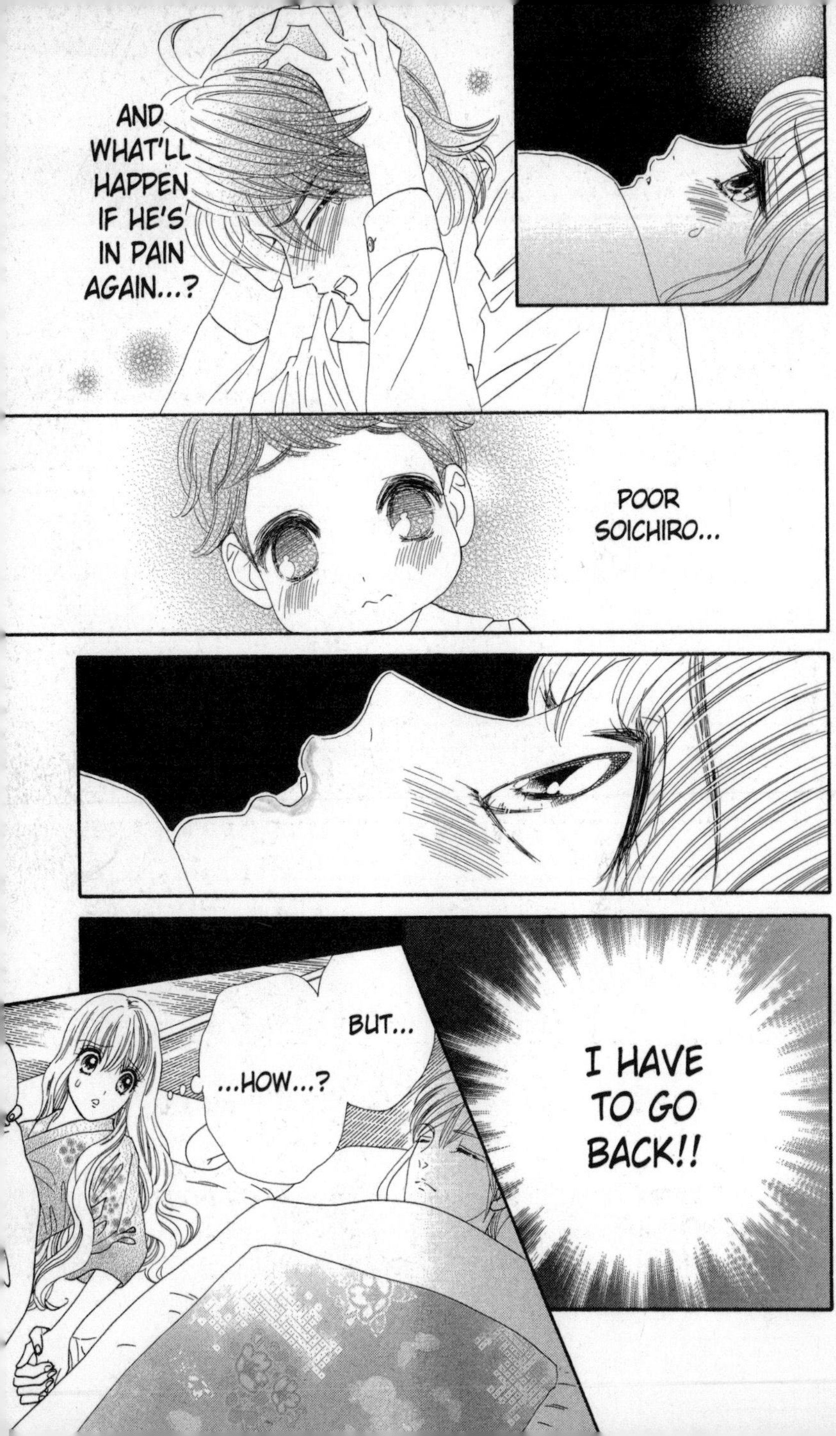
AND WHAT'LL HAPPEN IF HE'S IN PAIN AGAIN...?
POOR SOICHIRO...
I HAVE TO GO BACK!!
BUT...
...HOW...?

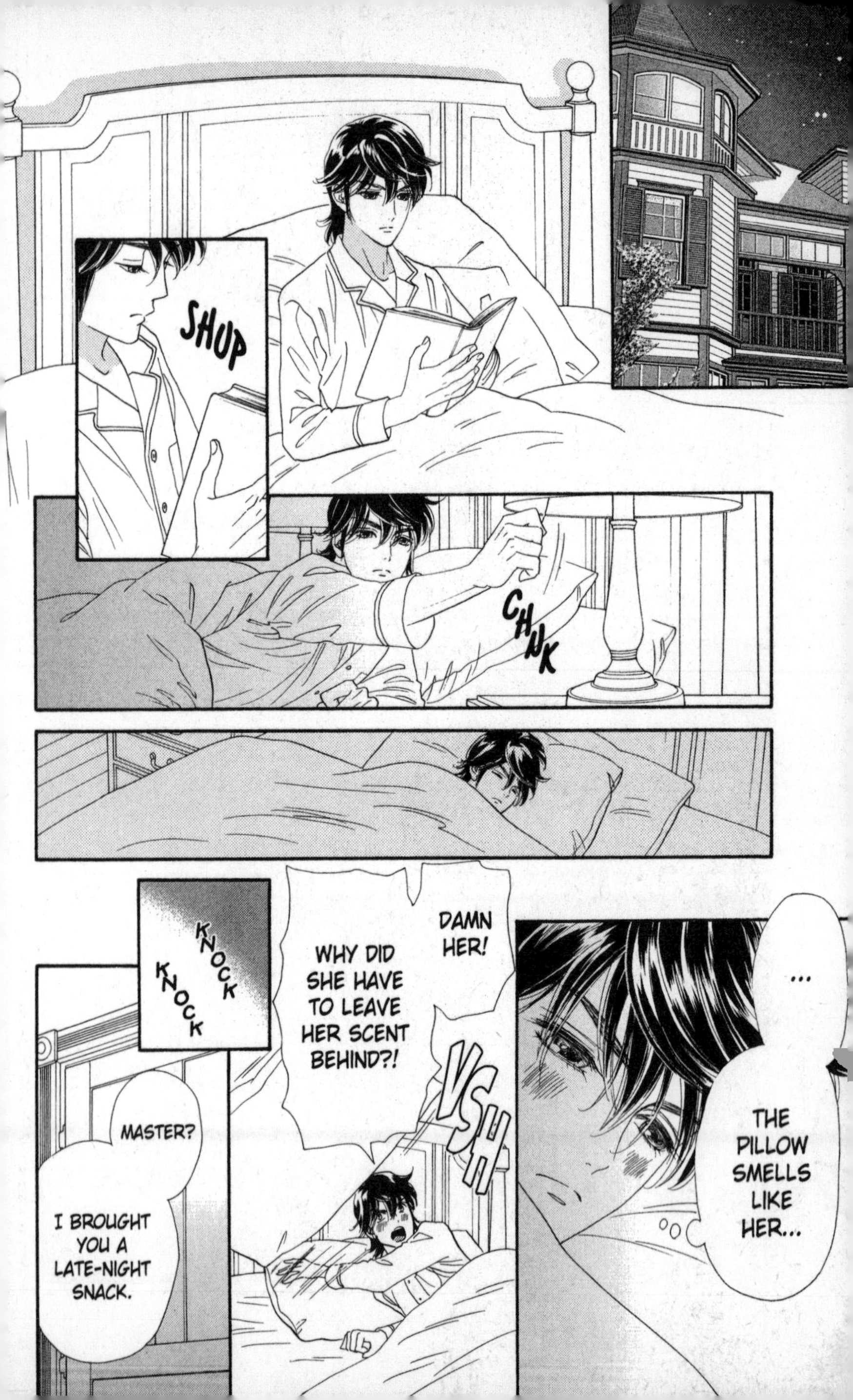
SHUP
CHNK
...
THE PILLOW SMELLS LIKE HER...
DAMN HER!
WHY DID SHE HAVE TO LEAVE HER SCENT BEHIND?!
VSH
KNOCK KNOCK
MASTER?
I BROUGHT YOU A LATE-NIGHT SNACK.

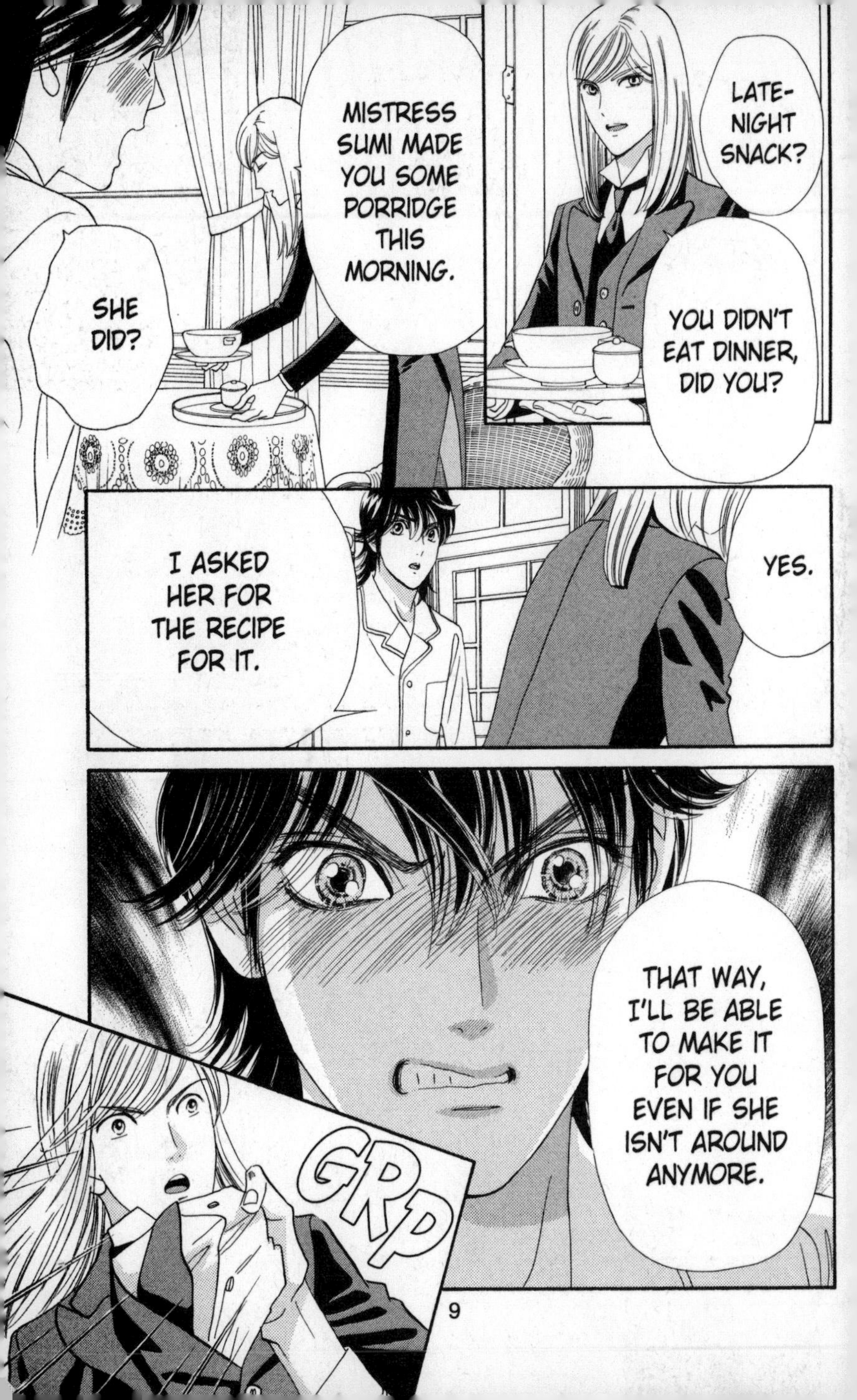
LATE-NIGHT SNACK?
YOU DIDN'T EAT DINNER, DID YOU?
MISTRESS SUMI MADE YOU SOME PORRIDGE THIS MORNING.
SHE DID?
YES.
I ASKED HER FOR THE RECIPE FOR IT.
THAT WAY, I'LL BE ABLE TO MAKE IT FOR YOU EVEN IF SHE ISN'T AROUND ANYMORE.
GRP

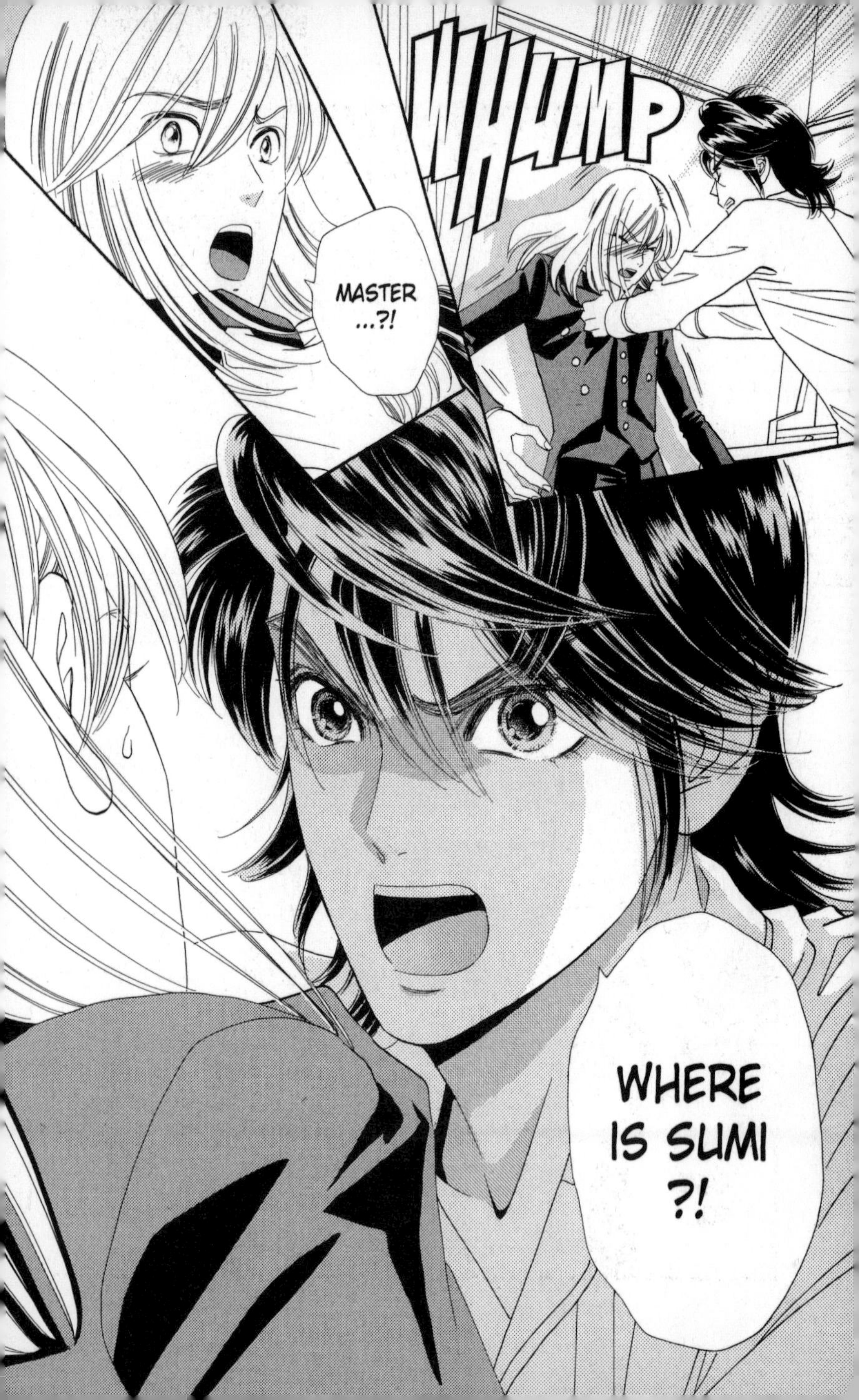
WHUMP
MASTER ...?!
WHERE IS SUMI ?!

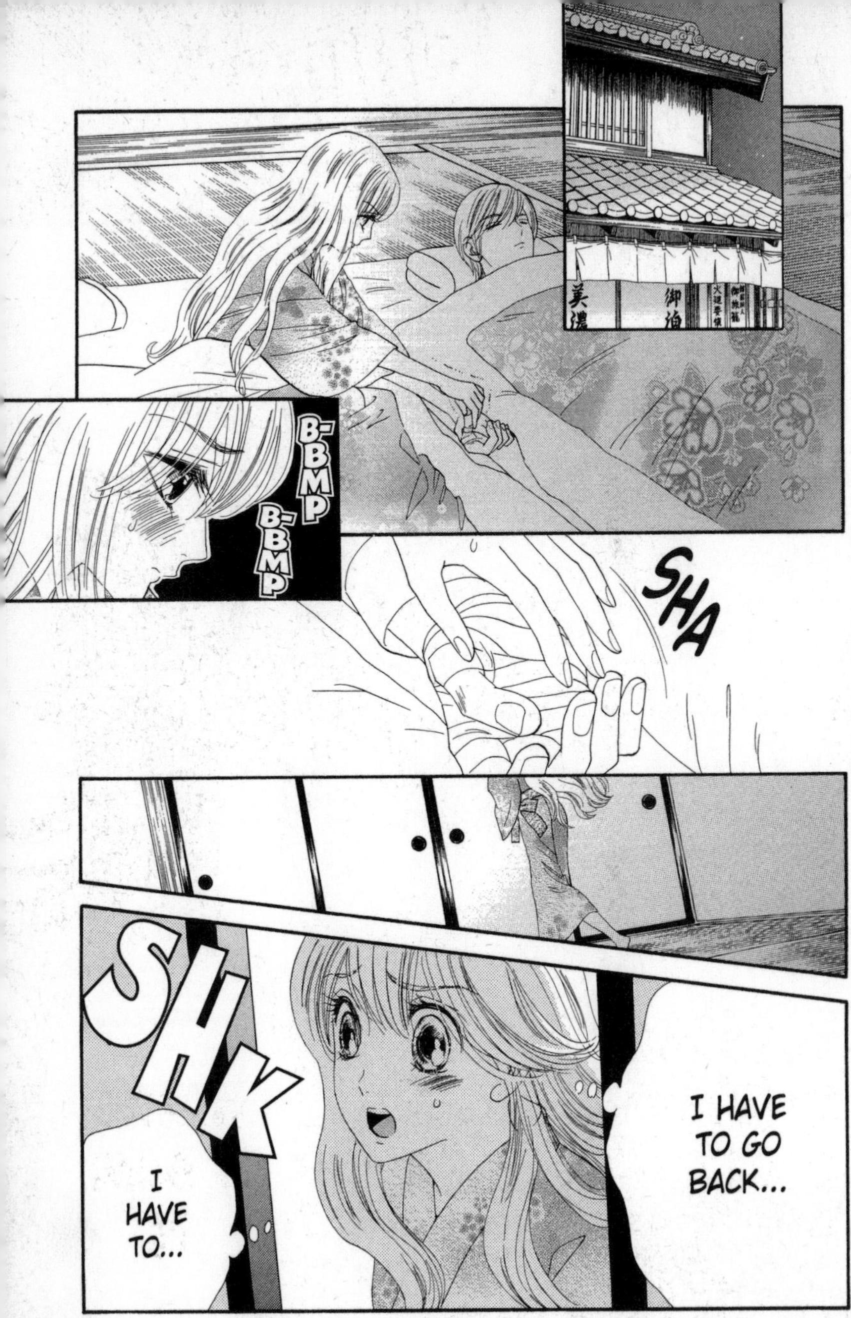
御泊
美濃
B-BMP
B-BMP
SHA
SHK
I HAVE TO GO BACK...
I HAVE TO...

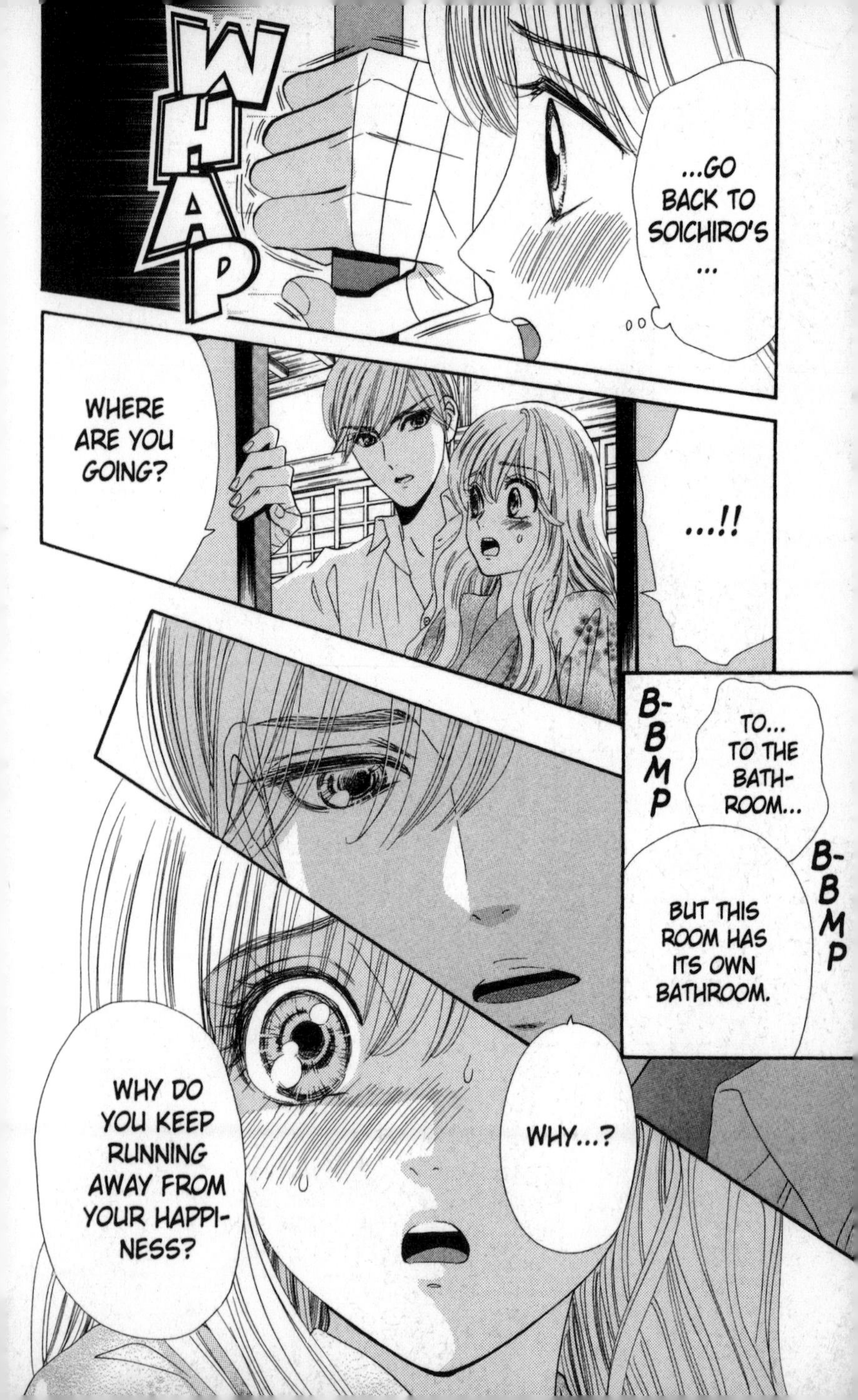

...GO BACK TO SOICHIRO'S ...
WHAP
WHERE ARE YOU GOING?
...!!
B-BMP
TO... TO THE BATH-ROOM...
B-BMP
BUT THIS ROOM HAS ITS OWN BATHROOM.
WHY...?
WHY DO YOU KEEP RUNNING AWAY FROM YOUR HAPPI-NESS?

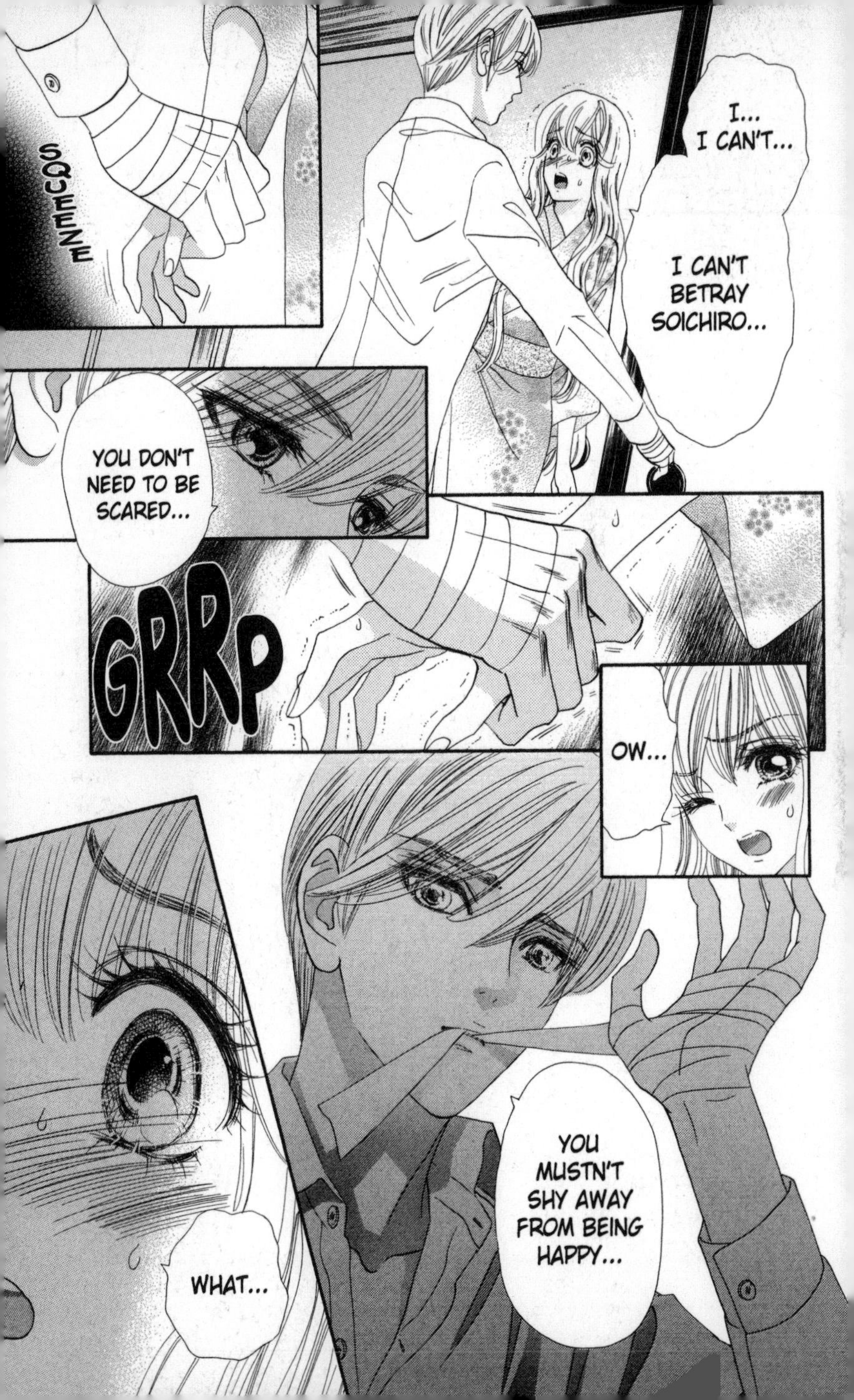
I...
I CAN'T...
I CAN'T BETRAY SOICHIRO...
SQUEEZE
YOU DON'T NEED TO BE SCARED...
GRRP
OW...
YOU MUSTN'T SHY AWAY FROM BEING HAPPY...
WHAT...

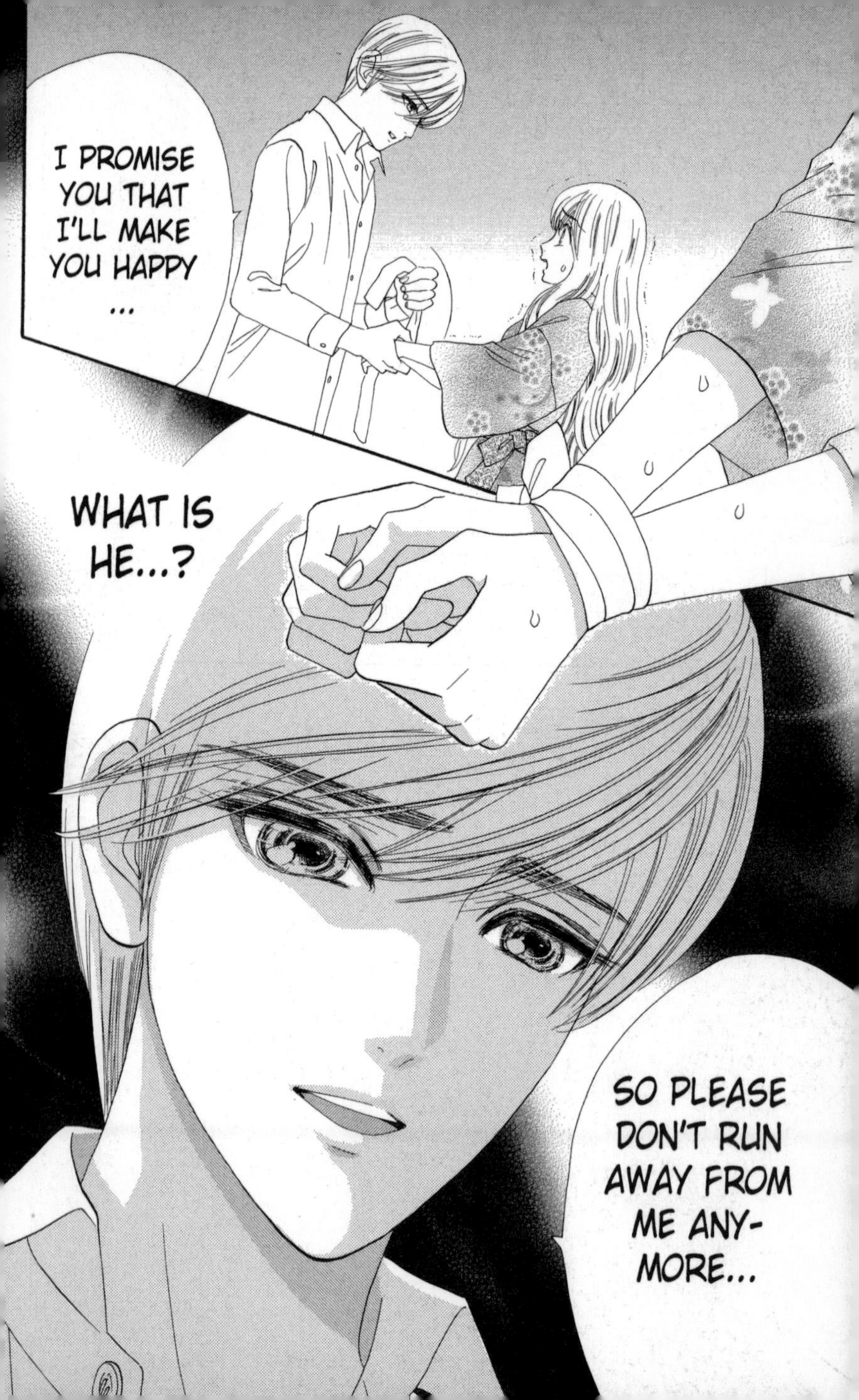
I PROMISE YOU THAT I'LL MAKE YOU HAPPY ...
WHAT IS HE...?
SO PLEASE DON'T RUN AWAY FROM ME ANY-MORE...

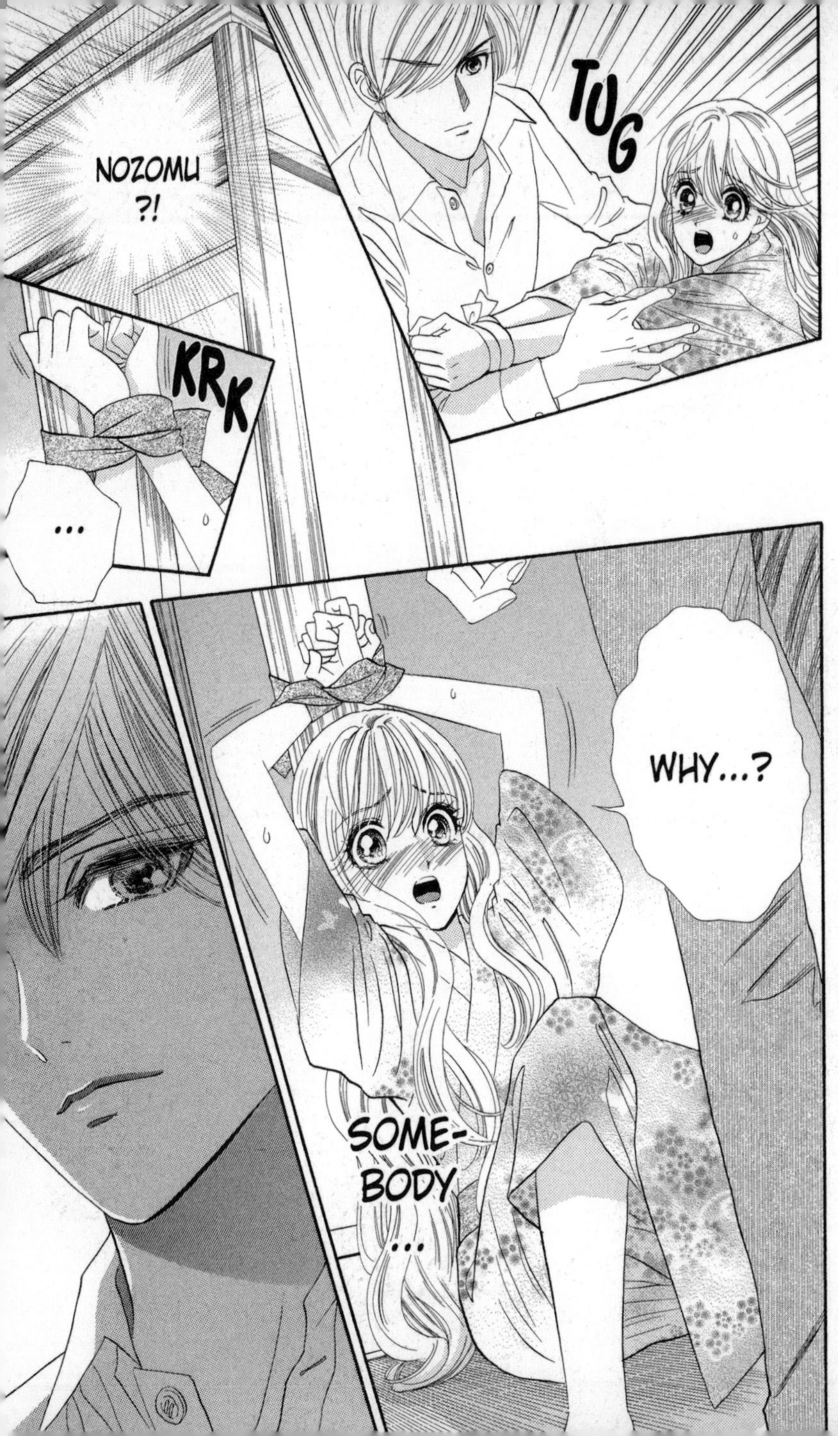
TUG
NOZOMU ?!
KRK
...
WHY...?
SOME-BODY ...

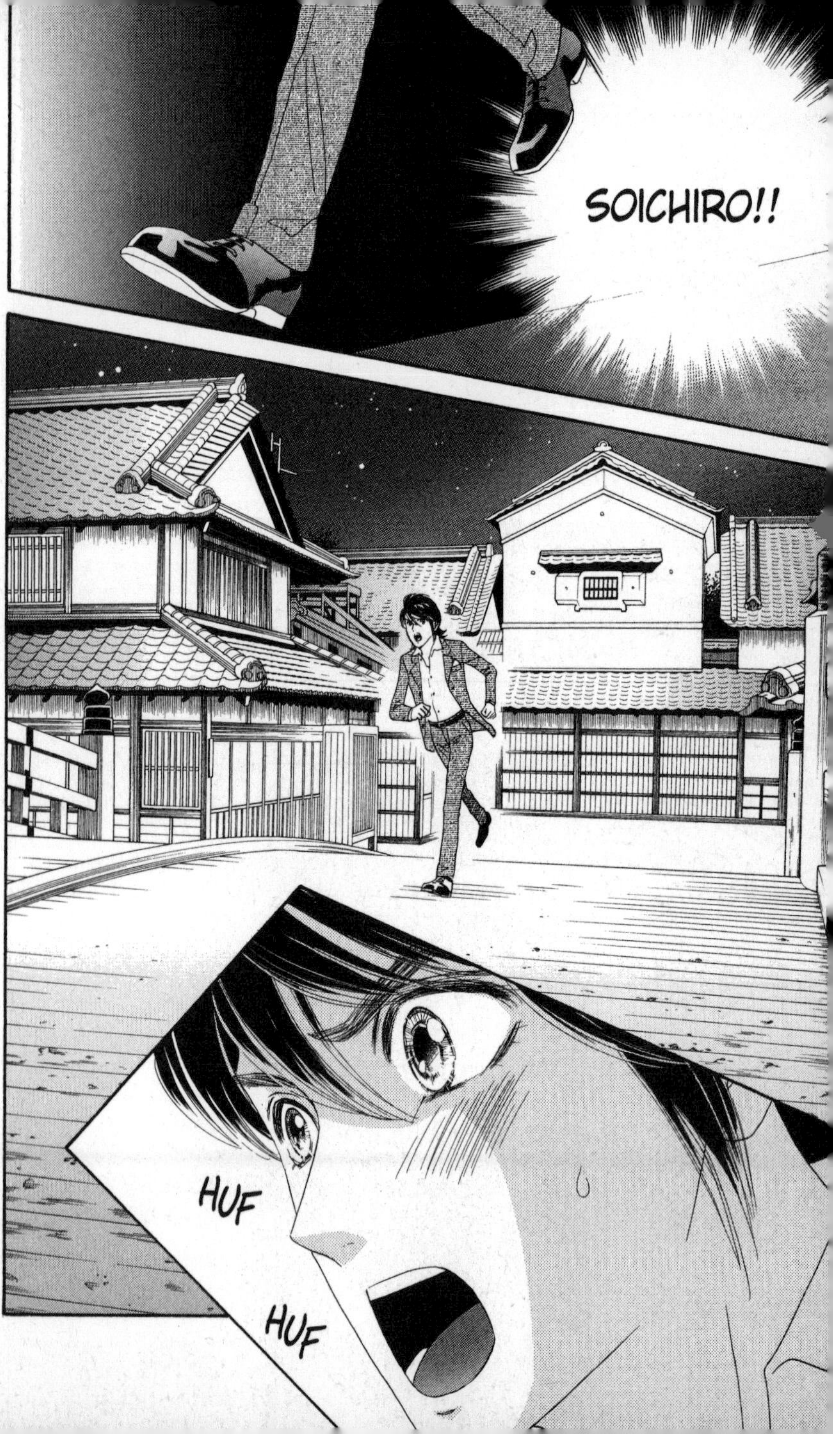
SOICHIRO!!
HUF
HUF

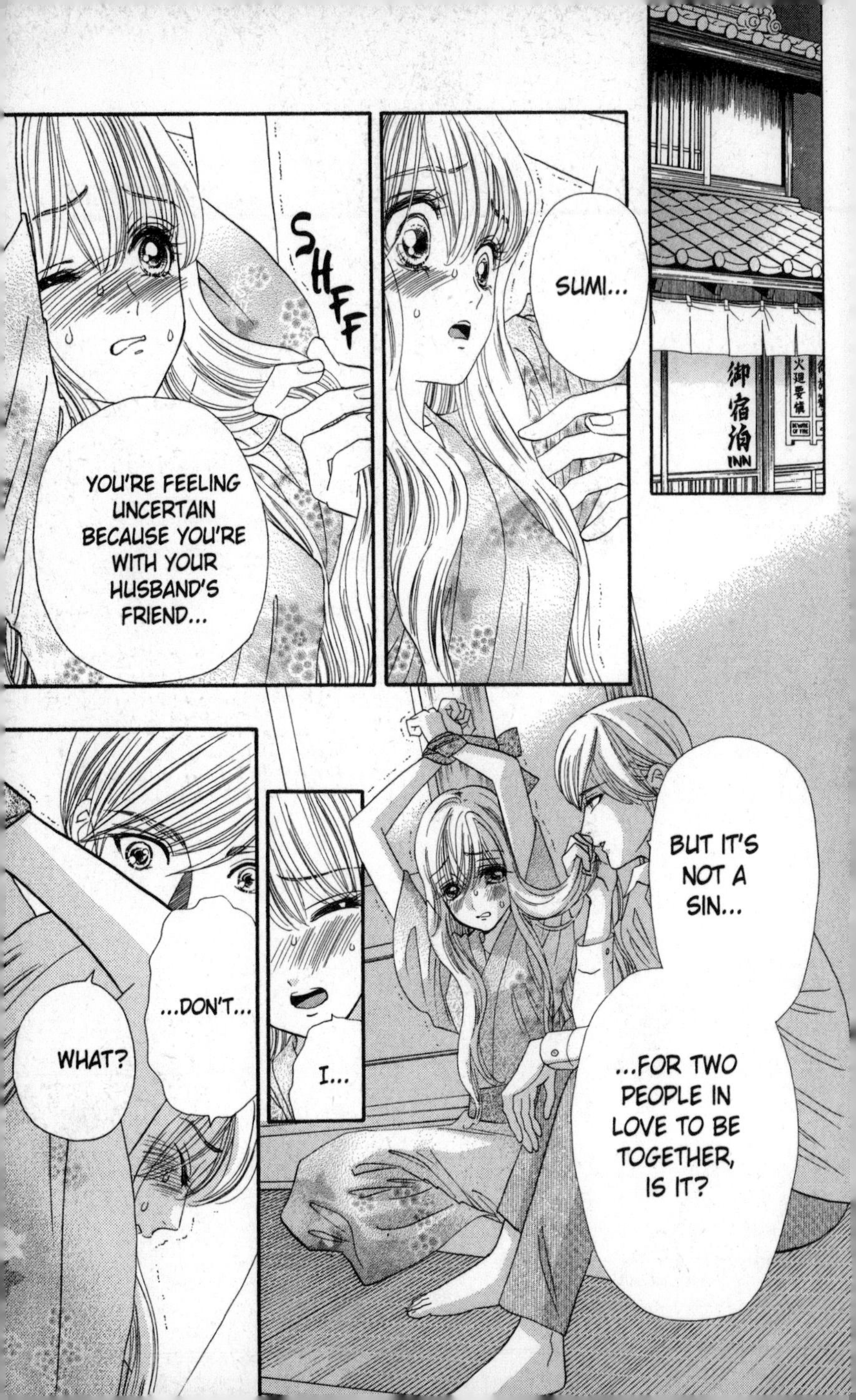
御宿泊
INN
SUMI...
SHFF
YOU'RE FEELING UNCERTAIN BECAUSE YOU'RE WITH YOUR HUSBAND'S FRIEND...
BUT IT'S NOT A SIN...
...FOR TWO PEOPLE IN LOVE TO BE TOGETHER, IS IT?
I...
...DON'T...
WHAT?

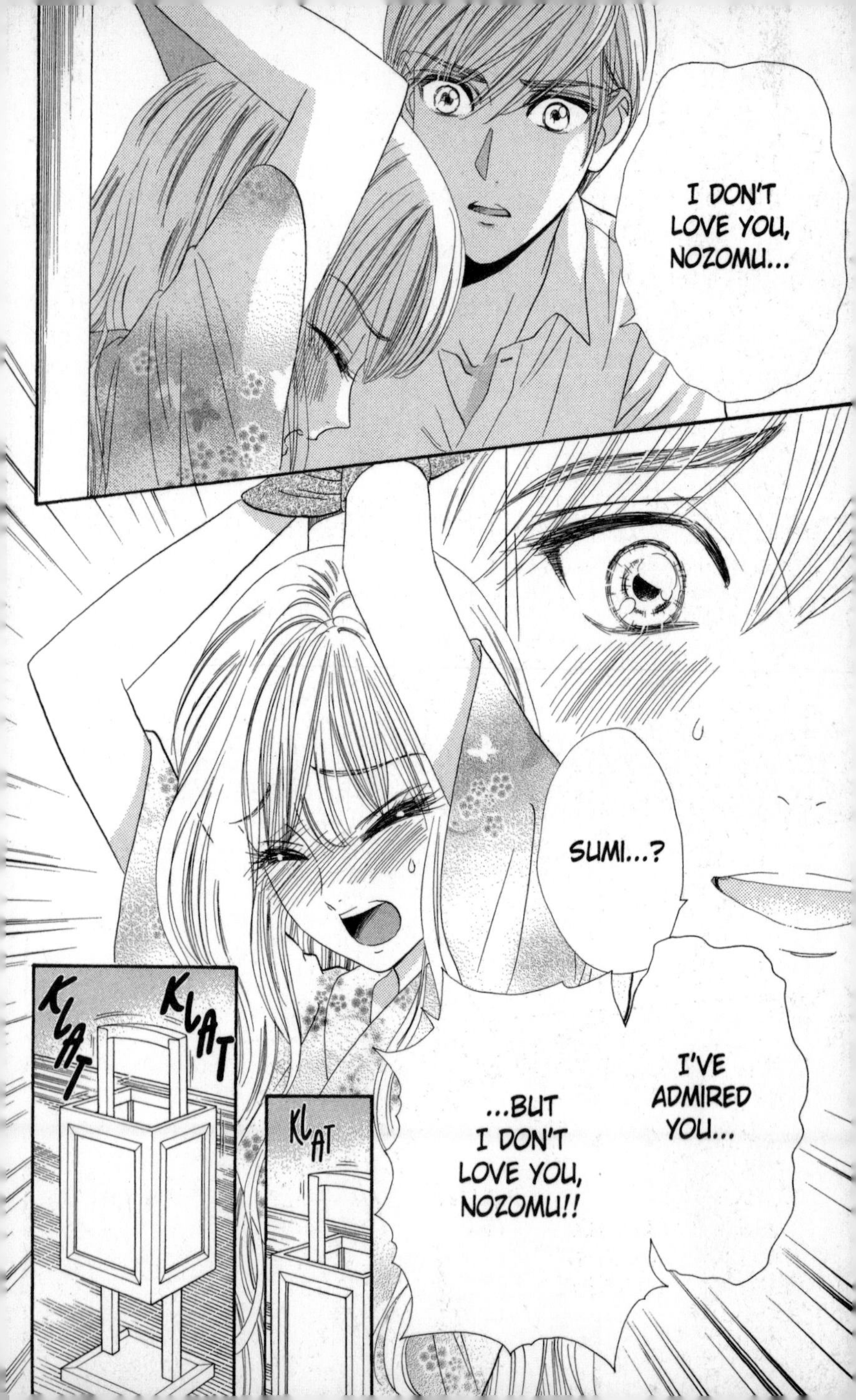
I DON'T LOVE YOU, NOZOMU...
SUMI...?
I'VE ADMIRED YOU...
...BUT I DON'T LOVE YOU, NOZOMU!!
KLAT
KLAT
KLAT

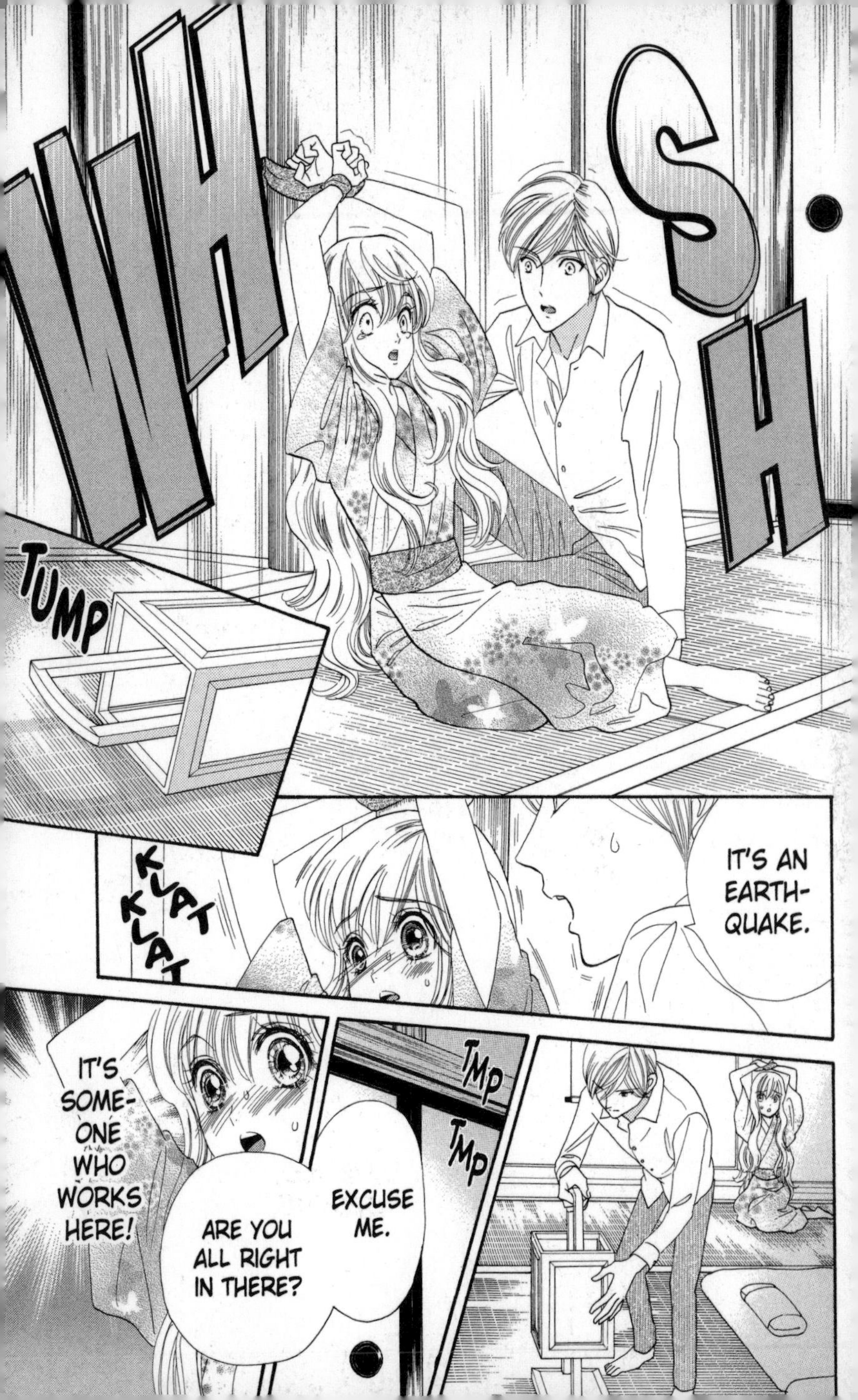
S·H
WHH
TUMP
IT'S AN EARTH-QUAKE.
KLAT KLAT
TMP TMP
EXCUSE ME.
ARE YOU ALL RIGHT IN THERE?
IT'S SOME-ONE WHO WORKS HERE!

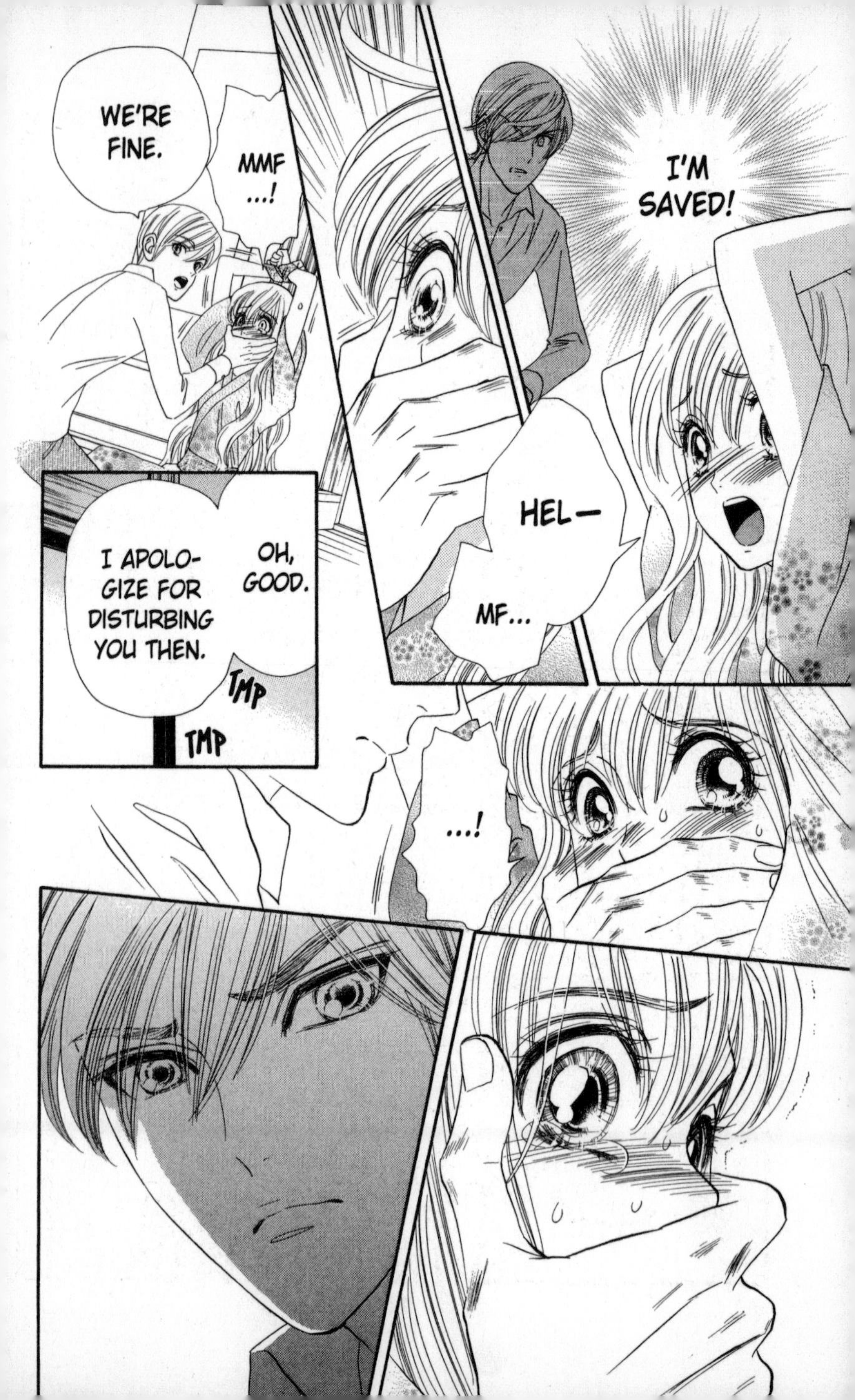

I'M SAVED!
HEL—
MF...
WE'RE FINE.
MMF ...!
OH, GOOD.
I APOLOGIZE FOR DISTURBING YOU THEN.
TMP
TMP
...!

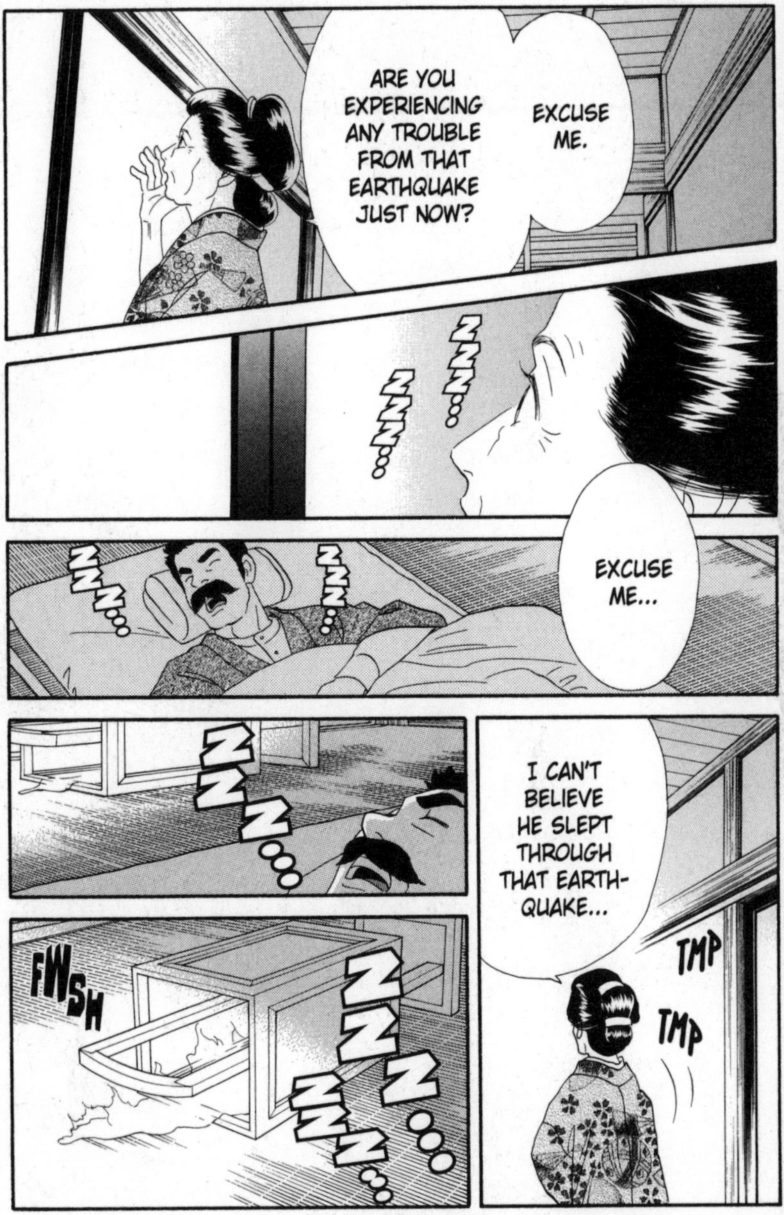

EXCUSE ME.
ARE YOU EXPERIENCING ANY TROUBLE FROM THAT EARTHQUAKE JUST NOW?
ZZZ...
ZZZ...
EXCUSE ME...
ZZZ...
ZZZ...
I CAN'T BELIEVE HE SLEPT THROUGH THAT EARTH-QUAKE...
TMP
TMP
ZZZ...
ZZZ...
ZZZ...
FWSH

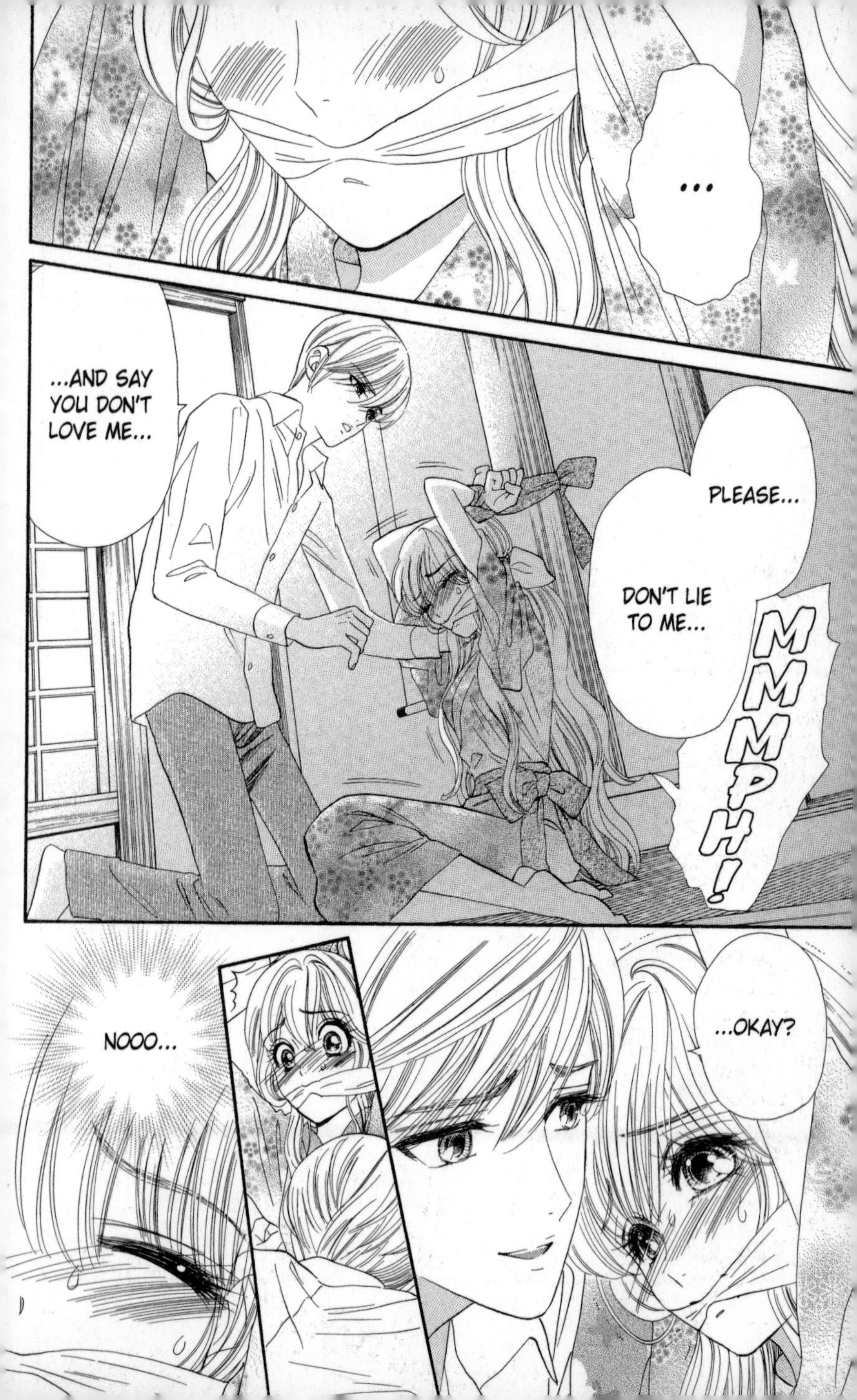
...
PLEASE...
DON'T LIE TO ME...
MMMPH!
...AND SAY YOU DON'T LOVE ME...
...OKAY?
NOOO...

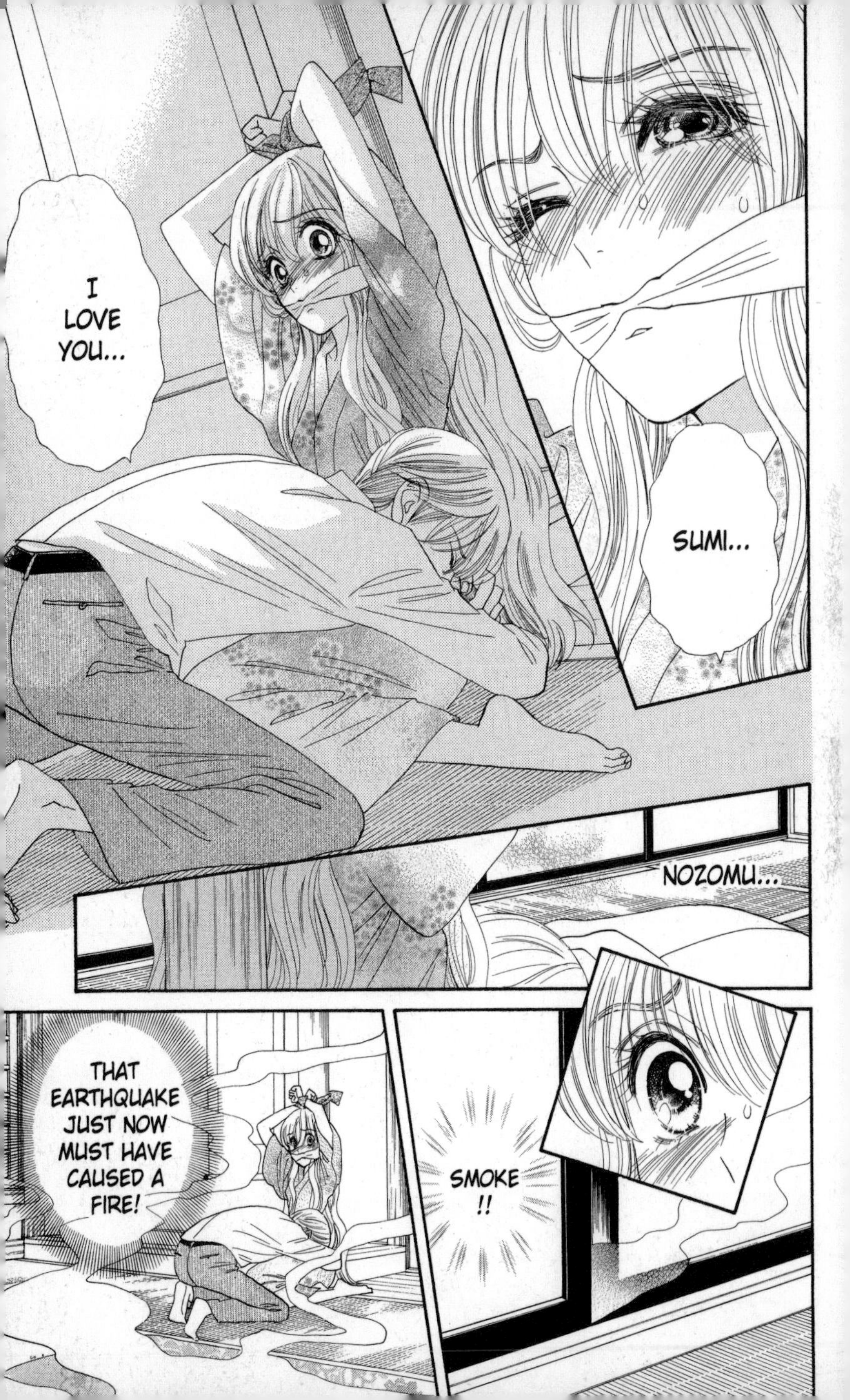
SUMI...
I LOVE YOU...
NOZOMU...
SMOKE !!
THAT EARTHQUAKE JUST NOW MUST HAVE CAUSED A FIRE!

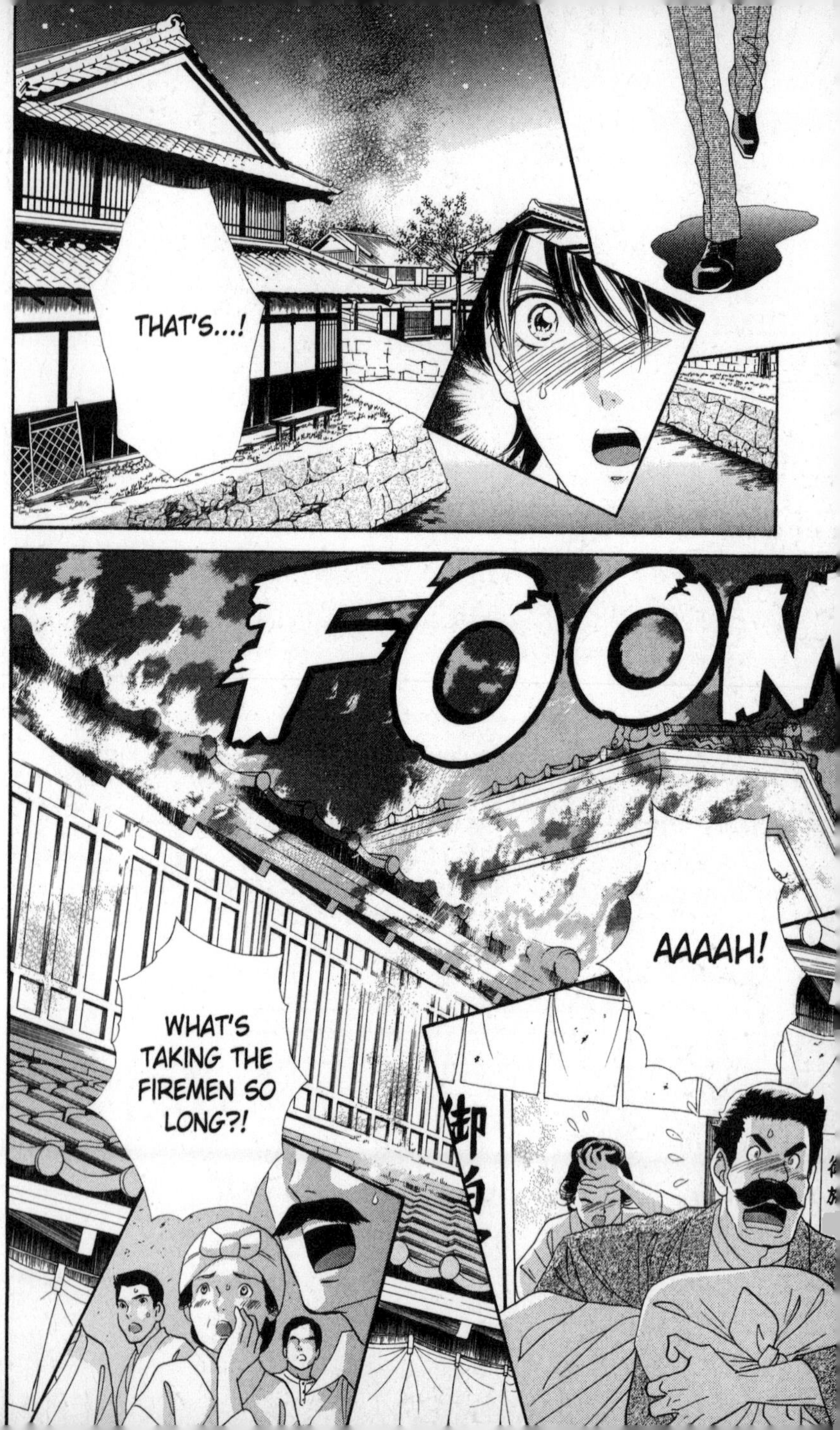
THAT'S...!
FOOM
AAAAH!
WHAT'S TAKING THE FIREMEN SO LONG?!

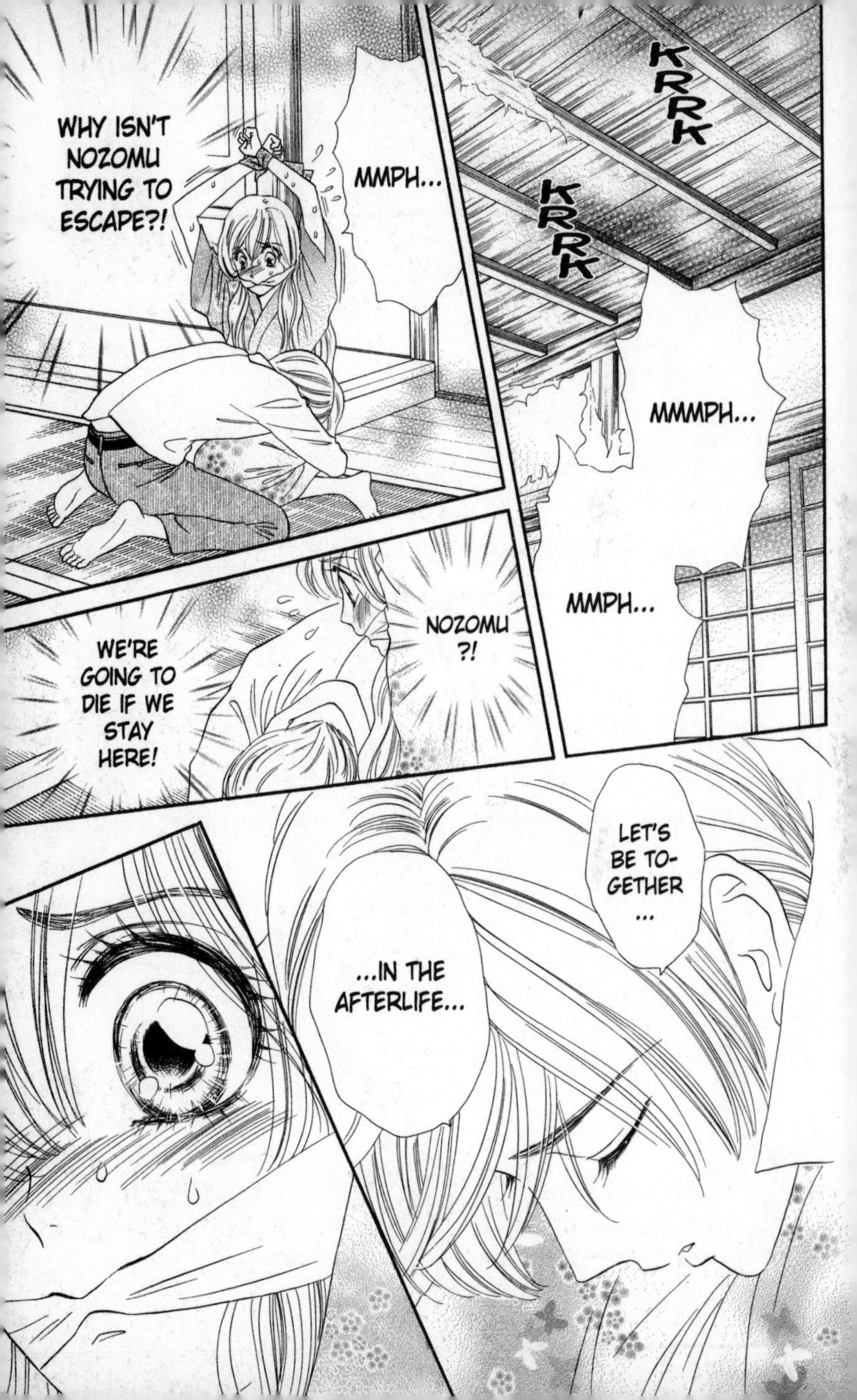
KRRK
KRRK
MMMPH...
MMPH...
MMPH...
WHY ISN'T NOZOMU TRYING TO ESCAPE?!
NOZOMU ?!
WE'RE GOING TO DIE IF WE STAY HERE!
LET'S BE TO-GETHER ...
...IN THE AFTERLIFE...

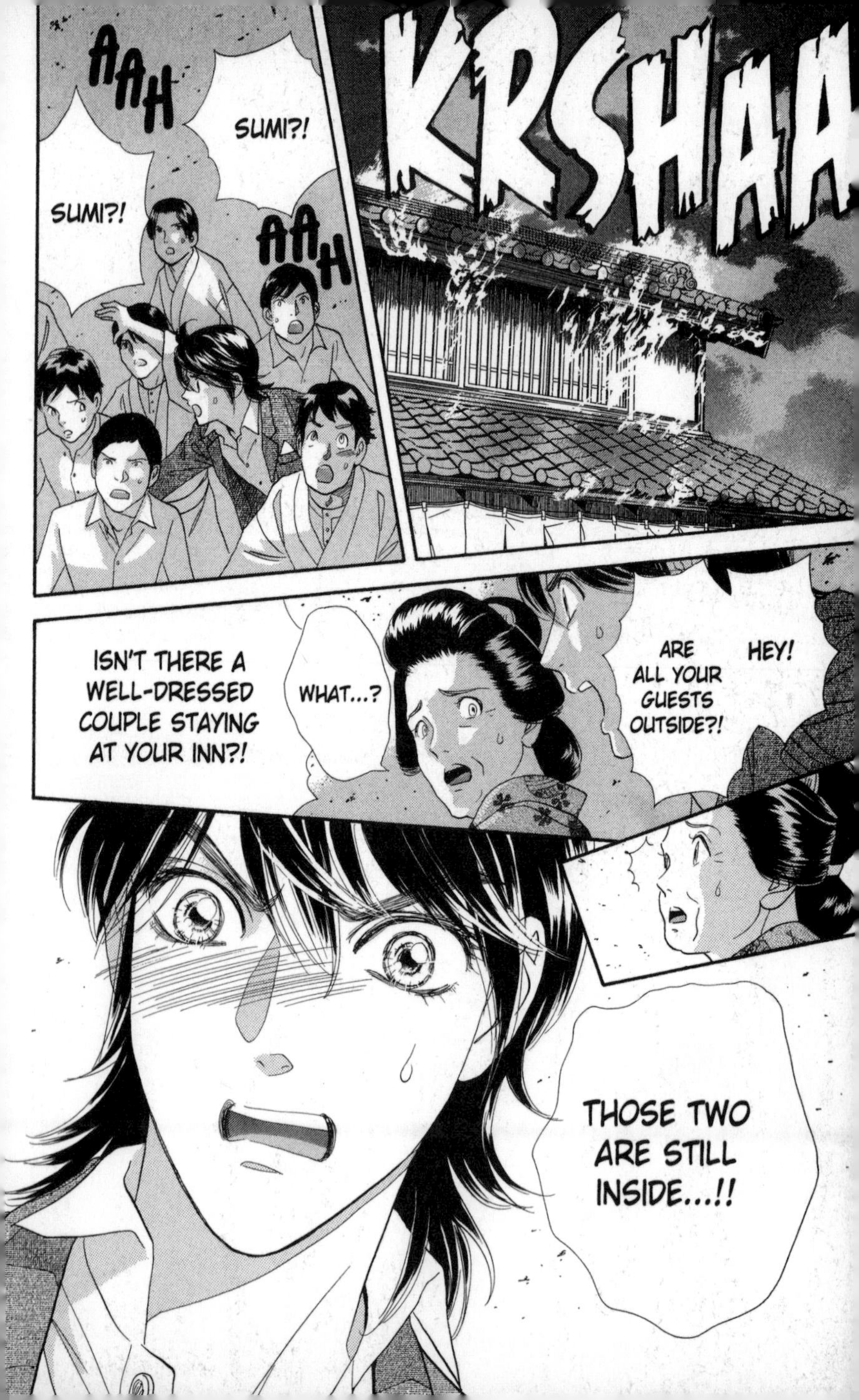
KRSHAA
AAH
SUMI?!
SUMI?!
AAH
HEY!
ARE ALL YOUR GUESTS OUTSIDE?!
WHAT...?
ISN'T THERE A WELL-DRESSED COUPLE STAYING AT YOUR INN?!
THOSE TWO ARE STILL INSIDE...!!

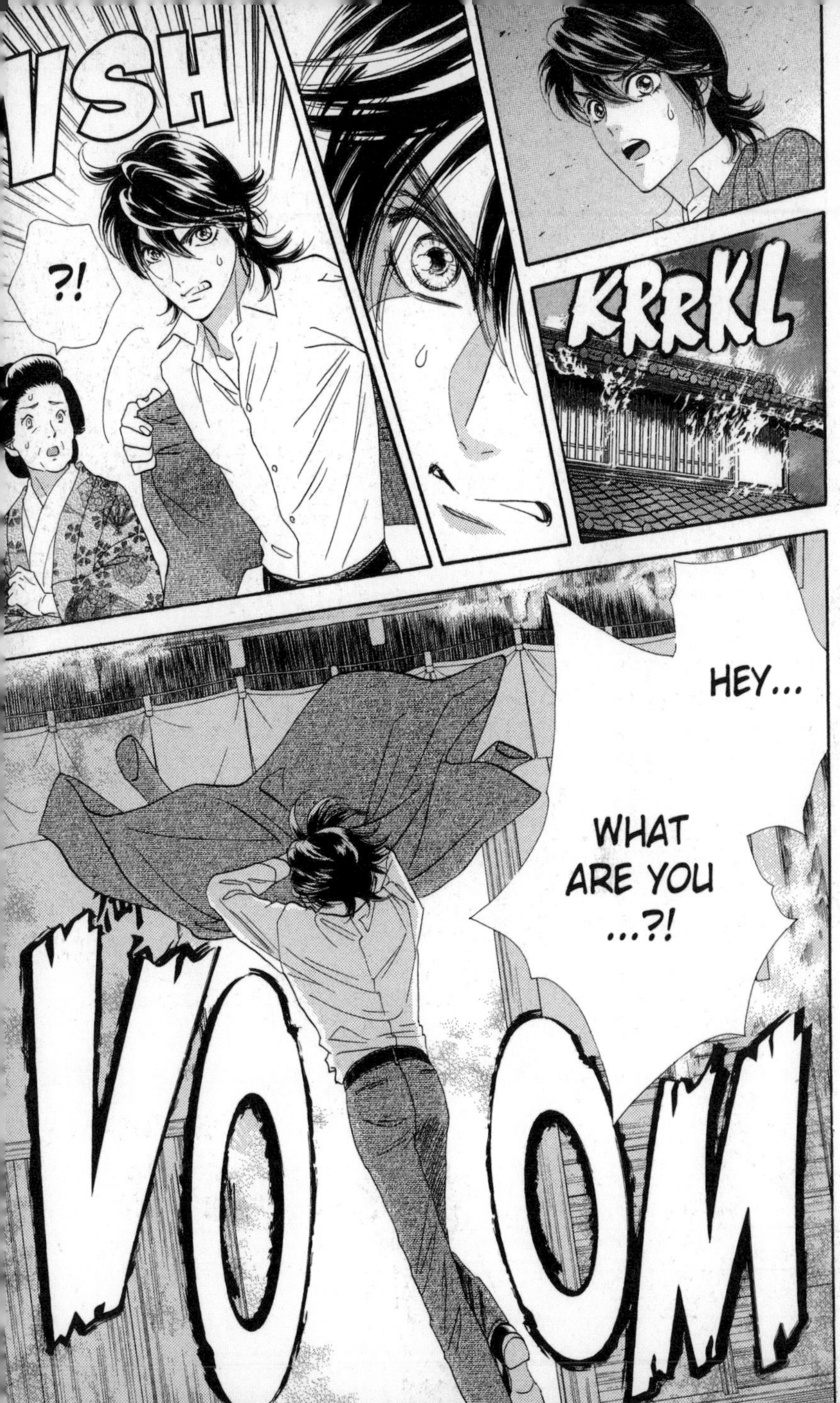
KRRKL
SH
?!
HEY... WHAT ARE YOU ...?!
VOOM

No.

STEPPING ON ROSES BACKSTAGE SECTION!! Date

❀ HELLO, IT'S UE-RIN!!

THANKS TO EVERYBODY'S SUPPORT, *STEPPING ON ROSES* WAS ABLE TO CELEBRATE ITS FIRST ONE-YEAR ANNIVERSARY IN *MARGARET*.

THANK YOU VERY MUCH!! HURRAY! CLAP CLAP!! (← KOMAI CLAPPING)

❀ BEFORE *TAIL OF THE MOON*, *MARGARET* GRAPHIC NOVEL COVERS ALL HAD THE SAME TITLE DESIGN THAT USED A SPECIFIC RED FONT. HOWEVER, STARTING WITH *STEPPING ON ROSES*, WE WERE GIVEN THE FREEDOM TO DO ANYTHING WE WANTED WITH THE COVER DESIGN. THAT'S WHY I WAS ABLE TO INCLUDE SPECIFIC ILLUSTRATIONS ON THE BACK COVERS.
IN VOLUME 3, YOU GET TO SEE YOU-KNOW-WHO STARING AT YOU. THE ORIGINAL ILLUSTRATION FOR THIS WAS ACTUALLY TWICE THE SIZE YOU SEE ON THE COVER ITSELF. IT WAS PRETTY MUCH LIFE-SIZE, AND I EVEN DREW THE RIGHT SIDE OF HIS FACE THAT ISN'T SHOWN ON THE COVER. DRAWING A LIFE-SIZE IMAGE OF NOZOMU IN THE MIDDLE OF THE NIGHT WITH A LOOMING DEADLINE WAS PRETTY SCARY.

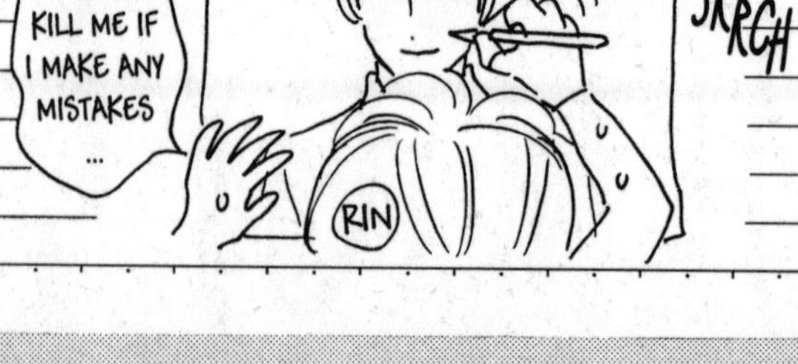
HE'LL PROBABLY KILL ME IF I MAKE ANY MISTAKES ...
SKRCH
SKRCH
RIN

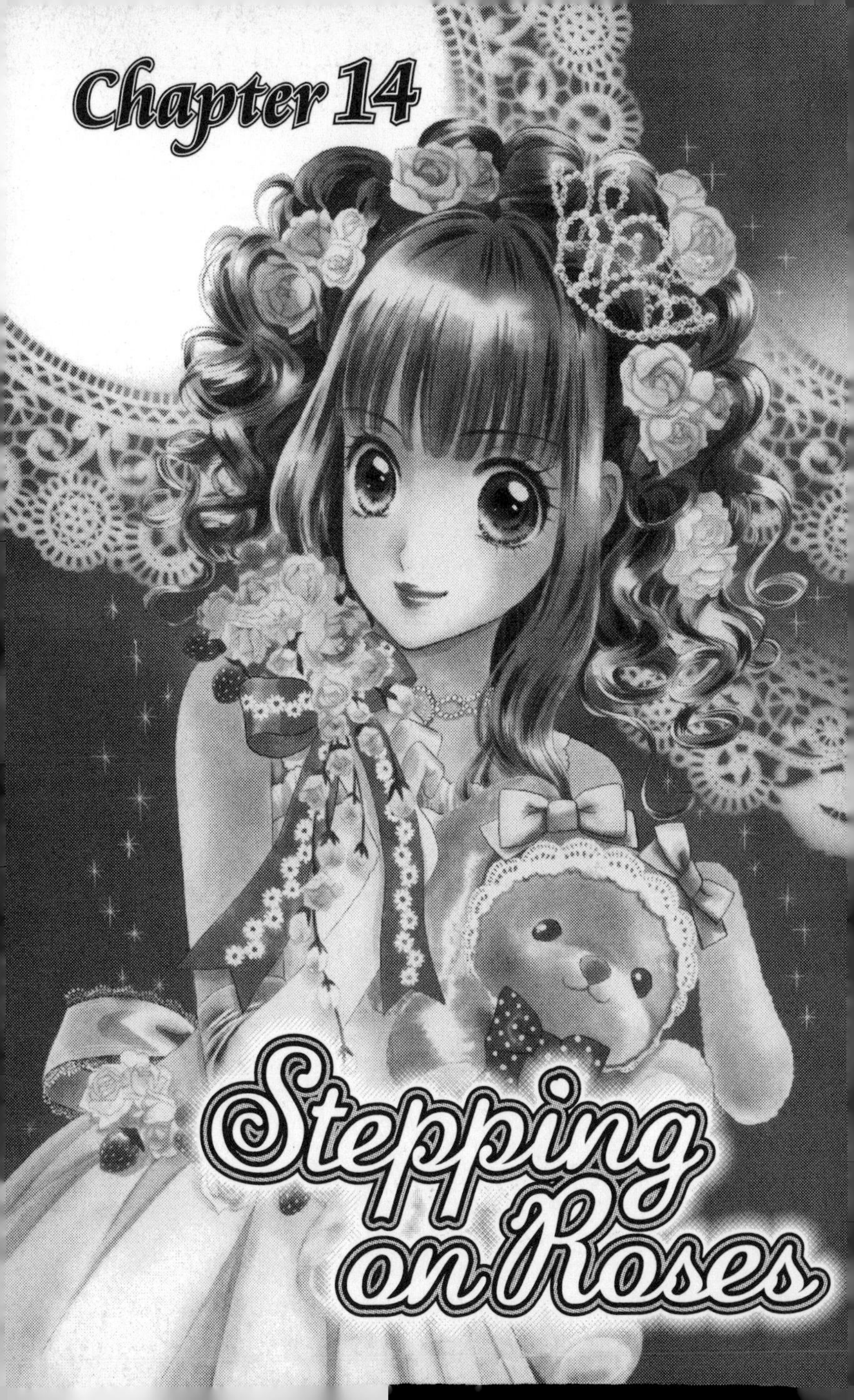
Chapter 14
Stepping on Roses

Stepping on Roses

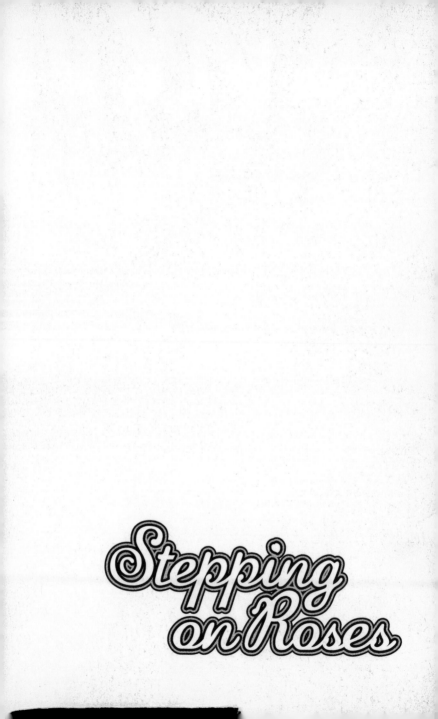

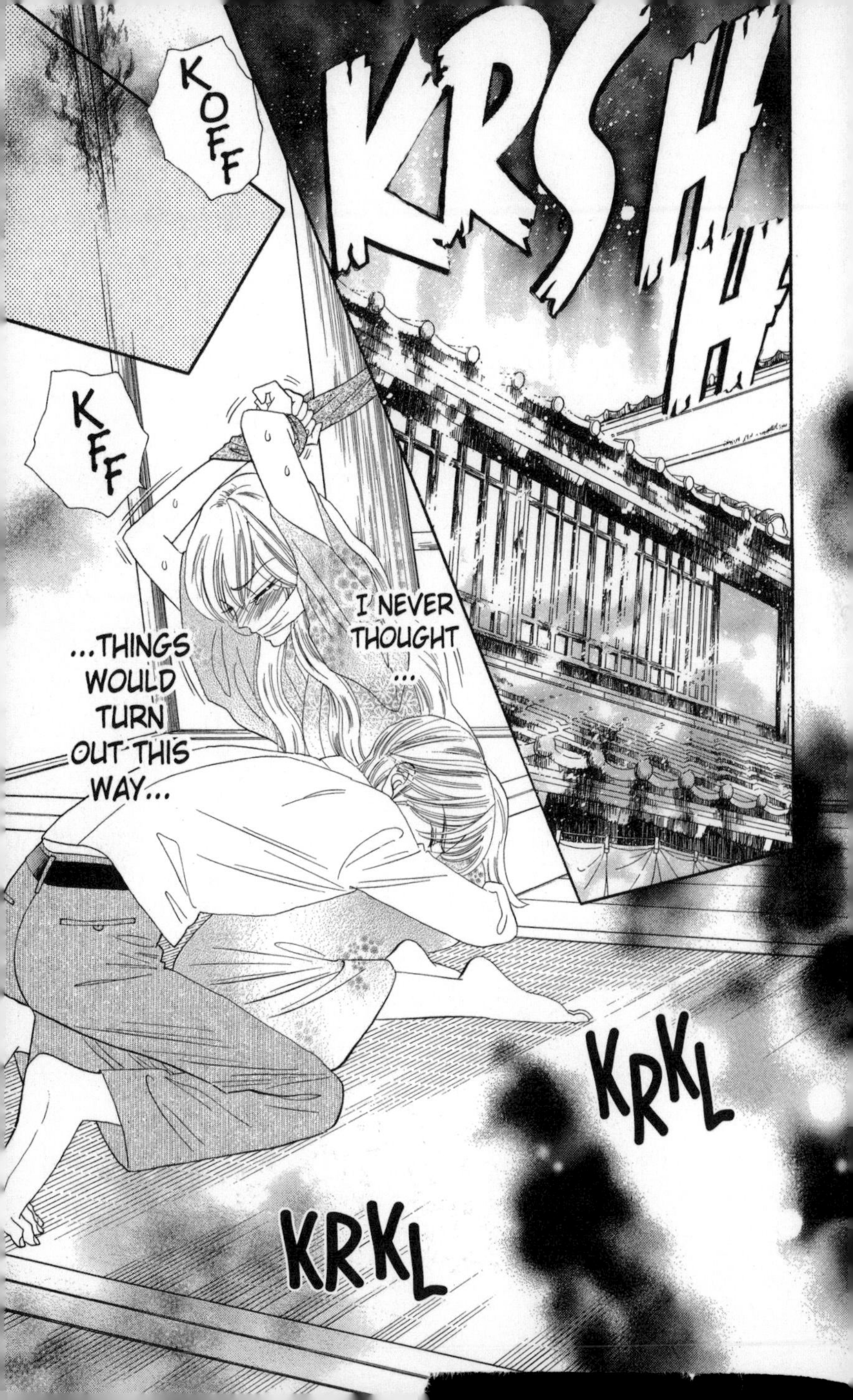
KRSHH
KOFF
KFF
I NEVER THOUGHT...
...THINGS WOULD TURN OUT THIS WAY...
KRKL
KRKL

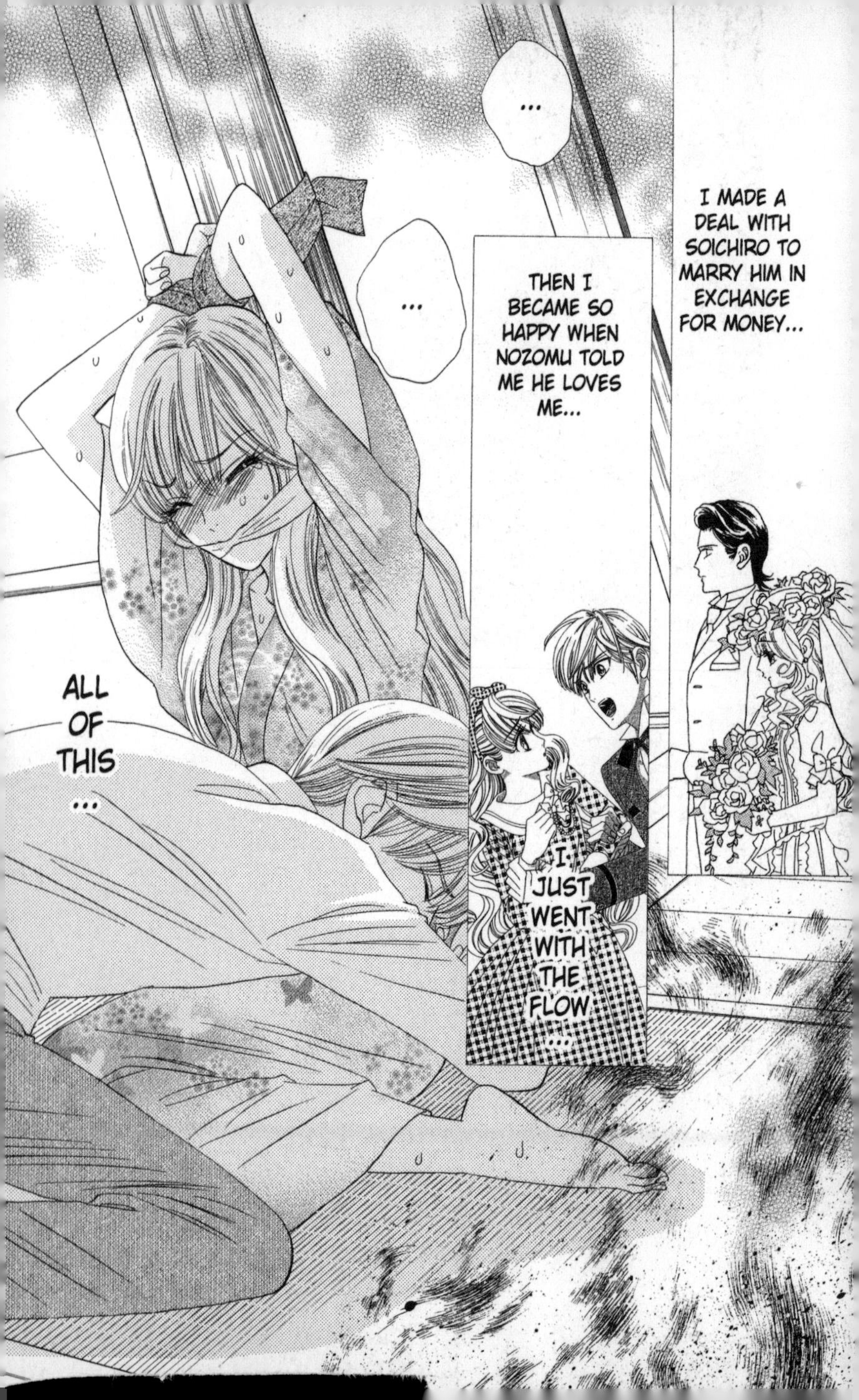
I MADE A DEAL WITH SOICHIRO TO MARRY HIM IN EXCHANGE FOR MONEY...
THEN I BECAME SO HAPPY WHEN NOZOMU TOLD ME HE LOVES ME...
I JUST WENT WITH THE FLOW...
...
...
ALL OF THIS...

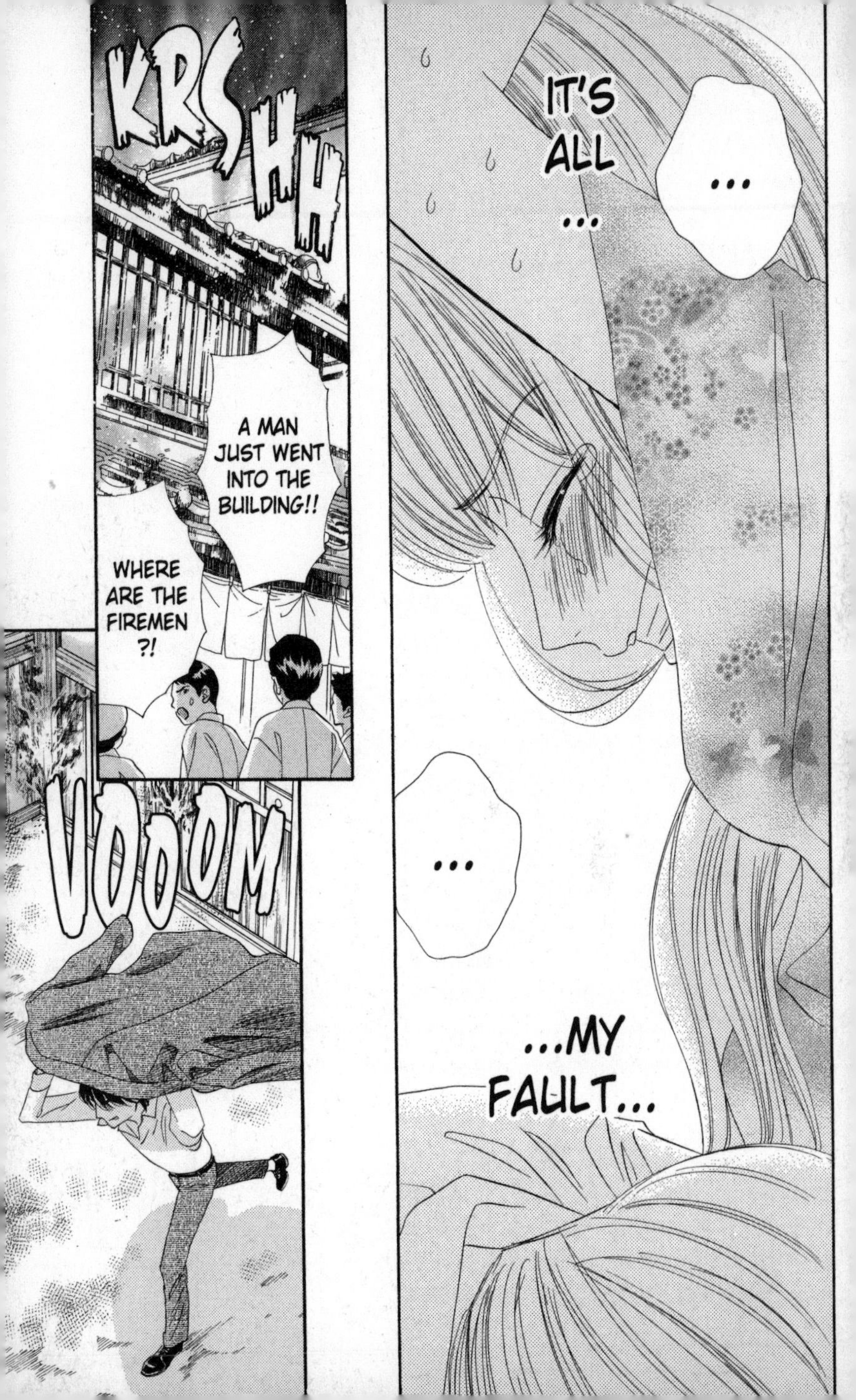
IT'S ALL ...
...
...
...MY FAULT...
KRSHH
A MAN JUST WENT INTO THE BUILDING!!
WHERE ARE THE FIREMEN?!
VOOOM

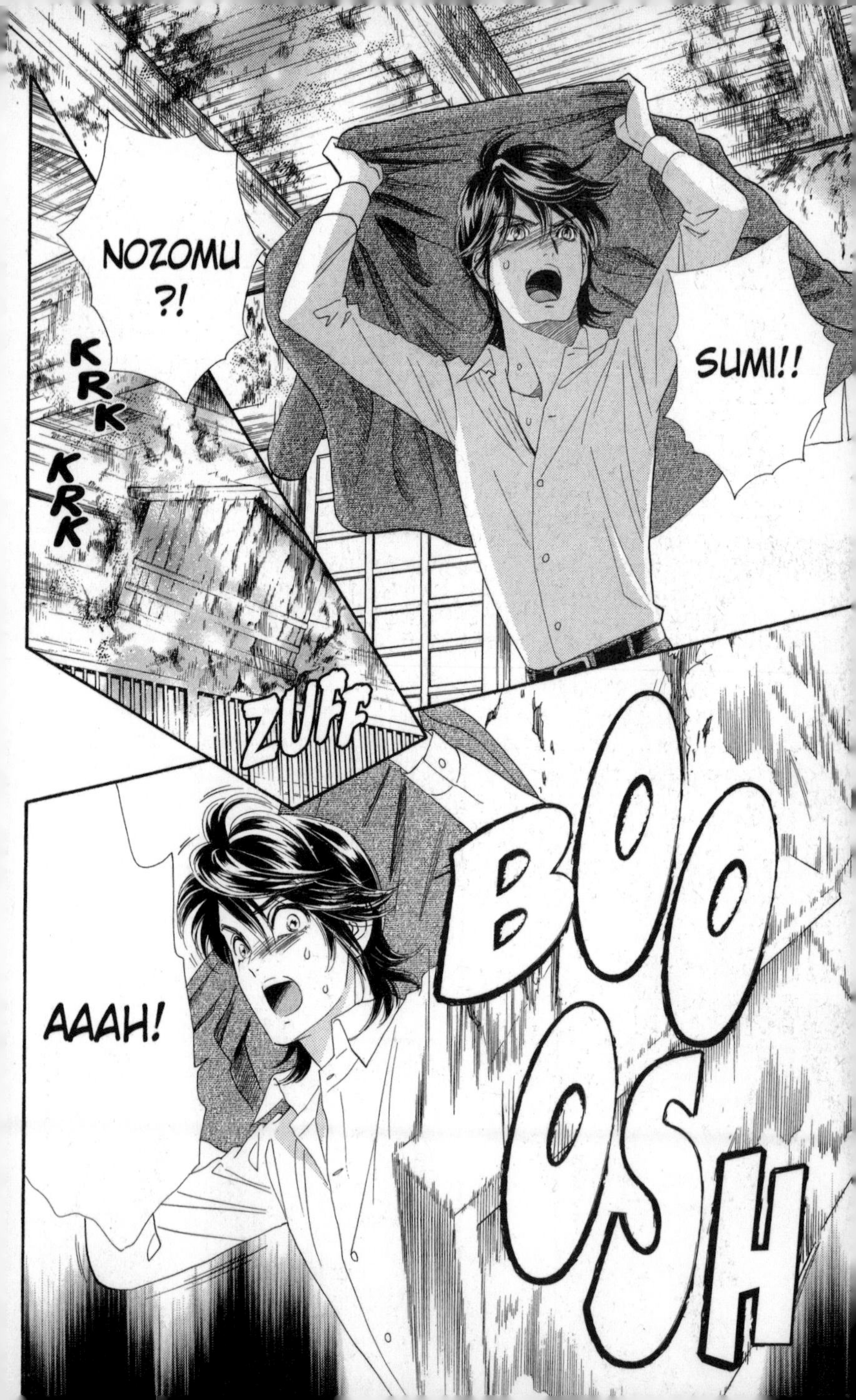
SUMI!!
NOZOMU ?!
KRK KRK
ZUFF
BOOOOSH
AAAH!

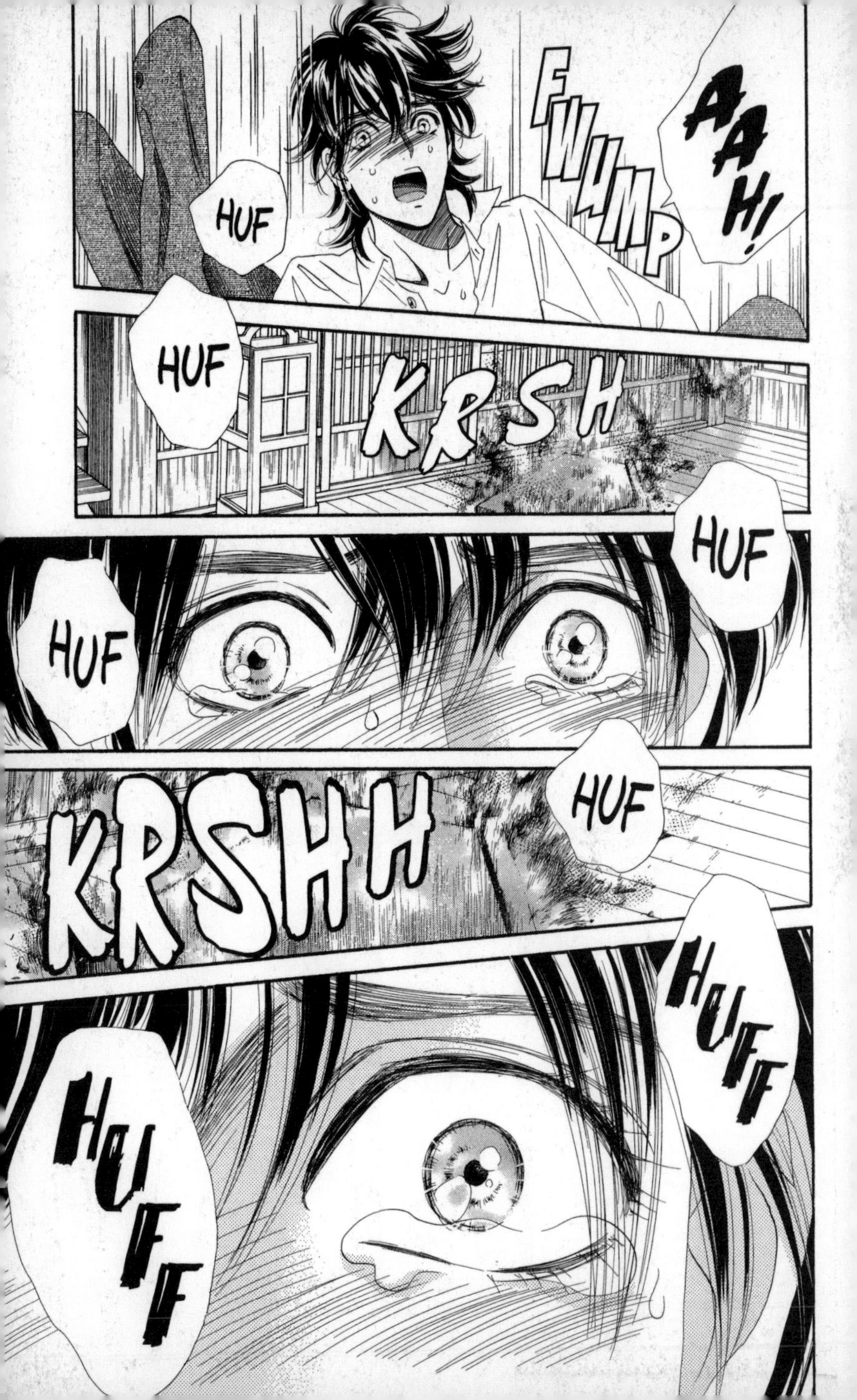
AAH!
FWUMP
HUF
KRSH
HUF
HUF
HUF
HUF
KRSHH
HUFF
HUFF

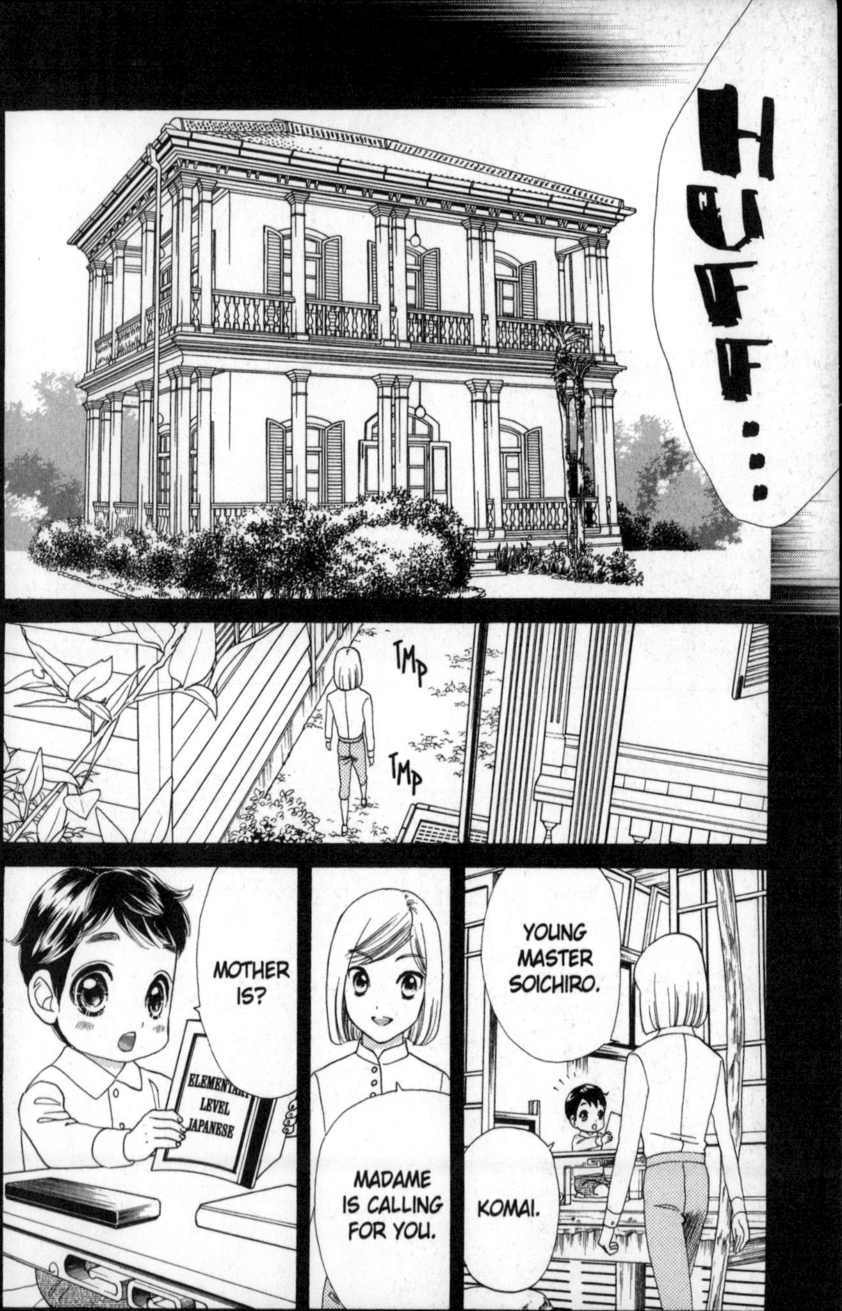
HUFF...
TMP
TMP
YOUNG MASTER SOICHIRO.
KOMAI.
MADAME IS CALLING FOR YOU.
MOTHER IS?
LEVEL

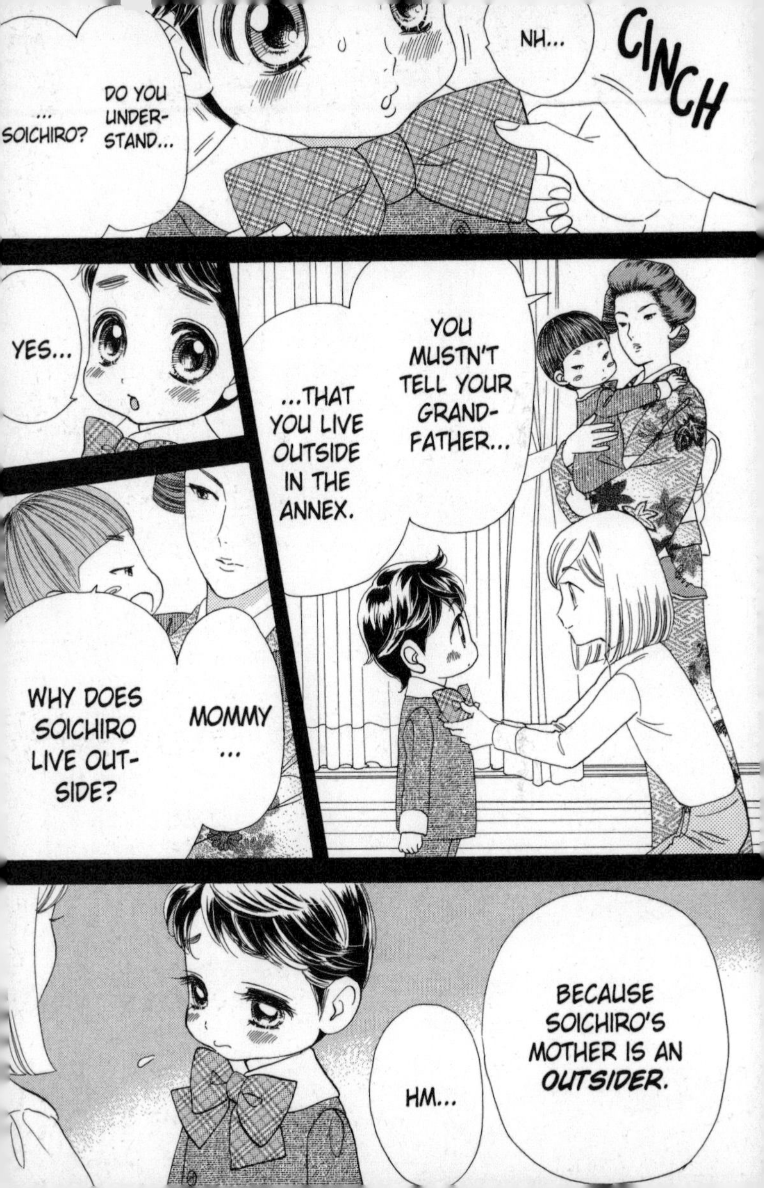
NH...
CINCH
DO YOU UNDERSTAND... ...SOICHIRO?
YOU MUSTN'T TELL YOUR GRANDFATHER...
...THAT YOU LIVE OUTSIDE IN THE ANNEX.
YES...
MOMMY...
WHY DOES SOICHIRO LIVE OUTSIDE?
BECAUSE SOICHIRO'S MOTHER IS AN *OUTSIDER.*
HM...

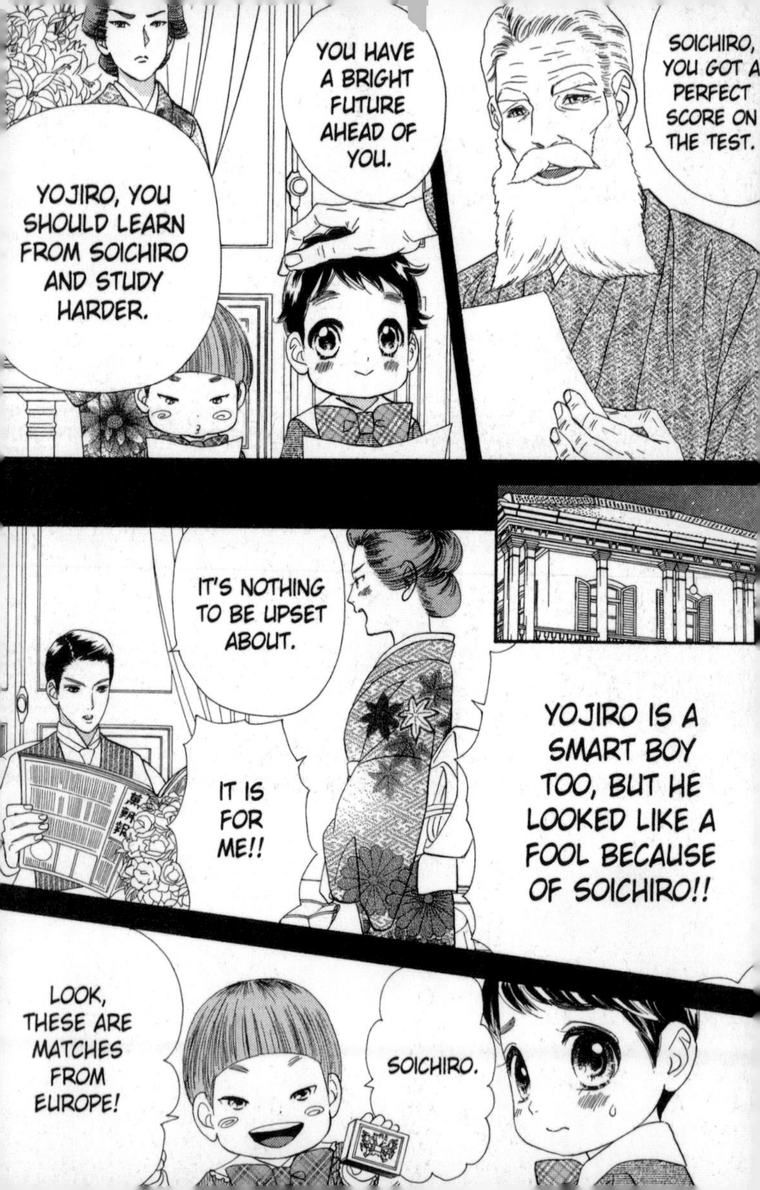
SOICHIRO, YOU GOT A PERFECT SCORE ON THE TEST.
YOU HAVE A BRIGHT FUTURE AHEAD OF YOU.
YOJIRO, YOU SHOULD LEARN FROM SOICHIRO AND STUDY HARDER.
YOJIRO IS A SMART BOY TOO, BUT HE LOOKED LIKE A FOOL BECAUSE OF SOICHIRO!!
IT'S NOTHING TO BE UPSET ABOUT.
IT IS FOR ME!!
SOICHIRO.
LOOK, THESE ARE MATCHES FROM EUROPE!

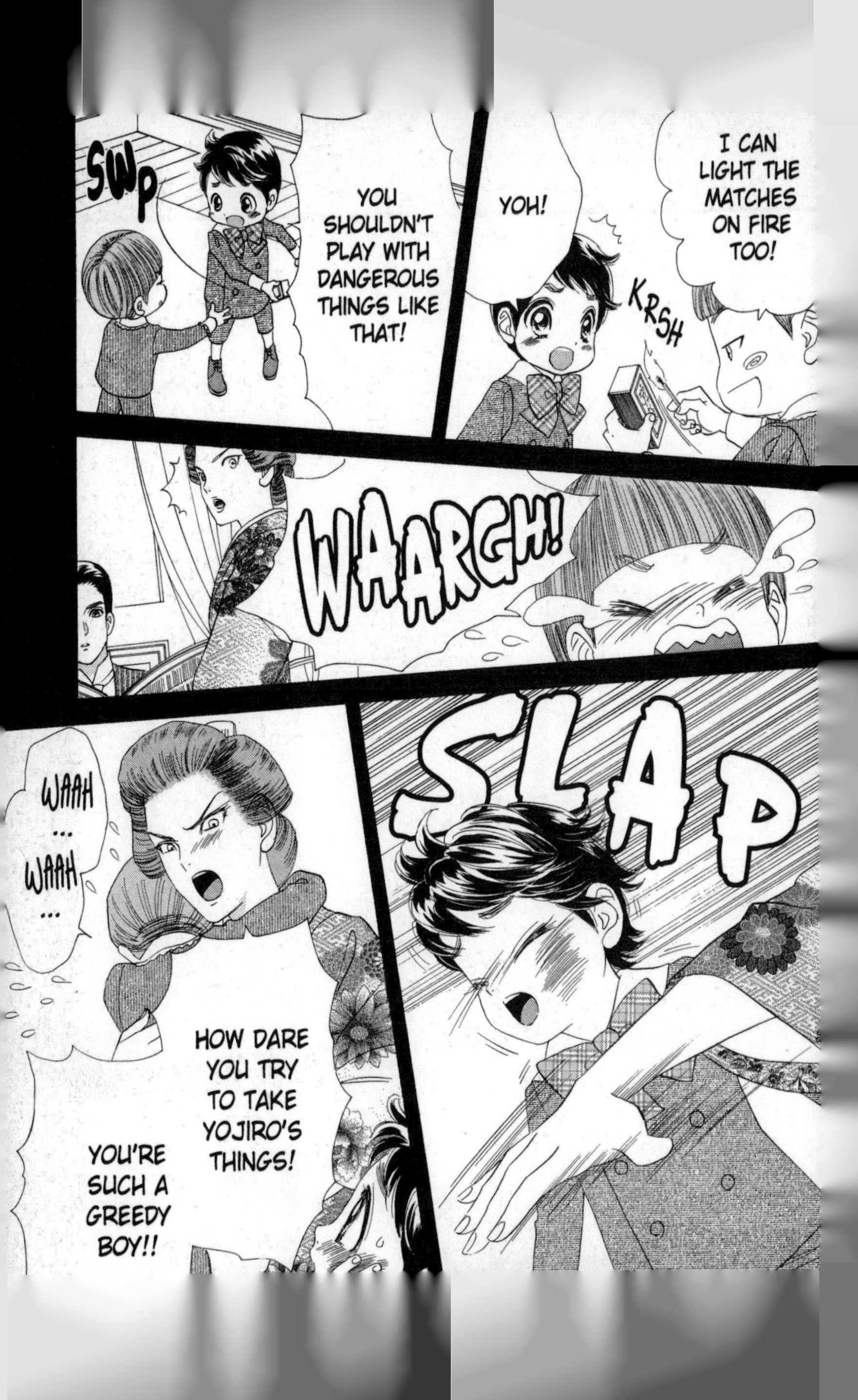
I CAN LIGHT THE MATCHES ON FIRE TOO!
KRSH
YOH!
YOU SHOULDN'T PLAY WITH DANGEROUS THINGS LIKE THAT!
SWP
WAARGH!
SLAP
HOW DARE YOU TRY TO TAKE YOJIRO'S THINGS!
YOU'RE SUCH A GREEDY BOY!!
WAAH ... WAAH ...

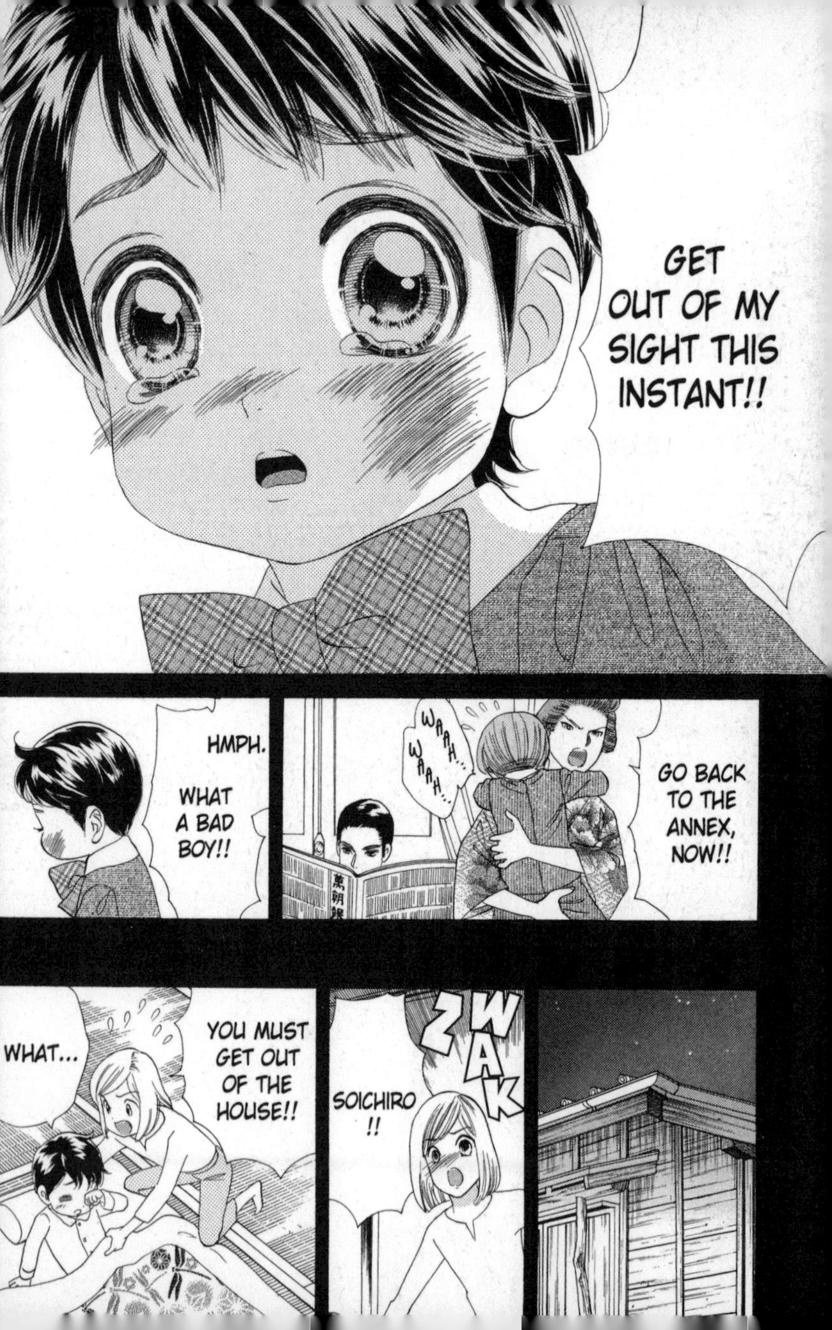
GET OUT OF MY SIGHT THIS INSTANT!!
GO BACK TO THE ANNEX, NOW!!
WAAH... WAAH...
HMPH.
WHAT A BAD BOY!!
ZWAK
SOICHIRO!!
YOU MUST GET OUT OF THE HOUSE!!
WHAT...

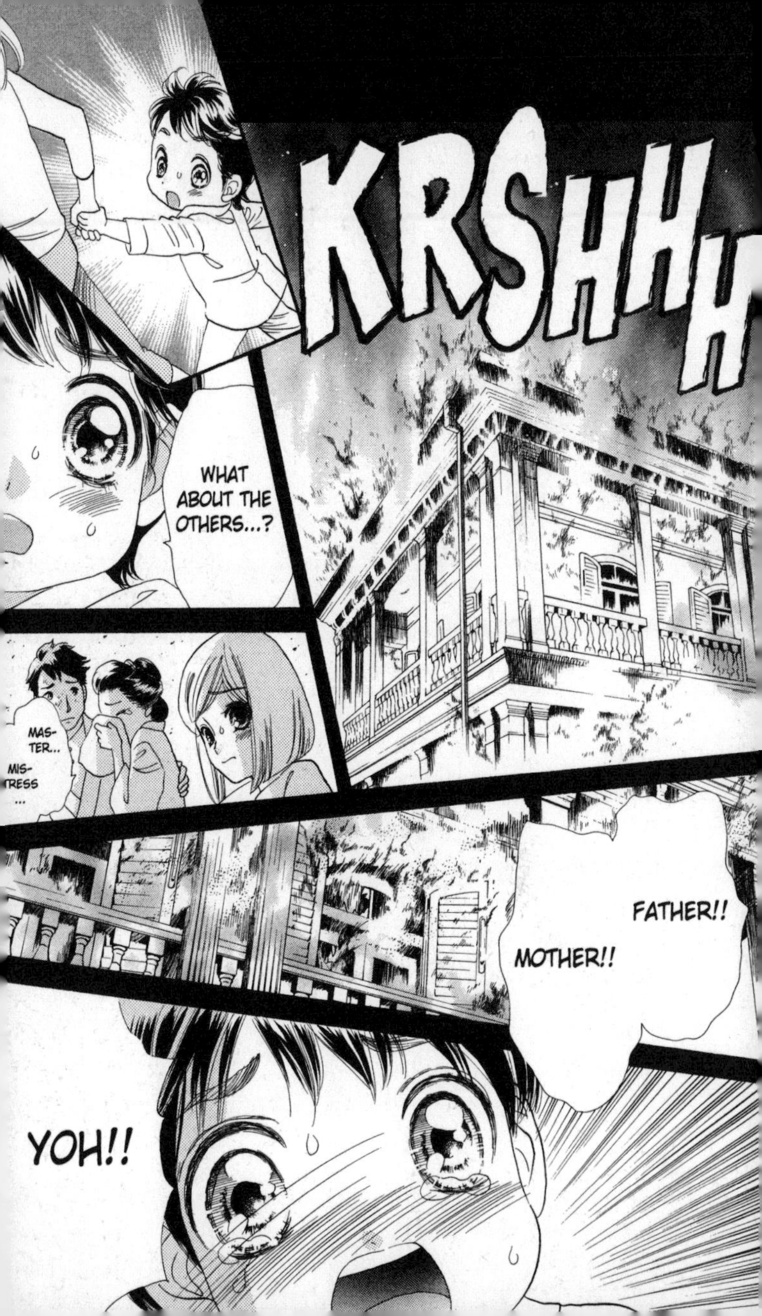
KRSHHH
WHAT ABOUT THE OTHERS...?
MASTER...
MISTRESS...
FATHER!!
MOTHER!!
YOH!!

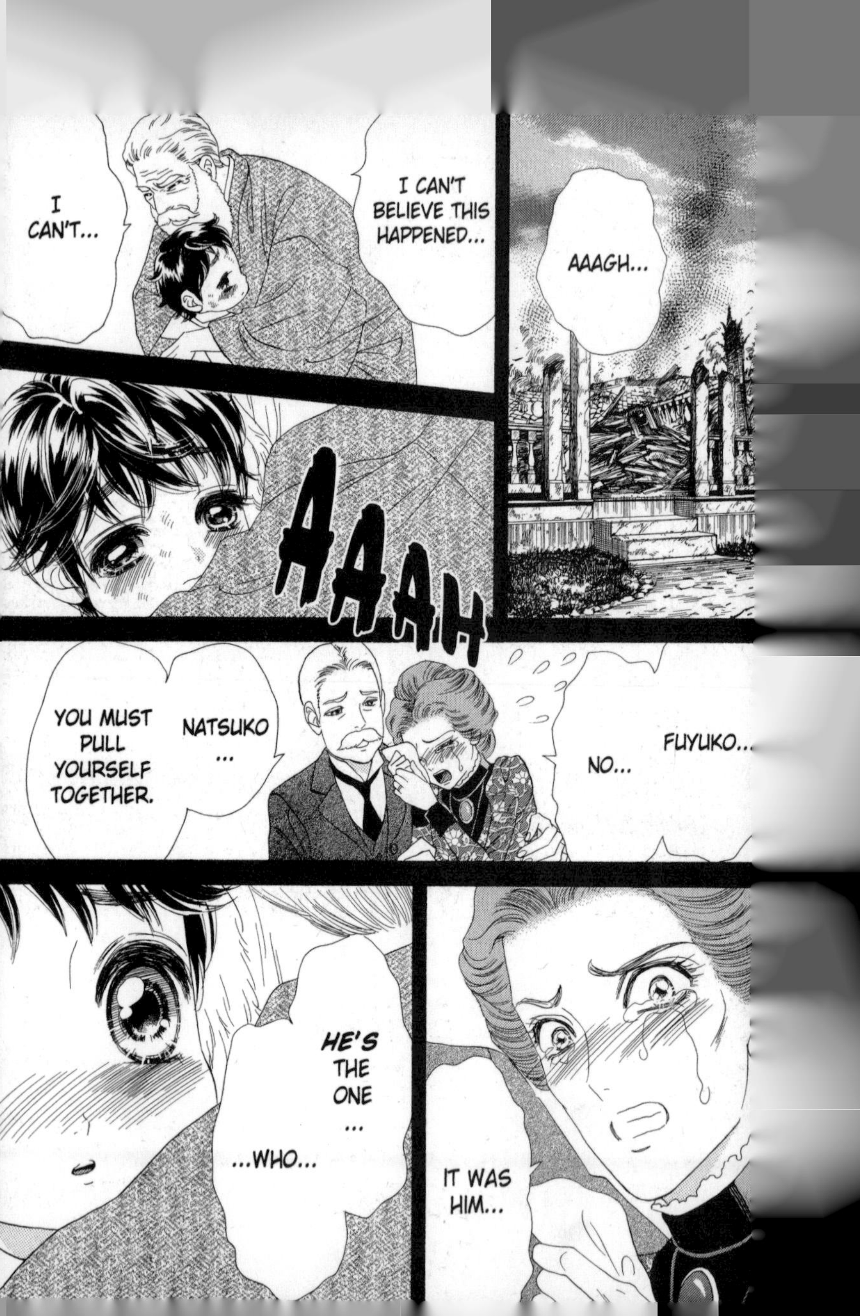
AAAGH...
I CAN'T BELIEVE THIS HAPPENED...
I CAN'T...
AAAH
FUYUKO...
NO...
NATSUKO ...
YOU MUST PULL YOURSELF TOGETHER.
IT WAS HIM...
HE'S THE ONE ...
...WHO...

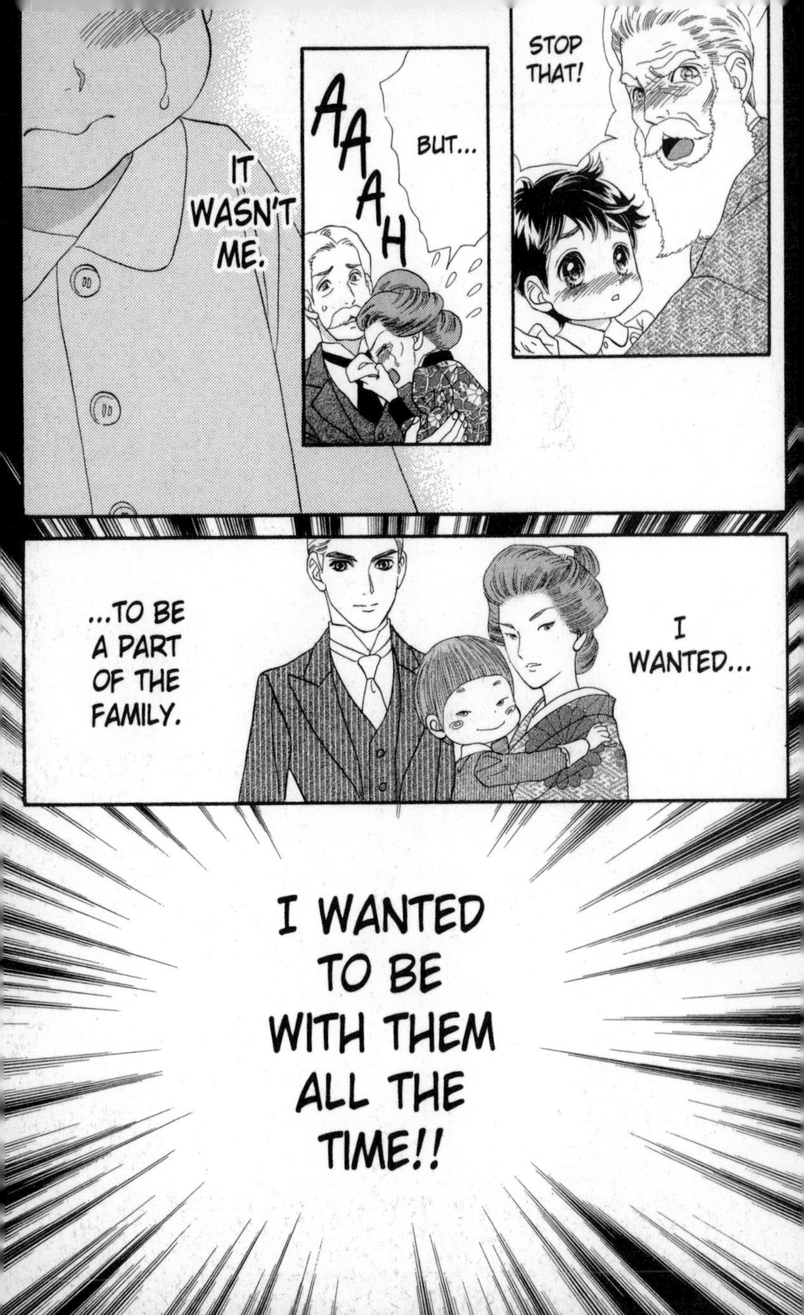
STOP THAT!
BUT...
AAAAH
IT WASN'T ME.
I WANTED...
...TO BE A PART OF THE FAMILY.
I WANTED TO BE WITH THEM ALL THE TIME!!

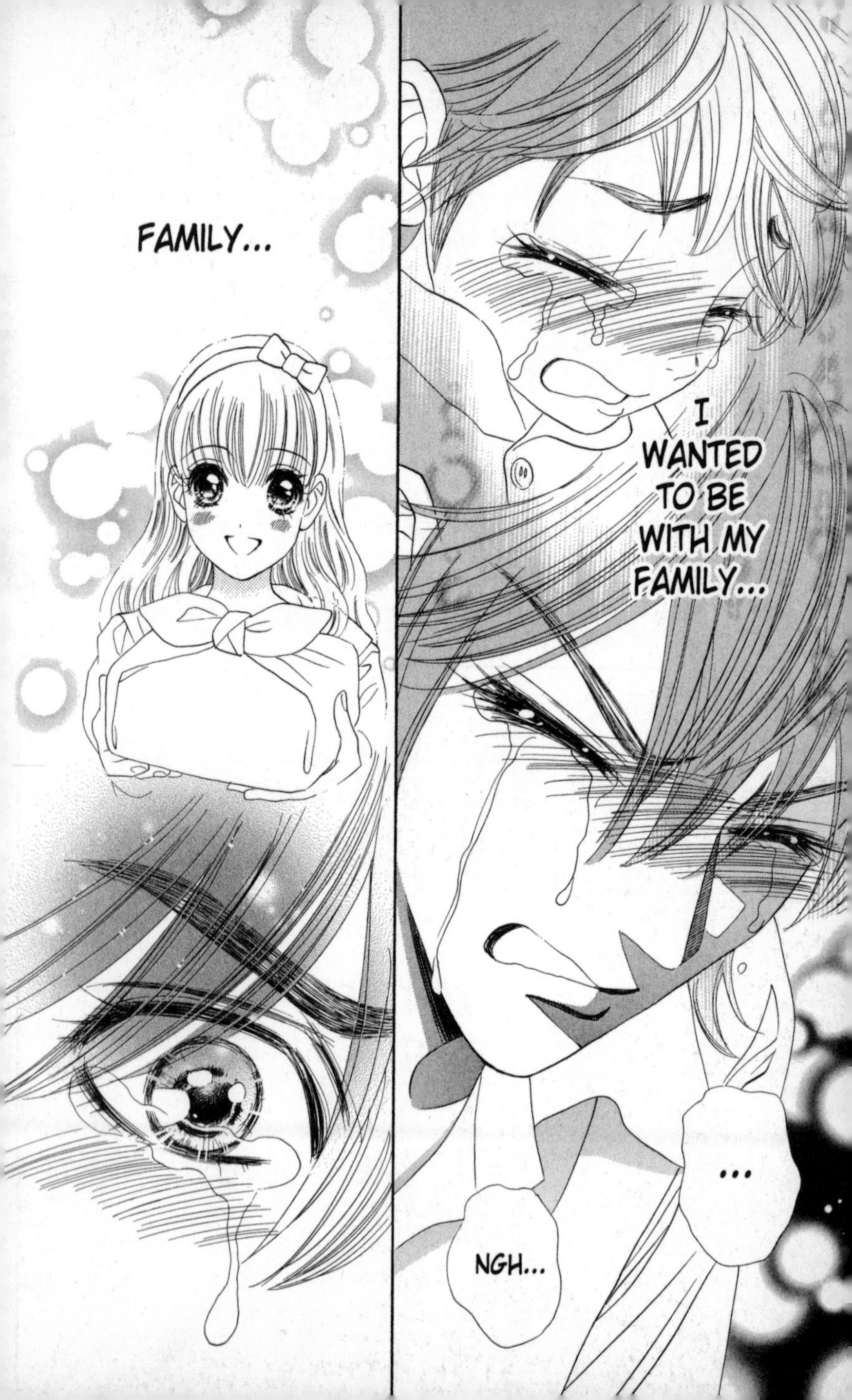
I WANTED TO BE WITH MY FAMILY...
...
NGH...
FAMILY...

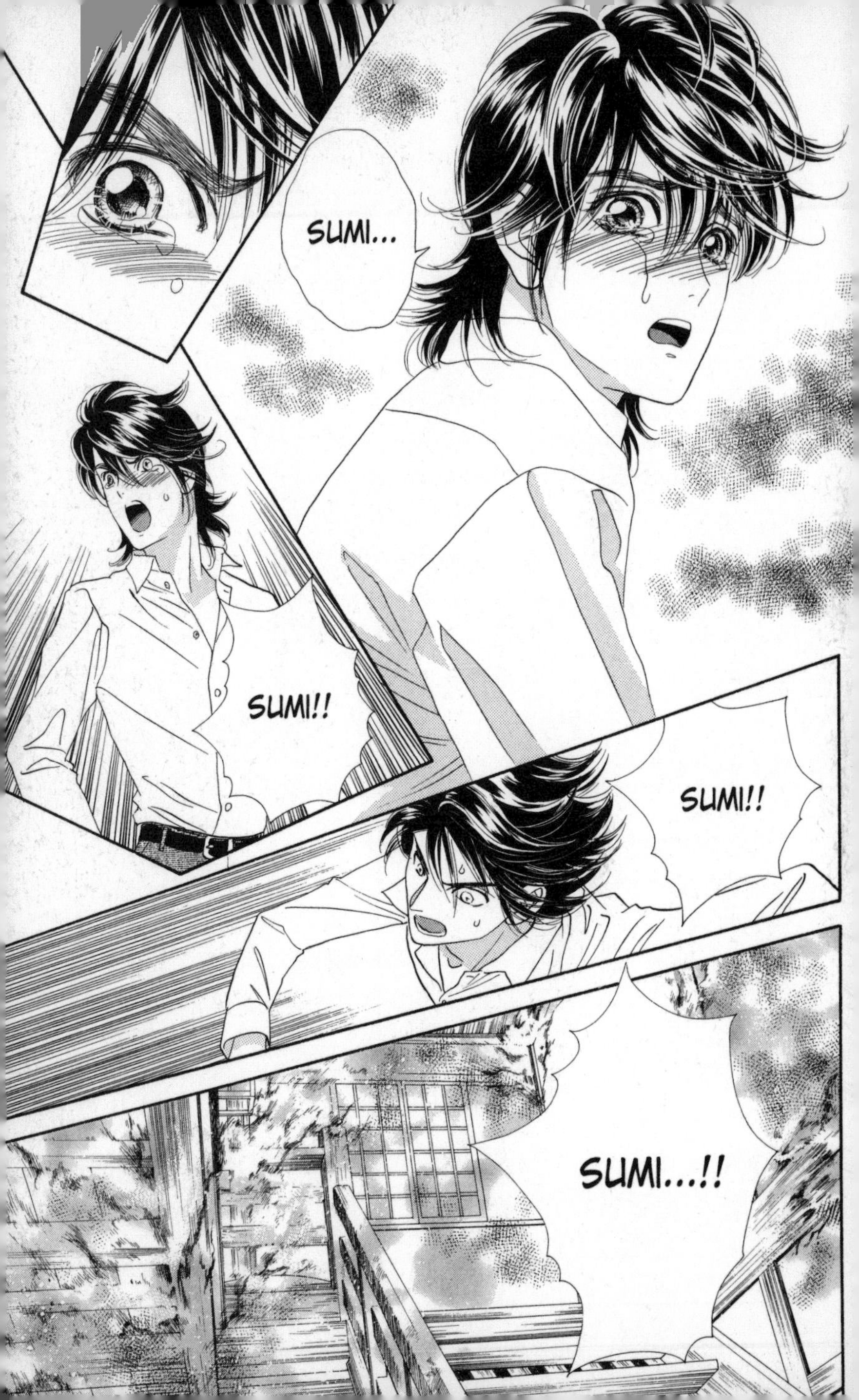
SUMI...
SUMI!!
SUMI!!
SUMI...!!

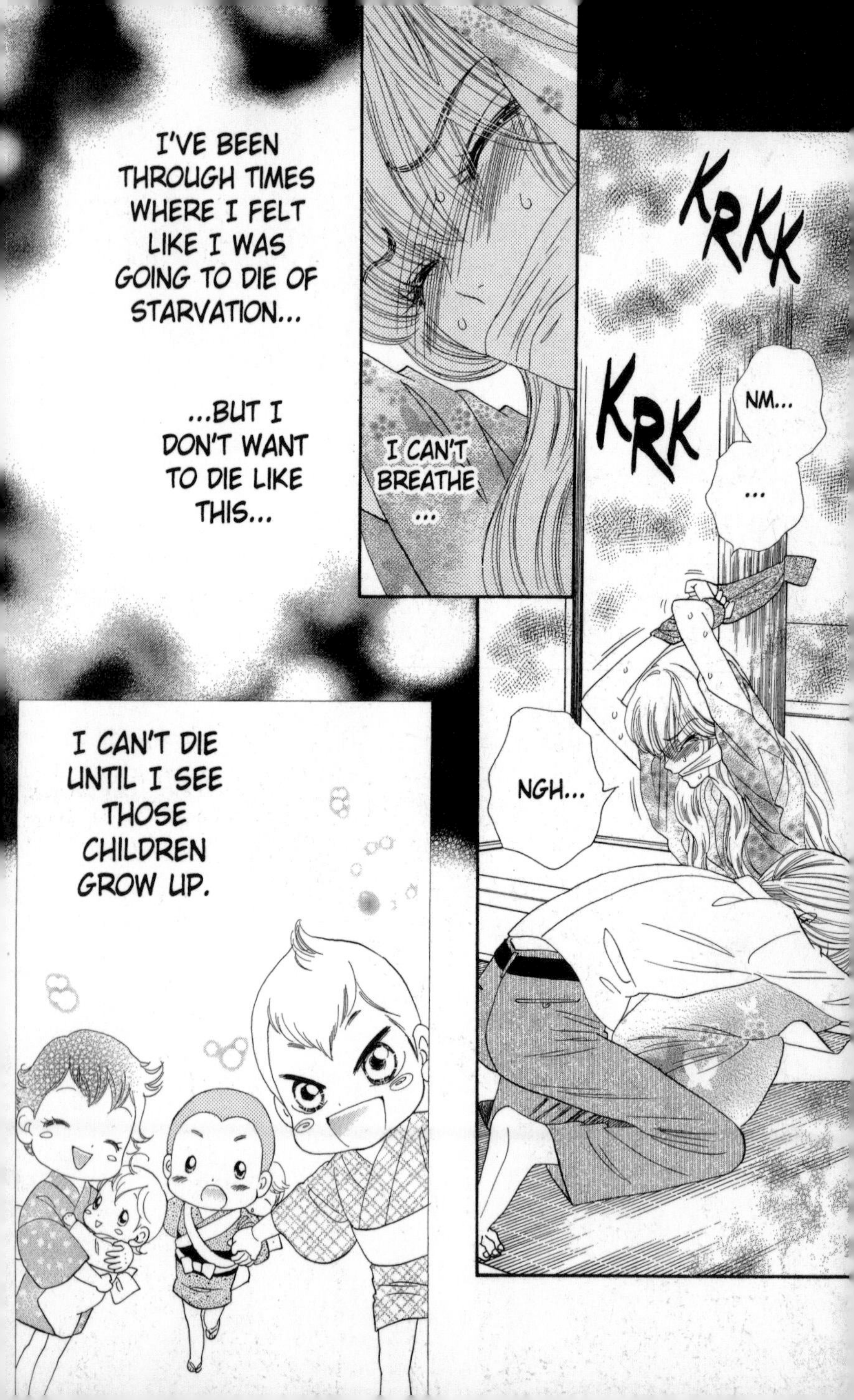
I CAN'T BREATHE ...
KRKK
KRK
NM...
...
NGH...
I'VE BEEN THROUGH TIMES WHERE I FELT LIKE I WAS GOING TO DIE OF STARVATION...
...BUT I DON'T WANT TO DIE LIKE THIS...
I CAN'T DIE UNTIL I SEE THOSE CHILDREN GROW UP.

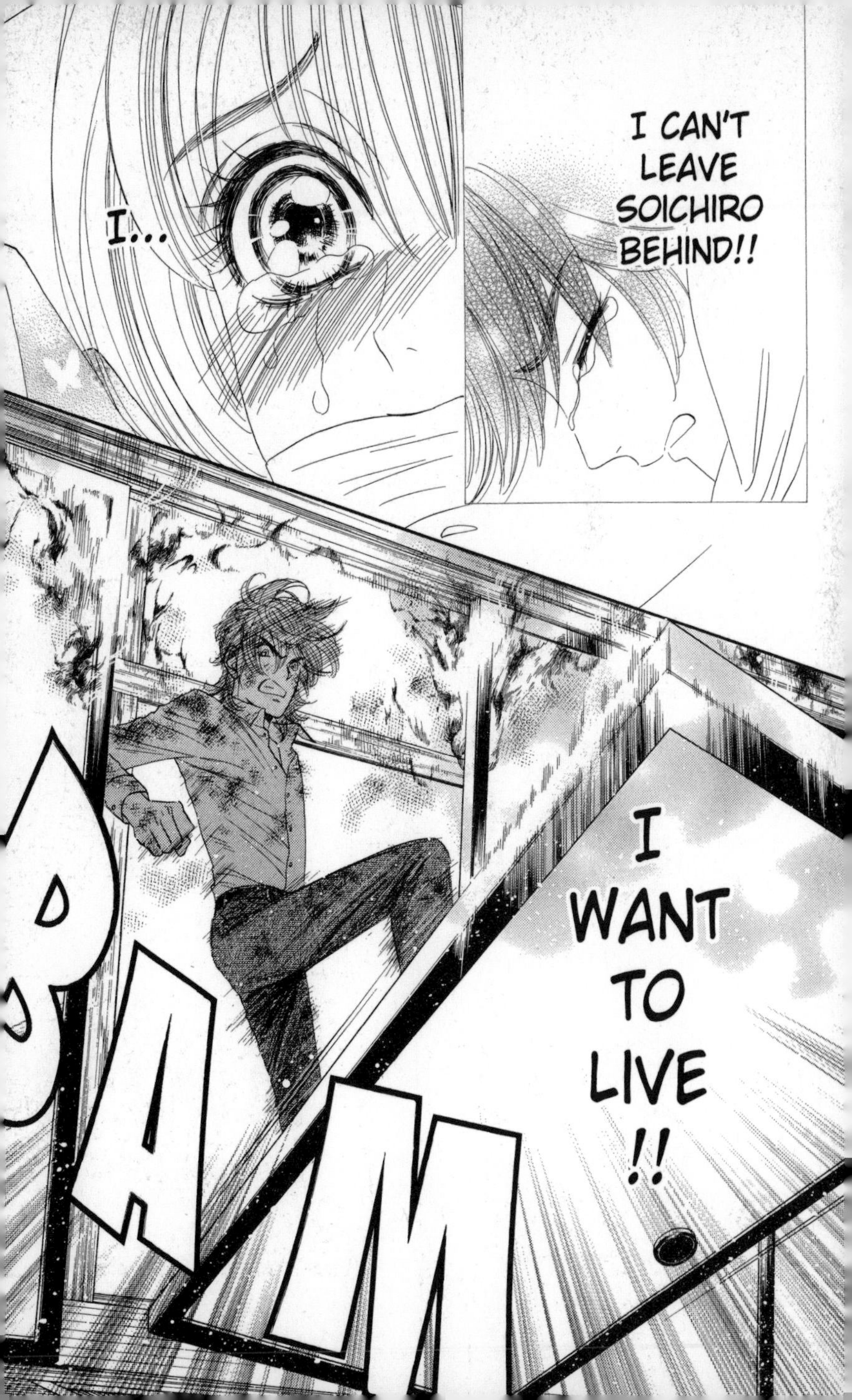
I CAN'T LEAVE SOICHIRO BEHIND!!
I...
I WANT TO LIVE!!

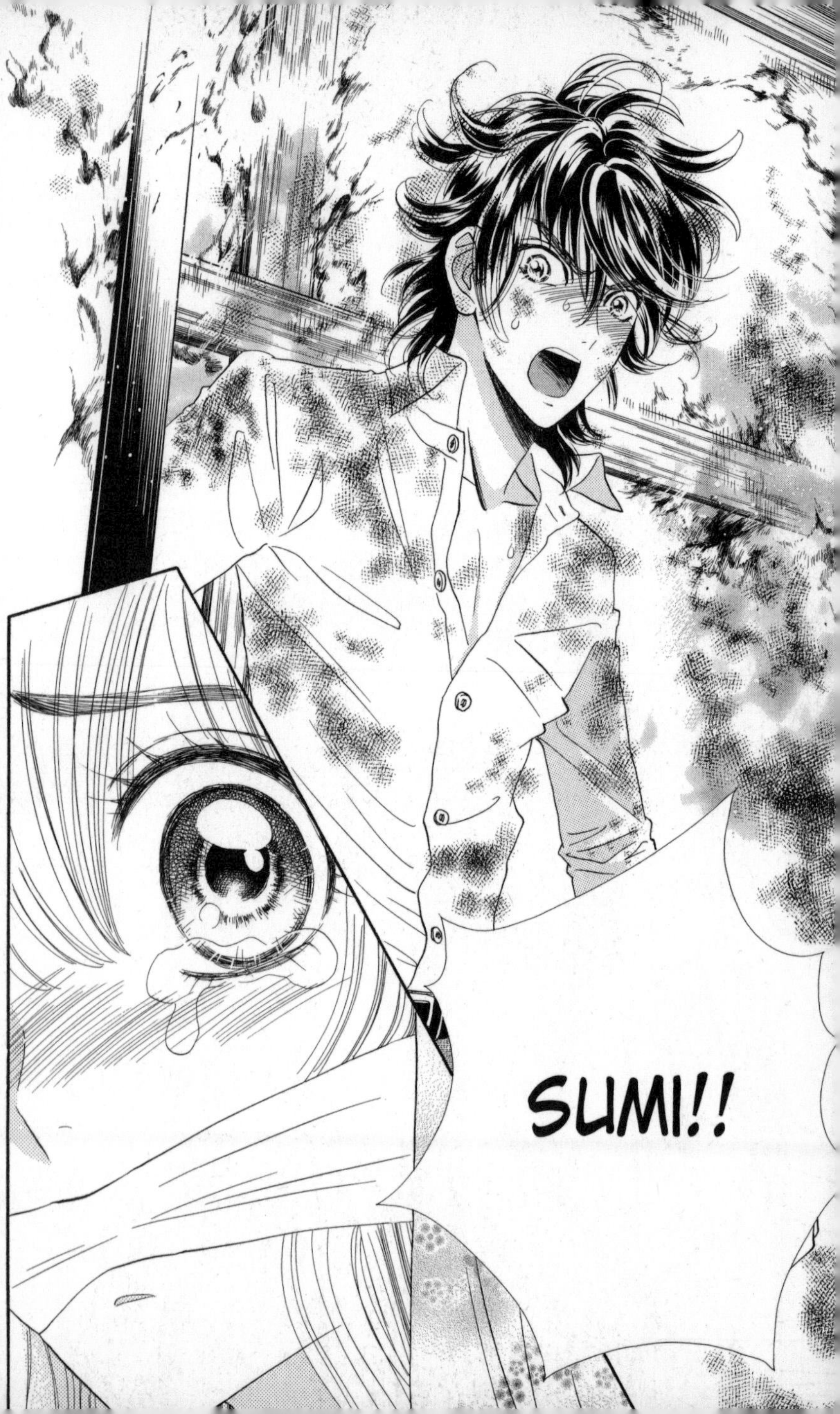
SUMI!!

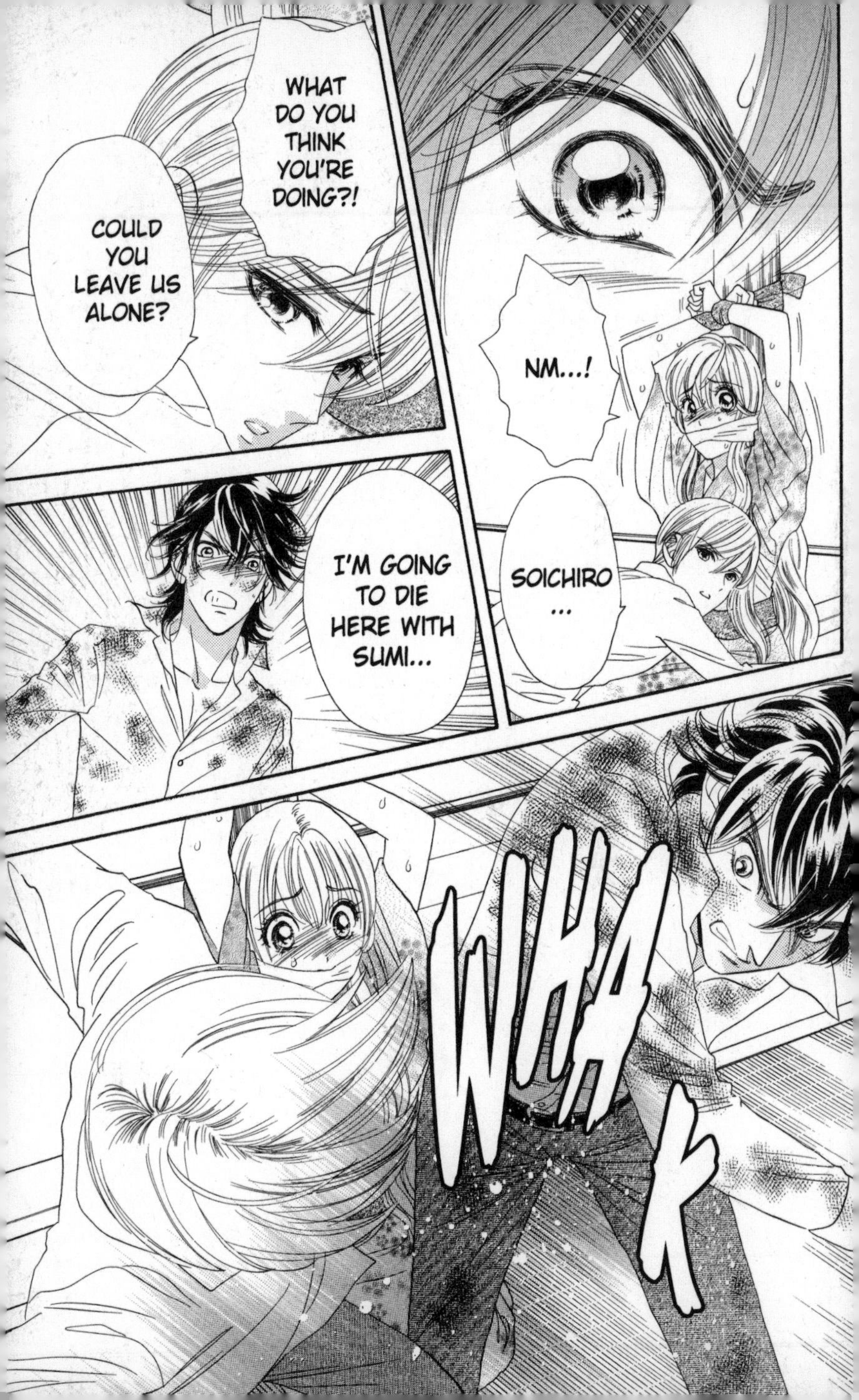
NM...!
WHAT DO YOU THINK YOU'RE DOING?!
COULD YOU LEAVE US ALONE?
SOICHIRO ...
I'M GOING TO DIE HERE WITH SUMI...
WHAK

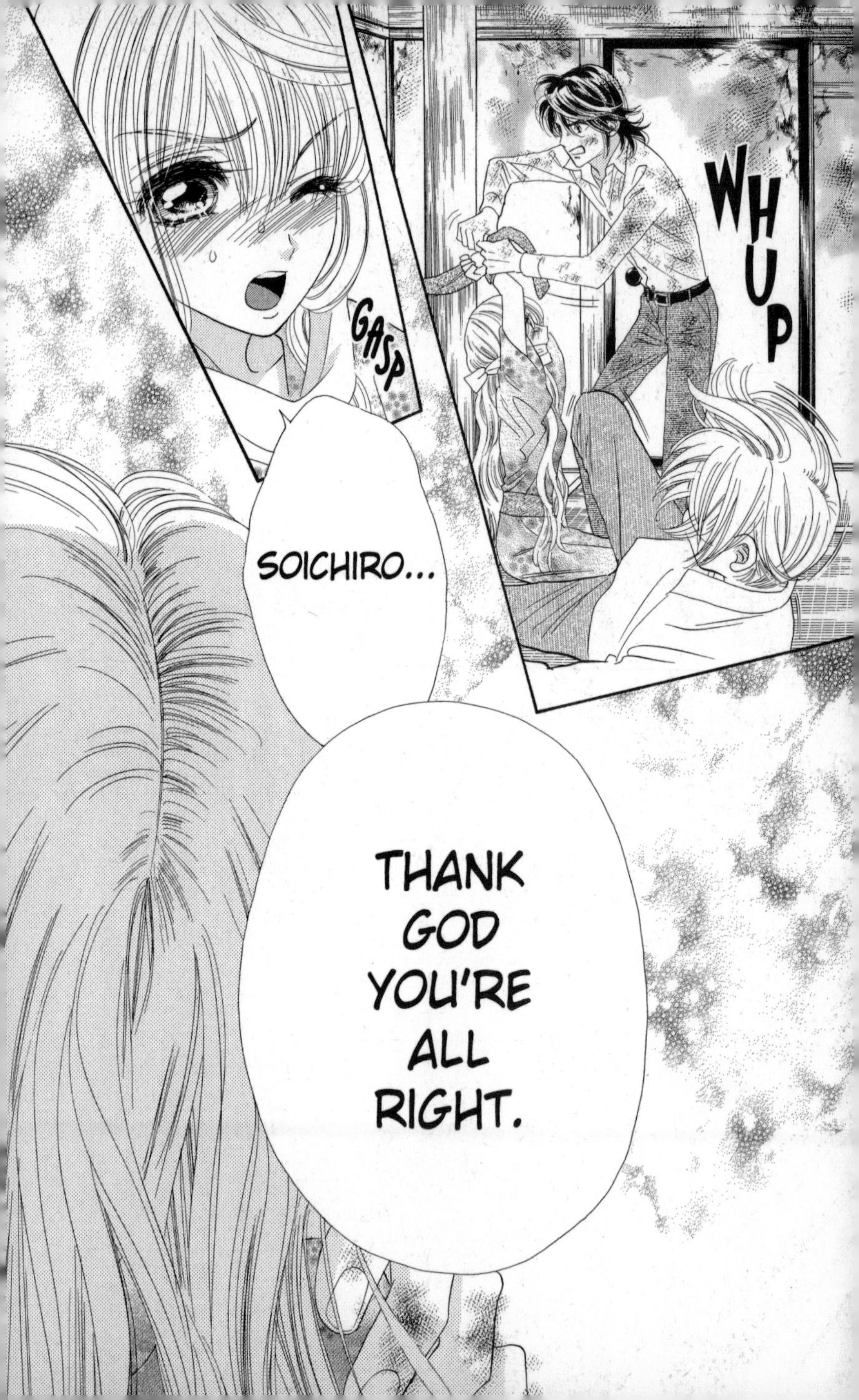
WHUP
GASP
SOICHIRO...
THANK GOD YOU'RE ALL RIGHT.

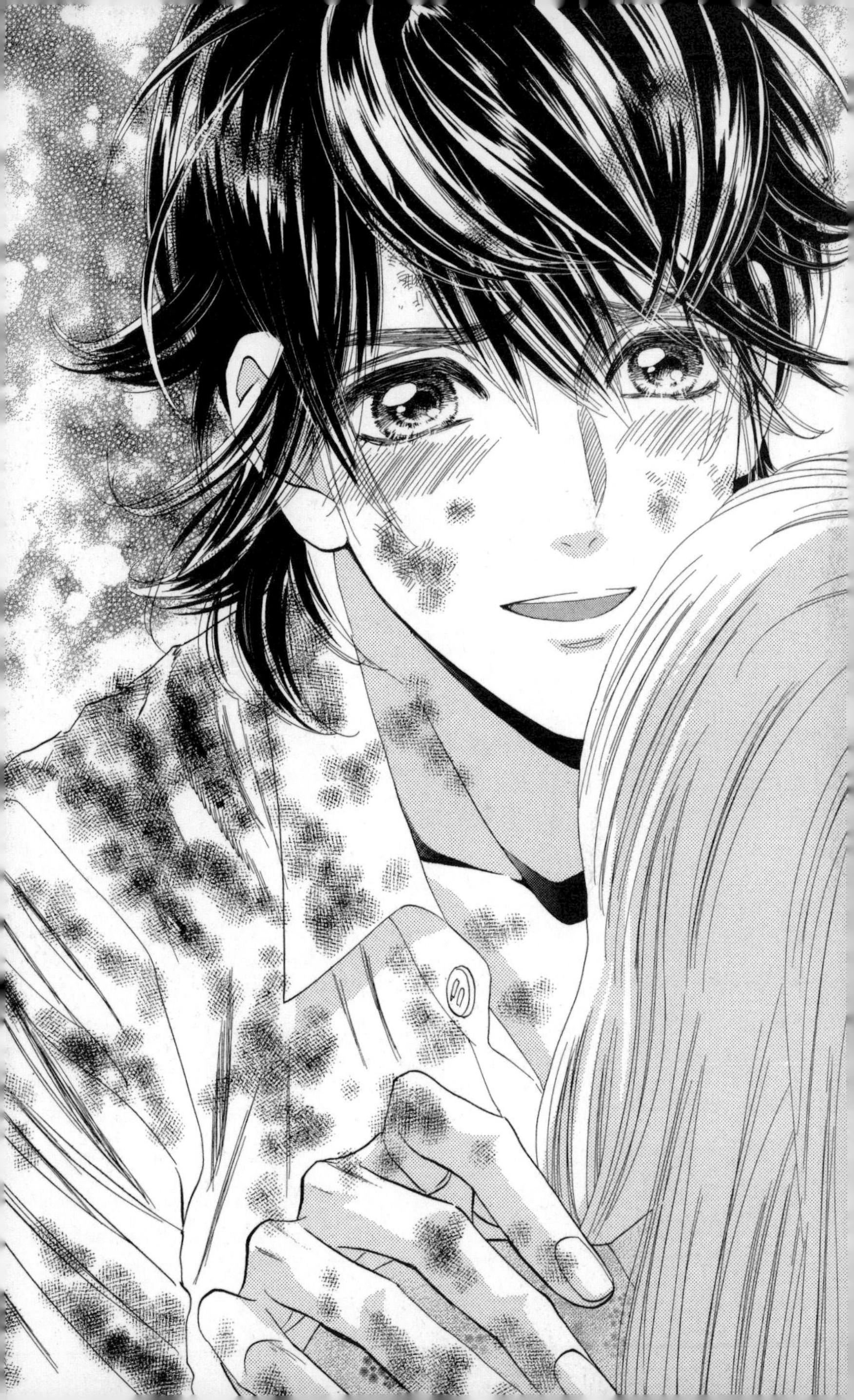

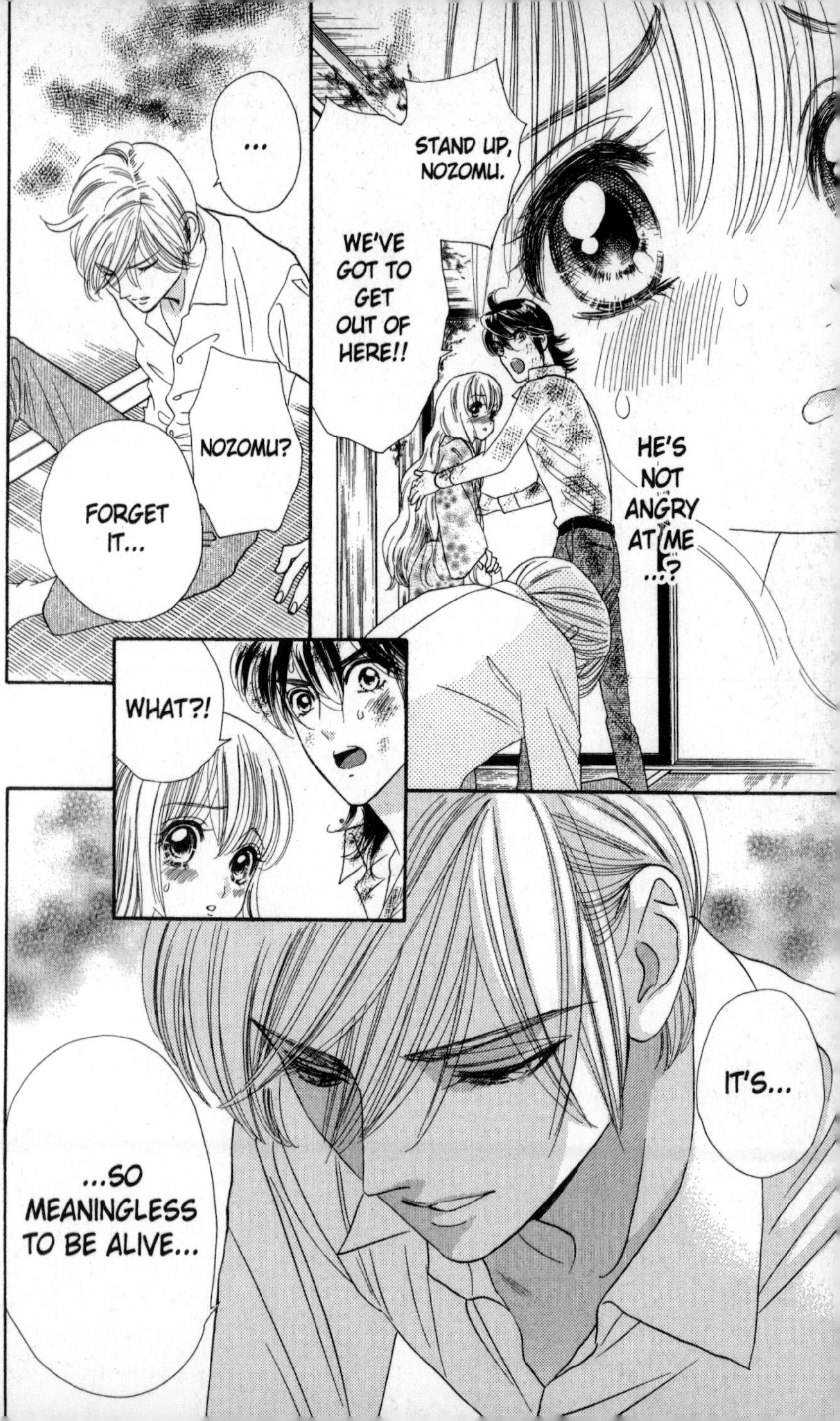
STAND UP, NOZOMU.
WE'VE GOT TO GET OUT OF HERE!!
HE'S NOT ANGRY AT ME ...?
...
NOZOMU?
FORGET IT...
WHAT?!
IT'S...
...SO MEANINGLESS TO BE ALIVE...

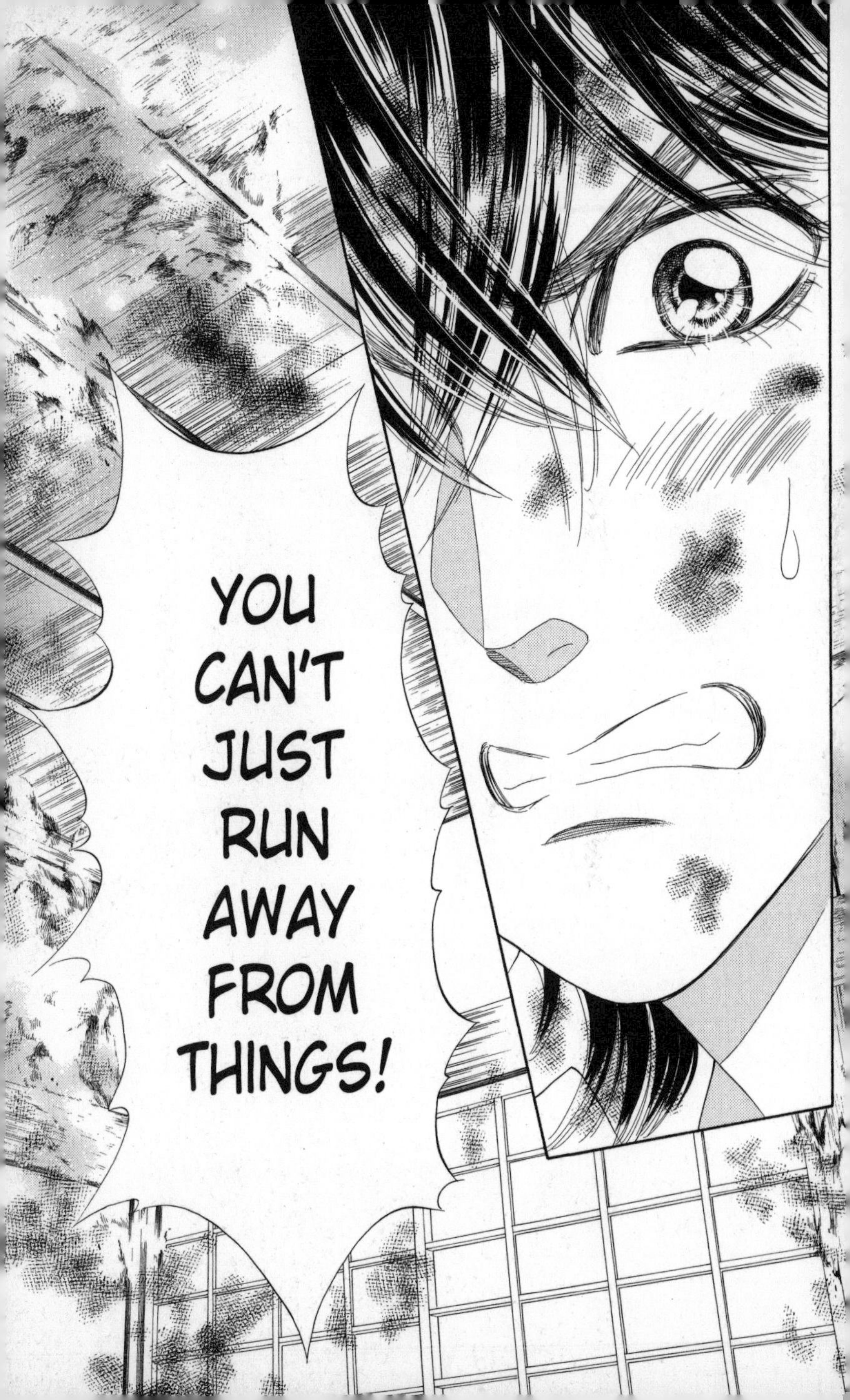
YOU CAN'T JUST RUN AWAY FROM THINGS!

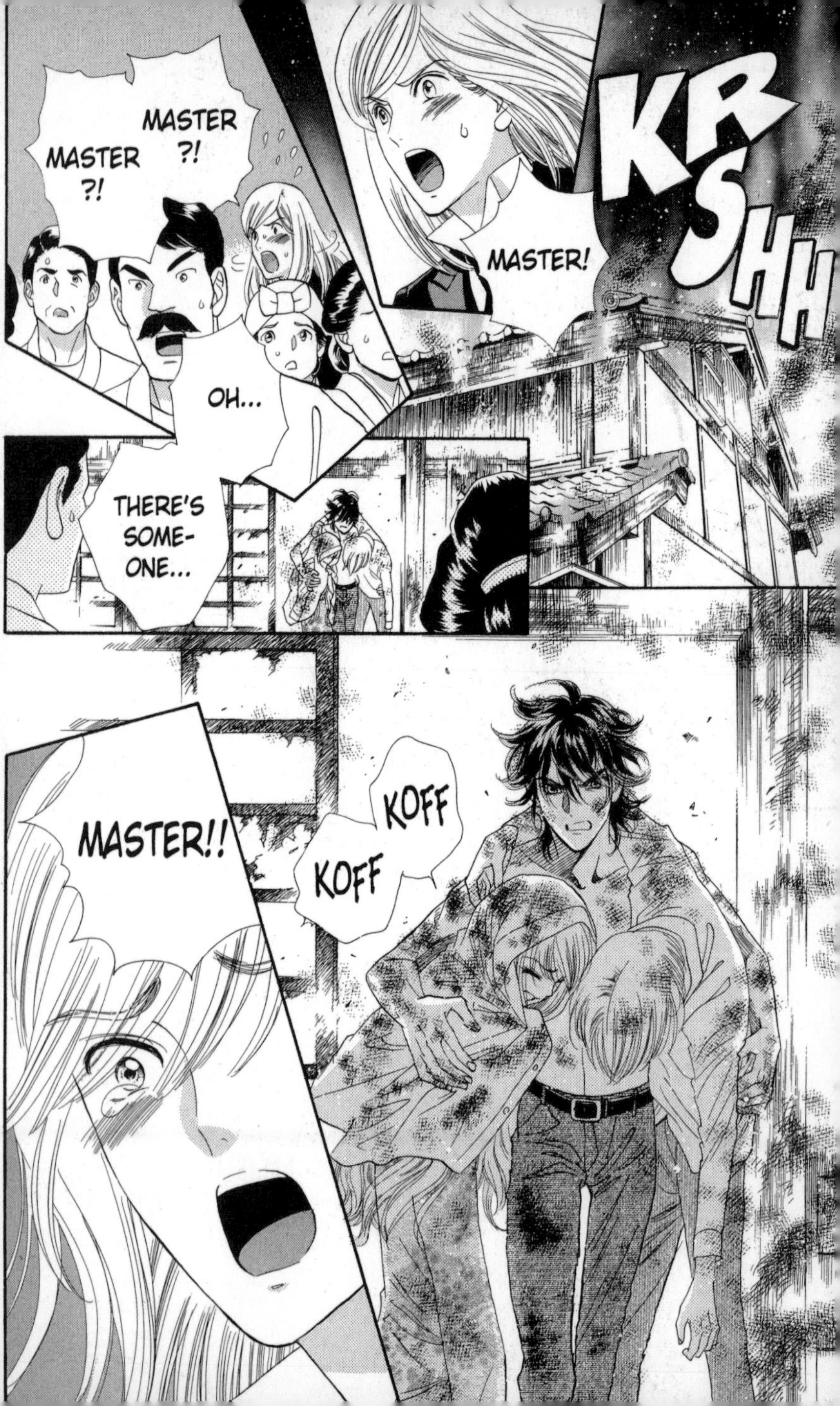
KRSHH
MASTER!
MASTER ?!
MASTER ?!
OH...
THERE'S SOME-ONE...
KOFF
KOFF
MASTER!!

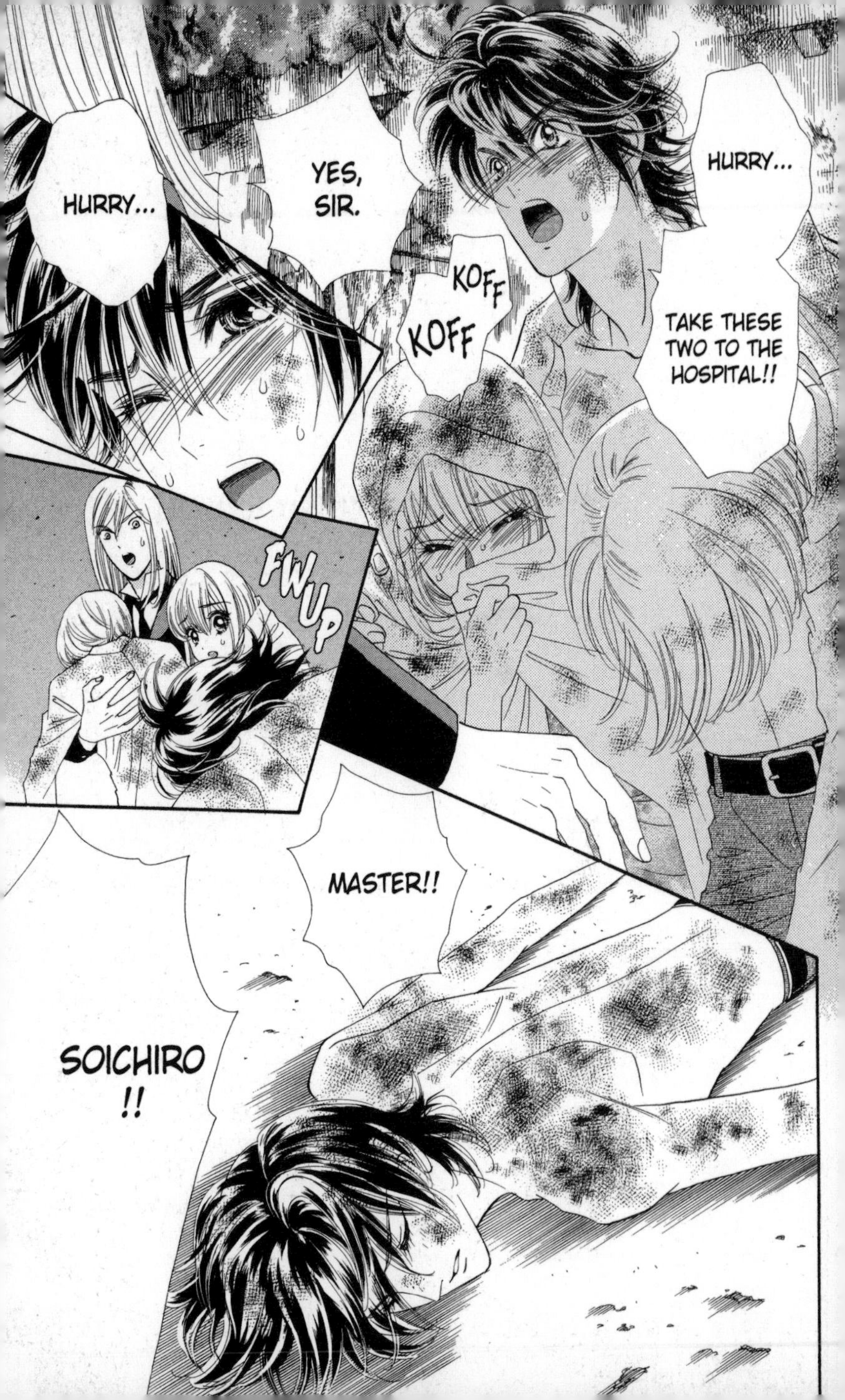
HURRY...
TAKE THESE TWO TO THE HOSPITAL!!
KOFF
KOFF
YES, SIR.
HURRY...
FWUP
MASTER!!
SOICHIRO !!

STEP STAGE ② (I WAS ON THE RADIO...)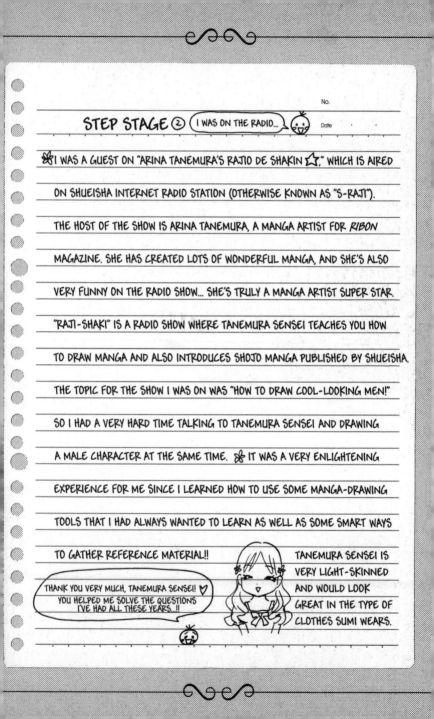

❀I WAS A GUEST ON "ARINA TANEMURA'S RAJIO DE SHAKIN ☆," WHICH IS AIRED

ON SHUEISHA INTERNET RADIO STATION (OTHERWISE KNOWN AS "S-RAJI").

THE HOST OF THE SHOW IS ARINA TANEMURA, A MANGA ARTIST FOR *RIBON*

MAGAZINE. SHE HAS CREATED LOTS OF WONDERFUL MANGA, AND SHE'S ALSO

VERY FUNNY ON THE RADIO SHOW... SHE'S TRULY A MANGA ARTIST SUPER STAR.

"RAJI-SHAKI" IS A RADIO SHOW WHERE TANEMURA SENSEI TEACHES YOU HOW

TO DRAW MANGA AND ALSO INTRODUCES SHOJO MANGA PUBLISHED BY SHUEISHA.

THE TOPIC FOR THE SHOW I WAS ON WAS "HOW TO DRAW COOL-LOOKING MEN!"

SO I HAD A VERY HARD TIME TALKING TO TANEMURA SENSEI AND DRAWING

A MALE CHARACTER AT THE SAME TIME. ✂ IT WAS A VERY ENLIGHTENING

EXPERIENCE FOR ME SINCE I LEARNED HOW TO USE SOME MANGA-DRAWING

TOOLS THAT I HAD ALWAYS WANTED TO LEARN AS WELL AS SOME SMART WAYS

TO GATHER REFERENCE MATERIAL!!

THANK YOU VERY MUCH, TANEMURA SENSEI! ♡
YOU HELPED ME SOLVE THE QUESTIONS
I'VE HAD ALL THESE YEARS...!!

TANEMURA SENSEI IS
VERY LIGHT-SKINNED
AND WOULD LOOK
GREAT IN THE TYPE OF
CLOTHES SUMI WEARS.

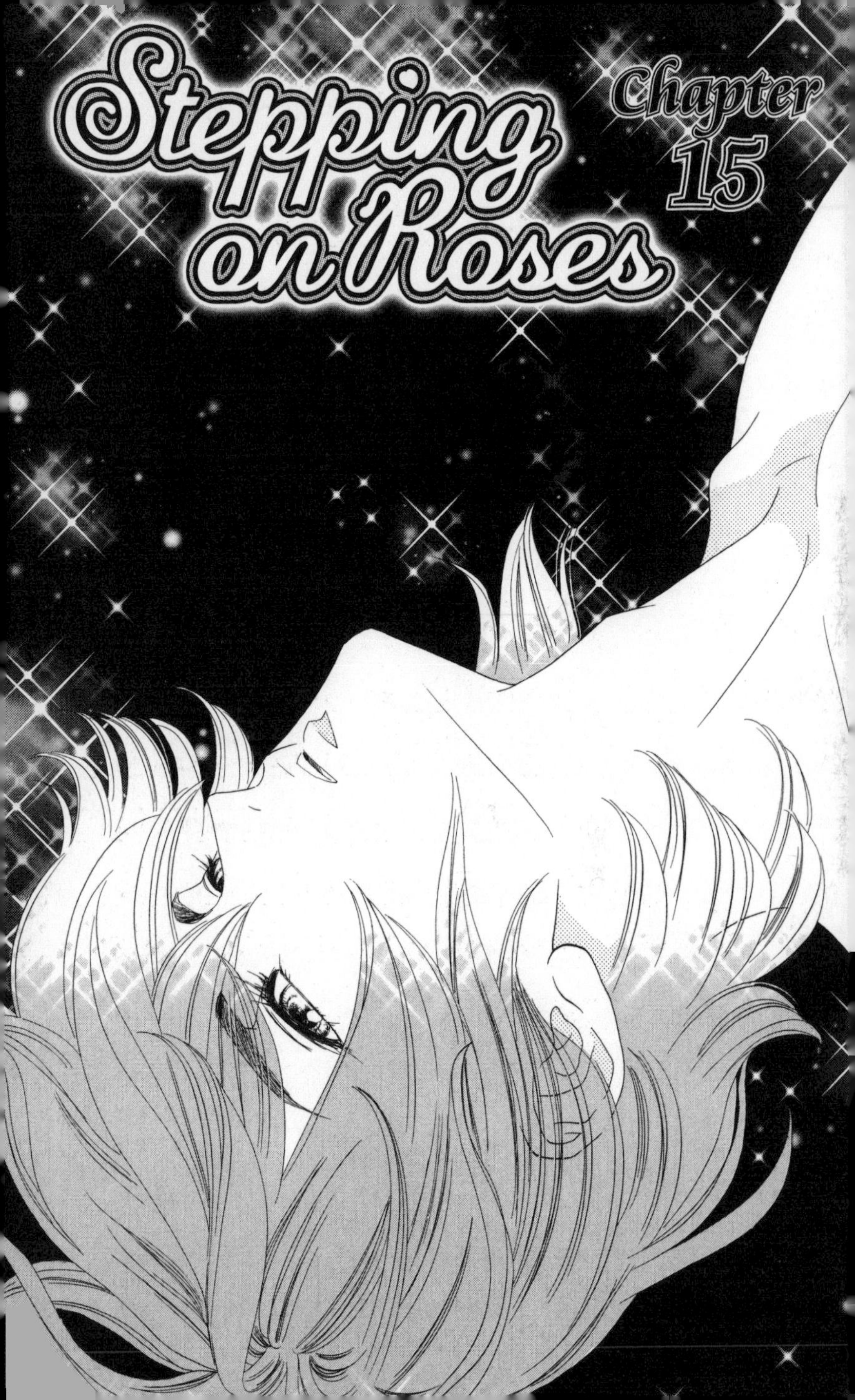
Stepping on Roses
Chapter 15

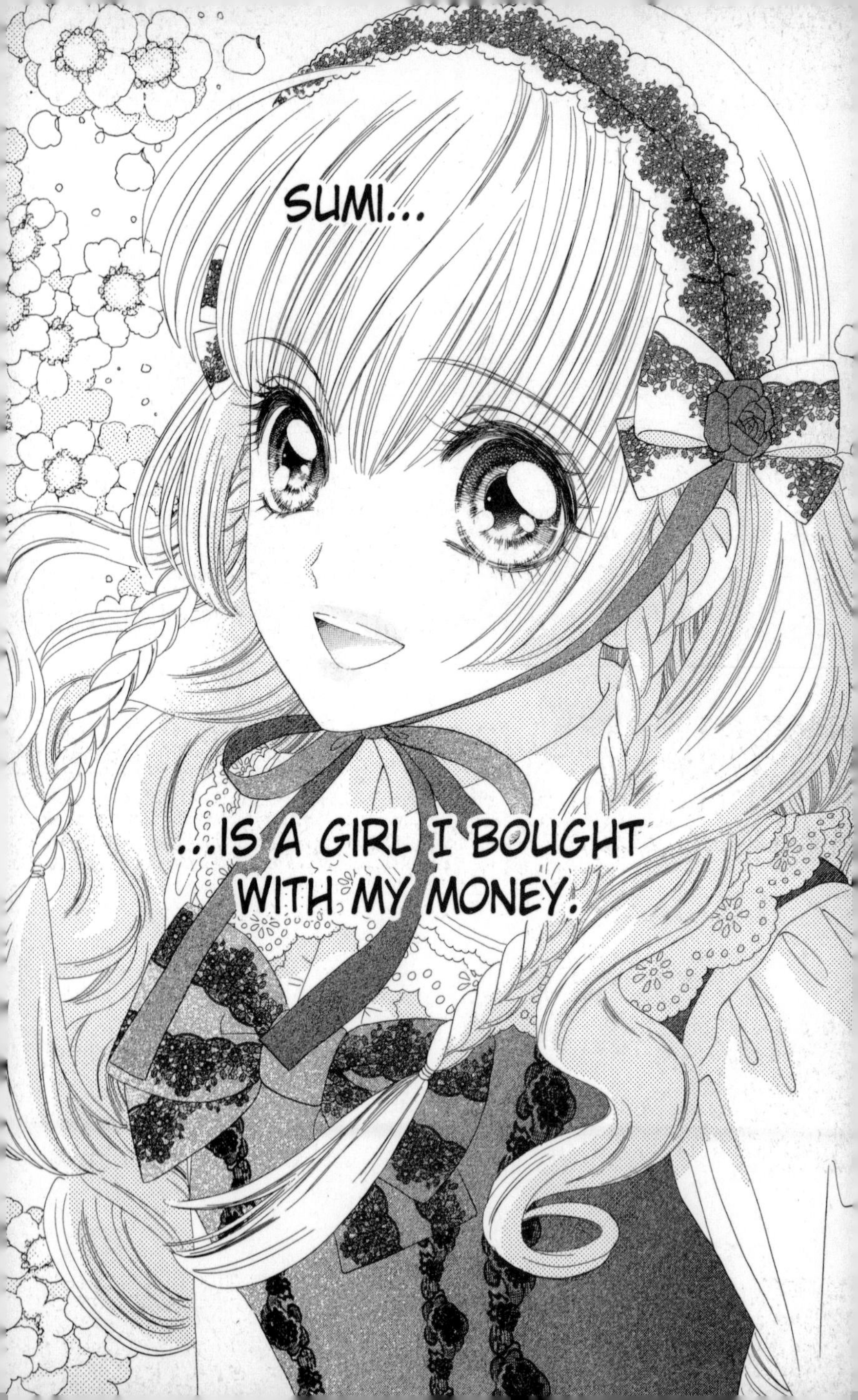
SUMI...
...IS A GIRL I BOUGHT WITH MY MONEY.

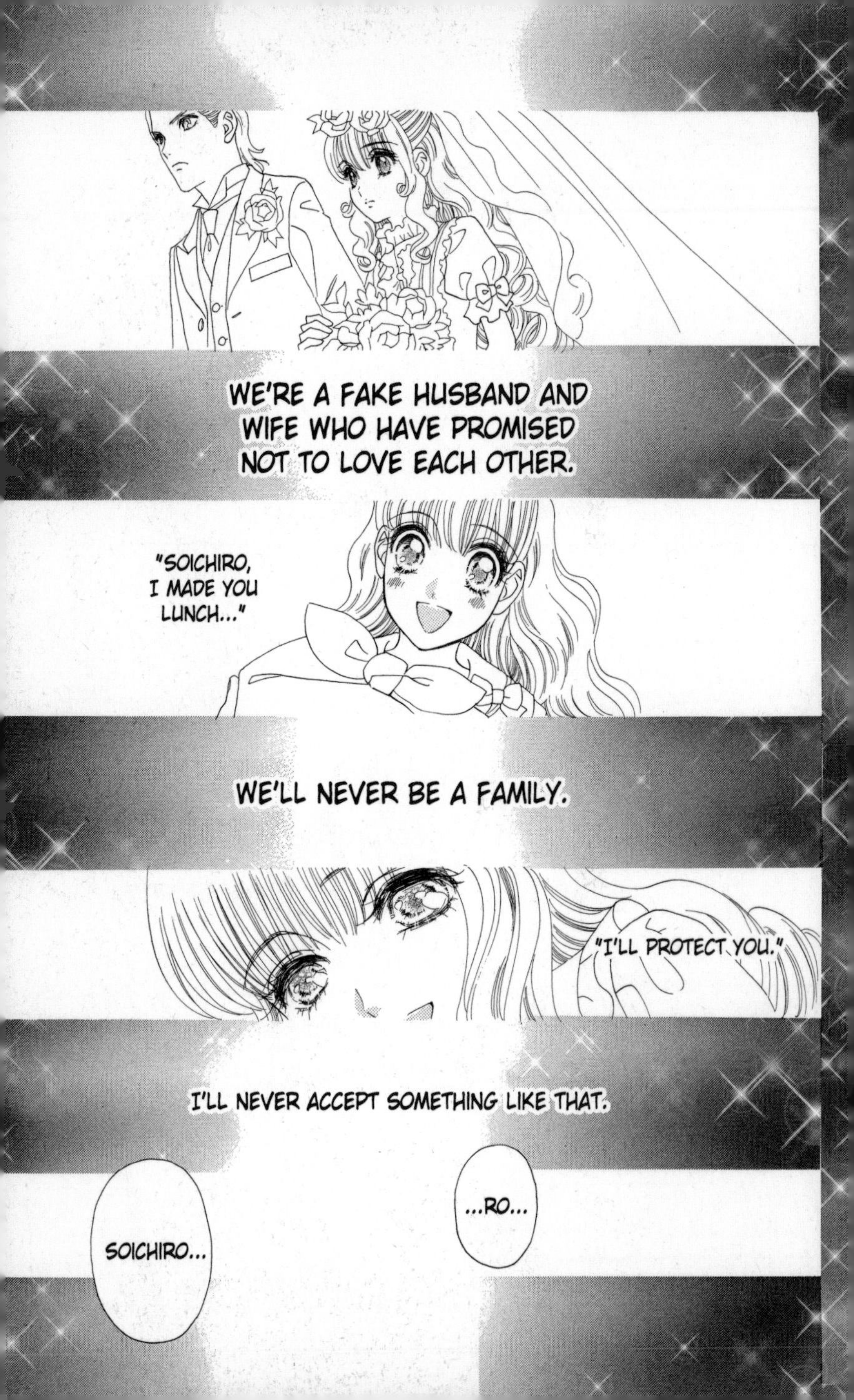
WE'RE A FAKE HUSBAND AND WIFE WHO HAVE PROMISED NOT TO LOVE EACH OTHER.
"SOICHIRO, I MADE YOU LUNCH..."
WE'LL NEVER BE A FAMILY.
"I'LL PROTECT YOU."
I'LL NEVER ACCEPT SOMETHING LIKE THAT.
...RO...
SOICHIRO...

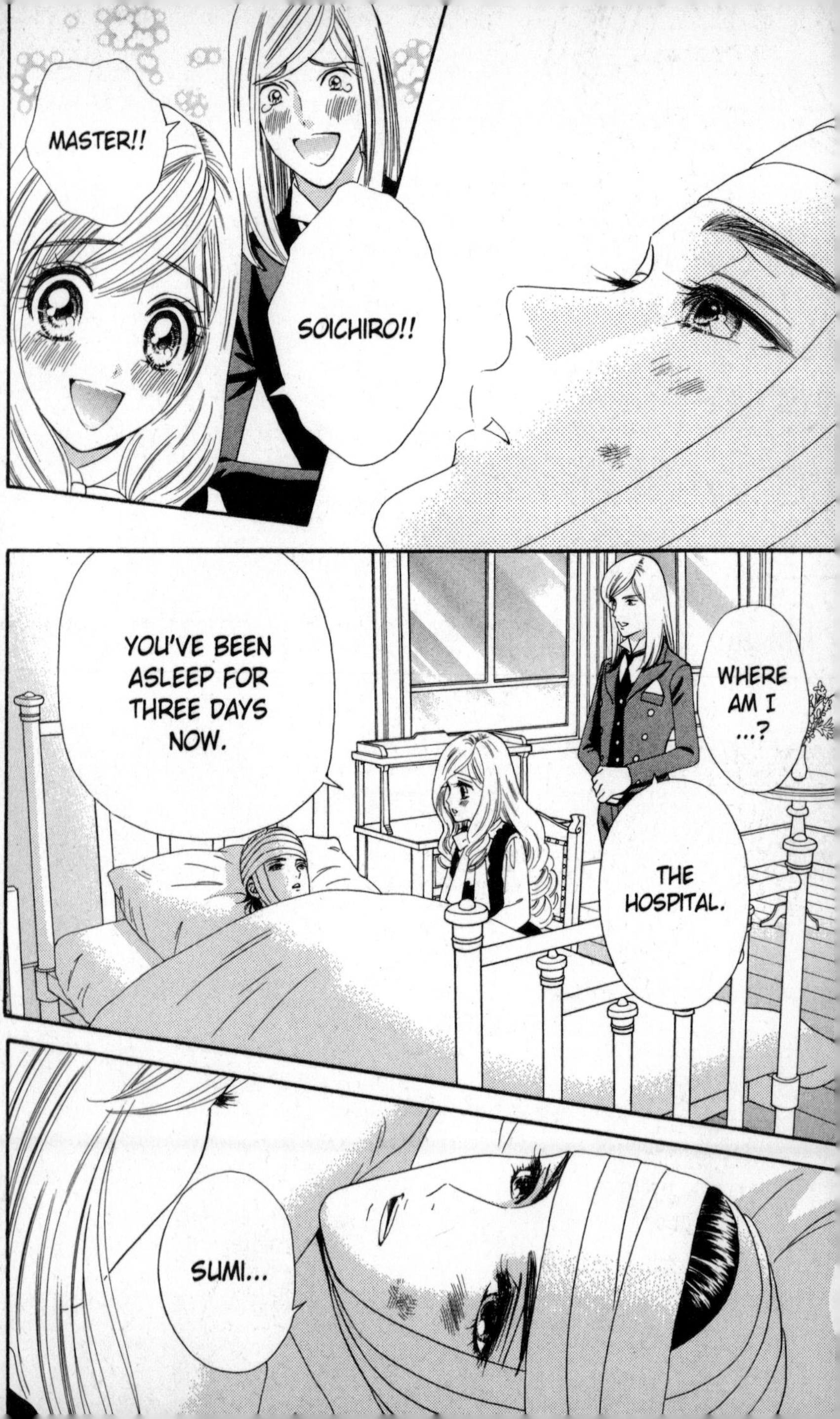
SOICHIRO!!
MASTER!!
WHERE AM I ...?
THE HOSPITAL.
YOU'VE BEEN ASLEEP FOR THREE DAYS NOW.
SUMI...

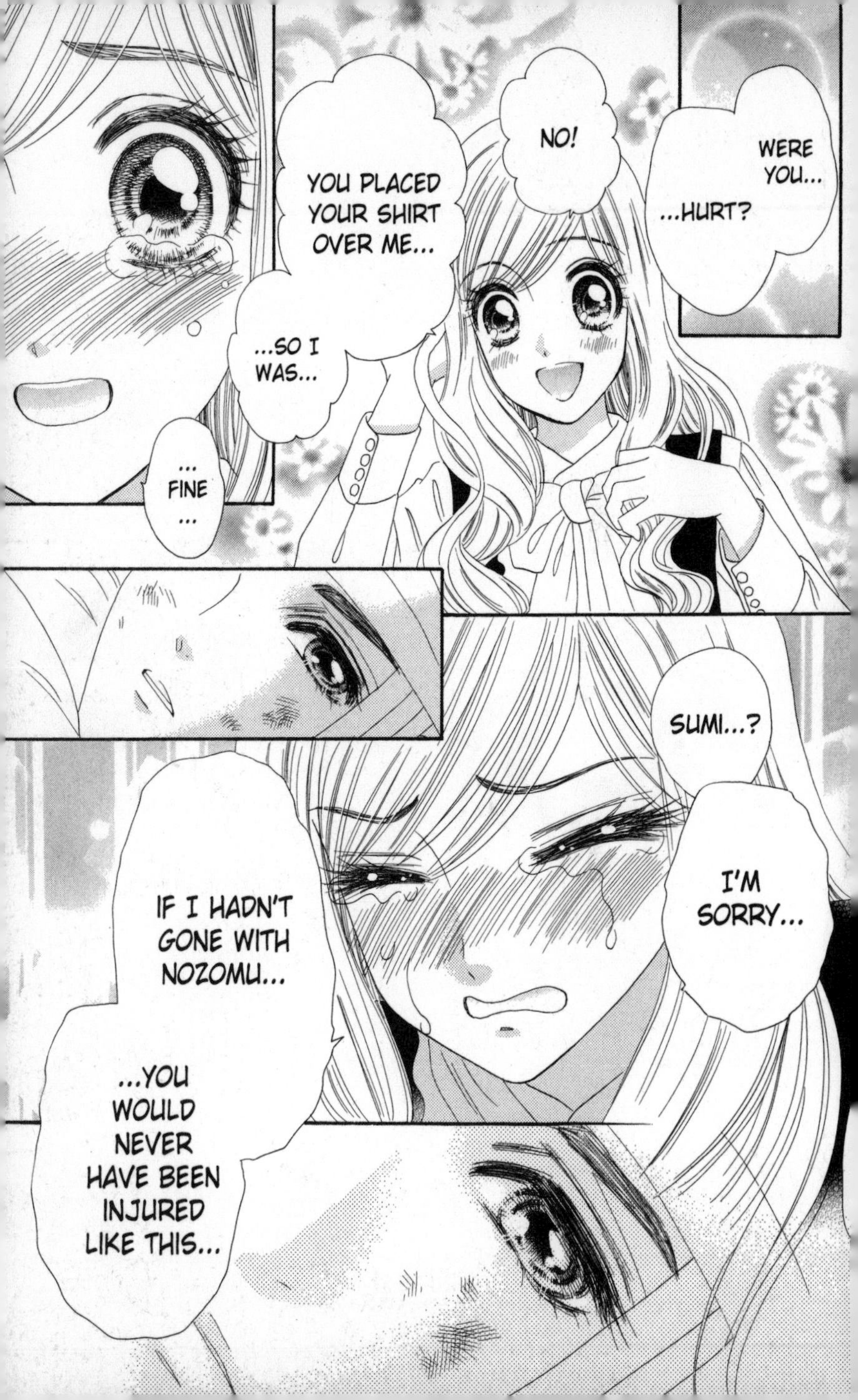
WERE YOU...
...HURT?
NO!
YOU PLACED YOUR SHIRT OVER ME...
...SO I WAS...
... FINE ...
SUMI...?
I'M SORRY...
IF I HADN'T GONE WITH NOZOMU...
...YOU WOULD NEVER HAVE BEEN INJURED LIKE THIS...

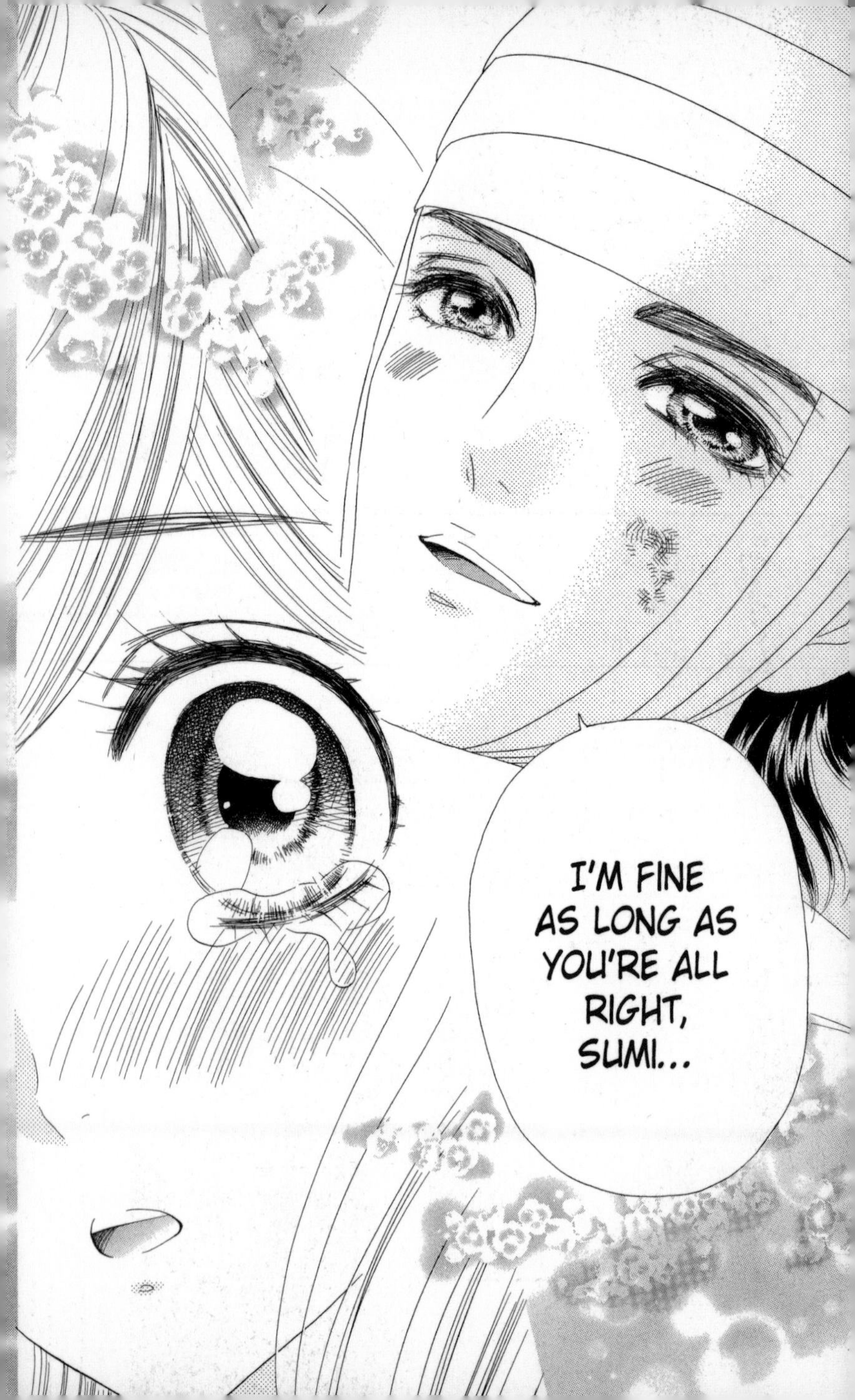
I'M FINE AS LONG AS YOU'RE ALL RIGHT, SUMI...

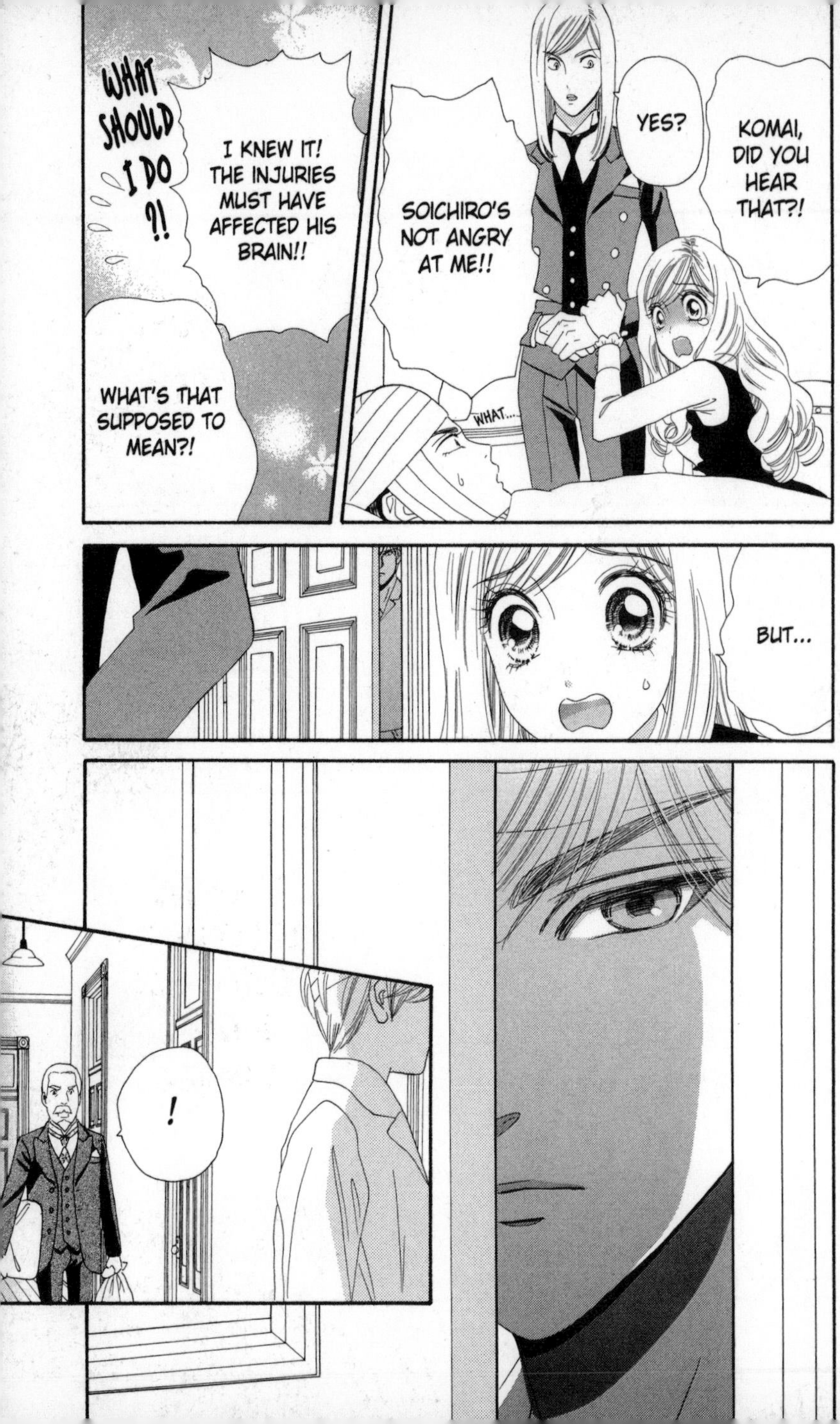
KOMAI, DID YOU HEAR THAT?!
YES?
SOICHIRO'S NOT ANGRY AT ME!!
WHAT...
I KNEW IT! THE INJURIES MUST HAVE AFFECTED HIS BRAIN!!
WHAT SHOULD I DO ?!
WHAT'S THAT SUPPOSED TO MEAN?!
BUT...
!

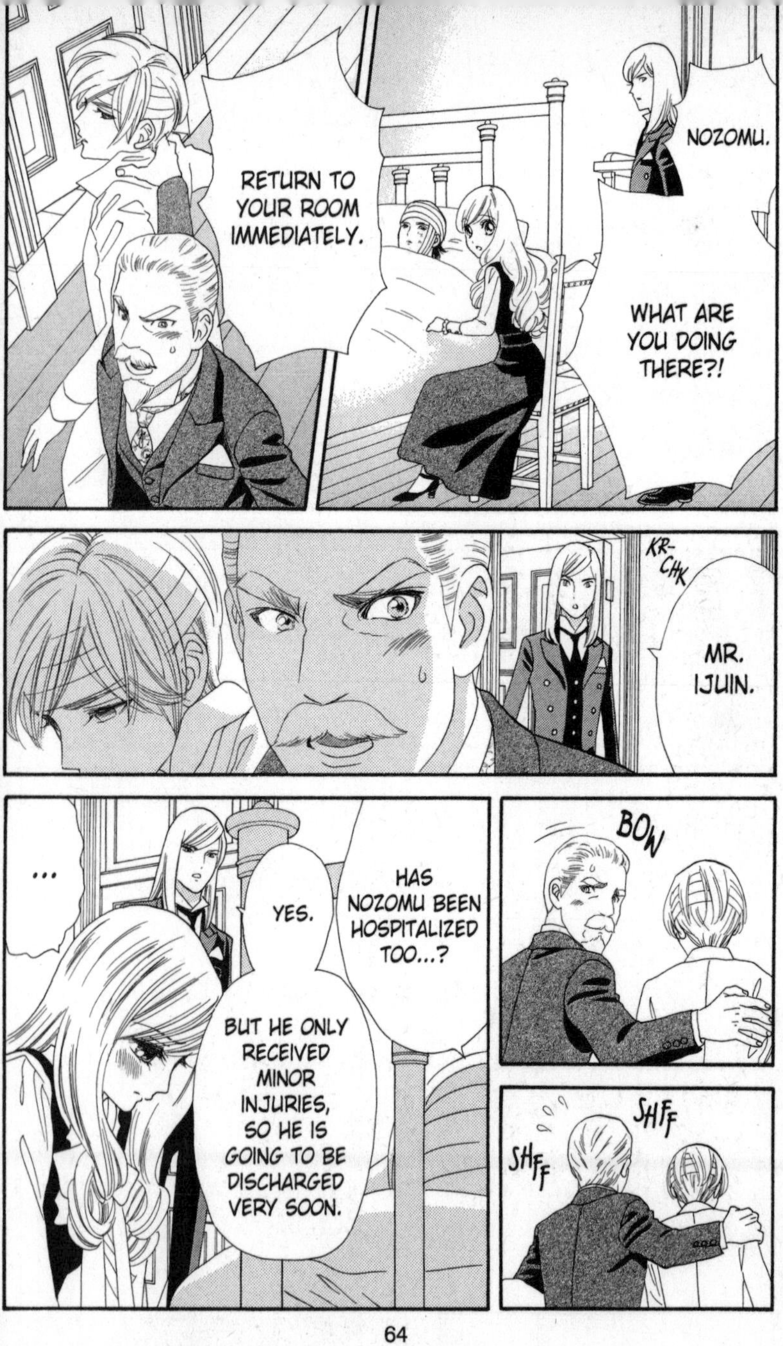

NOZOMU.
WHAT ARE YOU DOING THERE?!
RETURN TO YOUR ROOM IMMEDIATELY.
KR-CHK
MR. IJUIN.
BOW
SHFF
SHFF
HAS NOZOMU BEEN HOSPITALIZED TOO...?
YES.
BUT HE ONLY RECEIVED MINOR INJURIES, SO HE IS GOING TO BE DISCHARGED VERY SOON.
...

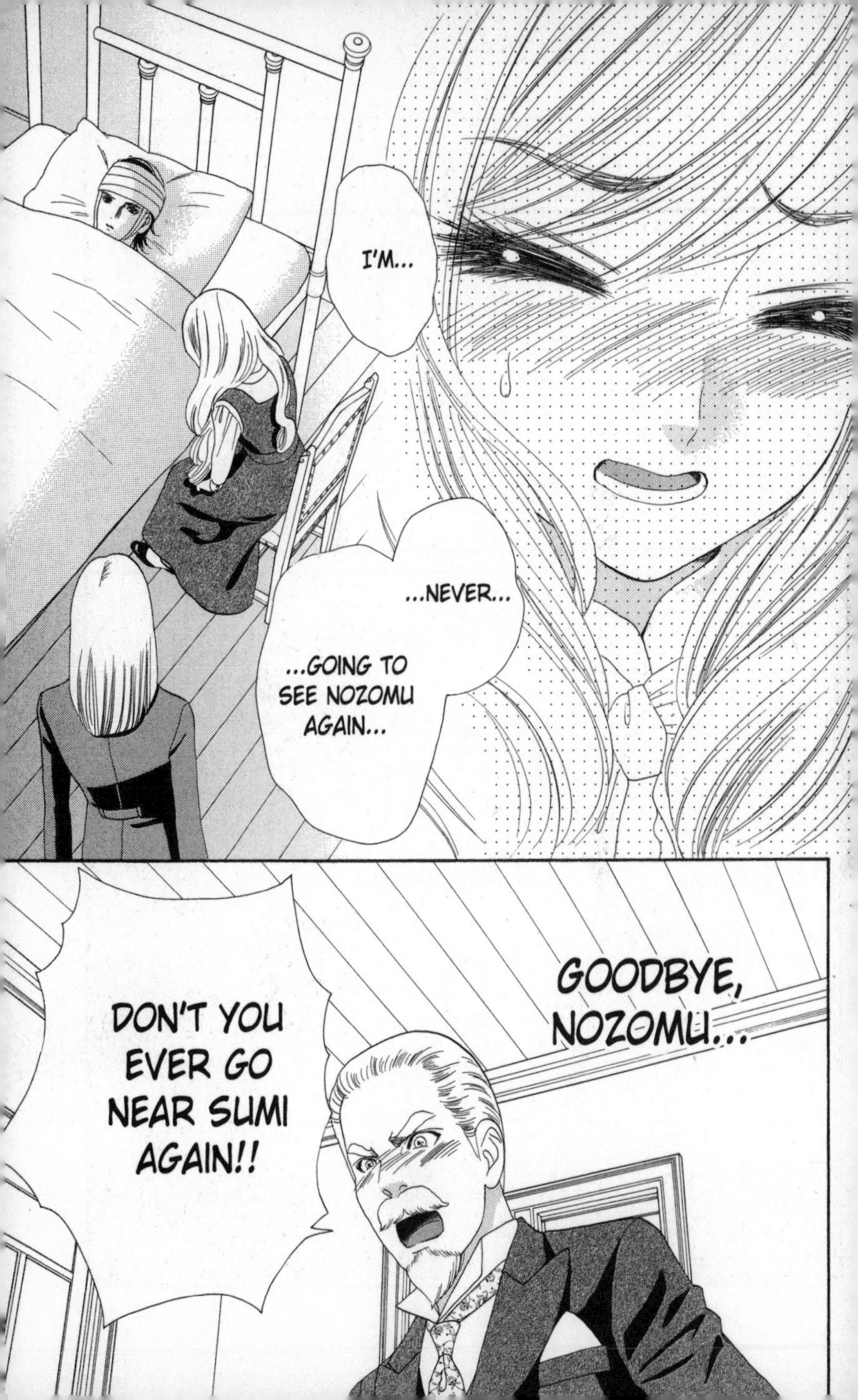
I'M...
...NEVER...
...GOING TO SEE NOZOMU AGAIN...
GOODBYE, NOZOMU...
DON'T YOU EVER GO NEAR SUMI AGAIN!!

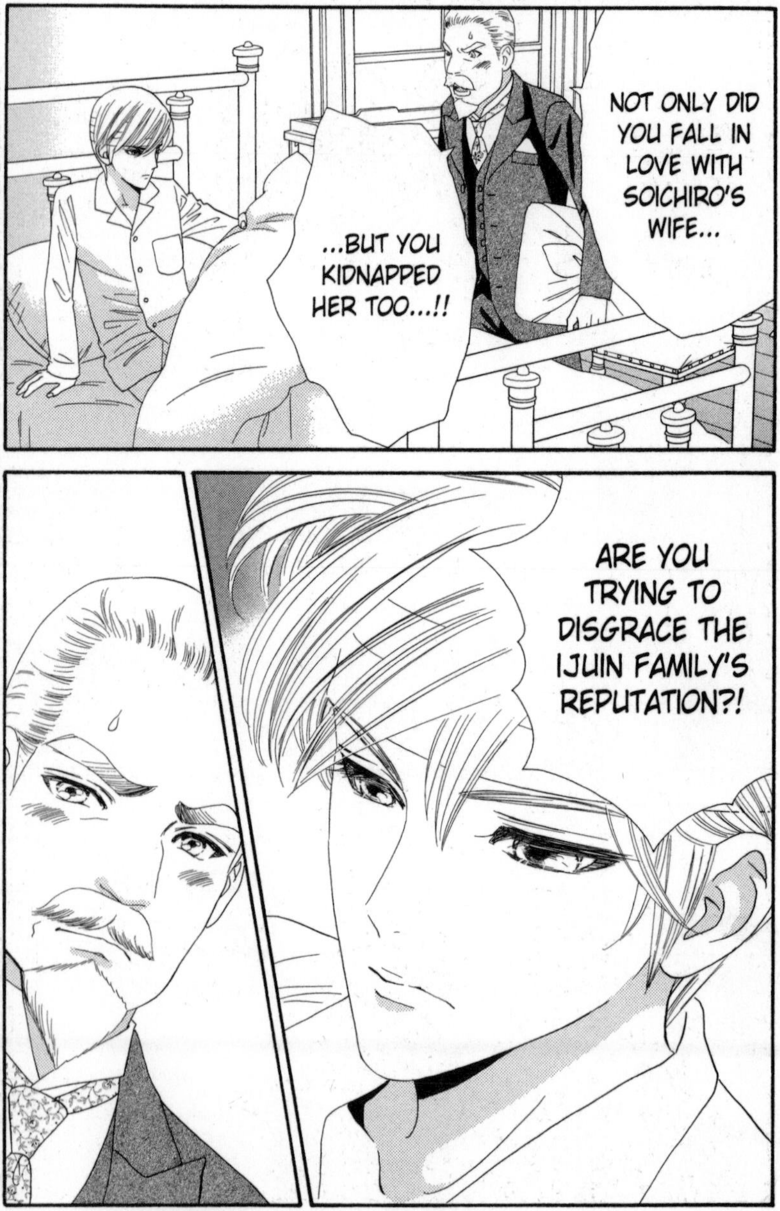
NOT ONLY DID YOU FALL IN LOVE WITH SOICHIRO'S WIFE...
...BUT YOU KIDNAPPED HER TOO...!!
ARE YOU TRYING TO DISGRACE THE IJUIN FAMILY'S REPUTATION?!

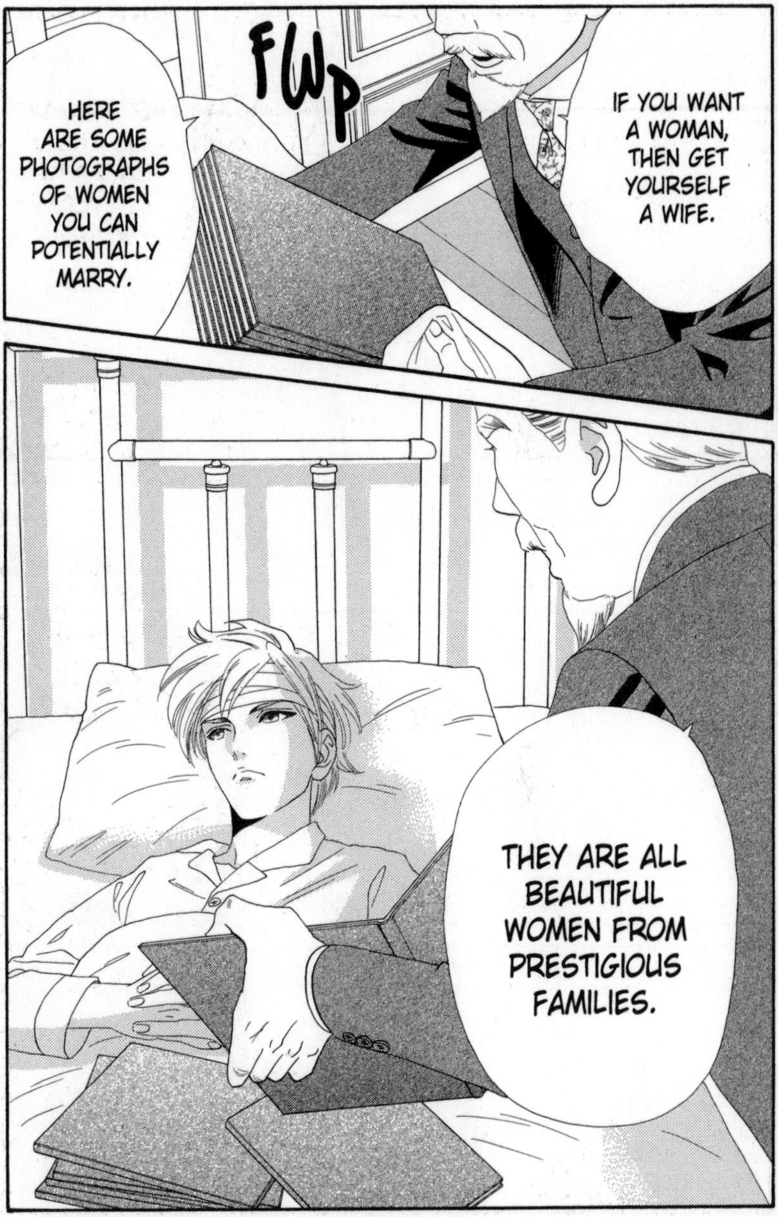
IF YOU WANT A WOMAN, THEN GET YOURSELF A WIFE.
FWP
HERE ARE SOME PHOTOGRAPHS OF WOMEN YOU CAN POTENTIALLY MARRY.
THEY ARE ALL BEAUTIFUL WOMEN FROM PRESTIGIOUS FAMILIES.

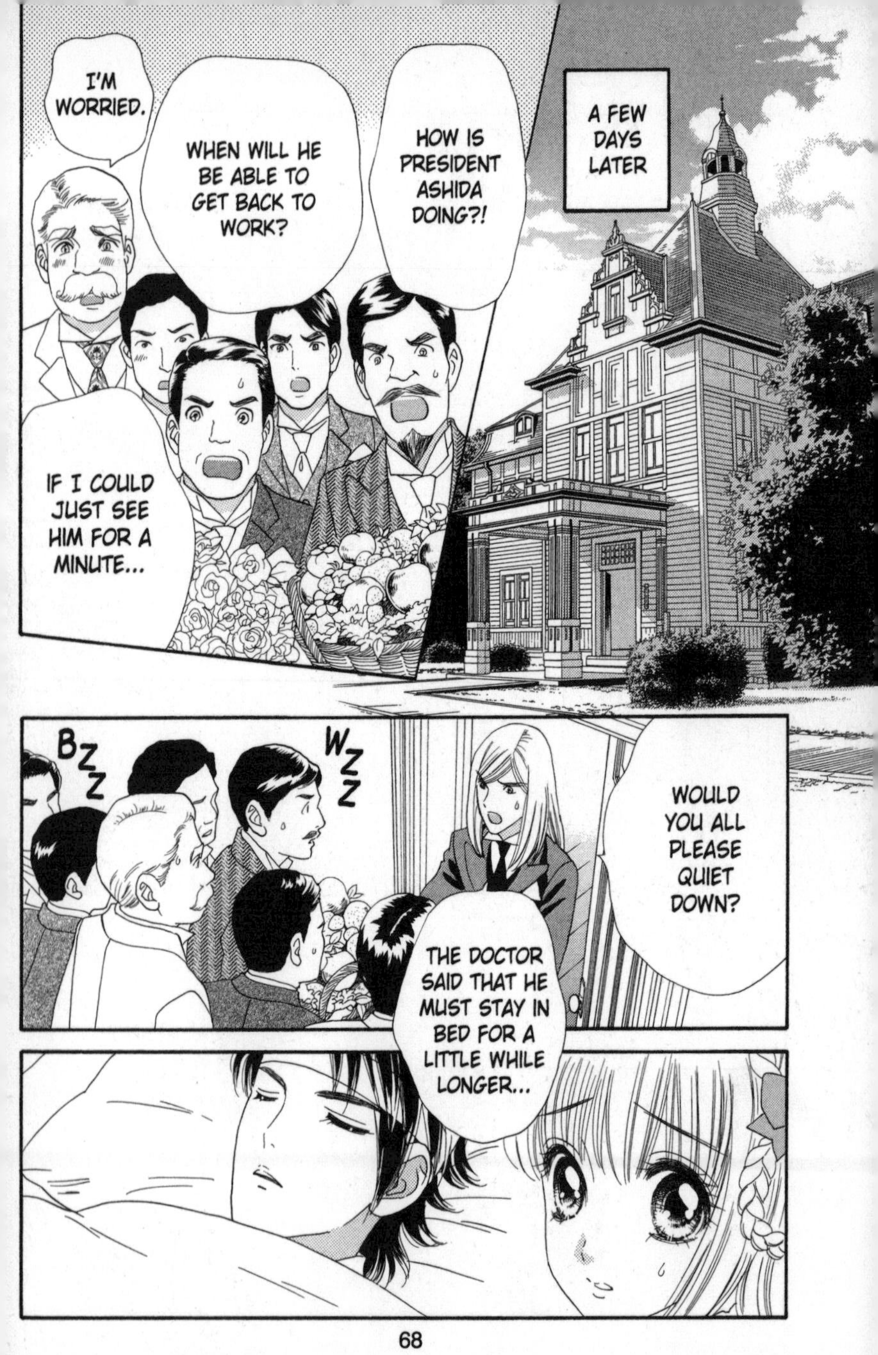
A FEW DAYS LATER
HOW IS PRESIDENT ASHIDA DOING?!
WHEN WILL HE BE ABLE TO GET BACK TO WORK?
I'M WORRIED.
IF I COULD JUST SEE HIM FOR A MINUTE...
WZZ
BZZ
WOULD YOU ALL PLEASE QUIET DOWN?
THE DOCTOR SAID THAT HE MUST STAY IN BED FOR A LITTLE WHILE LONGER...

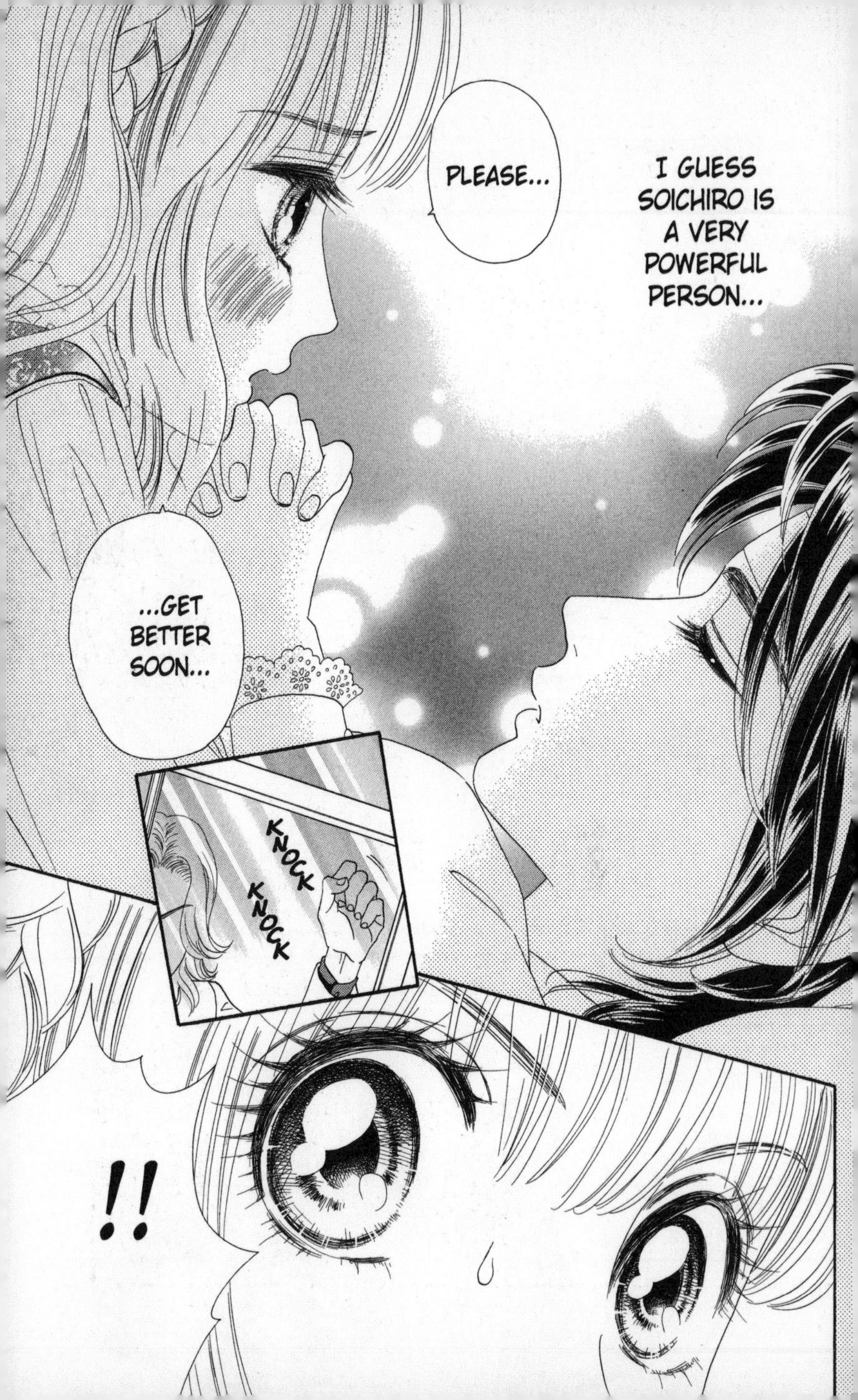
I GUESS SOICHIRO IS A VERY POWERFUL PERSON...
PLEASE...
...GET BETTER SOON...
KNOCK KNOCK
!!

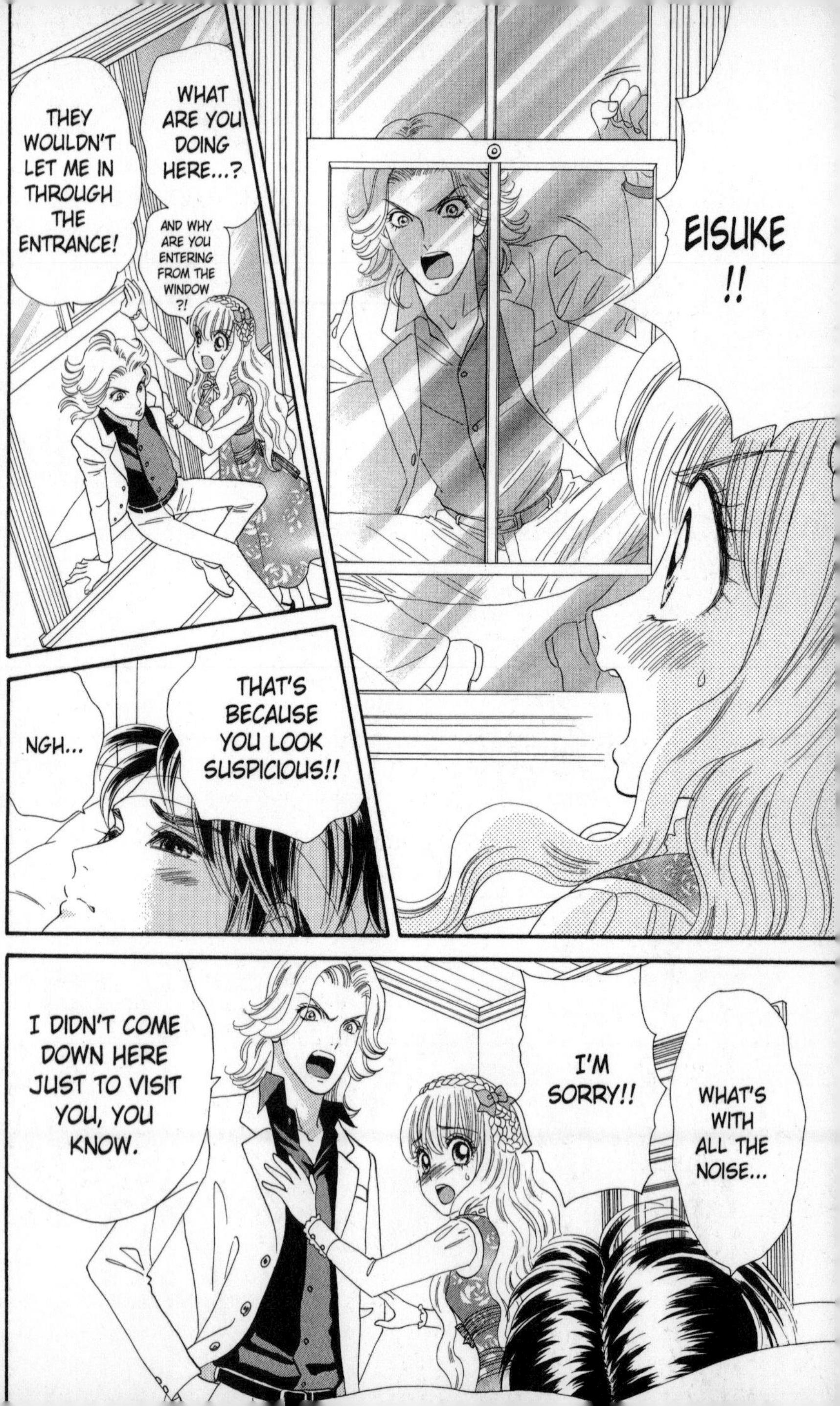
EISUKE !!
WHAT ARE YOU DOING HERE...?
AND WHY ARE YOU ENTERING FROM THE WINDOW ?!
THEY WOULDN'T LET ME IN THROUGH THE ENTRANCE!
THAT'S BECAUSE YOU LOOK SUSPICIOUS!!
NGH...
WHAT'S WITH ALL THE NOISE...
I'M SORRY!!
I DIDN'T COME DOWN HERE JUST TO VISIT YOU, YOU KNOW.

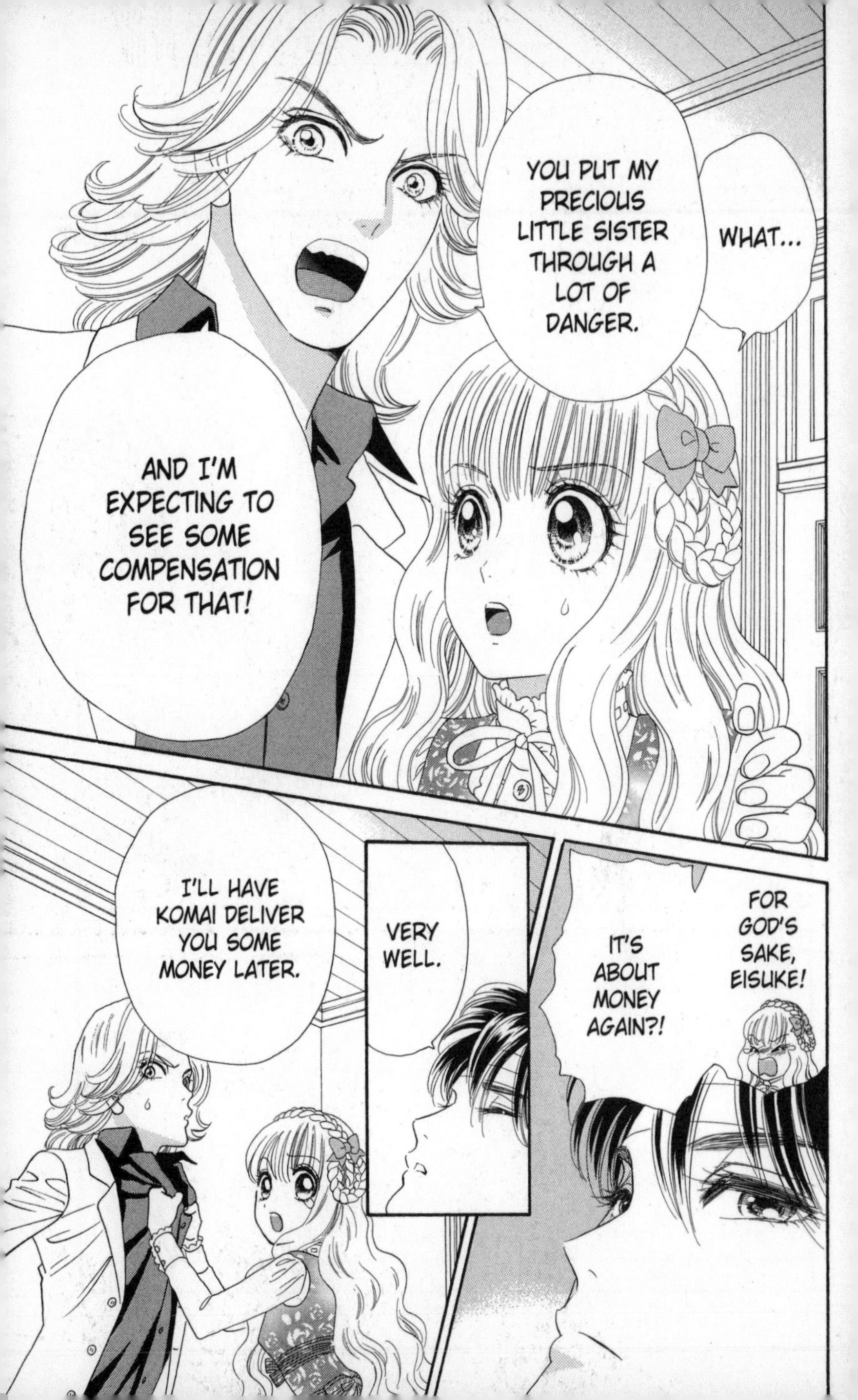
WHAT...
YOU PUT MY PRECIOUS LITTLE SISTER THROUGH A LOT OF DANGER.
AND I'M EXPECTING TO SEE SOME COMPENSATION FOR THAT!
FOR GOD'S SAKE, EISUKE!
IT'S ABOUT MONEY AGAIN?!
VERY WELL.
I'LL HAVE KOMAI DELIVER YOU SOME MONEY LATER.

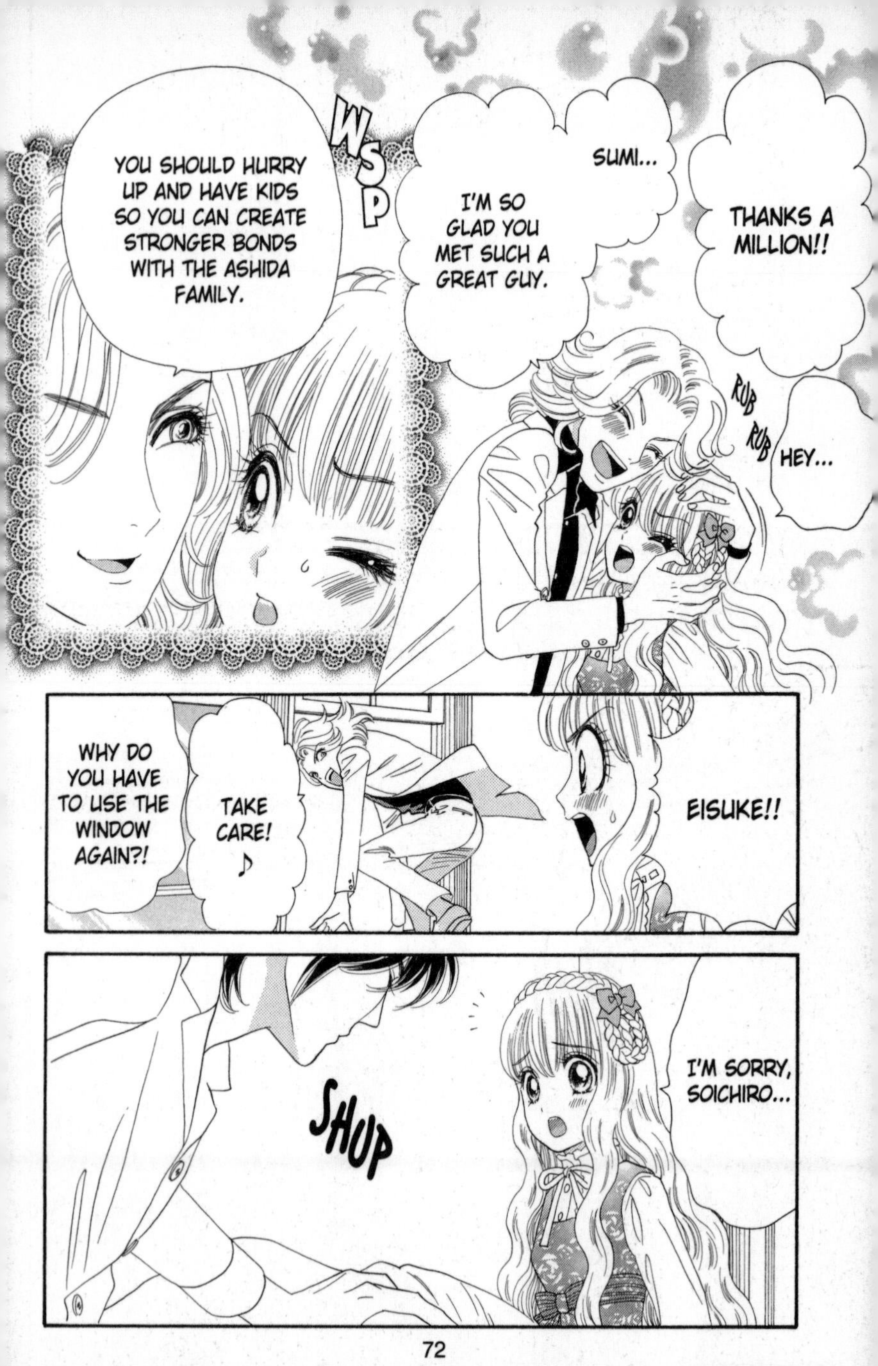
THANKS A MILLION!!
SUMI...
I'M SO GLAD YOU MET SUCH A GREAT GUY.
RUB RUB
HEY...
WSP
YOU SHOULD HURRY UP AND HAVE KIDS SO YOU CAN CREATE STRONGER BONDS WITH THE ASHIDA FAMILY.
EISUKE!!
TAKE CARE! ♪
WHY DO YOU HAVE TO USE THE WINDOW AGAIN?!
I'M SORRY, SOICHIRO...
SHUP

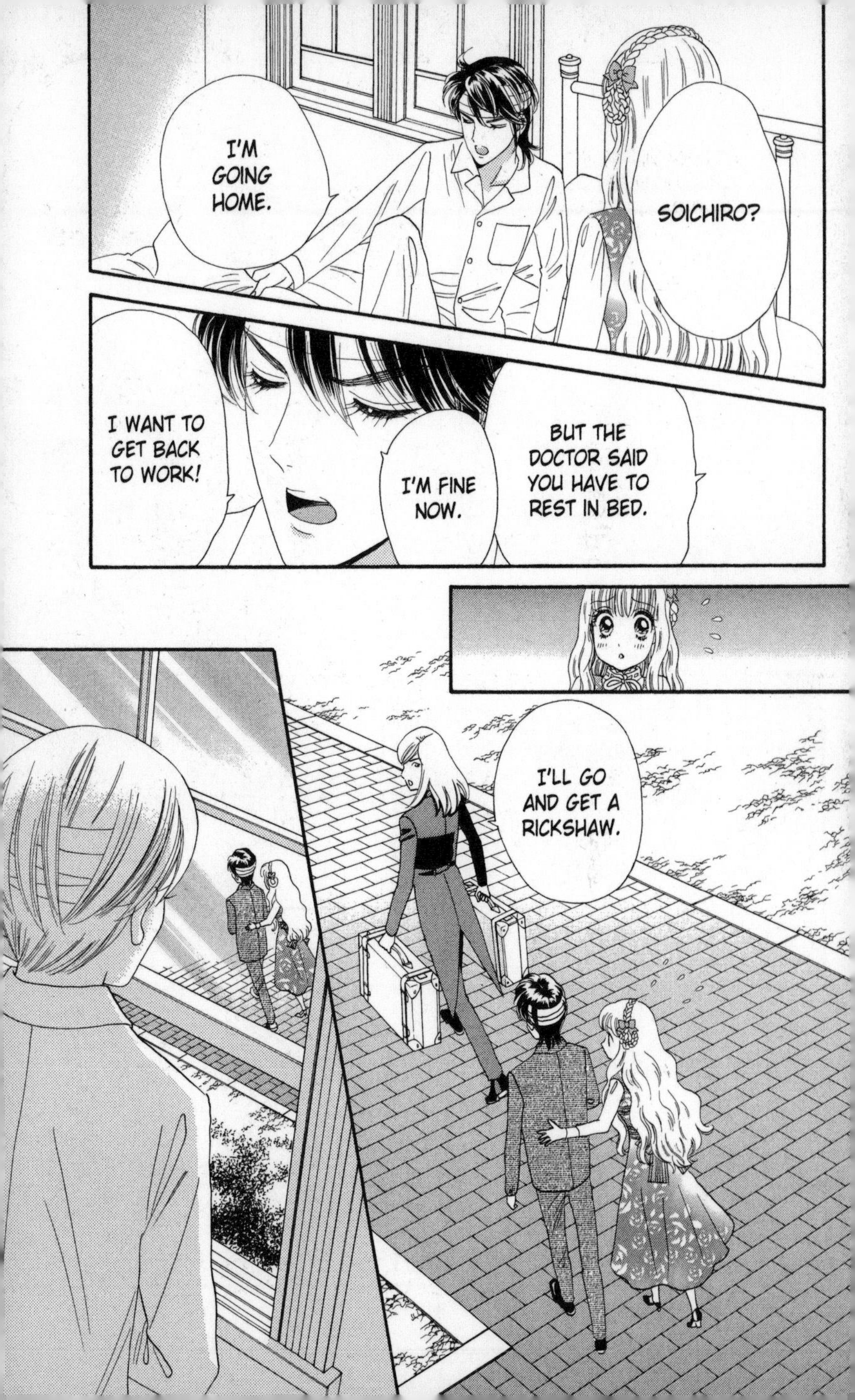
SOICHIRO?
I'M GOING HOME.
BUT THE DOCTOR SAID YOU HAVE TO REST IN BED.
I'M FINE NOW.
I WANT TO GET BACK TO WORK!
I'LL GO AND GET A RICKSHAW.

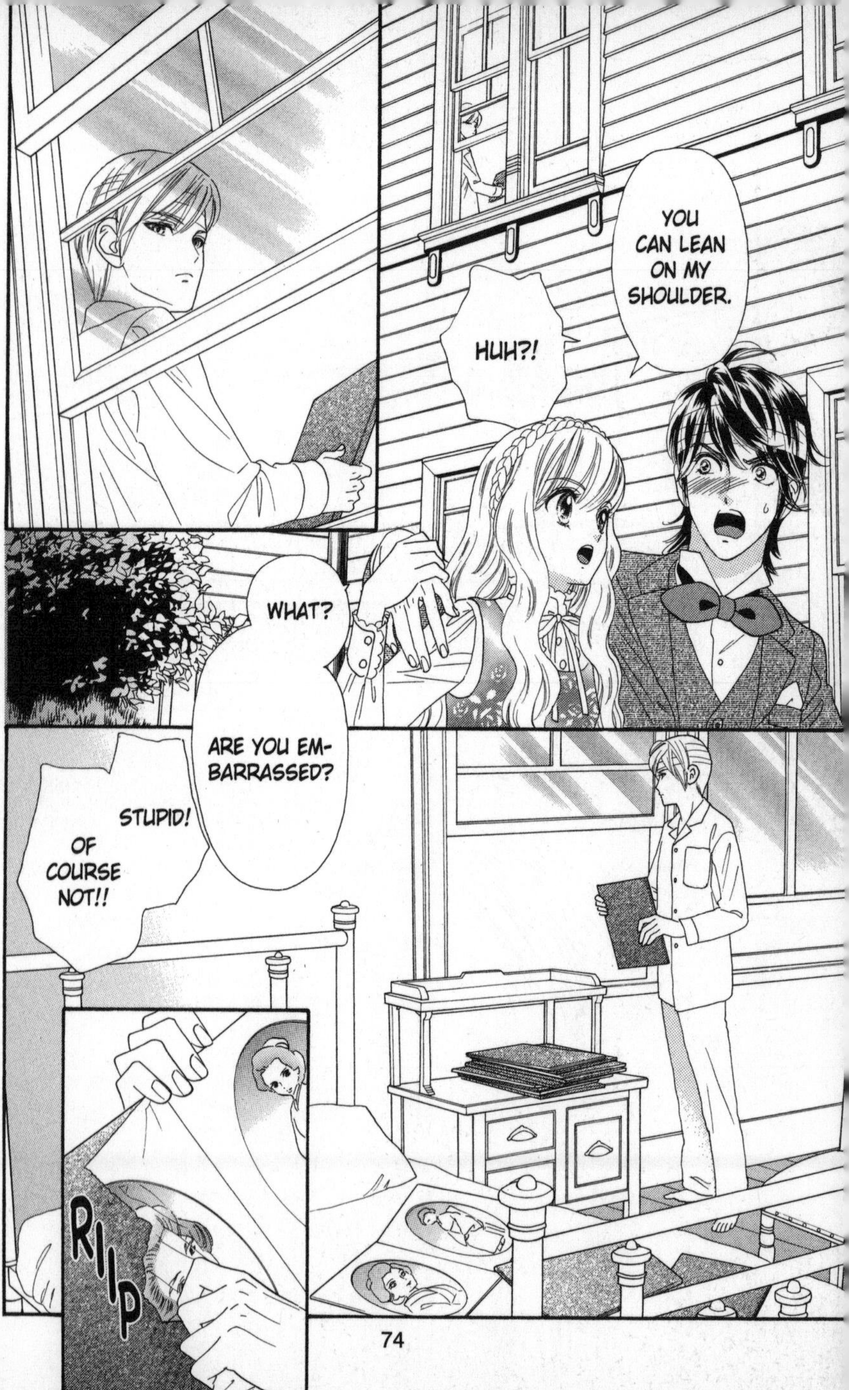
YOU CAN LEAN ON MY SHOULDER.
HUH?!
WHAT?
ARE YOU EM-BARRASSED?
STUPID! OF COURSE NOT!!
RIIP

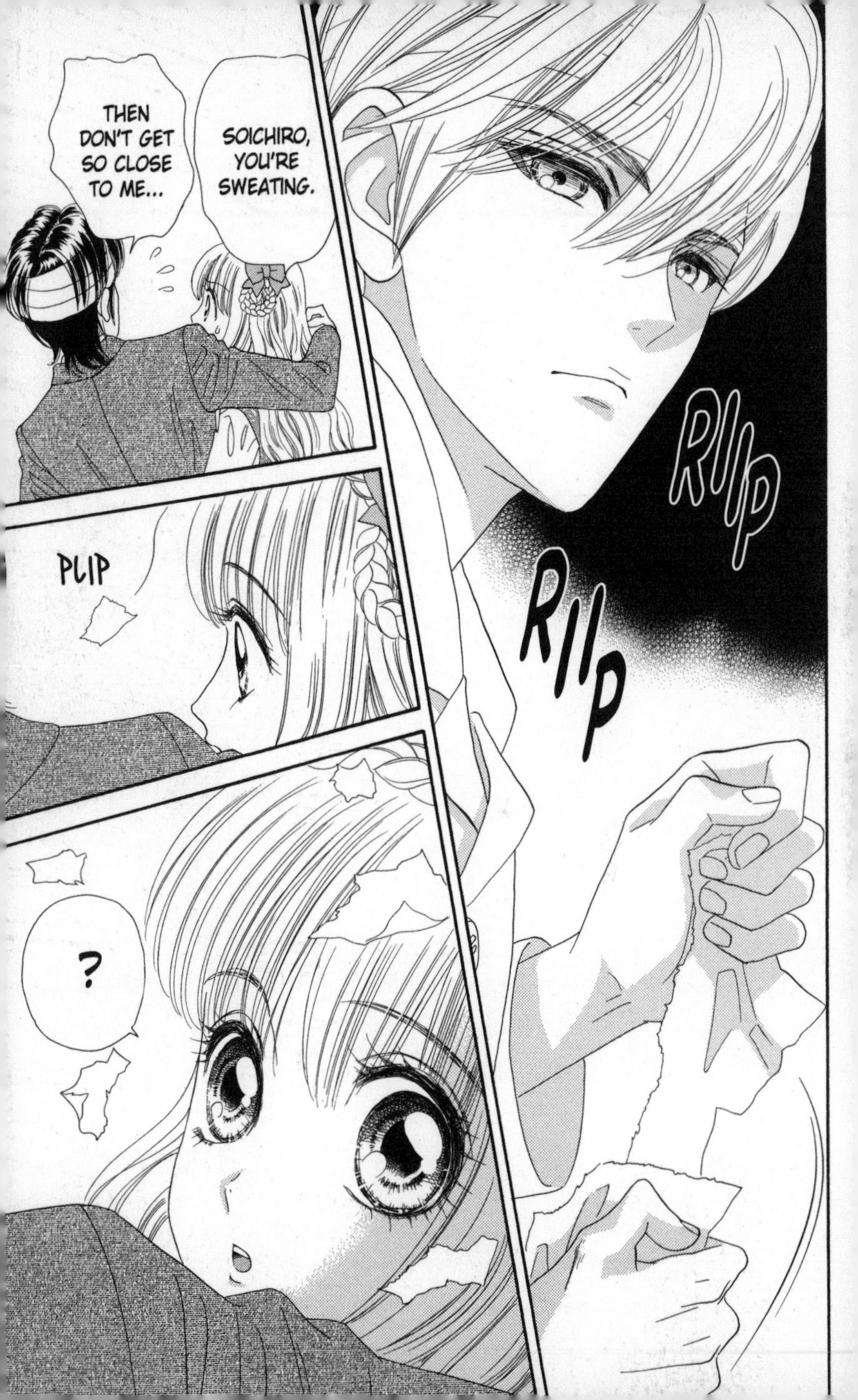
RIIP
RIIP
SOICHIRO, YOU'RE SWEATING.
THEN DON'T GET SO CLOSE TO ME...
PLIP
?

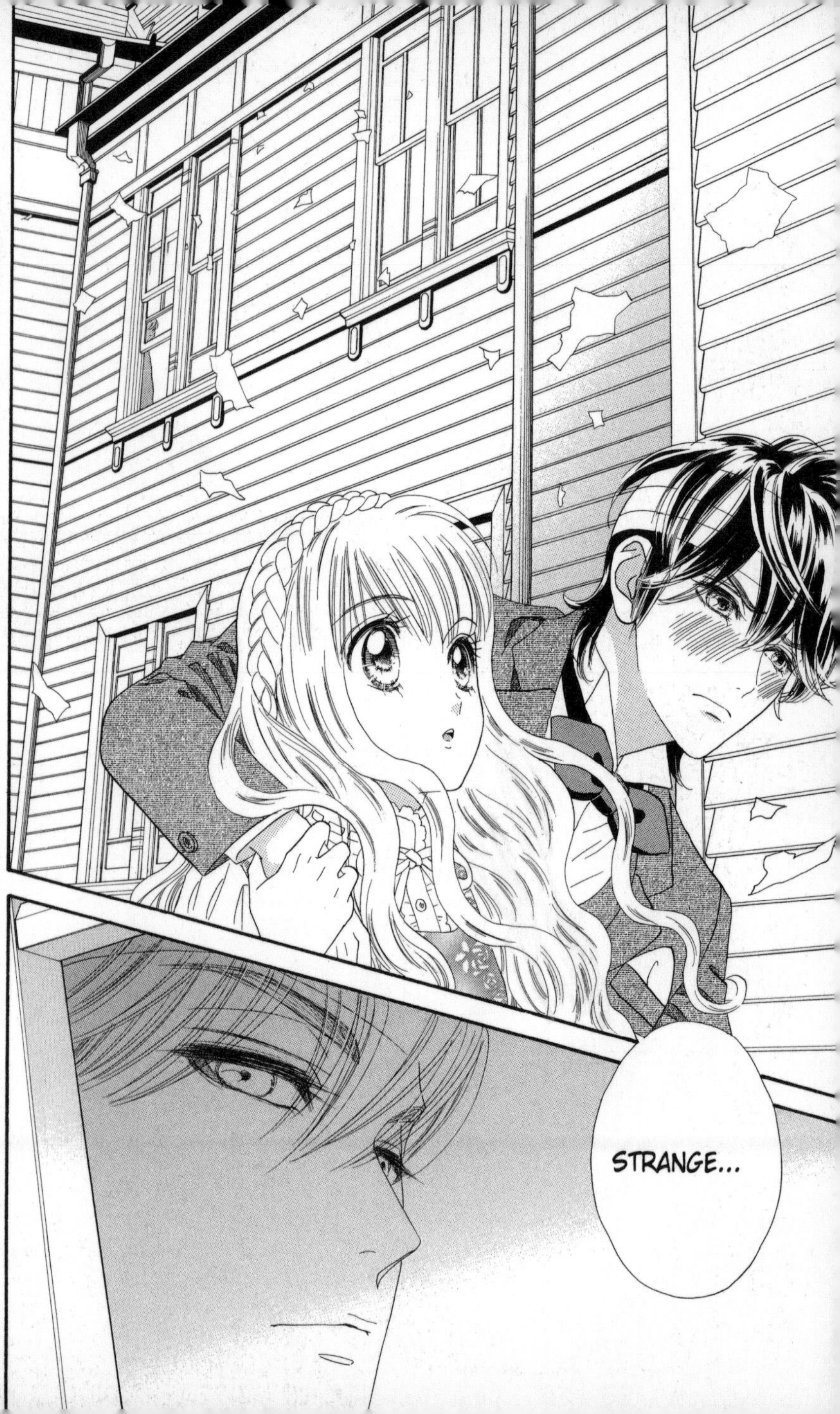
STRANGE...

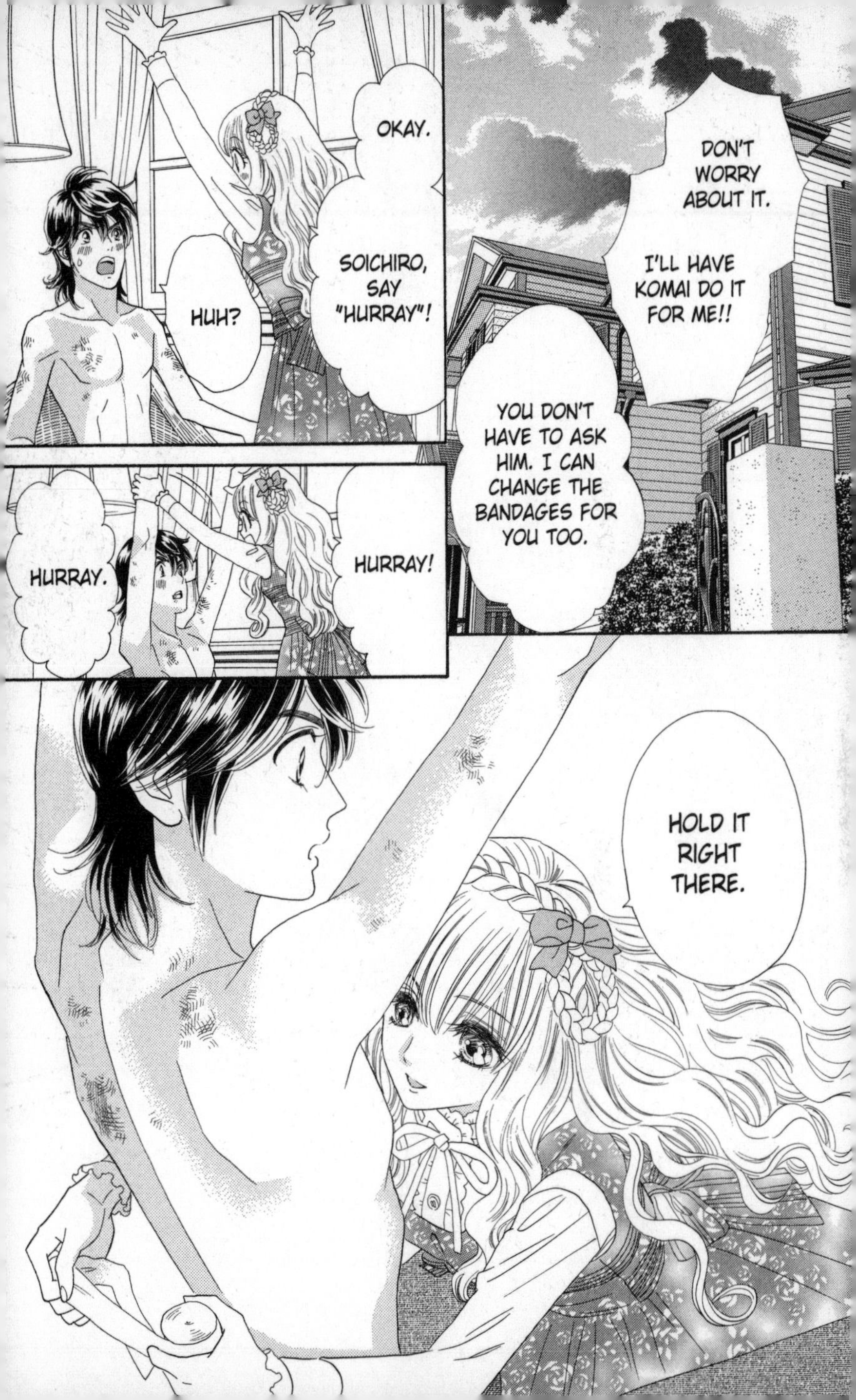
DON'T WORRY ABOUT IT.
I'LL HAVE KOMAI DO IT FOR ME!!
YOU DON'T HAVE TO ASK HIM. I CAN CHANGE THE BANDAGES FOR YOU TOO.
OKAY.
SOICHIRO, SAY "HURRAY"!
HUH?
HURRAY!
HURRAY.
HOLD IT RIGHT THERE.

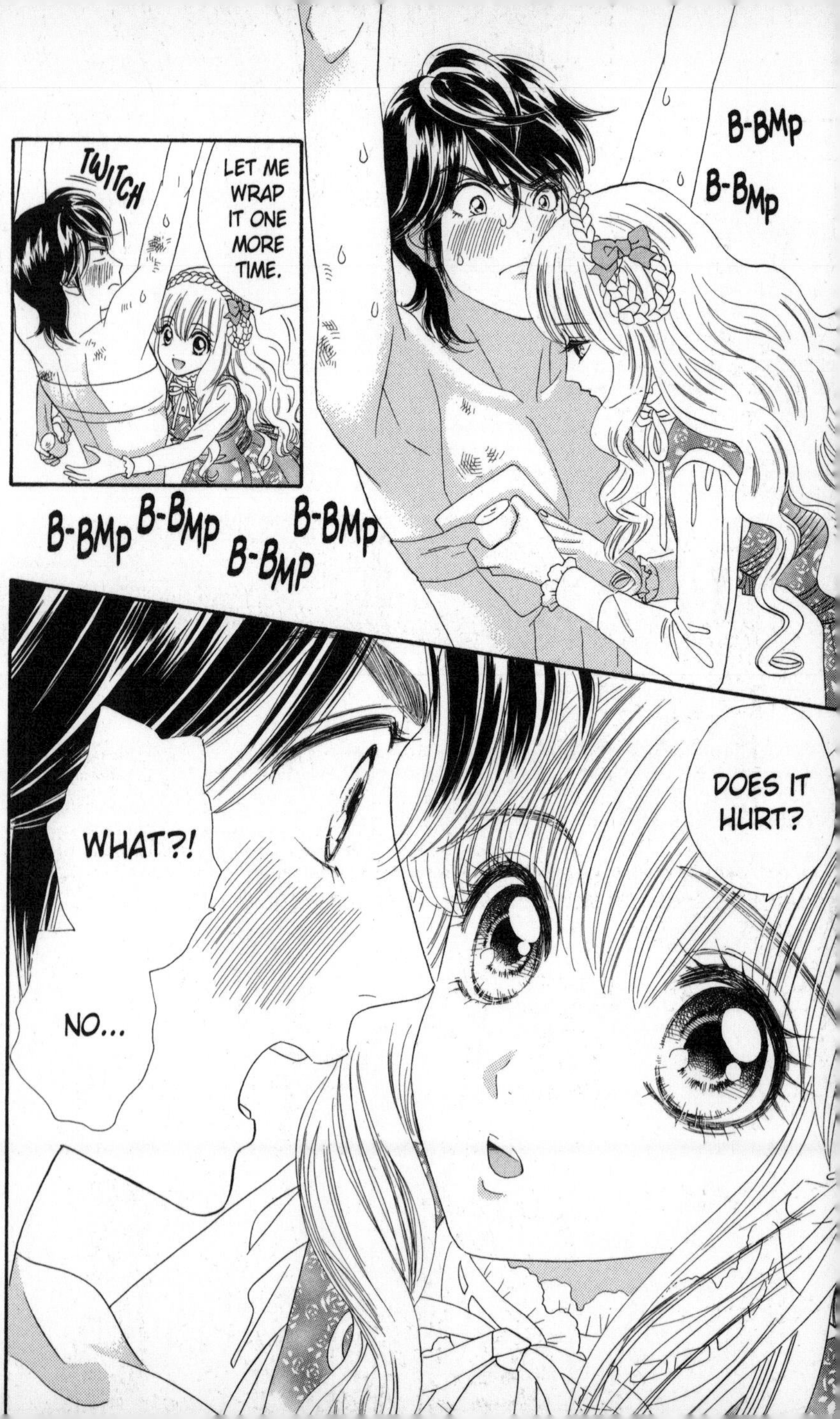
B-BMP
B-BMP
B-BMP
B-BMP
B-BMP
B-BMP
LET ME WRAP IT ONE MORE TIME.
TWITCH
DOES IT HURT?
WHAT?!
NO...

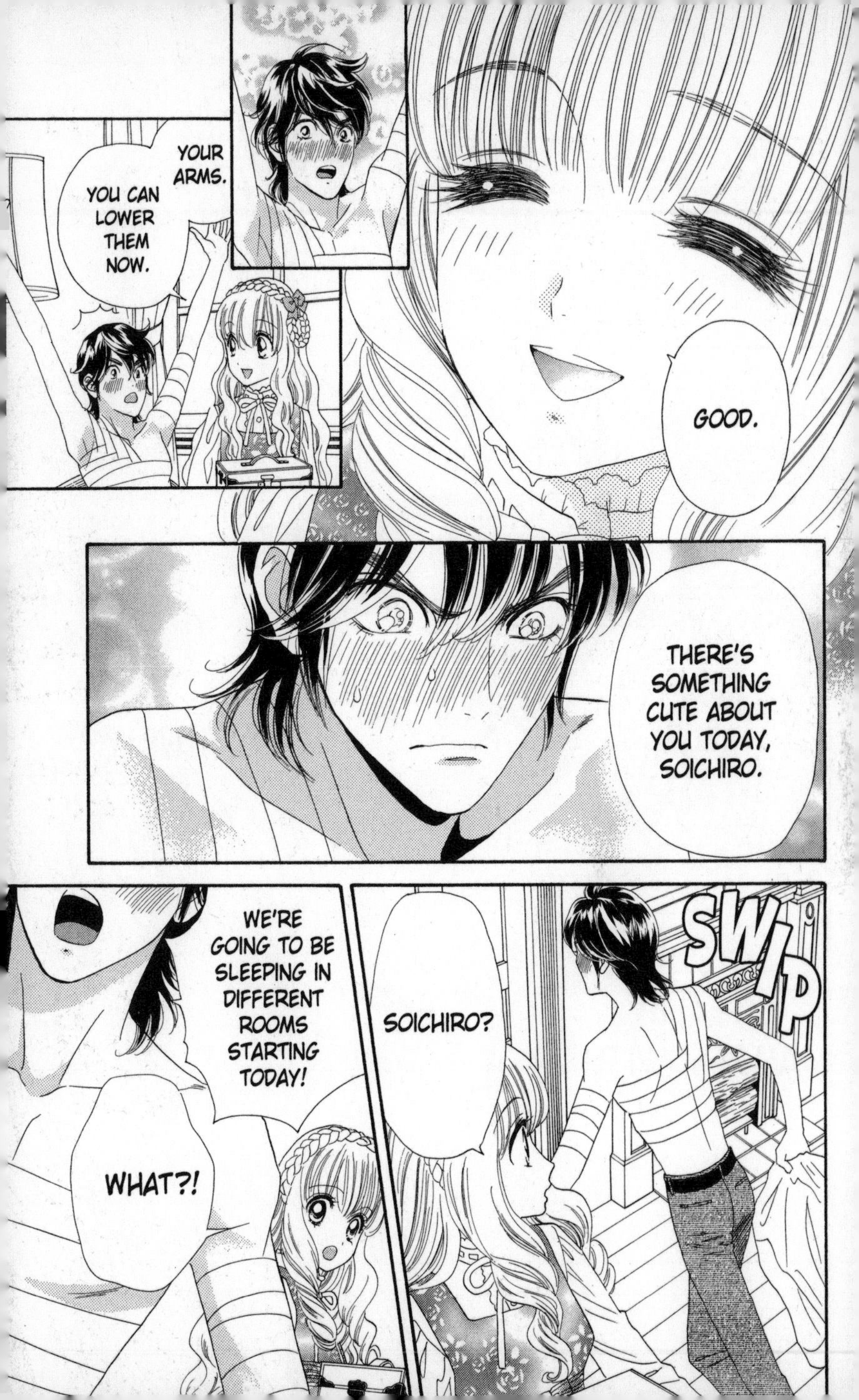
GOOD.
YOUR ARMS.
YOU CAN LOWER THEM NOW.
THERE'S SOMETHING CUTE ABOUT YOU TODAY, SOICHIRO.
SWIP
SOICHIRO?
WE'RE GOING TO BE SLEEPING IN DIFFERENT ROOMS STARTING TODAY!
WHAT?!

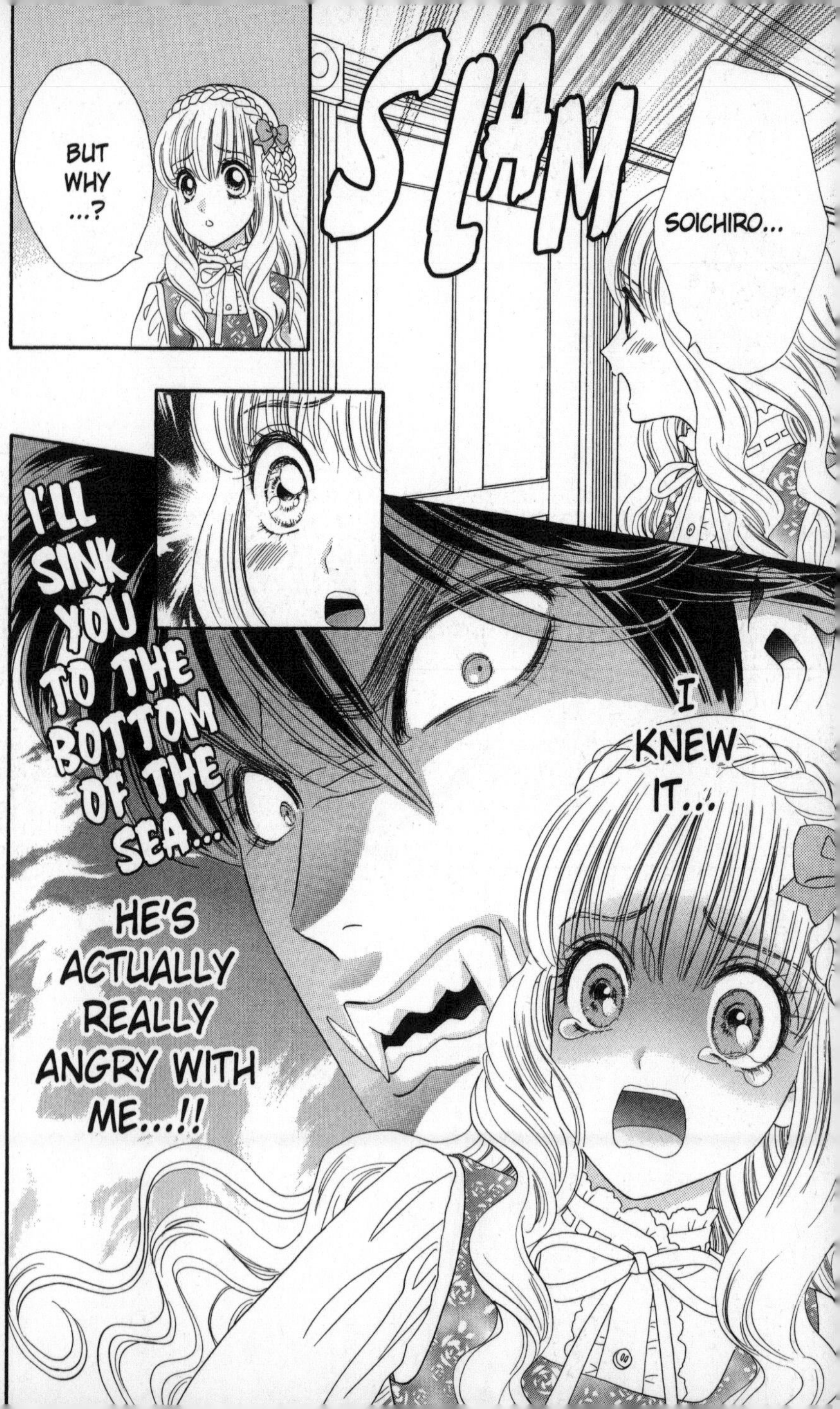
SLAM
SOICHIRO...
BUT WHY ...?
I'LL SINK YOU TO THE BOTTOM OF THE SEA...
I KNEW IT...
HE'S ACTUALLY REALLY ANGRY WITH ME...!!

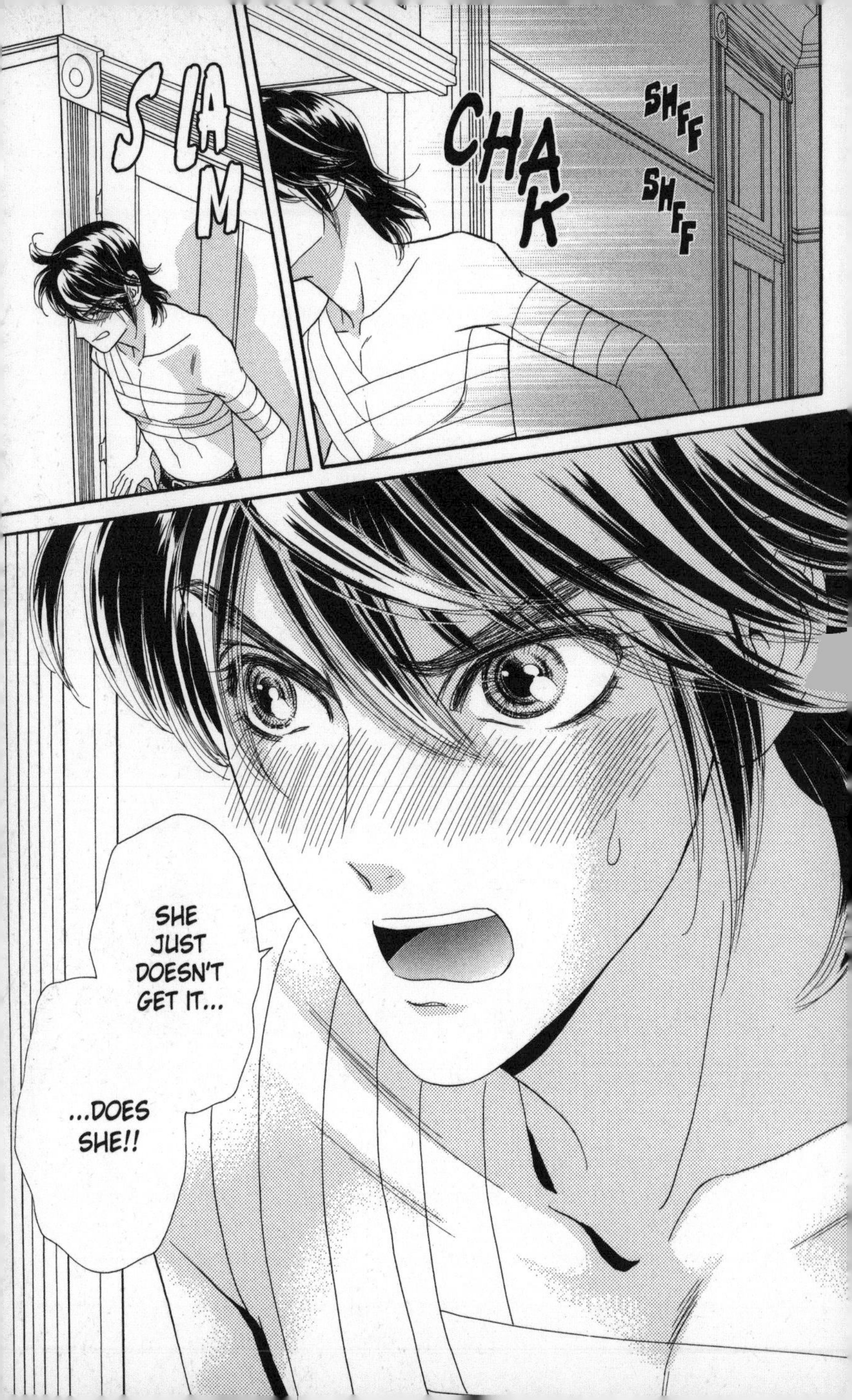
SHFF
SHFF
CHAK
SLAM
SHE JUST DOESN'T GET IT...
...DOES SHE!!

STEP STAGE ③

No.

Date · ·

❊ "RAJI-SHAKI" IS A SHOW STREAMED ONLINE, SO ANYONE WITH A COMPUTER CAN

LISTEN TO IT EVEN NOW (NOVEMBER 2008). IF YOU GO TO THE "S-RAJI" SITE

FROM SHUEISHA'S HOMEPAGE, YOU SHOULD BE ABLE TO FIND THE "RAJI-SHAKI"

CONTENTS THERE.

TANEMURA SENSEI'S ADVICE WAS VERY USEFUL, EVEN FOR A PROFESSIONAL

LIKE ME. IF ONLY THERE HAD BEEN A RADIO SHOW LIKE THIS ONE WHEN I

WAS A CHILD...!!

NOT ONLY DO YOU GET TO HEAR HER TALK ABOUT MANGA, BUT YOU CAN ALSO

WATCH THE VIDEO CLIPS ON THE SITE AND SEE HER DRAW. IT'S AMAZING!!

YOU ALSO GET TO SEE ME DRAW TOO, SO PLEASE DROP BY THE SITE AND

TAKE A LOOK.

BY THE WAY, IT'S REALLY A SURPRISE TO HEAR YOUR OWN VOICE ON THE RADIO

SINCE IT SOUNDS NOTHING LIKE WHAT YOU'D EXPECT. IT WAS HARD TO KEEP

CALM WHILE I LISTENED TO IT...

BECAUSE OF THE MONEY, I PROMISED THAT I WOULD NEVER FALL IN LOVE WITH HIM.
THAT WAS THE LIFE I CHOSE ...

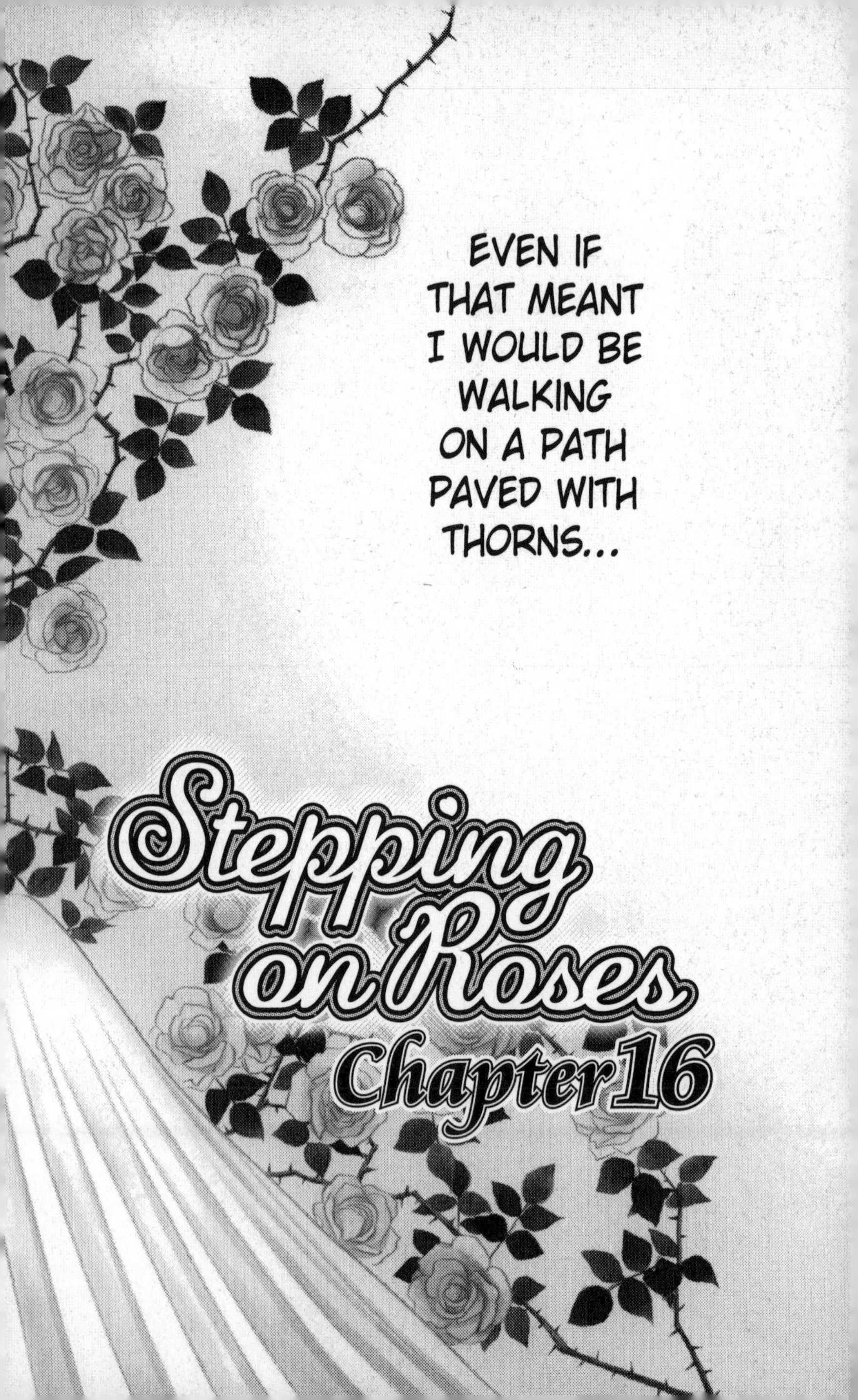
EVEN IF THAT MEANT I WOULD BE WALKING ON A PATH PAVED WITH THORNS...
Stepping on Roses
Chapter 16

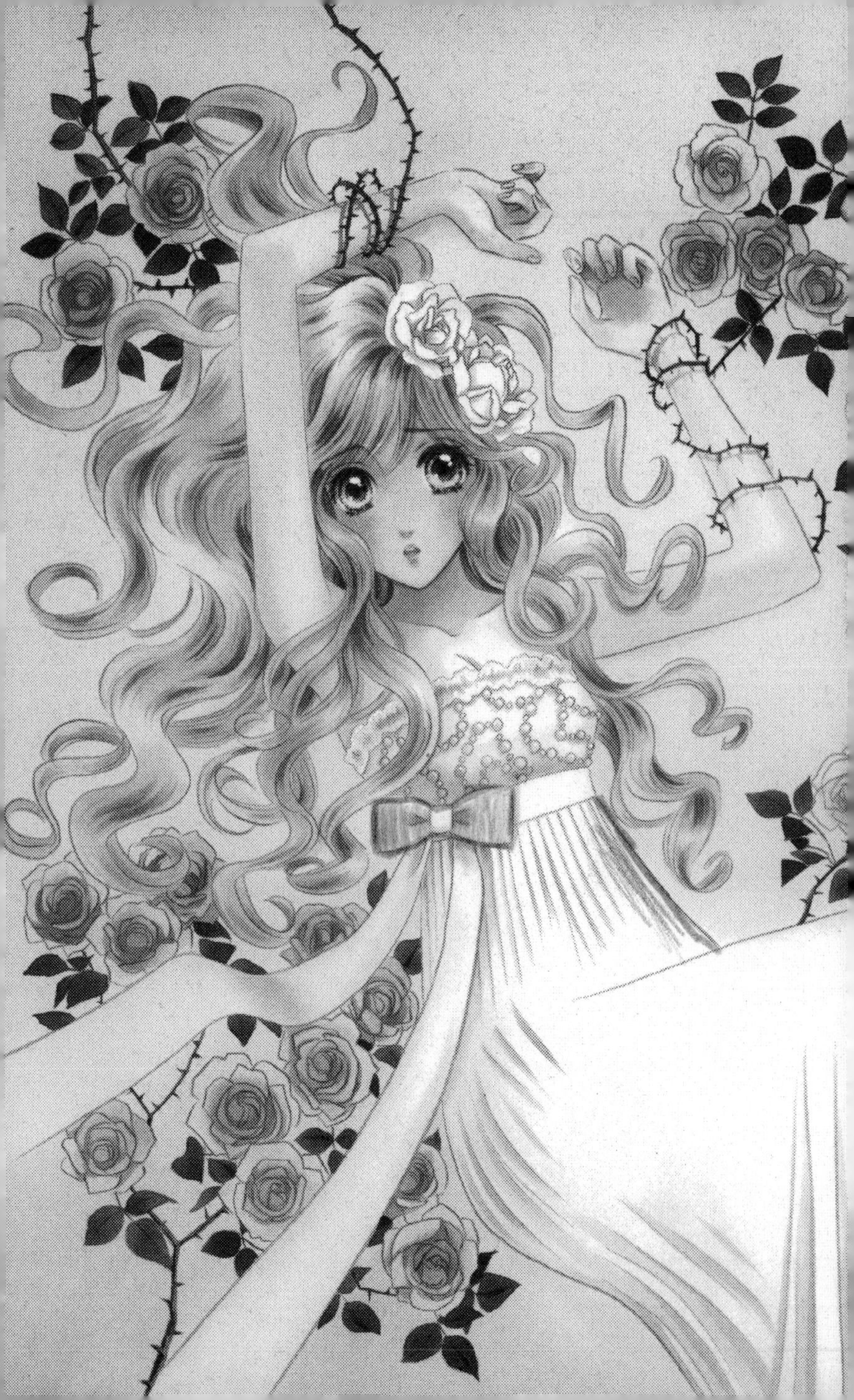

Stepping on Roses

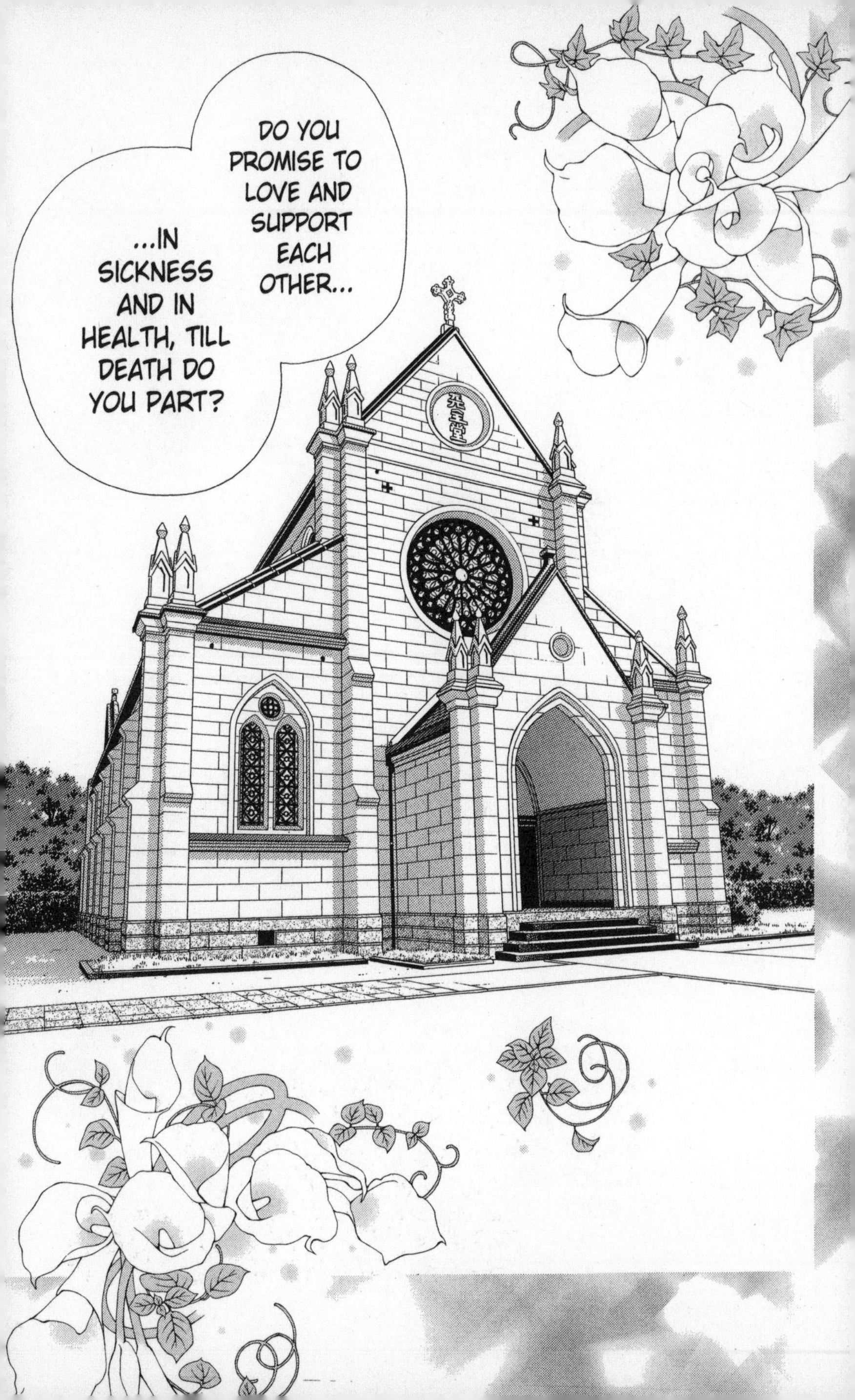
DO YOU PROMISE TO LOVE AND SUPPORT EACH OTHER... ...IN SICKNESS AND IN HEALTH, TILL DEATH DO YOU PART?

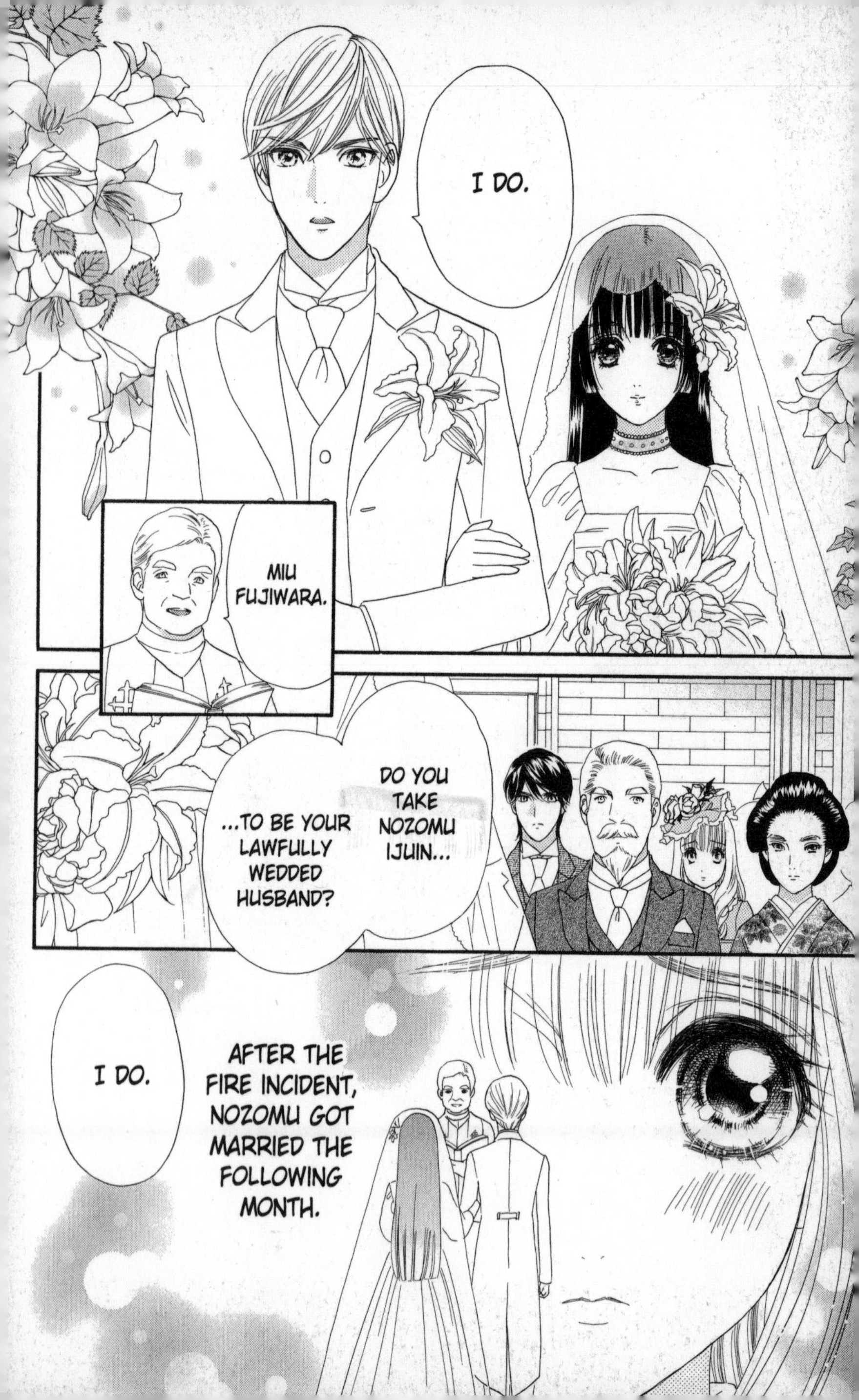

I DO.
MIU FUJIWARA.
DO YOU TAKE NOZOMU IJUIN...
...TO BE YOUR LAWFULLY WEDDED HUSBAND?
AFTER THE FIRE INCIDENT, NOZOMU GOT MARRIED THE FOLLOWING MONTH.
I DO.

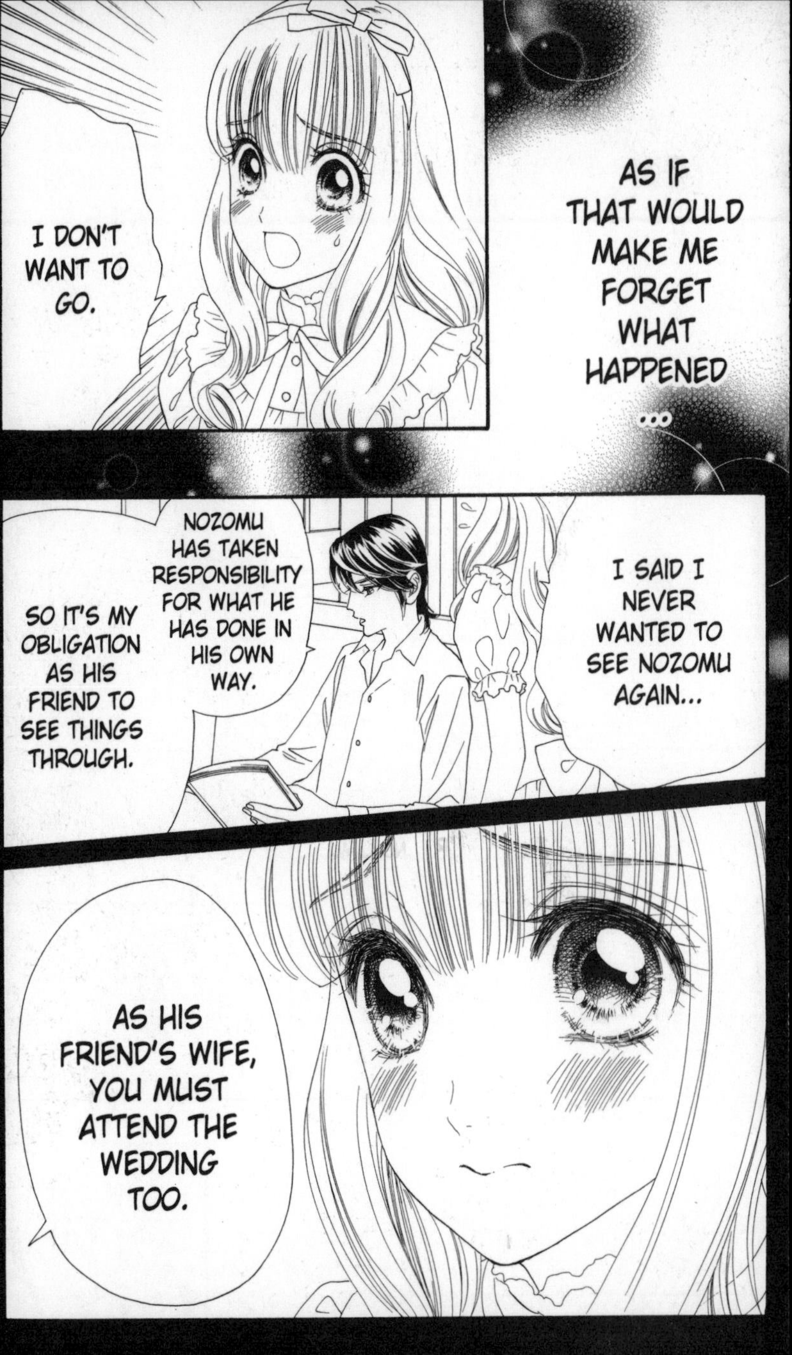
AS IF THAT WOULD MAKE ME FORGET WHAT HAPPENED...
I DON'T WANT TO GO.
I SAID I NEVER WANTED TO SEE NOZOMU AGAIN...
NOZOMU HAS TAKEN RESPONSIBILITY FOR WHAT HE HAS DONE IN HIS OWN WAY.
SO IT'S MY OBLIGATION AS HIS FRIEND TO SEE THINGS THROUGH.
AS HIS FRIEND'S WIFE, YOU MUST ATTEND THE WEDDING TOO.

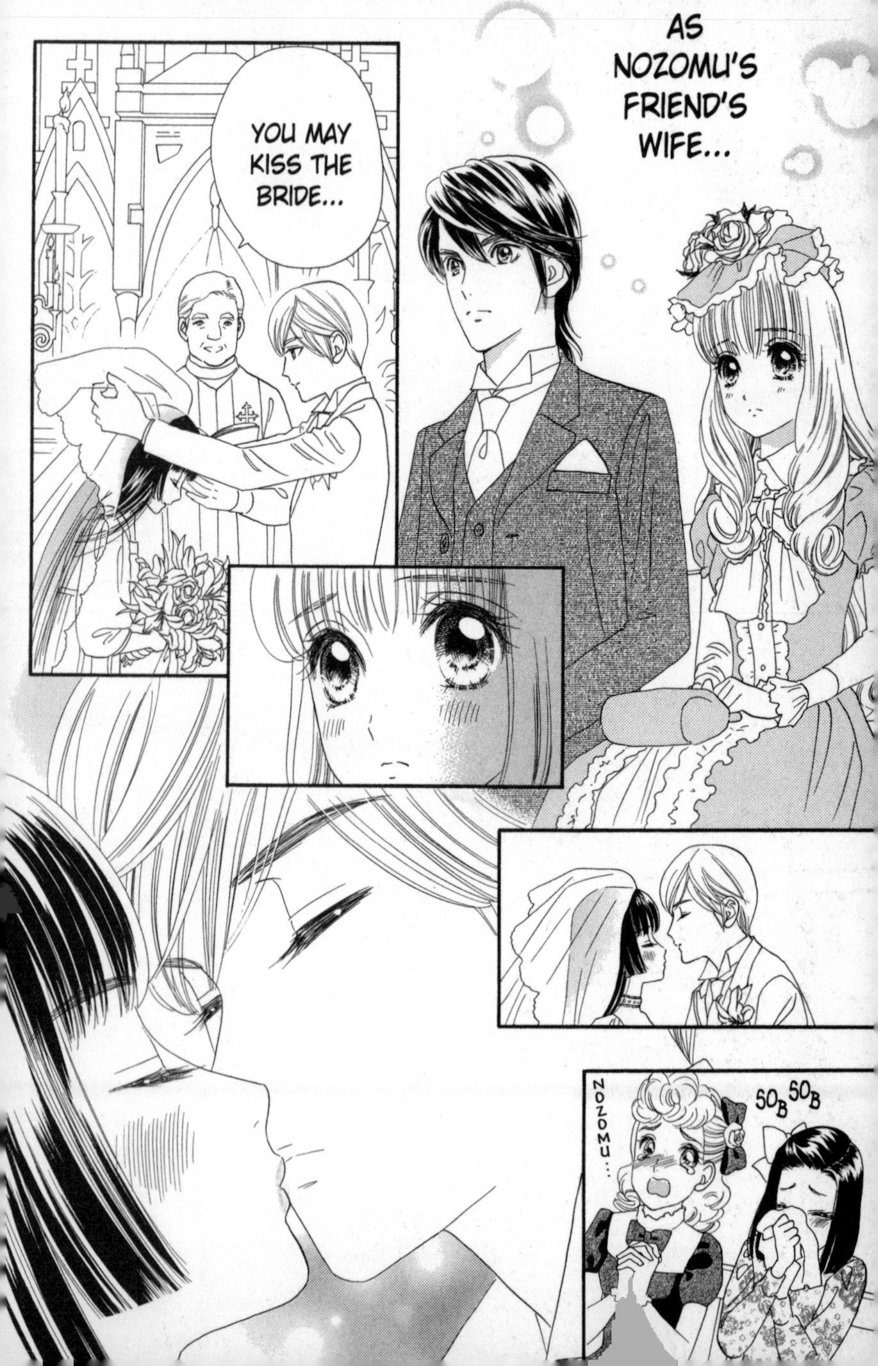
AS NOZOMU'S FRIEND'S WIFE...
YOU MAY KISS THE BRIDE...
SOB SOB
NOZOMU...

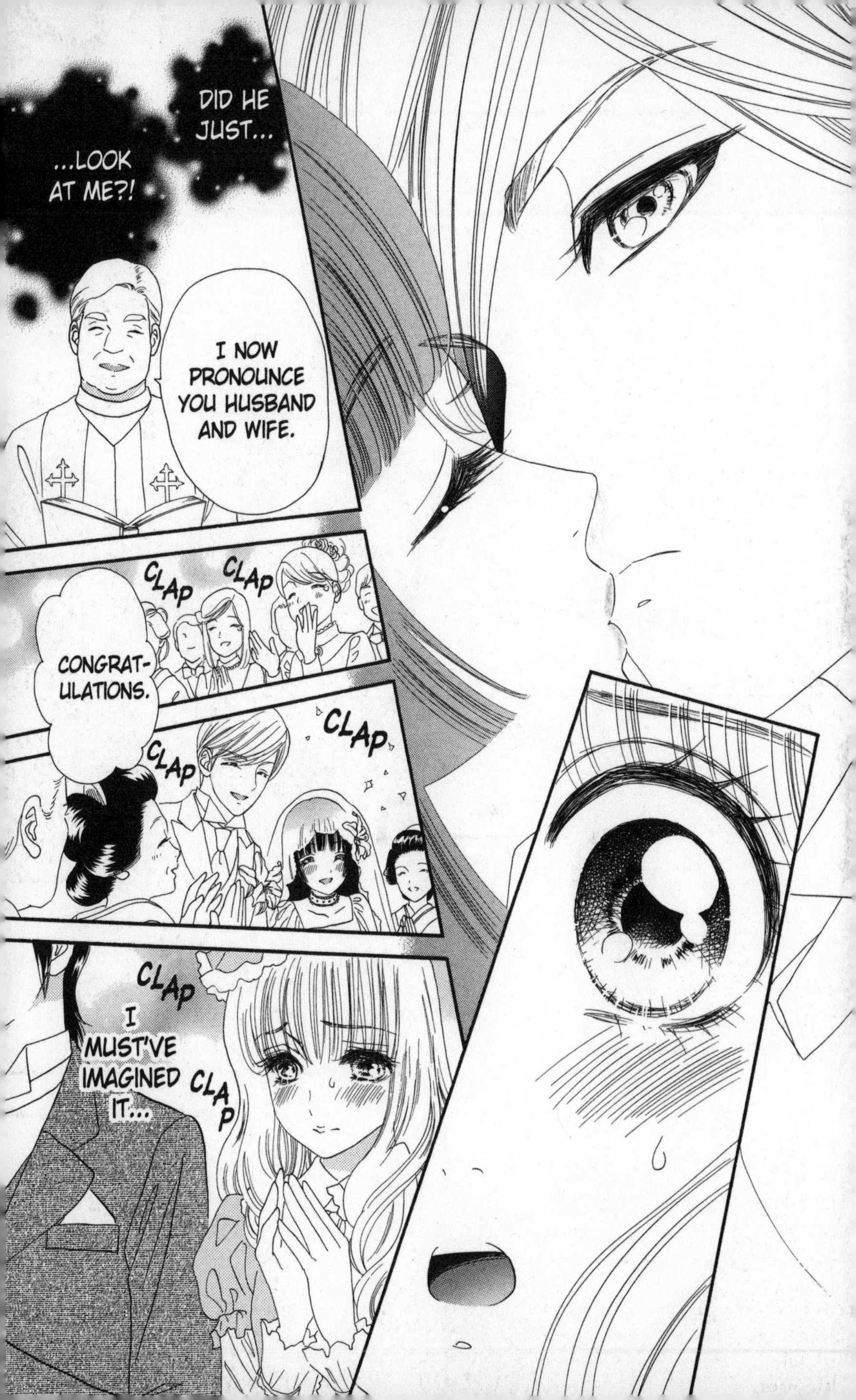
DID HE JUST...
...LOOK AT ME?!
I NOW PRONOUNCE YOU HUSBAND AND WIFE.
CLAP
CLAP
CONGRAT-ULATIONS.
CLAP
CLAP
CLAP
I MUST'VE IMAGINED IT...
CLAP

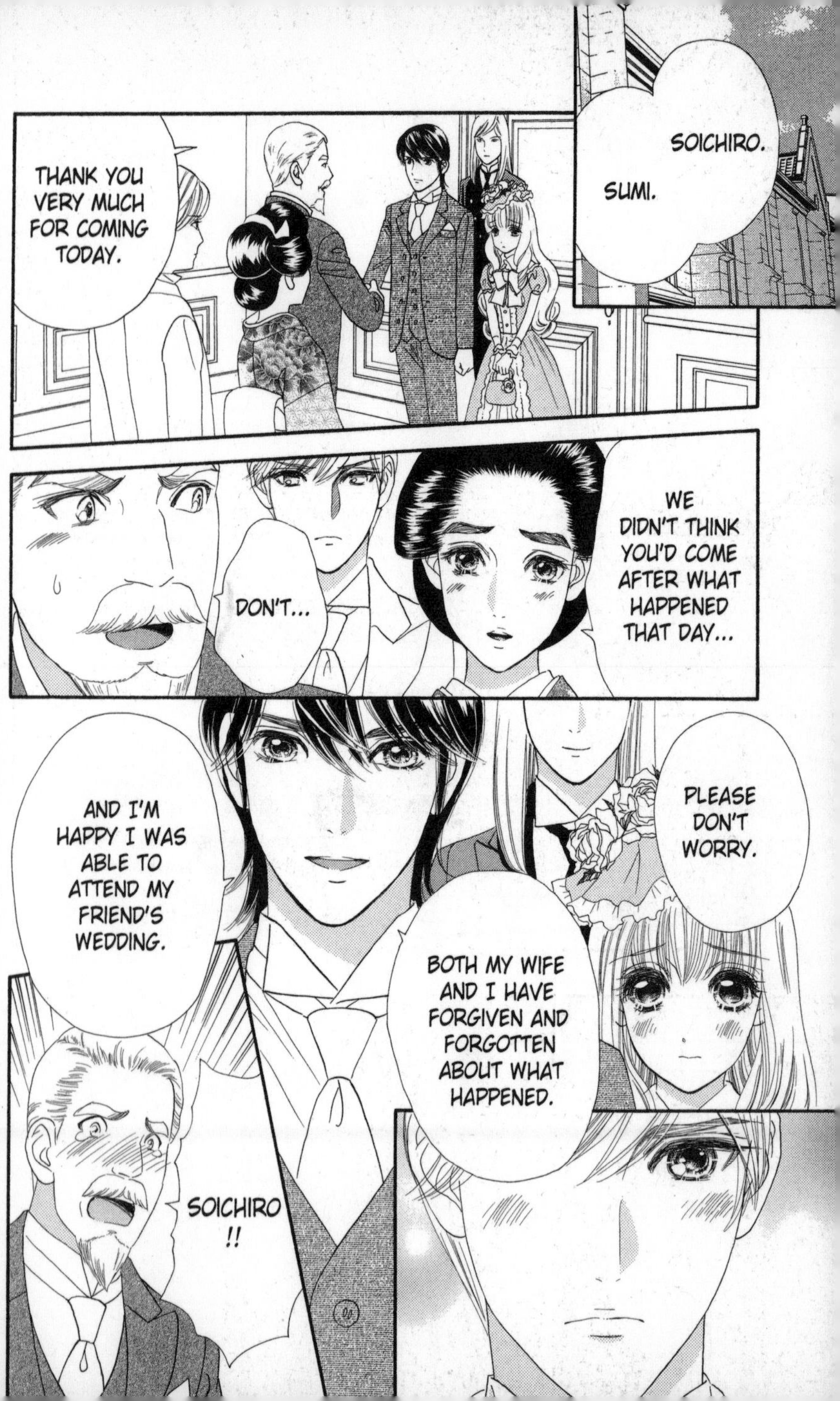
SOICHIRO.
SUMI.
THANK YOU VERY MUCH FOR COMING TODAY.
WE DIDN'T THINK YOU'D COME AFTER WHAT HAPPENED THAT DAY...
DON'T...
PLEASE DON'T WORRY.
BOTH MY WIFE AND I HAVE FORGIVEN AND FORGOTTEN ABOUT WHAT HAPPENED.
AND I'M HAPPY I WAS ABLE TO ATTEND MY FRIEND'S WEDDING.
SOICHIRO !!

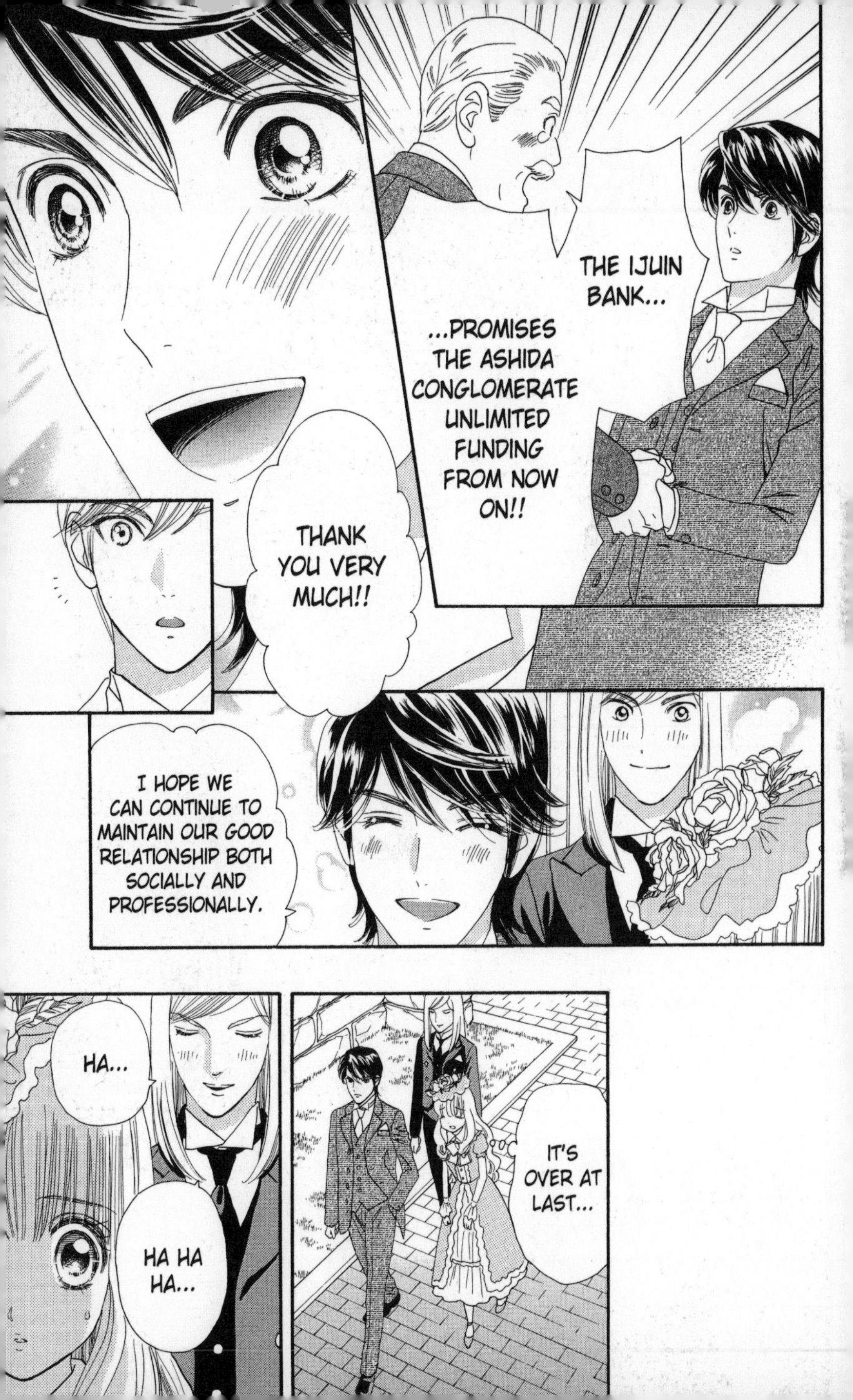
THE IJUIN BANK...
...PROMISES THE ASHIDA CONGLOMERATE UNLIMITED FUNDING FROM NOW ON!!
THANK YOU VERY MUCH!!
I HOPE WE CAN CONTINUE TO MAINTAIN OUR GOOD RELATIONSHIP BOTH SOCIALLY AND PROFESSIONALLY.
IT'S OVER AT LAST...
HA...
HA HA HA...

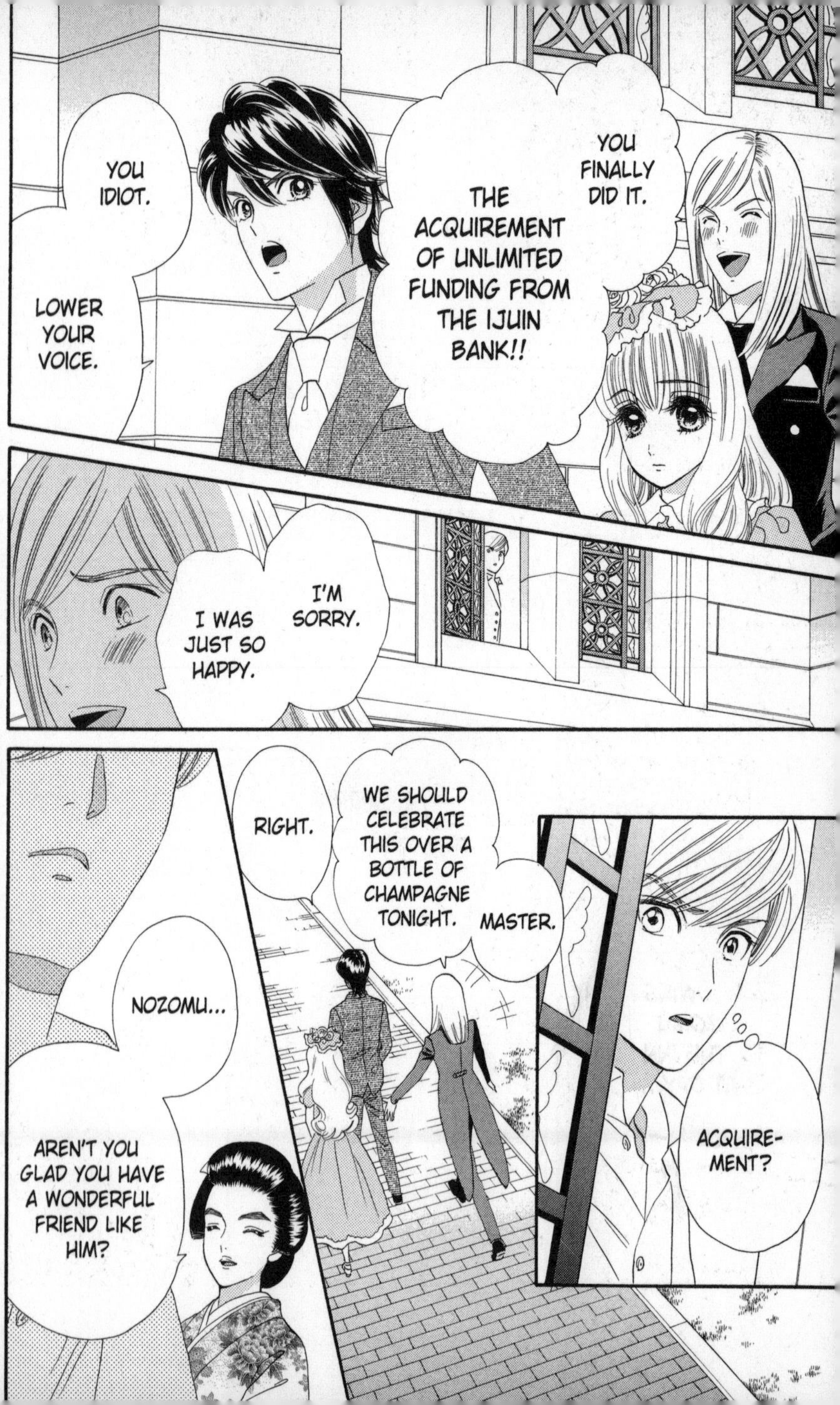
YOU FINALLY DID IT.
THE ACQUIREMENT OF UNLIMITED FUNDING FROM THE IJUIN BANK!!
YOU IDIOT.
LOWER YOUR VOICE.
I'M SORRY.
I WAS JUST SO HAPPY.
ACQUIRE-MENT?
MASTER.
WE SHOULD CELEBRATE THIS OVER A BOTTLE OF CHAMPAGNE TONIGHT.
RIGHT.
NOZOMU...
AREN'T YOU GLAD YOU HAVE A WONDERFUL FRIEND LIKE HIM?

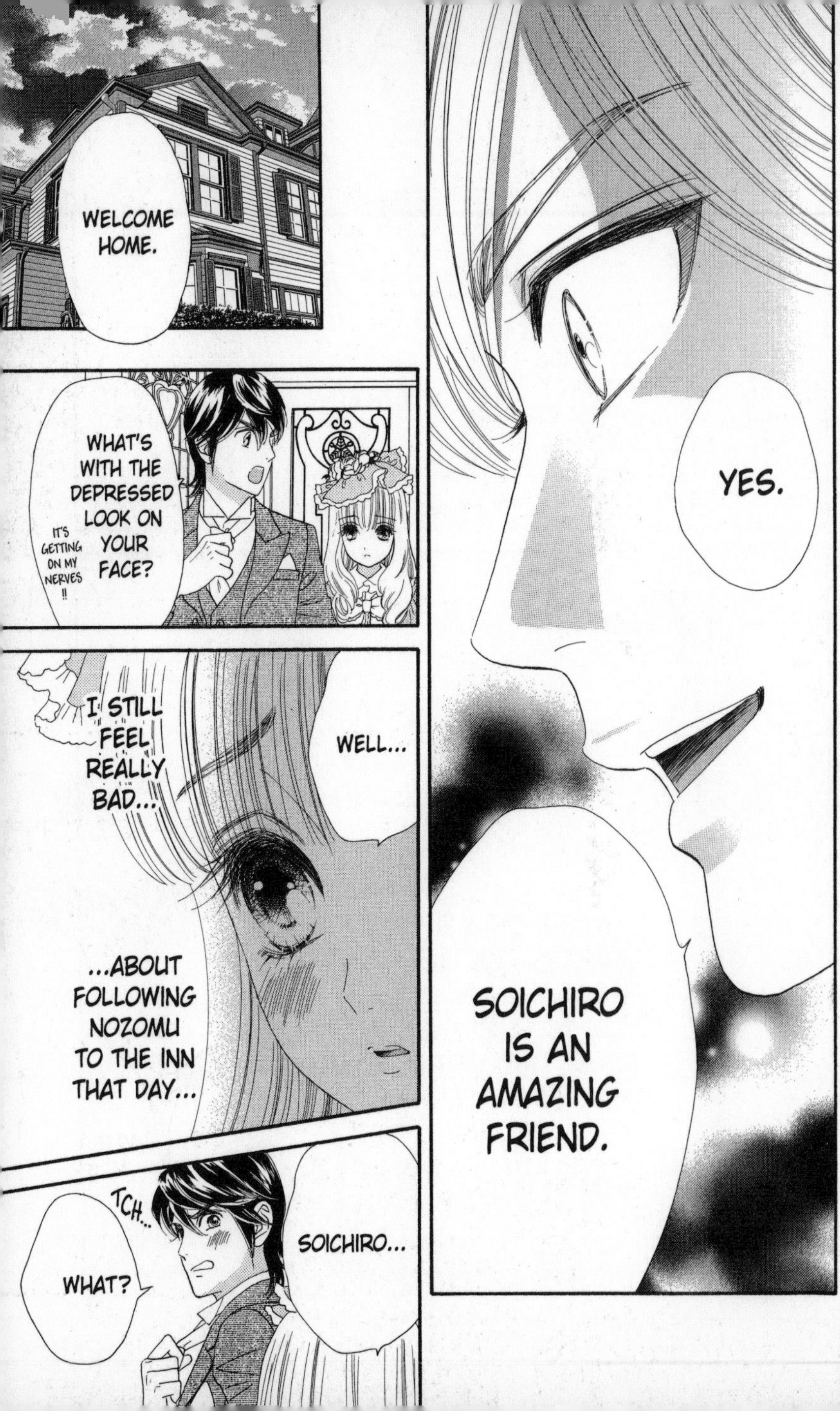
YES.
SOICHIRO IS AN AMAZING FRIEND.
WELCOME HOME.
WHAT'S WITH THE DEPRESSED LOOK ON YOUR FACE?
IT'S GETTING ON MY NERVES!!
WELL...
I STILL FEEL REALLY BAD...
...ABOUT FOLLOWING NOZOMU TO THE INN THAT DAY...
SOICHIRO...
TCH...
WHAT?

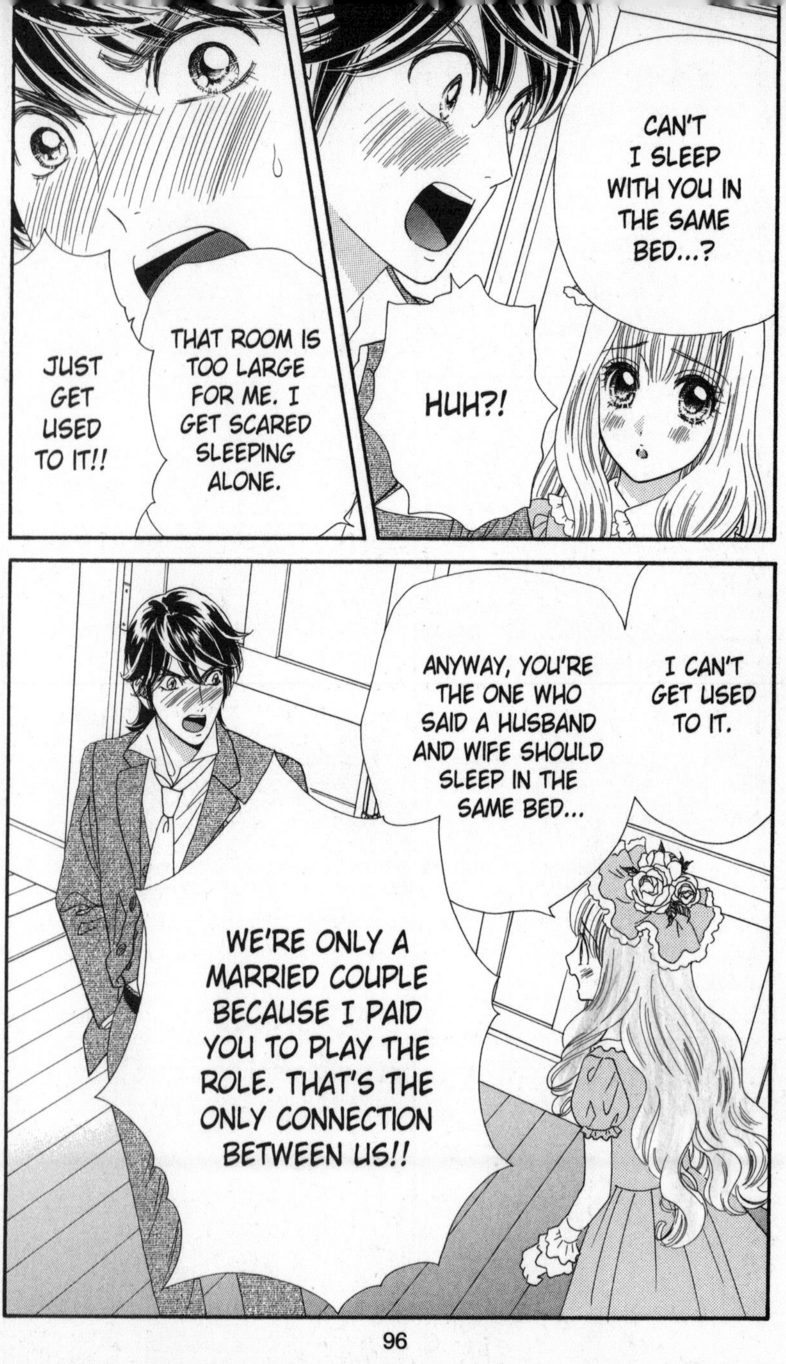
CAN'T I SLEEP WITH YOU IN THE SAME BED...?
HUH?!
THAT ROOM IS TOO LARGE FOR ME. I GET SCARED SLEEPING ALONE.
JUST GET USED TO IT!!
I CAN'T GET USED TO IT.
ANYWAY, YOU'RE THE ONE WHO SAID A HUSBAND AND WIFE SHOULD SLEEP IN THE SAME BED...
WE'RE ONLY A MARRIED COUPLE BECAUSE I PAID YOU TO PLAY THE ROLE. THAT'S THE ONLY CONNECTION BETWEEN US!!

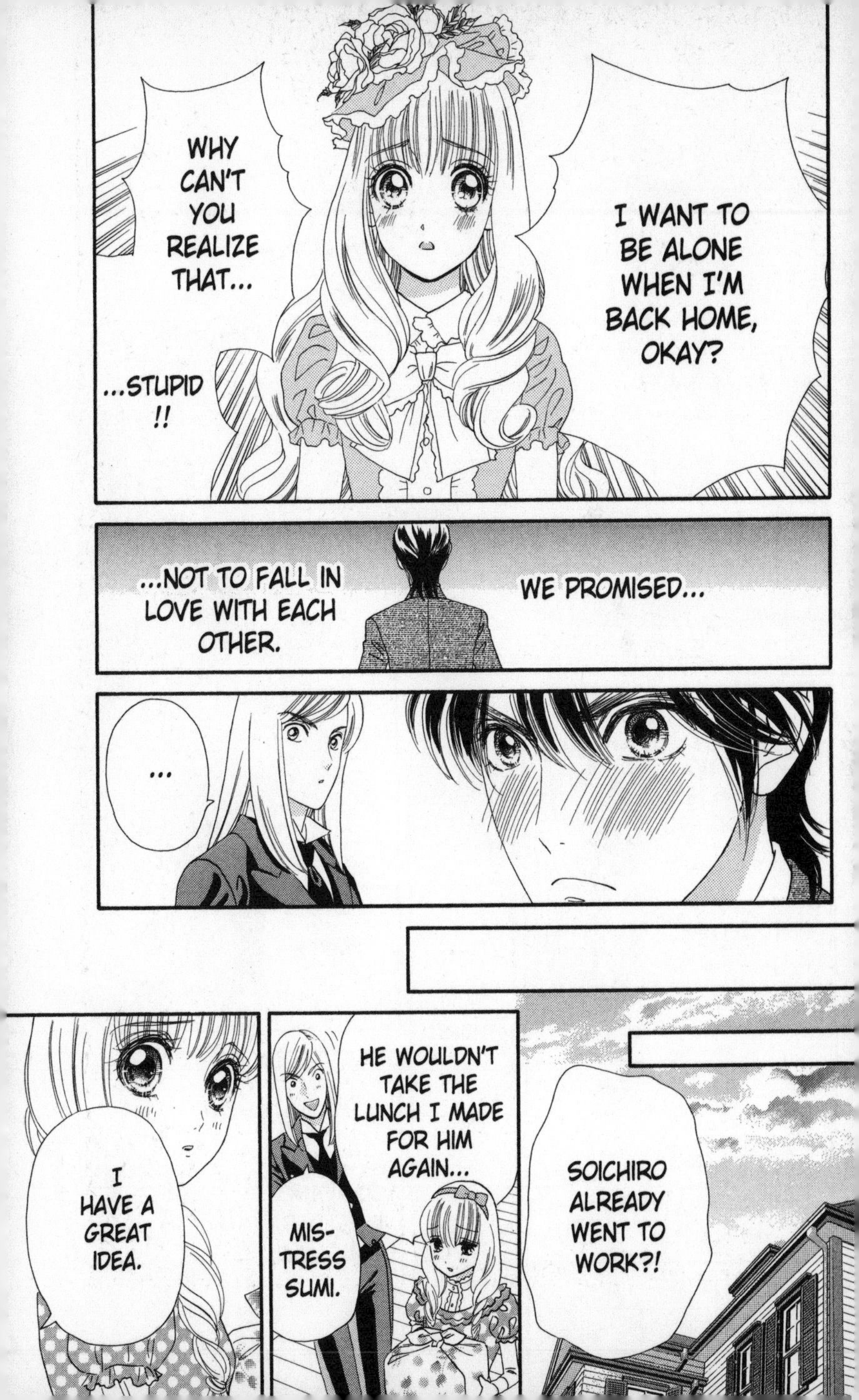
I WANT TO BE ALONE WHEN I'M BACK HOME, OKAY?
WHY CAN'T YOU REALIZE THAT...
...STUPID !!
WE PROMISED...
...NOT TO FALL IN LOVE WITH EACH OTHER.
...
SOICHIRO ALREADY WENT TO WORK?!
HE WOULDN'T TAKE THE LUNCH I MADE FOR HIM AGAIN...
MIS-TRESS SUMI.
I HAVE A GREAT IDEA.

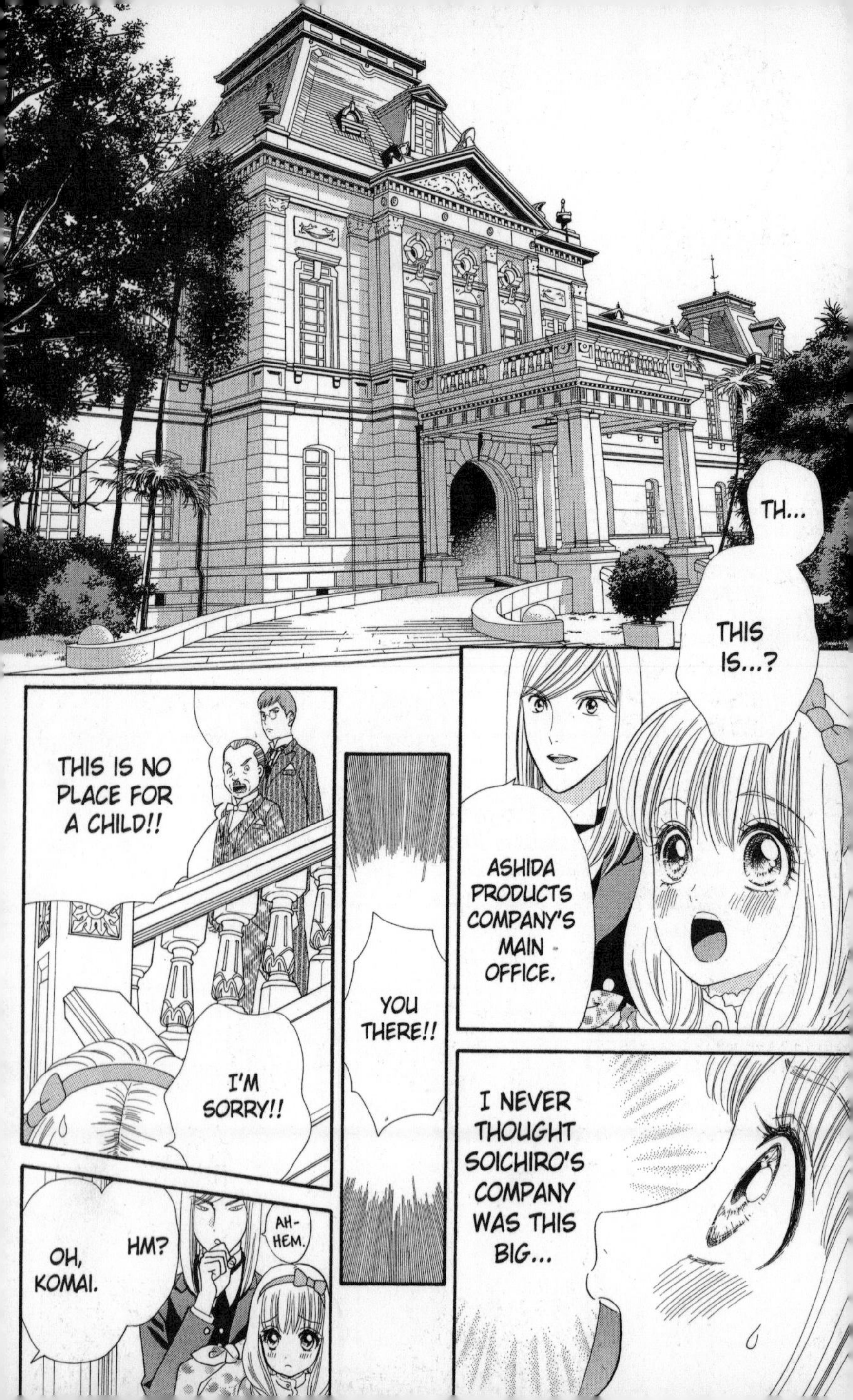
TH...
THIS IS...?
ASHIDA PRODUCTS COMPANY'S MAIN OFFICE.
I NEVER THOUGHT SOICHIRO'S COMPANY WAS THIS BIG...
YOU THERE!!
THIS IS NO PLACE FOR A CHILD!!
I'M SORRY!!
AH-HEM.
HM?
OH, KOMAI.

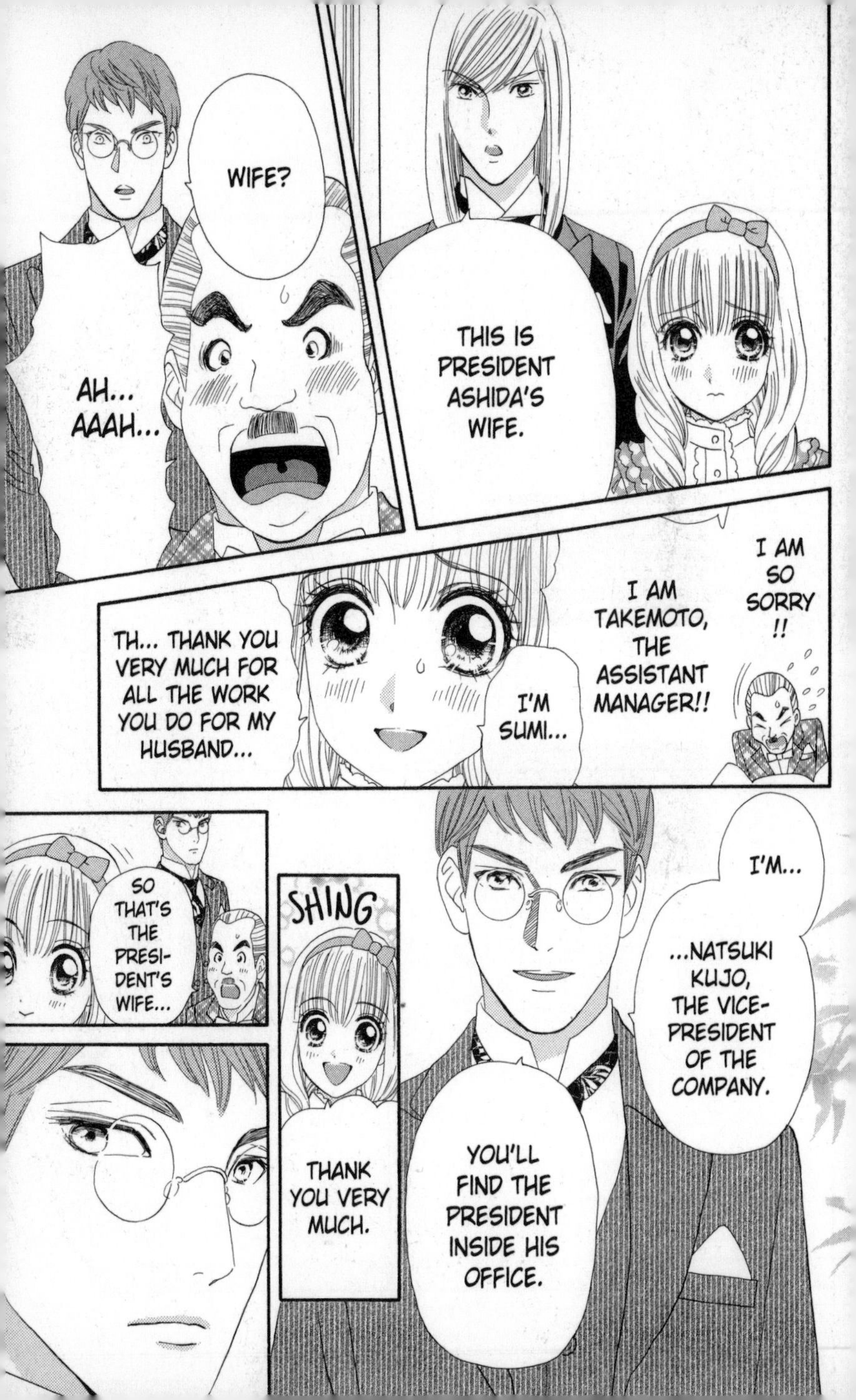
THIS IS PRESIDENT ASHIDA'S WIFE.
WIFE?
AH... AAAH...
I AM SO SORRY!!
I AM TAKEMOTO, THE ASSISTANT MANAGER!!
I'M SUMI...
TH... THANK YOU VERY MUCH FOR ALL THE WORK YOU DO FOR MY HUSBAND...
I'M...
...NATSUKI KUJO, THE VICE-PRESIDENT OF THE COMPANY.
YOU'LL FIND THE PRESIDENT INSIDE HIS OFFICE.
SHING
THANK YOU VERY MUCH.
SO THAT'S THE PRESI-DENT'S WIFE...

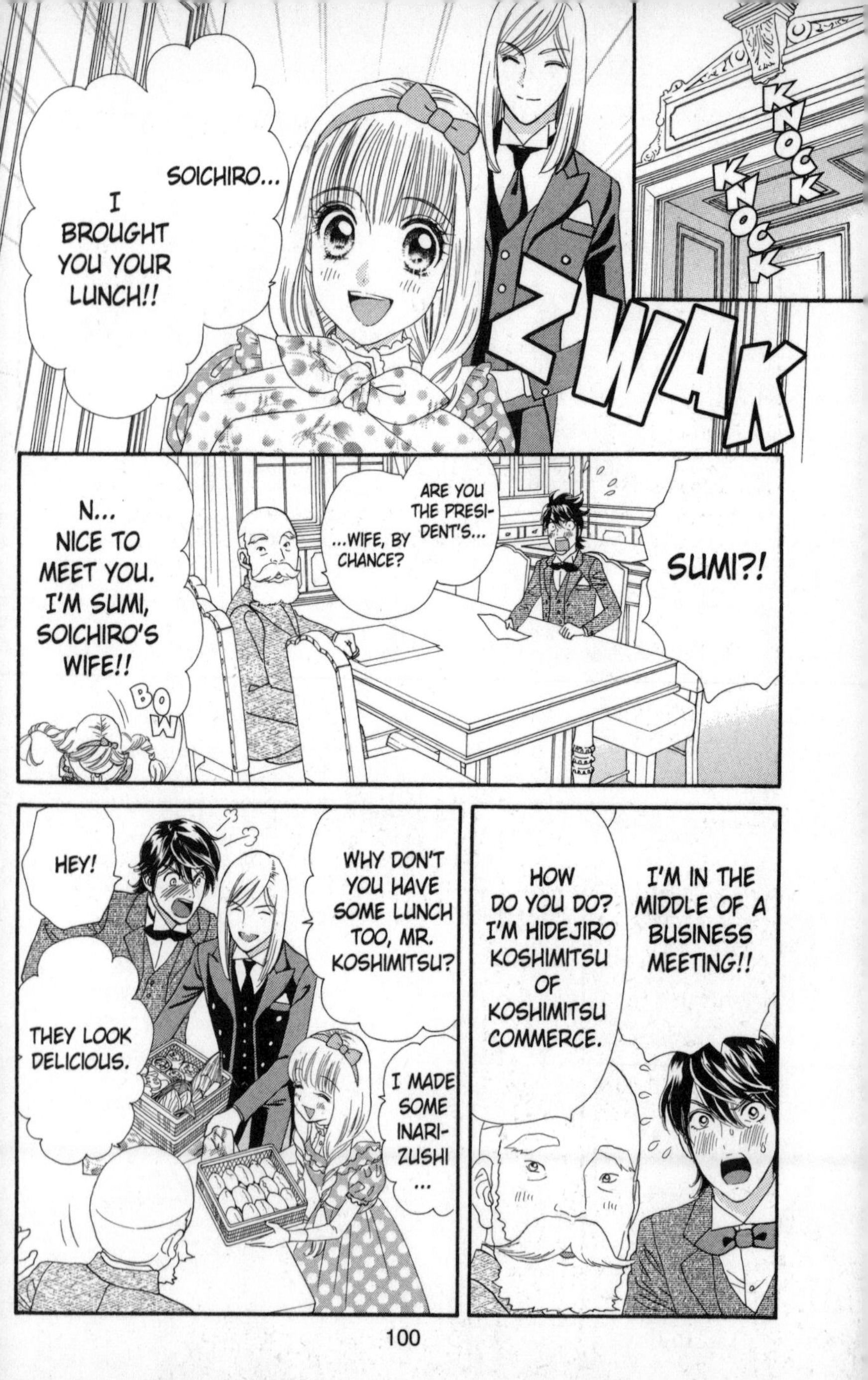
KNOCK
KNOCK
ZWAK
SOICHIRO...
I BROUGHT YOU YOUR LUNCH!!
SUMI?!
ARE YOU THE PRESI-DENT'S...
...WIFE, BY CHANCE?
N... NICE TO MEET YOU. I'M SUMI, SOICHIRO'S WIFE!!
BOW
I'M IN THE MIDDLE OF A BUSINESS MEETING!!
HOW DO YOU DO? I'M HIDEJIRO KOSHIMITSU OF KOSHIMITSU COMMERCE.
WHY DON'T YOU HAVE SOME LUNCH TOO, MR. KOSHIMITSU?
HEY!
I MADE SOME INARI-ZUSHI...
THEY LOOK DELICIOUS.

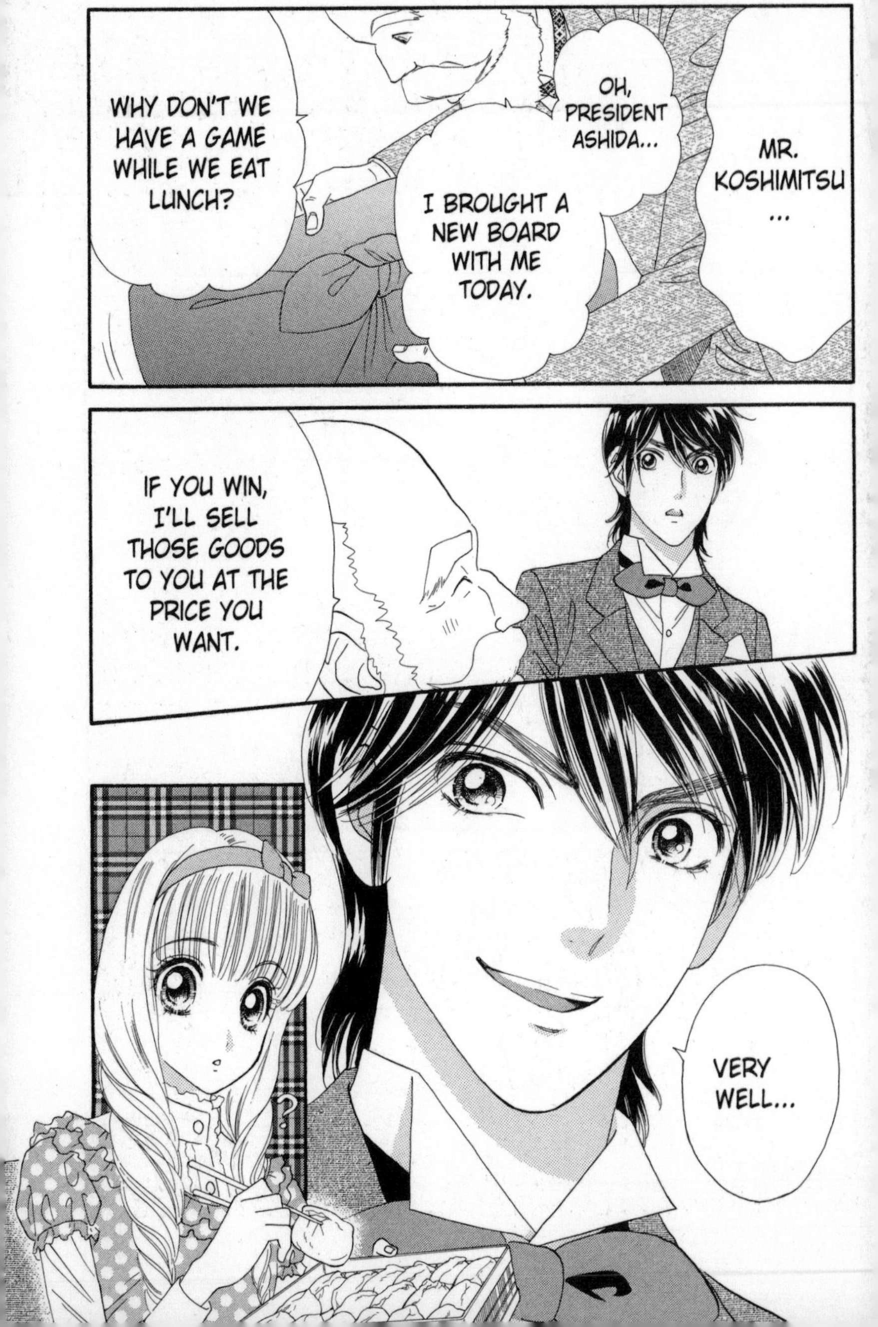
MR. KOSHIMITSU ...
OH, PRESIDENT ASHIDA...
I BROUGHT A NEW BOARD WITH ME TODAY.
WHY DON'T WE HAVE A GAME WHILE WE EAT LUNCH?
IF YOU WIN, I'LL SELL THOSE GOODS TO YOU AT THE PRICE YOU WANT.
VERY WELL...

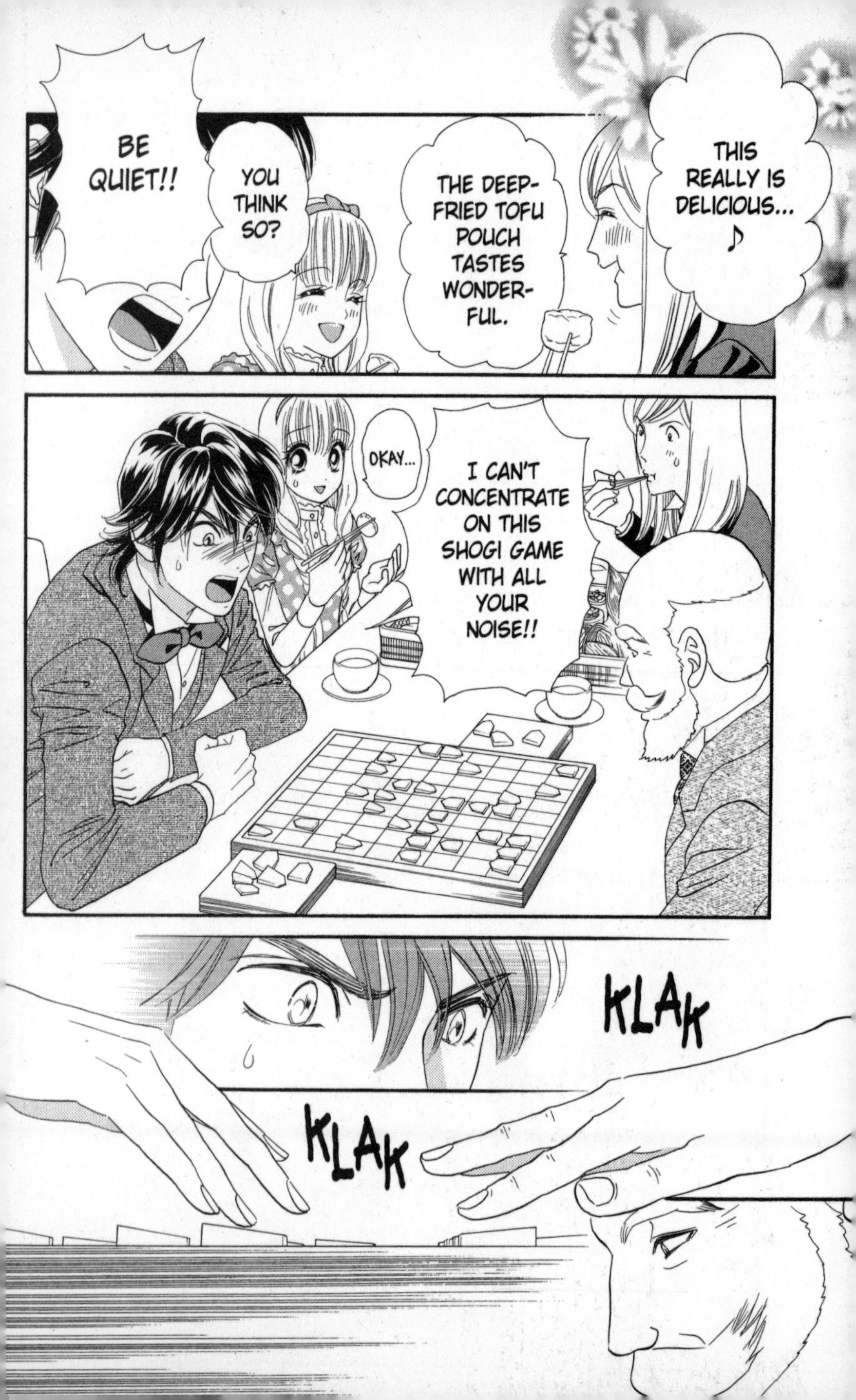
THIS REALLY IS DELICIOUS... ♪
THE DEEP-FRIED TOFU POUCH TASTES WONDERFUL.
YOU THINK SO?
BE QUIET!!
I CAN'T CONCENTRATE ON THIS SHOGI GAME WITH ALL YOUR NOISE!!
OKAY...
KLAK
KLAK

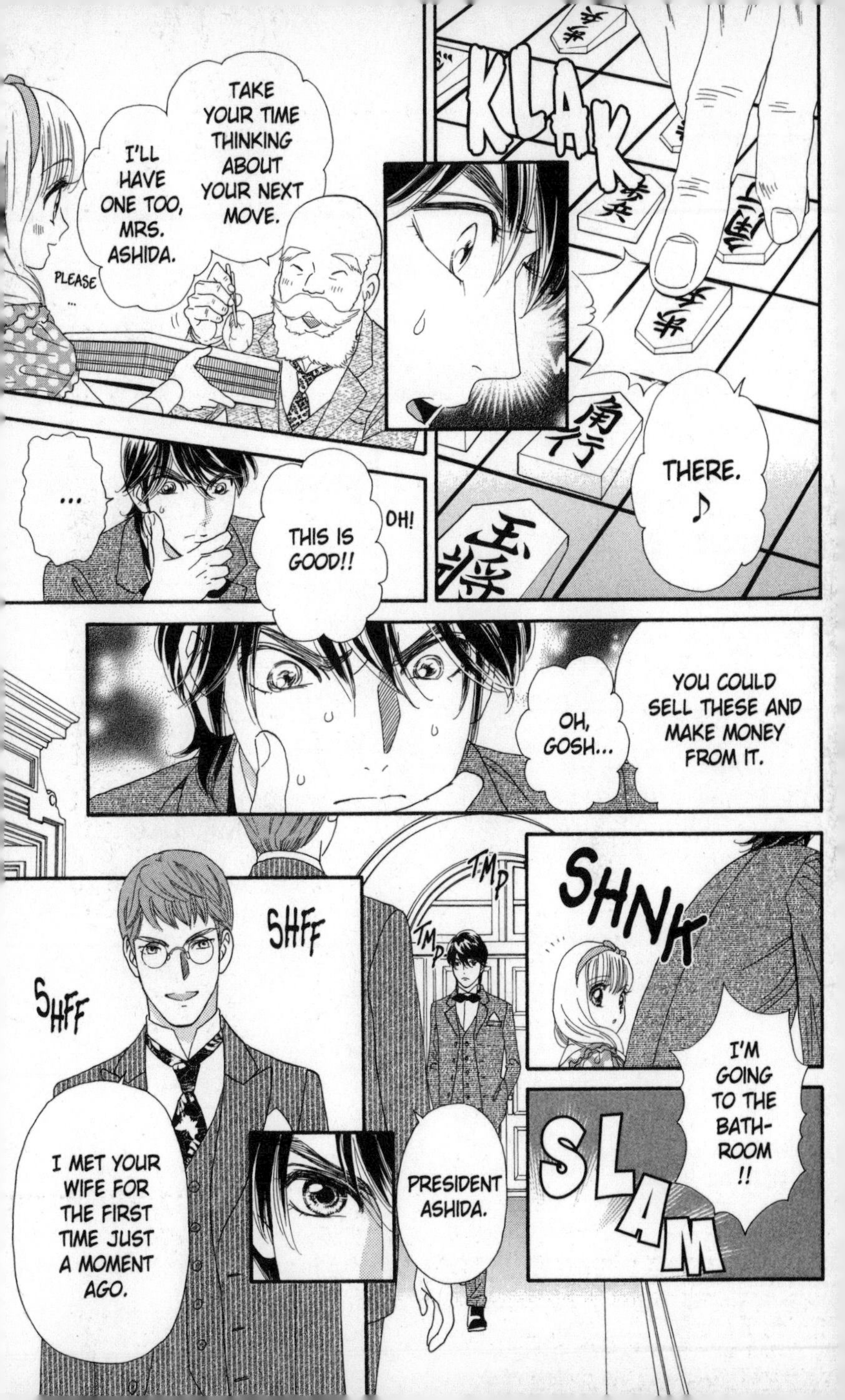
KLAK
角行
THERE. ♪
TAKE YOUR TIME THINKING ABOUT YOUR NEXT MOVE.
I'LL HAVE ONE TOO, MRS. ASHIDA.
PLEASE ...
OH!
THIS IS GOOD!!
...
YOU COULD SELL THESE AND MAKE MONEY FROM IT.
OH, GOSH...
SHNK
I'M GOING TO THE BATH-ROOM !!
SLAM
TMP
TMP
PRESIDENT ASHIDA.
SHFF
SHFF
I MET YOUR WIFE FOR THE FIRST TIME JUST A MOMENT AGO.

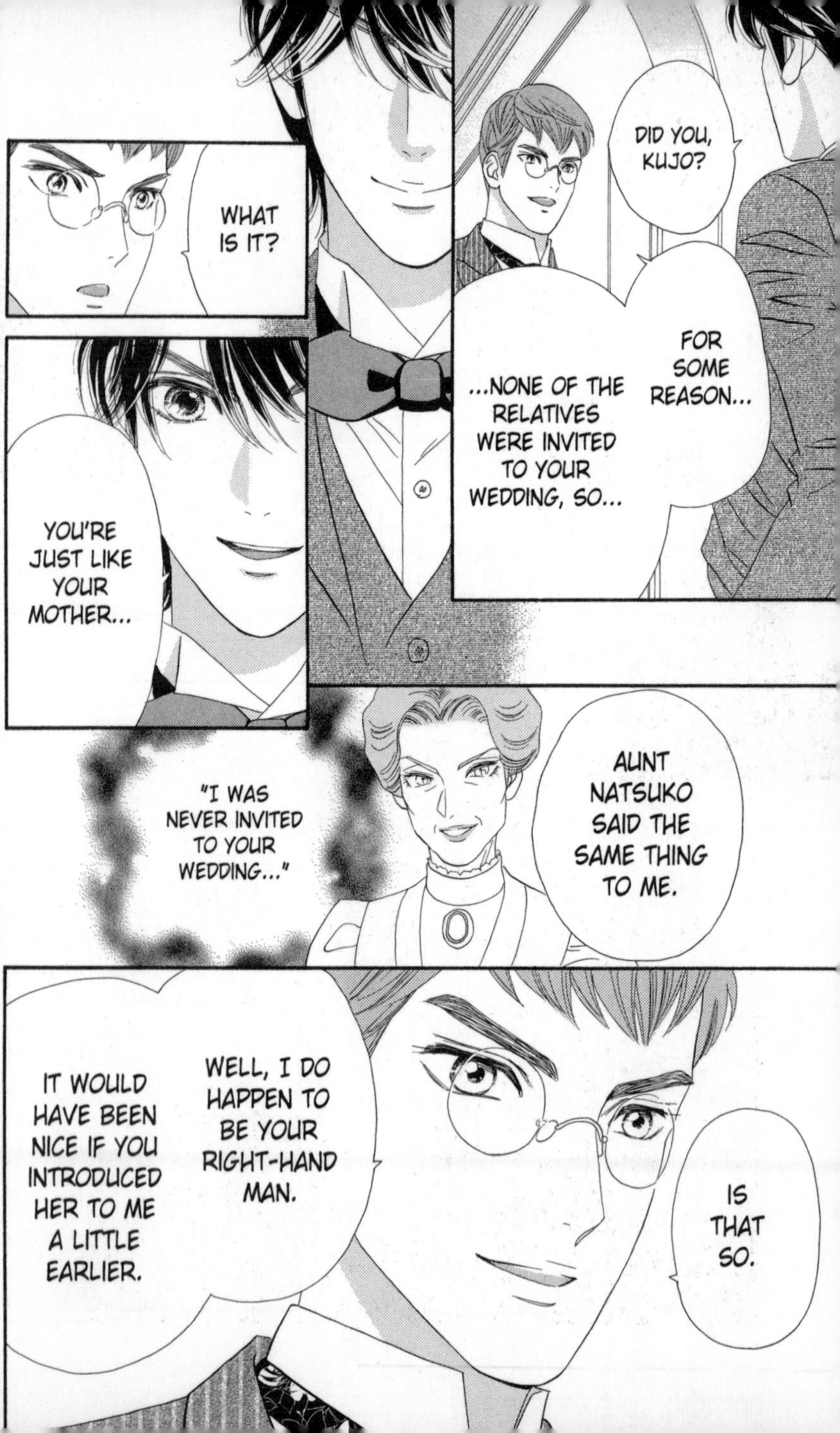
DID YOU, KUJO?
FOR SOME REASON...
...NONE OF THE RELATIVES WERE INVITED TO YOUR WEDDING, SO...
WHAT IS IT?
YOU'RE JUST LIKE YOUR MOTHER...
AUNT NATSUKO SAID THE SAME THING TO ME.
"I WAS NEVER INVITED TO YOUR WEDDING..."
IS THAT SO.
WELL, I DO HAPPEN TO BE YOUR RIGHT-HAND MAN.
IT WOULD HAVE BEEN NICE IF YOU INTRODUCED HER TO ME A LITTLE EARLIER.

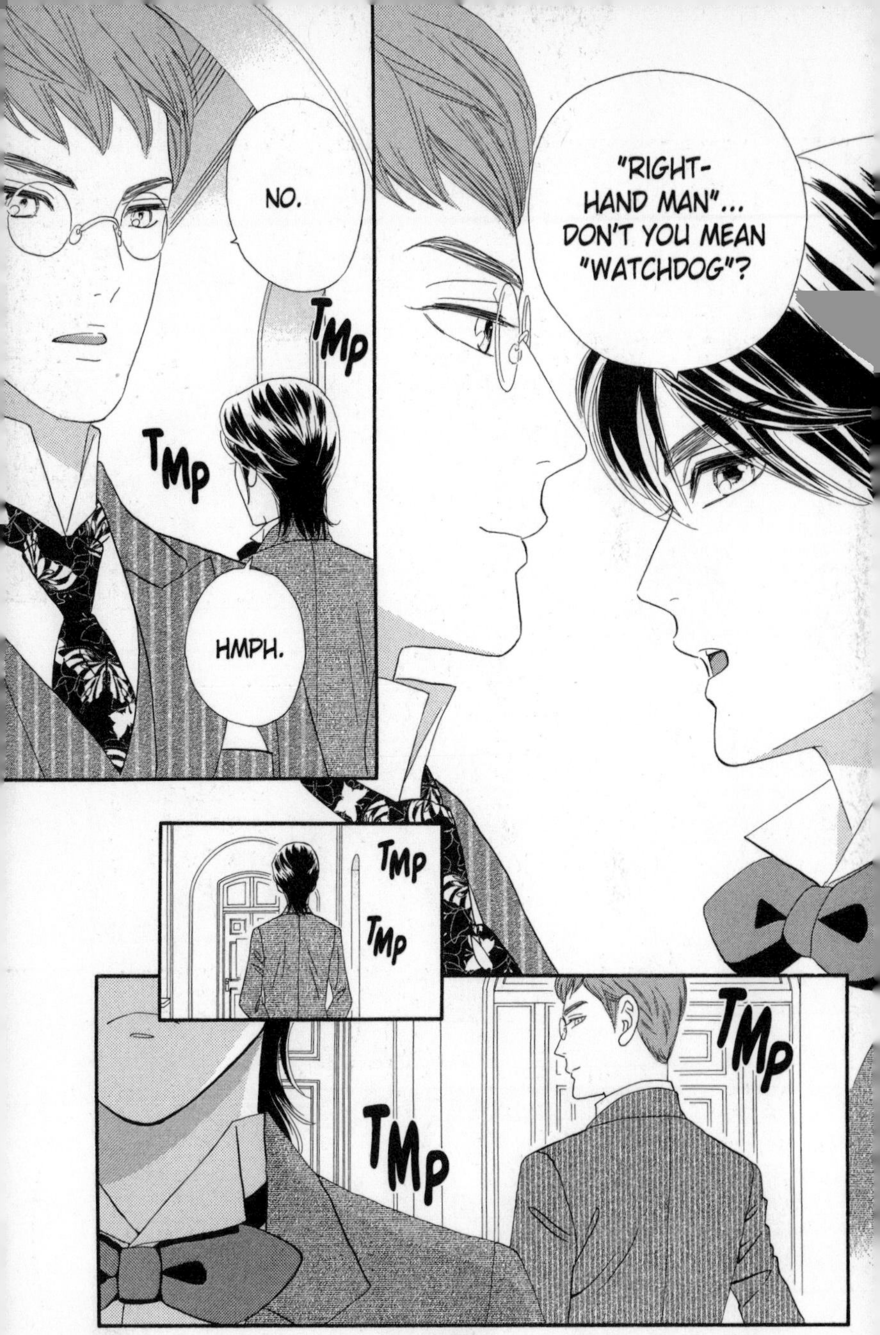
"RIGHT-HAND MAN"... DON'T YOU MEAN "WATCHDOG"?
NO.
TMP
TMP
HMPH.
TMP
TMP
TMP
TMP

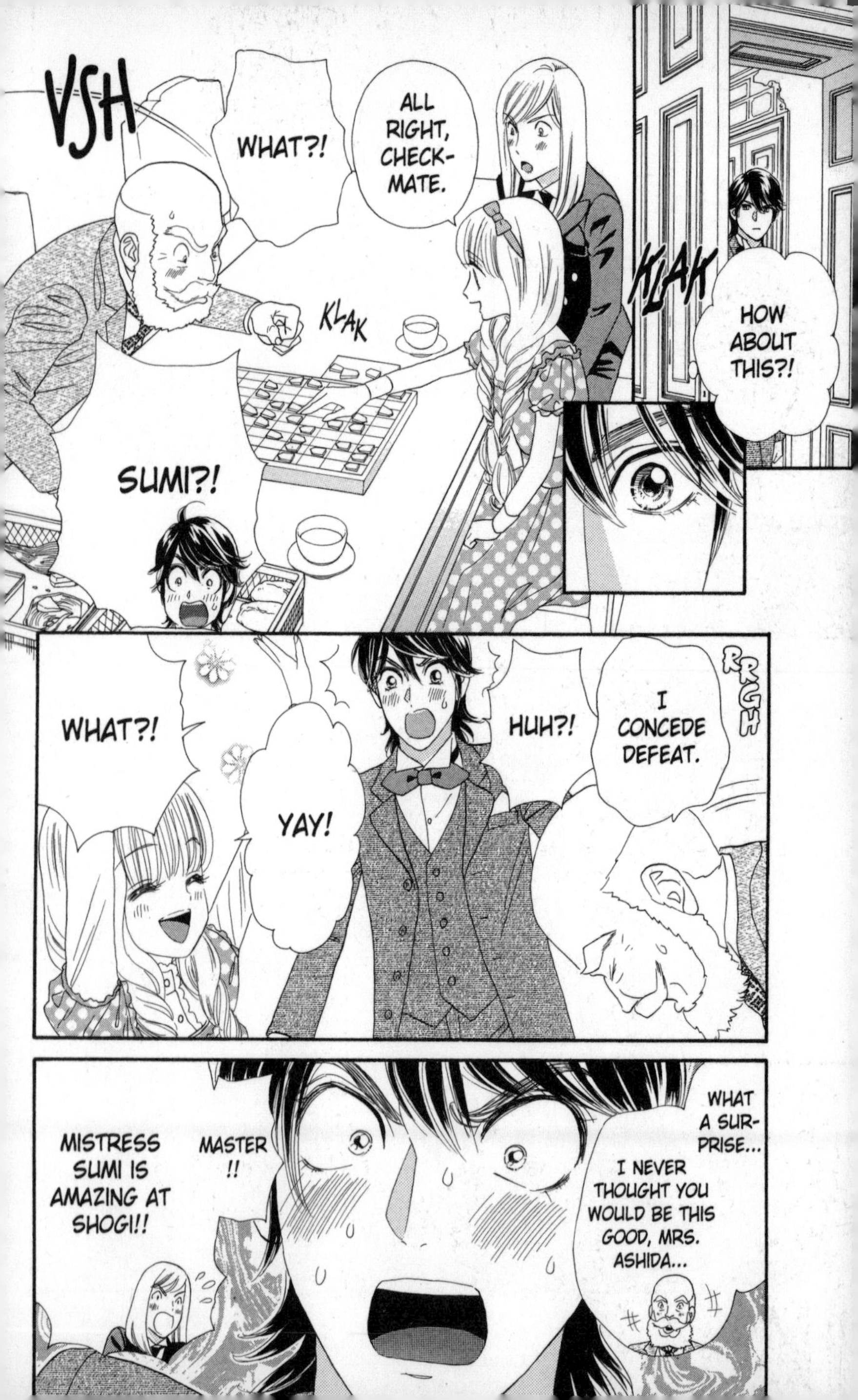
KLAK
HOW ABOUT THIS?!
ALL RIGHT, CHECKMATE.
WHAT?!
VSH
KLAK
SUMI?!
RRGH
I CONCEDE DEFEAT.
HUH?!
YAY!
WHAT?!
WHAT A SURPRISE...
I NEVER THOUGHT YOU WOULD BE THIS GOOD, MRS. ASHIDA...
MASTER!!
MISTRESS SUMI IS AMAZING AT SHOGI!!

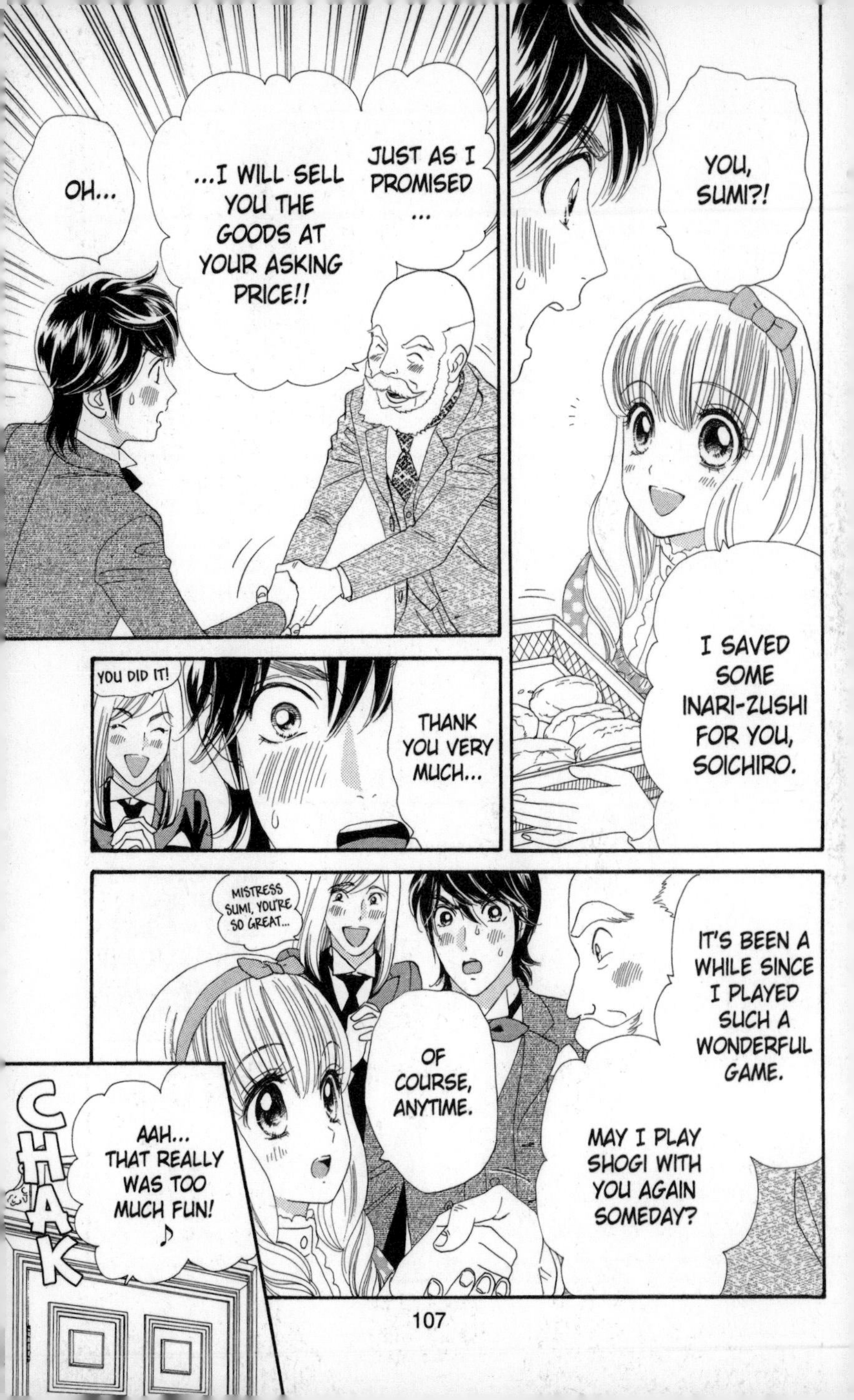
YOU, SUMI?!
I SAVED SOME INARI-ZUSHI FOR YOU, SOICHIRO.
JUST AS I PROMISED ...
...I WILL SELL YOU THE GOODS AT YOUR ASKING PRICE!!
OH...
THANK YOU VERY MUCH...
YOU DID IT!
IT'S BEEN A WHILE SINCE I PLAYED SUCH A WONDERFUL GAME.
MAY I PLAY SHOGI WITH YOU AGAIN SOMEDAY?
MISTRESS SUMI, YOU'RE SO GREAT...
OF COURSE, ANYTIME.
AAH... THAT REALLY WAS TOO MUCH FUN! ♪
CHAK

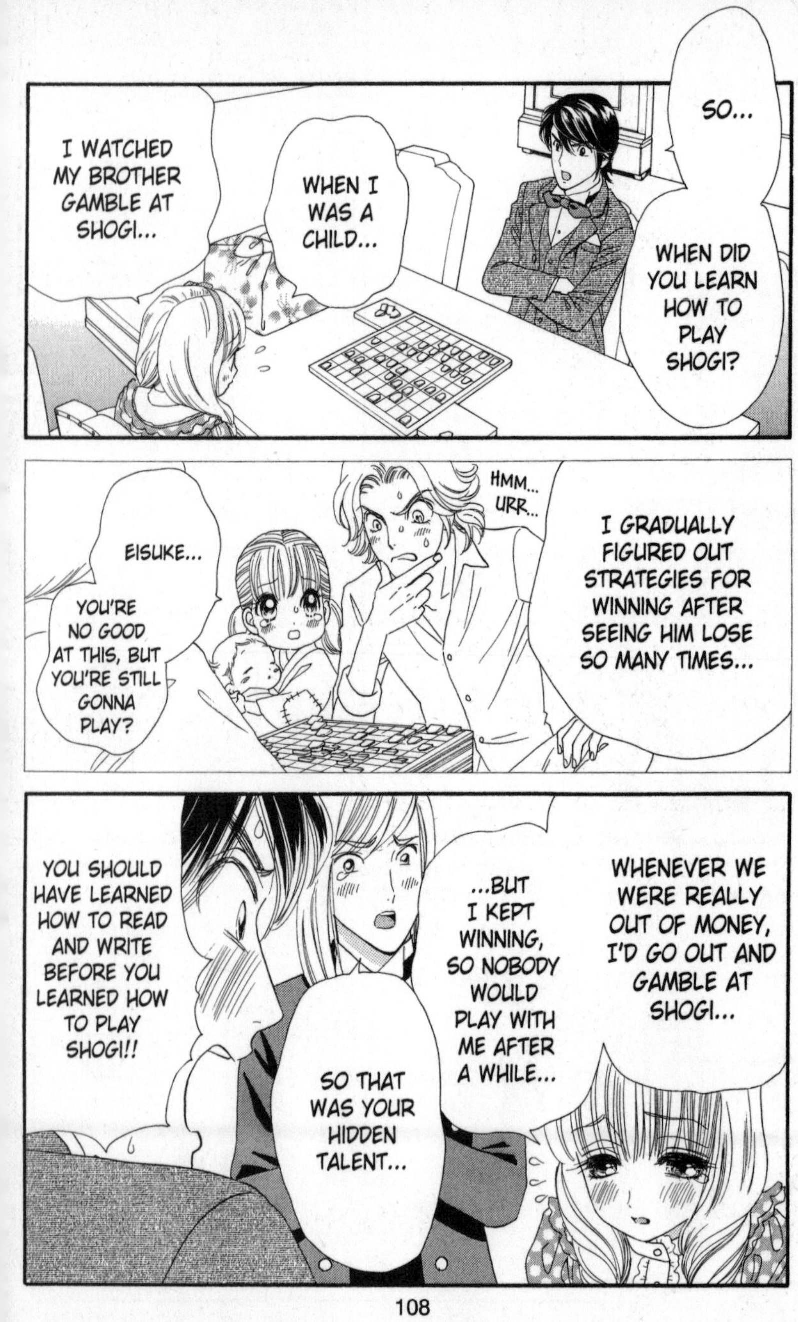
SO...
WHEN DID YOU LEARN HOW TO PLAY SHOGI?
WHEN I WAS A CHILD...
I WATCHED MY BROTHER GAMBLE AT SHOGI...
I GRADUALLY FIGURED OUT STRATEGIES FOR WINNING AFTER SEEING HIM LOSE SO MANY TIMES...
HMM... URR...
EISUKE...
YOU'RE NO GOOD AT THIS, BUT YOU'RE STILL GONNA PLAY?
WHENEVER WE WERE REALLY OUT OF MONEY, I'D GO OUT AND GAMBLE AT SHOGI...
...BUT I KEPT WINNING, SO NOBODY WOULD PLAY WITH ME AFTER A WHILE...
SO THAT WAS YOUR HIDDEN TALENT...
YOU SHOULD HAVE LEARNED HOW TO READ AND WRITE BEFORE YOU LEARNED HOW TO PLAY SHOGI!!

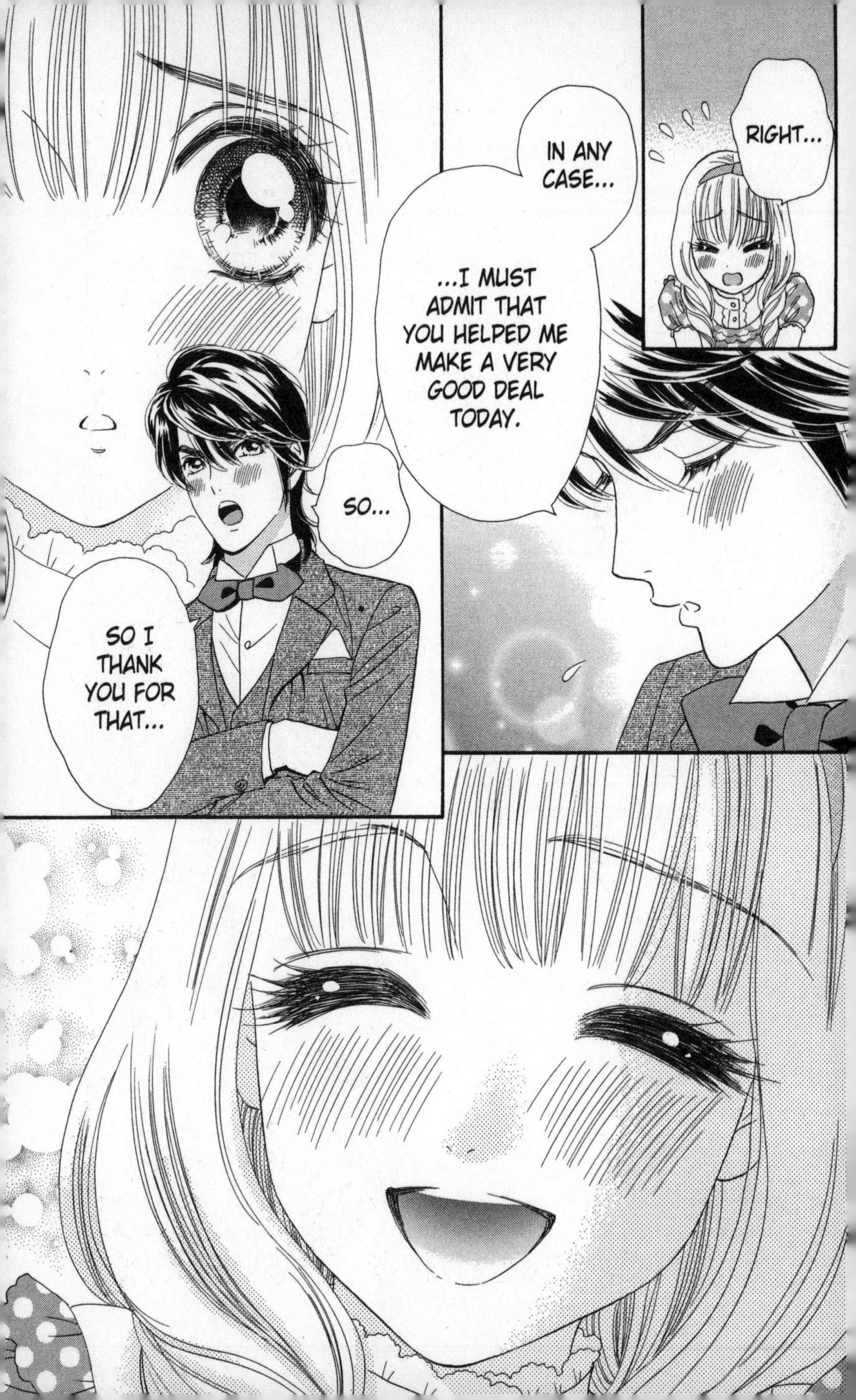
RIGHT...
IN ANY CASE...
...I MUST ADMIT THAT YOU HELPED ME MAKE A VERY GOOD DEAL TODAY.
SO...
SO I THANK YOU FOR THAT...

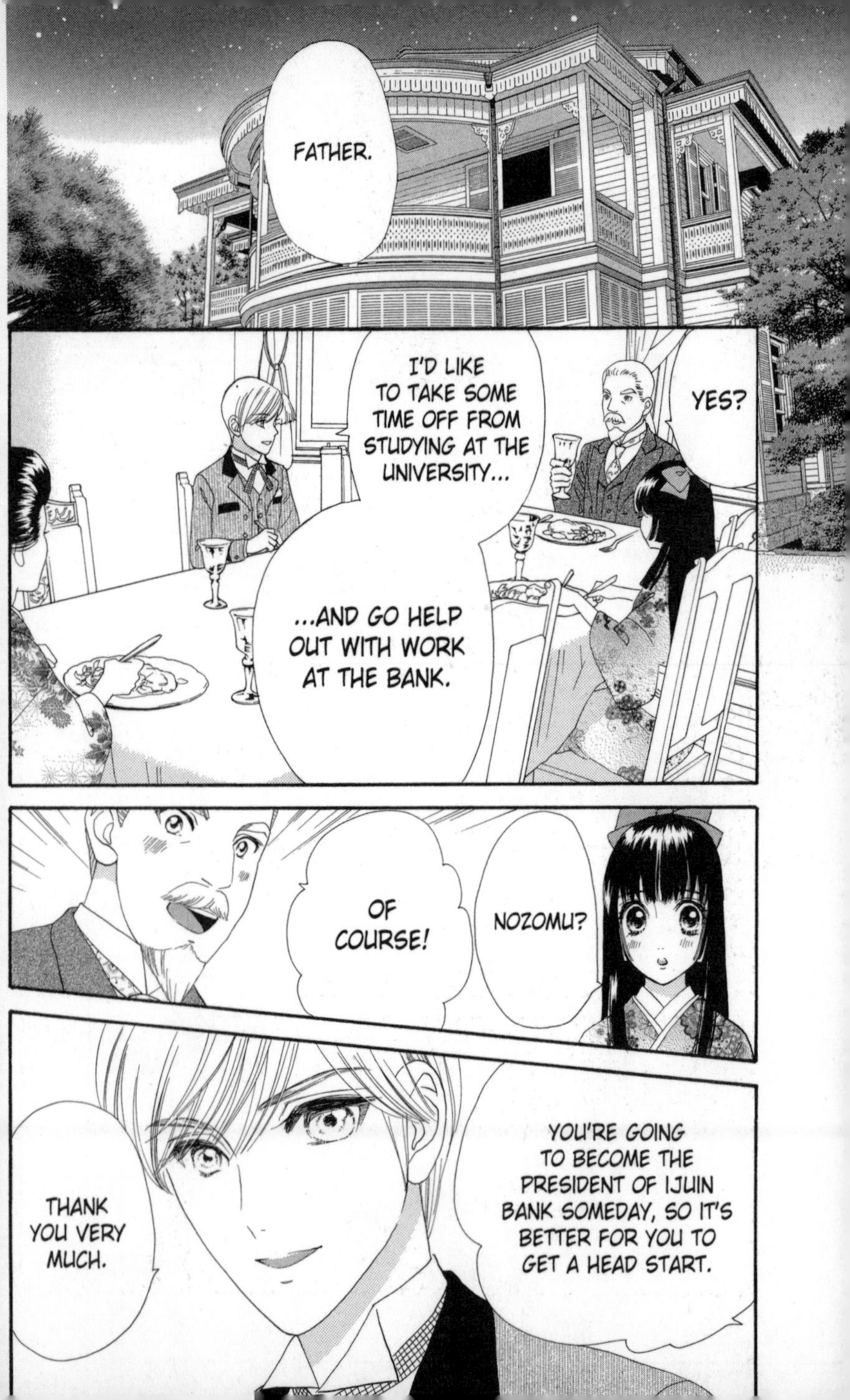
FATHER.
YES?
I'D LIKE TO TAKE SOME TIME OFF FROM STUDYING AT THE UNIVERSITY...
...AND GO HELP OUT WITH WORK AT THE BANK.
NOZOMU?
OF COURSE!
YOU'RE GOING TO BECOME THE PRESIDENT OF IJUIN BANK SOMEDAY, SO IT'S BETTER FOR YOU TO GET A HEAD START.
THANK YOU VERY MUCH.

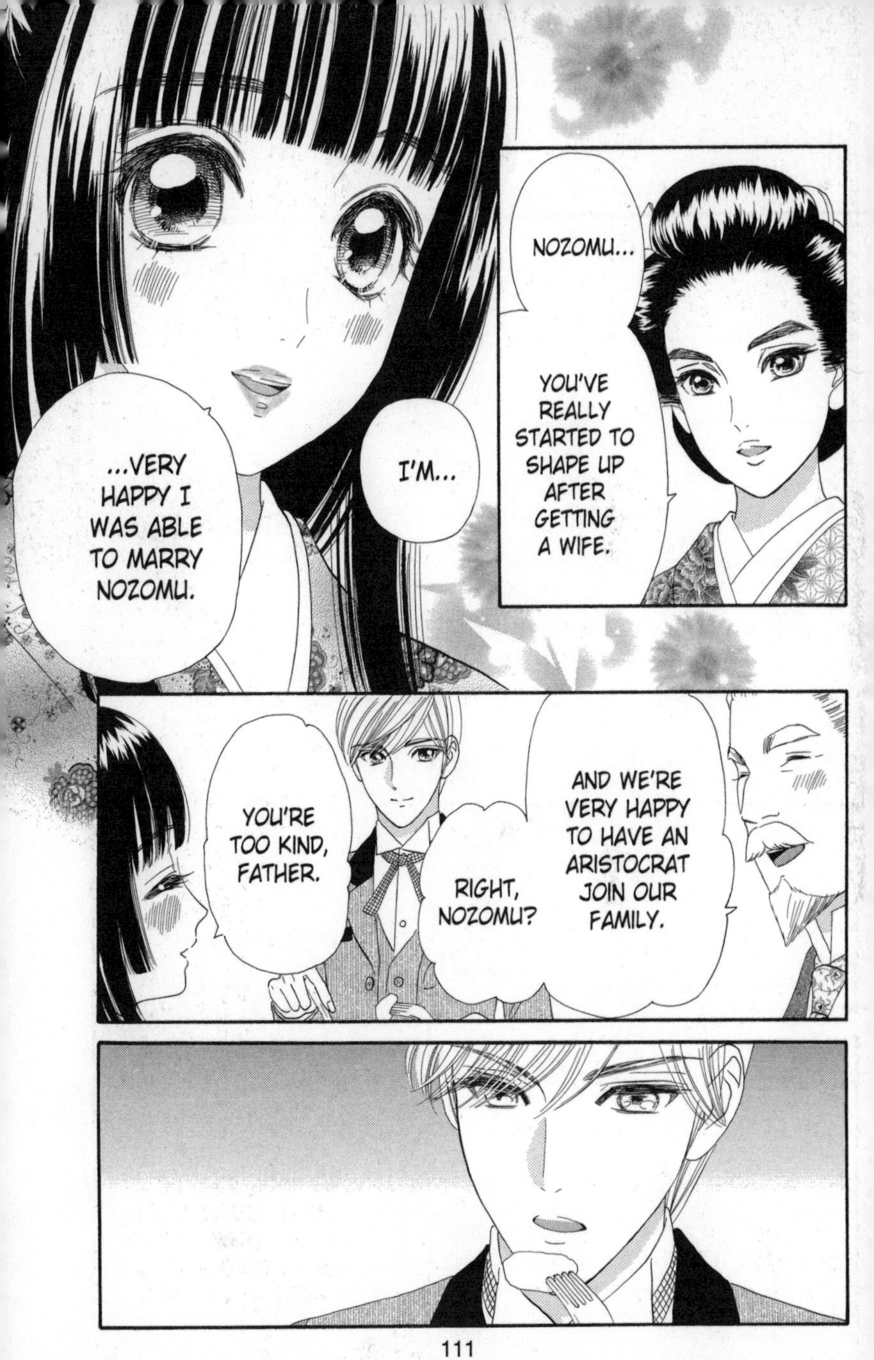
NOZOMU...
YOU'VE REALLY STARTED TO SHAPE UP AFTER GETTING A WIFE.
I'M...
...VERY HAPPY I WAS ABLE TO MARRY NOZOMU.
AND WE'RE VERY HAPPY TO HAVE AN ARISTOCRAT JOIN OUR FAMILY.
RIGHT, NOZOMU?
YOU'RE TOO KIND, FATHER.

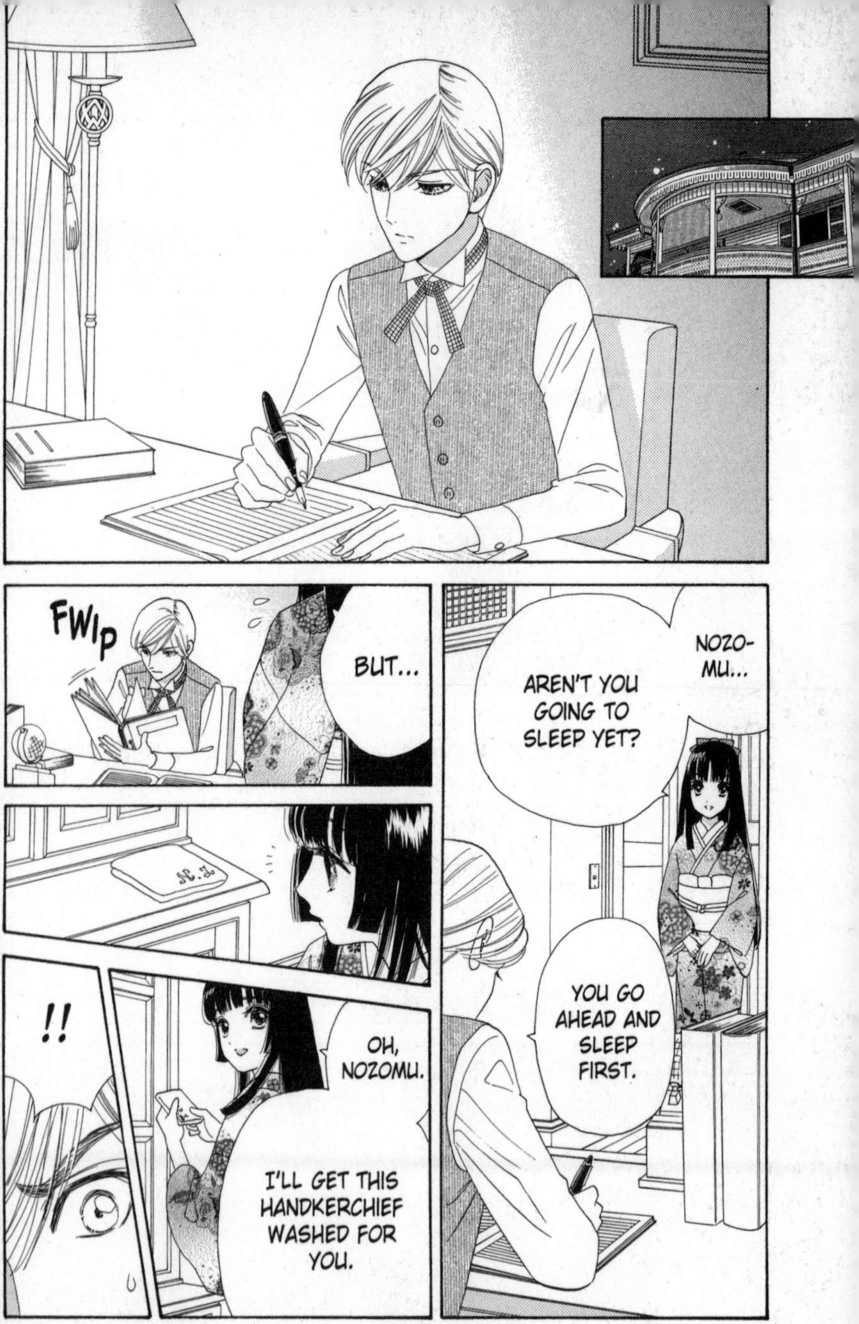
NOZOMU...
AREN'T YOU GOING TO SLEEP YET?
YOU GO AHEAD AND SLEEP FIRST.
FWIP
BUT...
OH, NOZOMU.
I'LL GET THIS HANDKERCHIEF WASHED FOR YOU.
!!

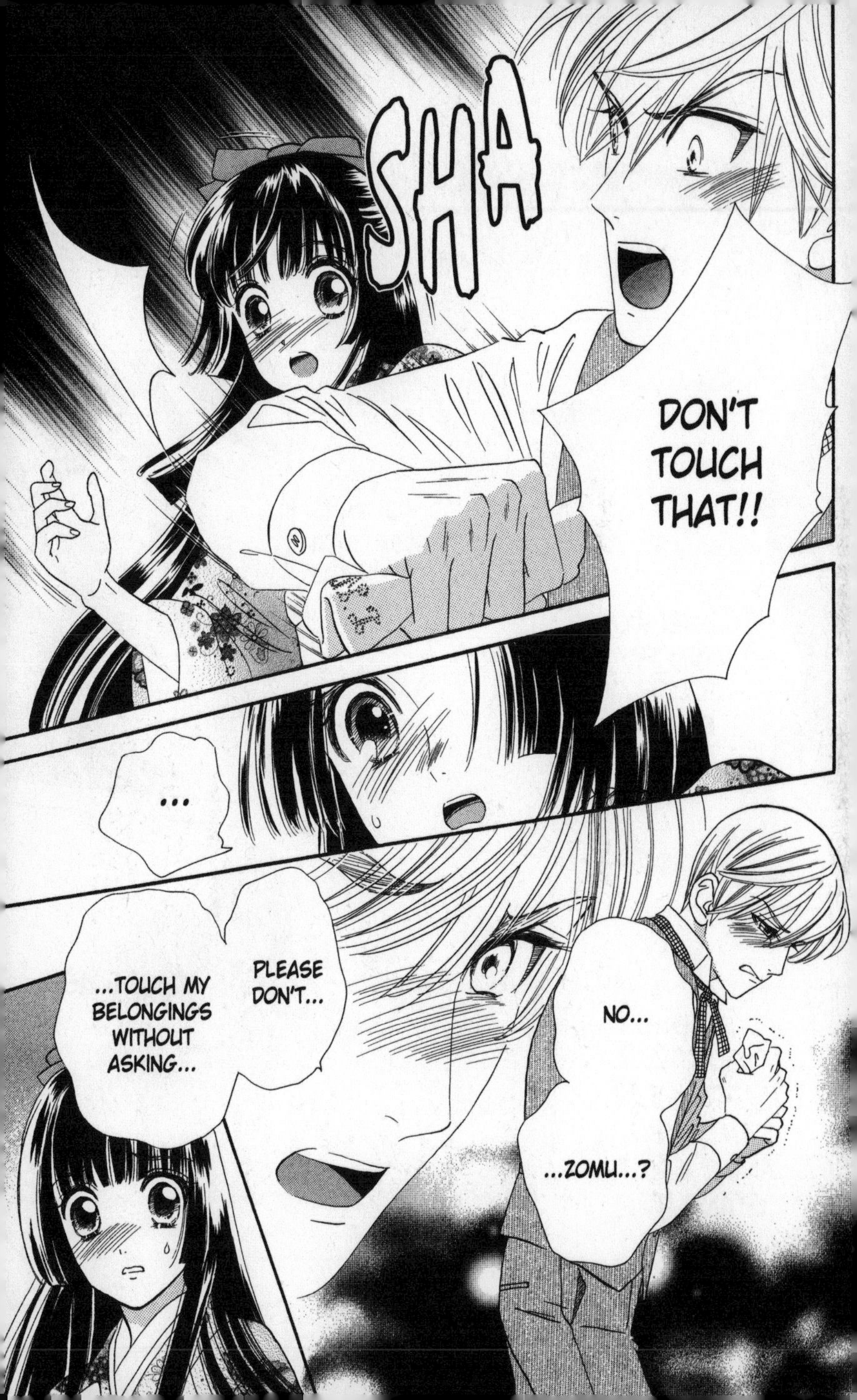
SHA
DON'T TOUCH THAT!!
...
NO...
...ZOMU...?
PLEASE DON'T...
...TOUCH MY BELONGINGS WITHOUT ASKING...

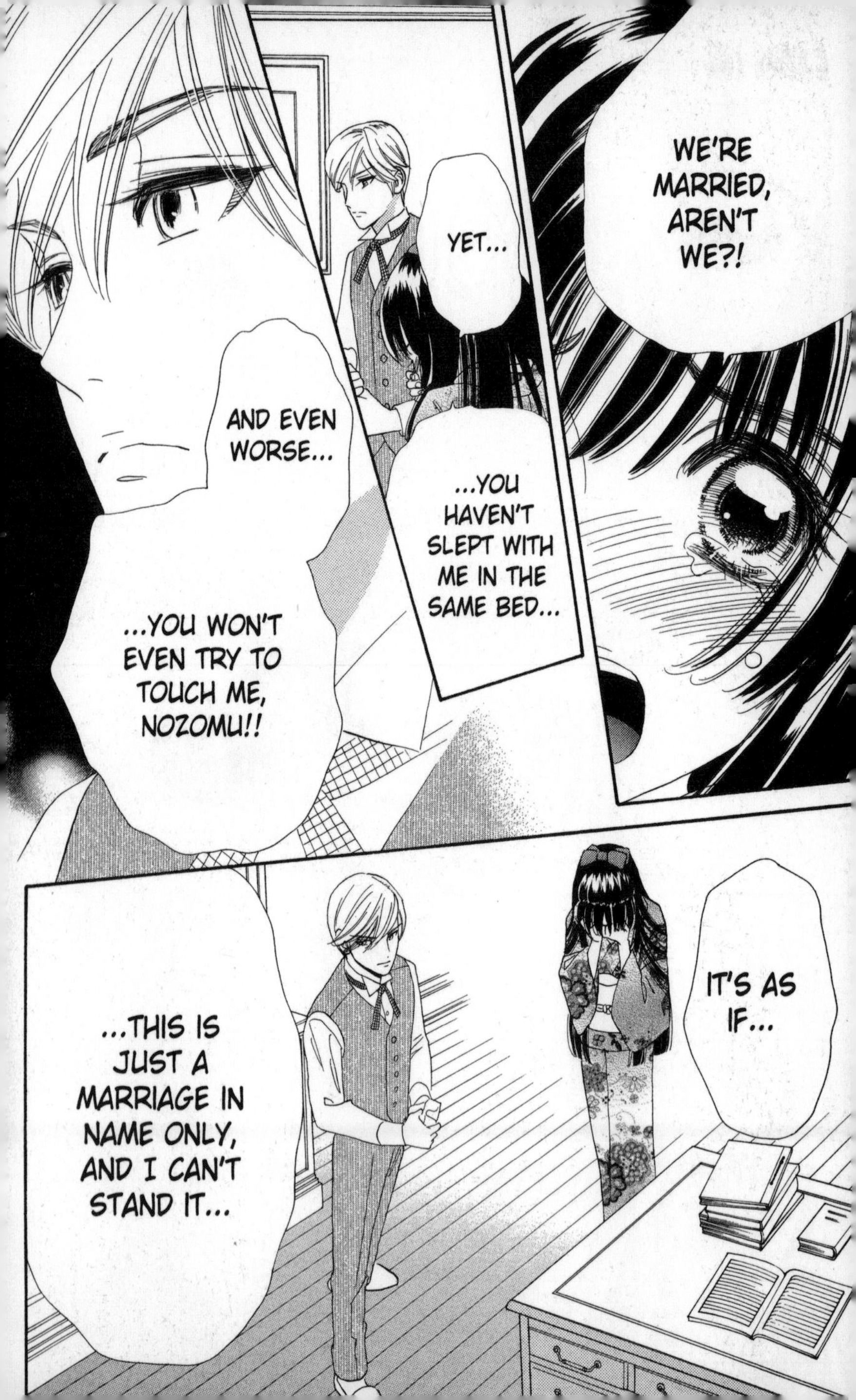
WE'RE MARRIED, AREN'T WE?!
YET...
...YOU HAVEN'T SLEPT WITH ME IN THE SAME BED...
AND EVEN WORSE...
...YOU WON'T EVEN TRY TO TOUCH ME, NOZOMU!!
IT'S AS IF...
...THIS IS JUST A MARRIAGE IN NAME ONLY, AND I CAN'T STAND IT...

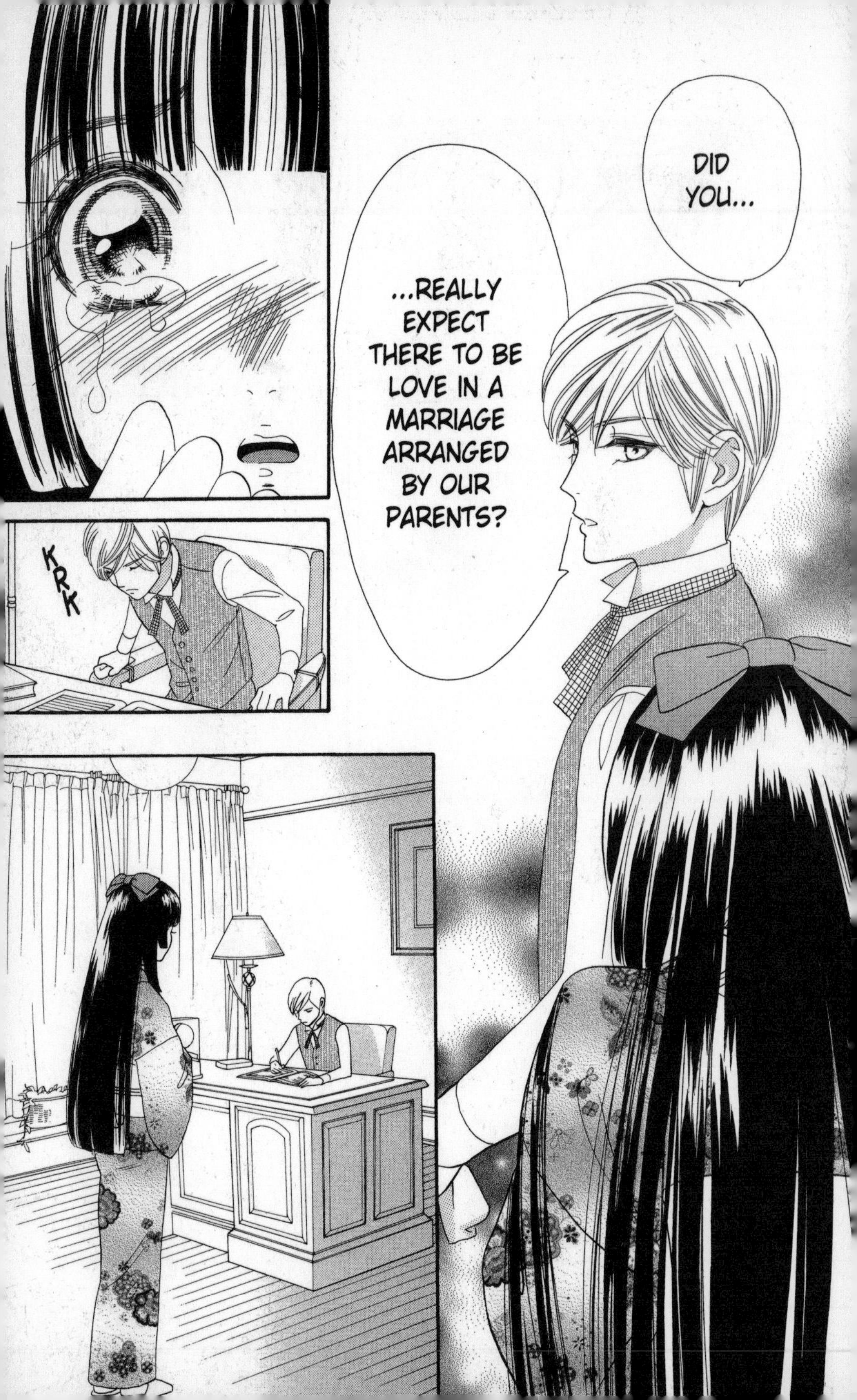
DID YOU...
...REALLY EXPECT THERE TO BE LOVE IN A MARRIAGE ARRANGED BY OUR PARENTS?
KRK

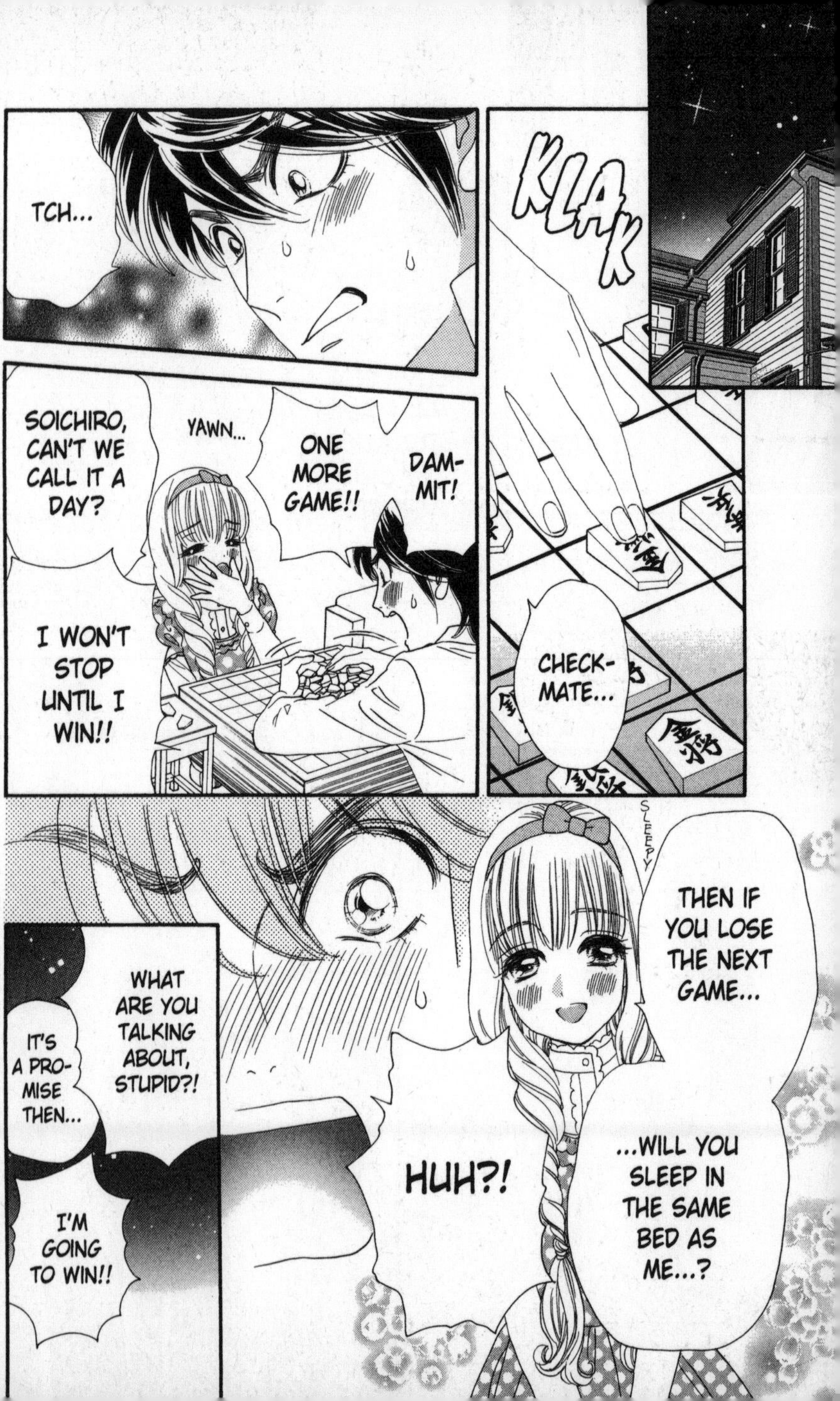
KLAK
CHECK-MATE...
TCH...
DAM-MIT!
ONE MORE GAME!!
YAWN...
SOICHIRO, CAN'T WE CALL IT A DAY?
I WON'T STOP UNTIL I WIN!!
SLEEPY
THEN IF YOU LOSE THE NEXT GAME...
...WILL YOU SLEEP IN THE SAME BED AS ME...?
HUH?!
WHAT ARE YOU TALKING ABOUT, STUPID?!
IT'S A PRO-MISE THEN...
I'M GOING TO WIN!!

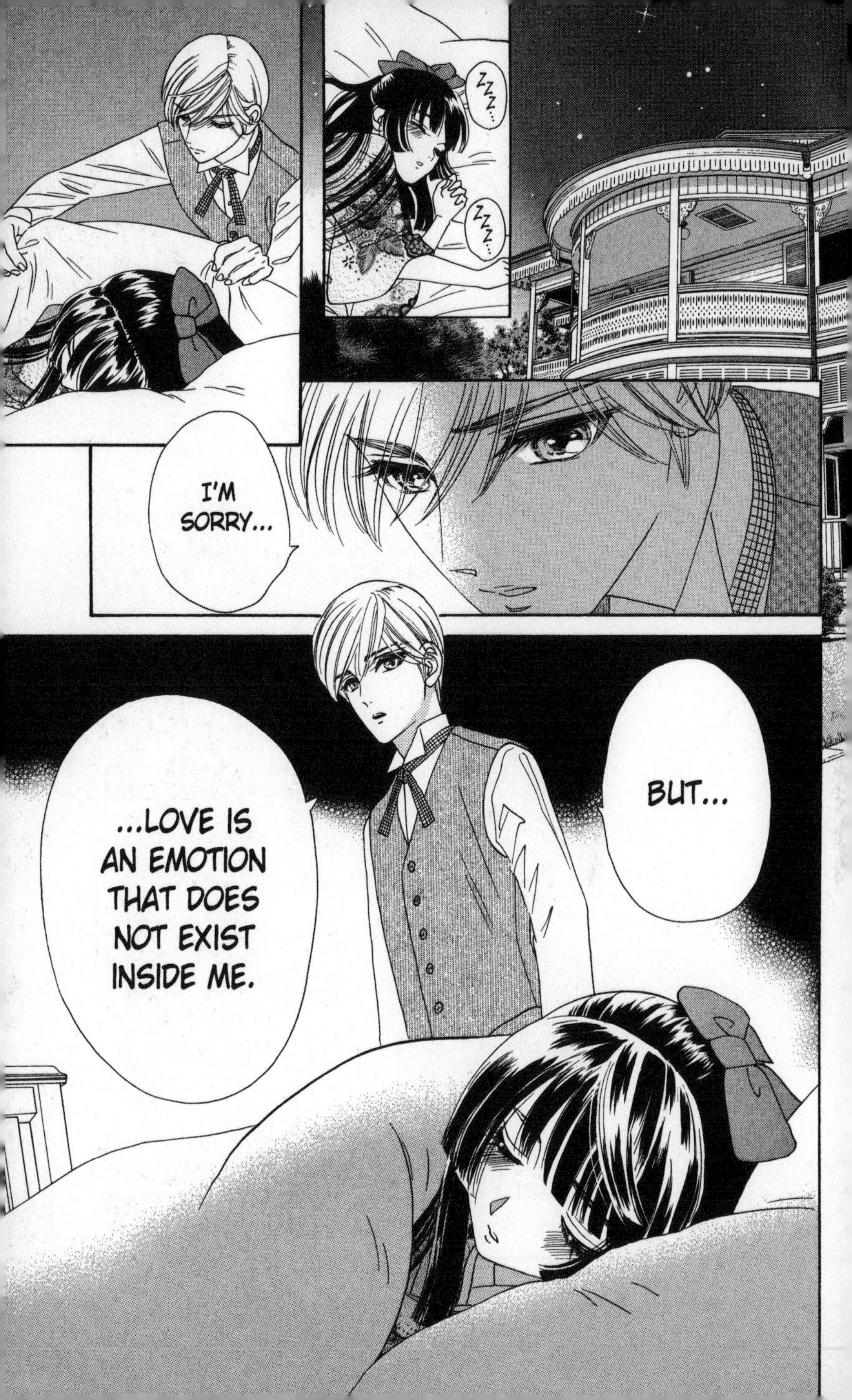
Zzz...
Zzz...
I'M SORRY...
BUT...
...LOVE IS AN EMOTION THAT DOES NOT EXIST INSIDE ME.

STEP STAGE ④

No.

Date   .   .

THIS IS THE FIRST ROUGH DRAFT I DREW FOR THE ILLUSTRATION THAT'S ON THE CHAPTER

16 TITLE PAGE SPREAD. IT'S BASICALLY A REDRAWN VERSION OF A ROUGH SKETCH I DREW

BEFORE THE SERIES STARTED. I STARTED GETTING THE FEELING THAT A COLORED IMAGE

OF THE MAIN CHARACTER BEING NAKED WOULDN'T LOOK GOOD IN *MARGARET* THOUGH,

SO I DECIDED TO SCRAP THIS DRAWING AND HAVE HER WEAR CLOTHES.

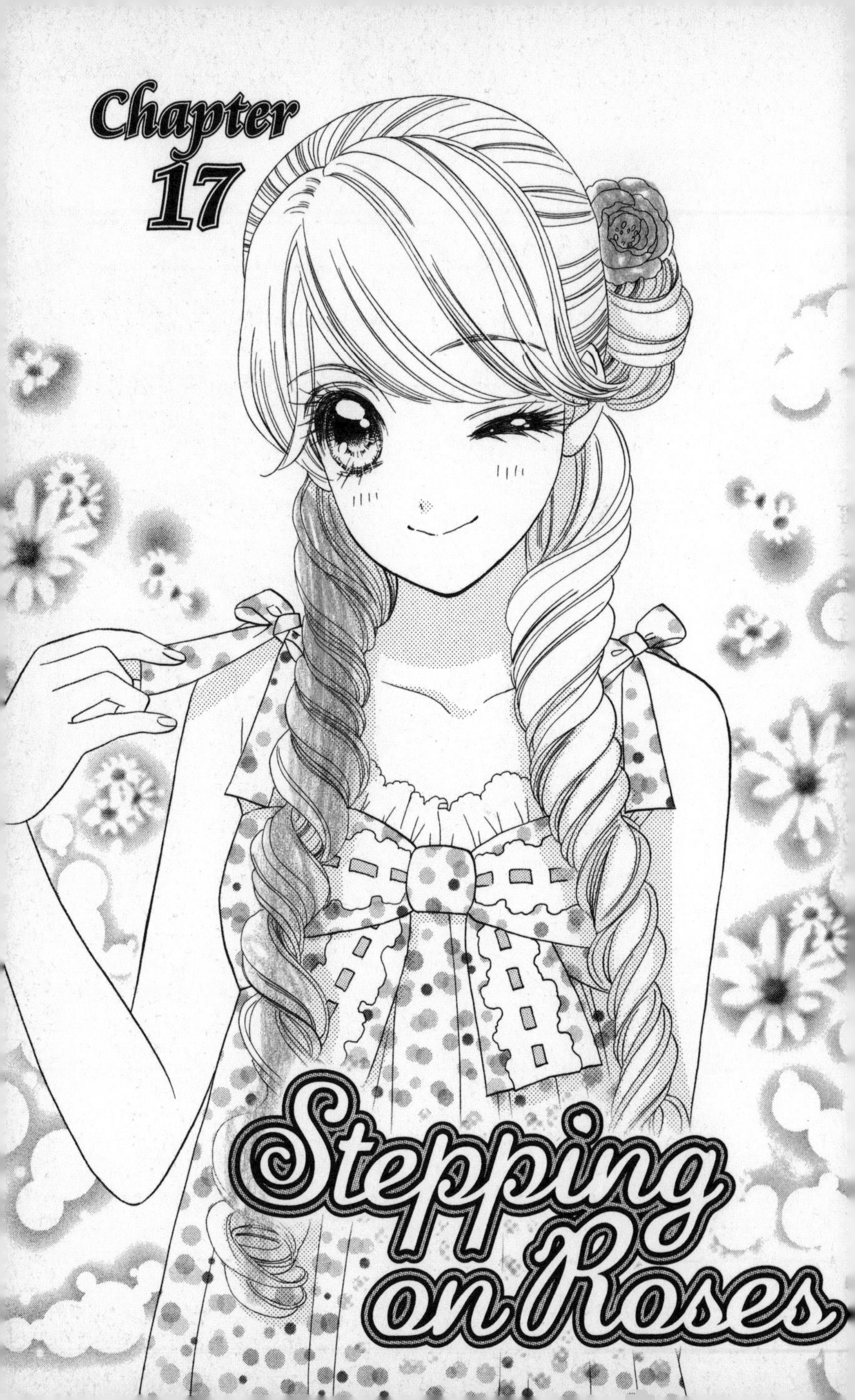
Chapter
17
Stepping on Roses

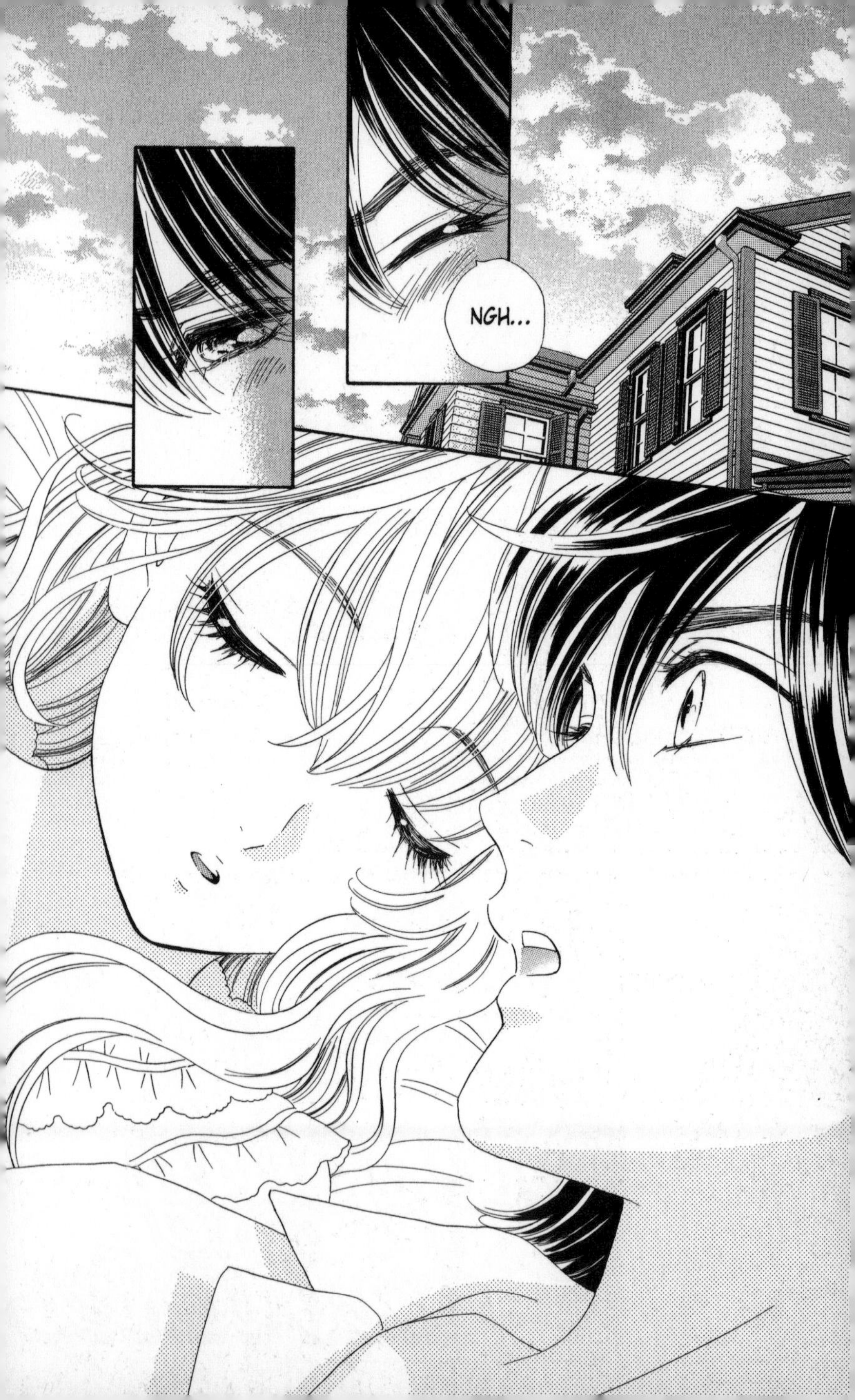
NGH...

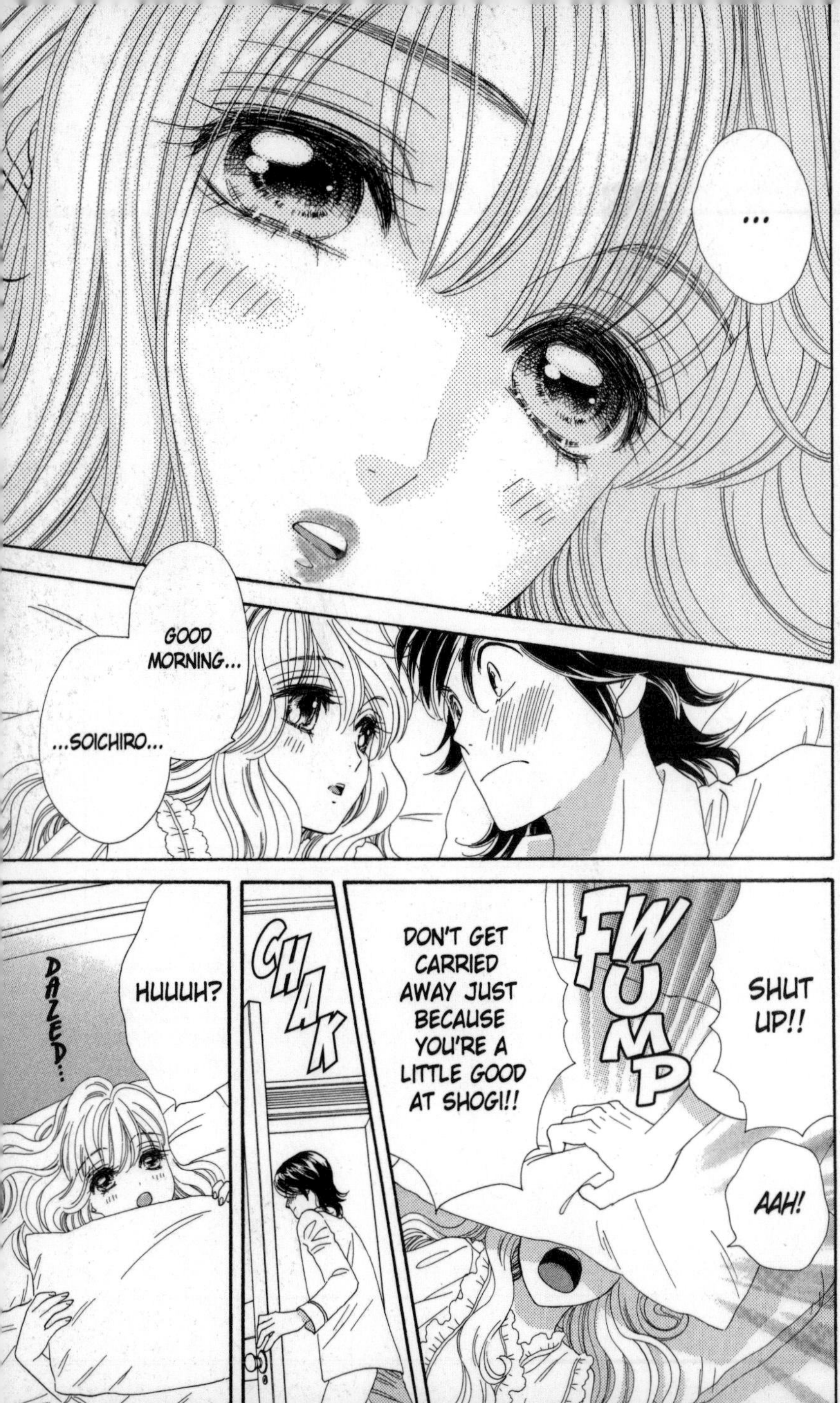
...
GOOD MORNING...
...SOICHIRO...
FWUMP
SHUT UP!!
AAH!
DON'T GET CARRIED AWAY JUST BECAUSE YOU'RE A LITTLE GOOD AT SHOGI!!
CHAK
HUUUH?
DAZED...

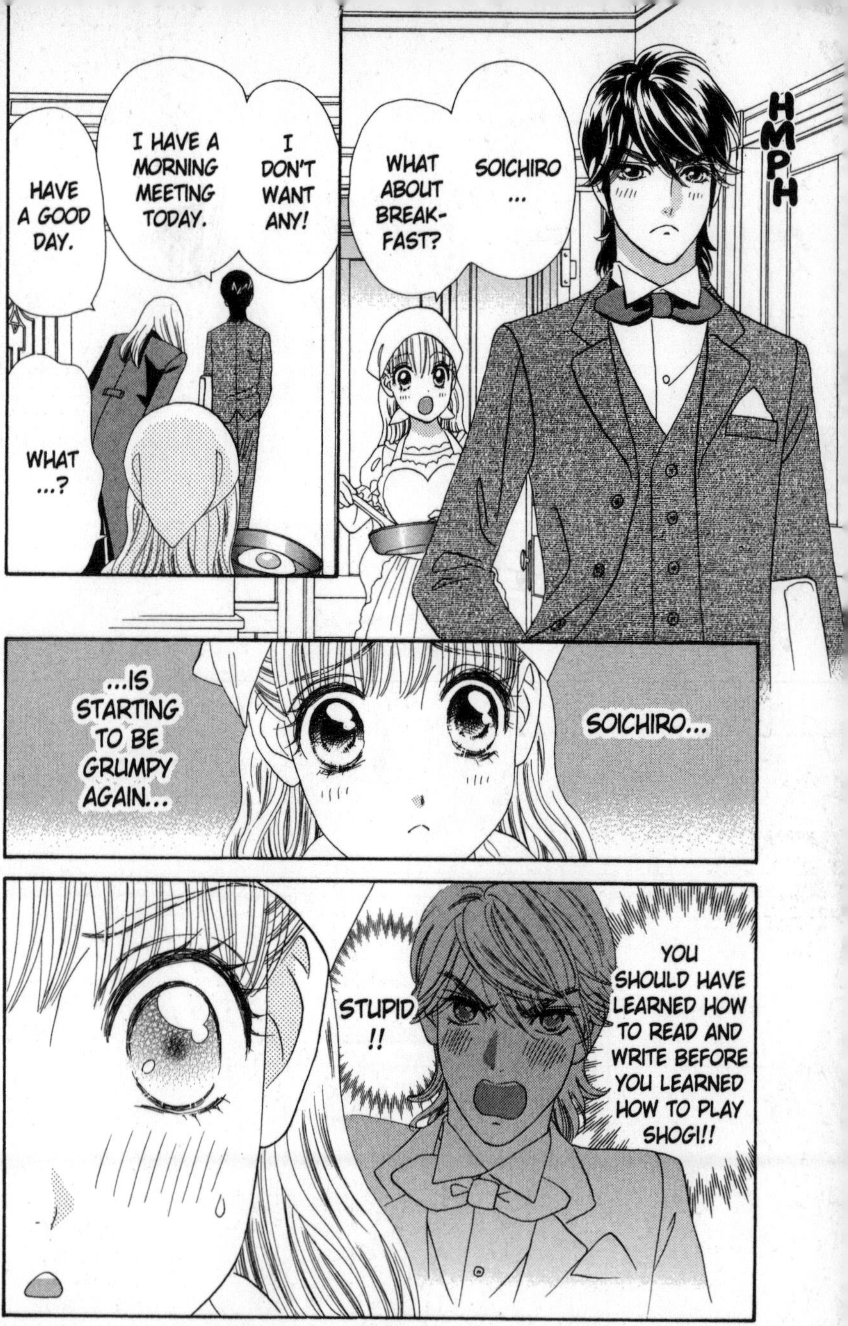
HMPH
SOICHIRO ...
WHAT ABOUT BREAK-FAST?
I DON'T WANT ANY!
I HAVE A MORNING MEETING TODAY.
HAVE A GOOD DAY.
WHAT ...?
SOICHIRO...
...IS STARTING TO BE GRUMPY AGAIN...
YOU SHOULD HAVE LEARNED HOW TO READ AND WRITE BEFORE YOU LEARNED HOW TO PLAY SHOGI!!
STUPID !!

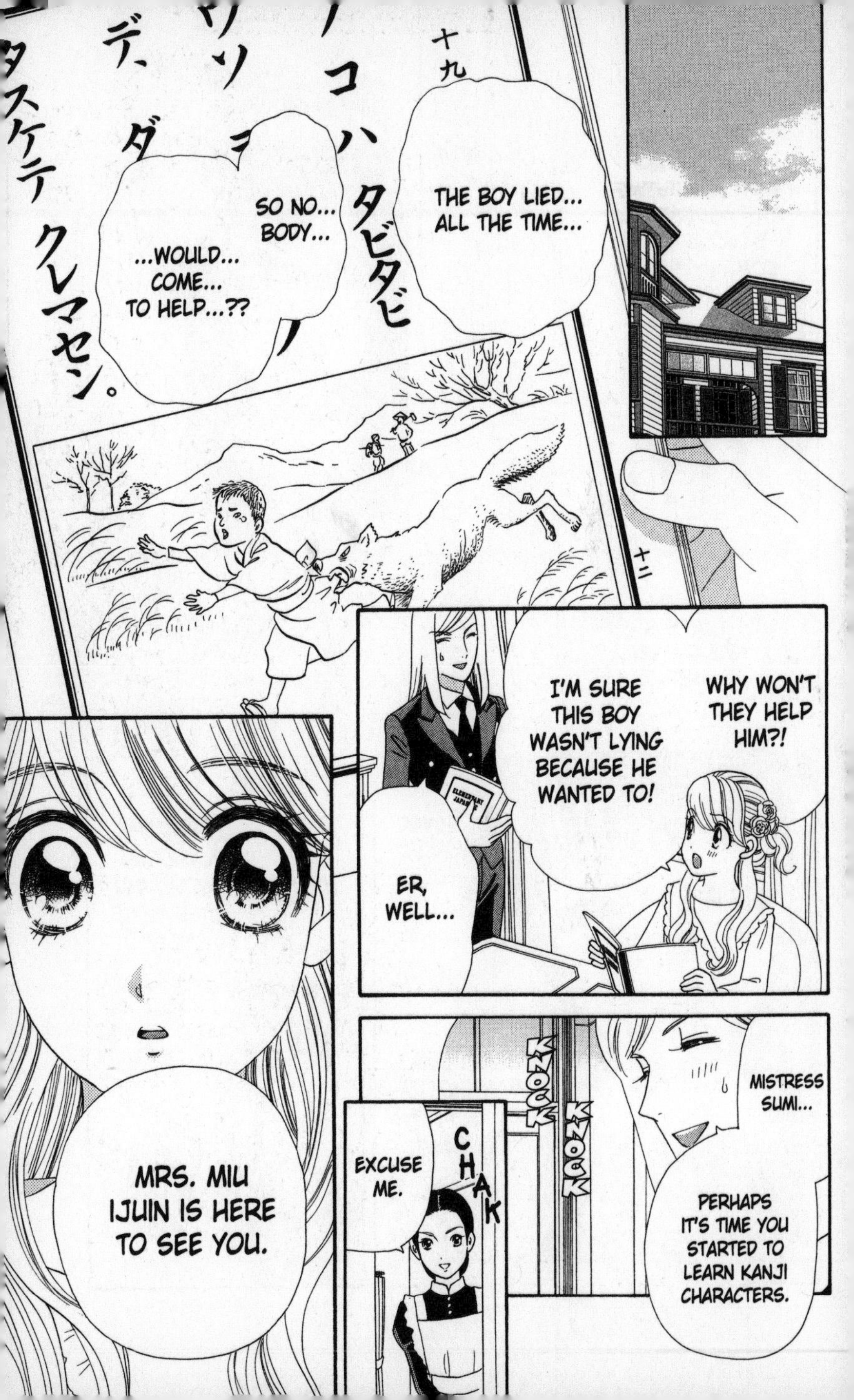
十九
ノコハタビタビ
デ、ダ
タスケテクレマセン。
THE BOY LIED... ALL THE TIME...
SO NO... BODY...
...WOULD... COME... TO HELP...??
十二
WHY WON'T THEY HELP HIM?!
I'M SURE THIS BOY WASN'T LYING BECAUSE HE WANTED TO!
ER, WELL...
MISTRESS SUMI...
PERHAPS IT'S TIME YOU STARTED TO LEARN KANJI CHARACTERS.
KNOCK
KNOCK
CHAK
EXCUSE ME.
MRS. MIU IJUIN IS HERE TO SEE YOU.

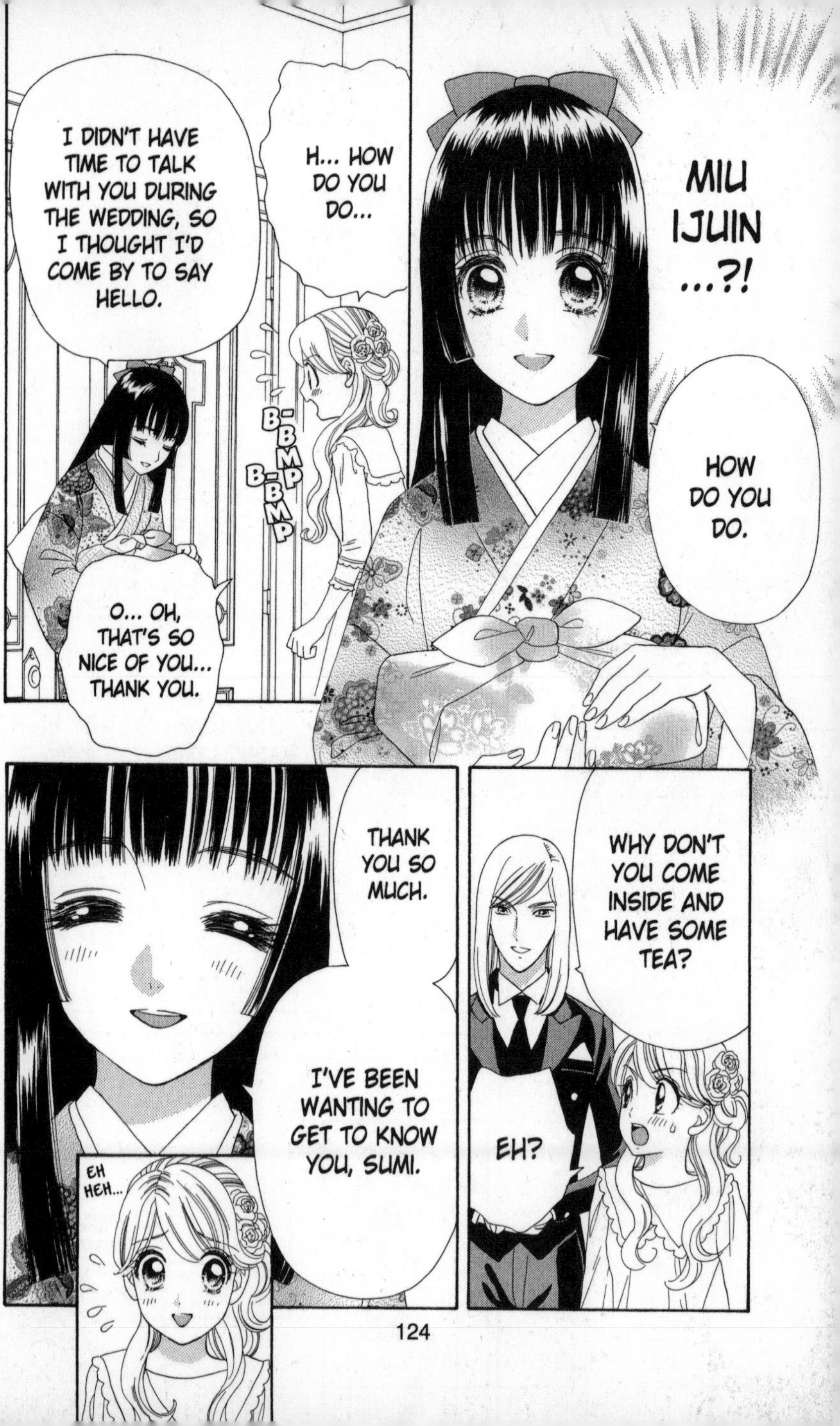
MIU IJUIN ...?!
HOW DO YOU DO.
H... HOW DO YOU DO...
I DIDN'T HAVE TIME TO TALK WITH YOU DURING THE WEDDING, SO I THOUGHT I'D COME BY TO SAY HELLO.
B-BMP B-BMP
O... OH, THAT'S SO NICE OF YOU... THANK YOU.
WHY DON'T YOU COME INSIDE AND HAVE SOME TEA?
EH?
THANK YOU SO MUCH.
I'VE BEEN WANTING TO GET TO KNOW YOU, SUMI.
EH HEH...

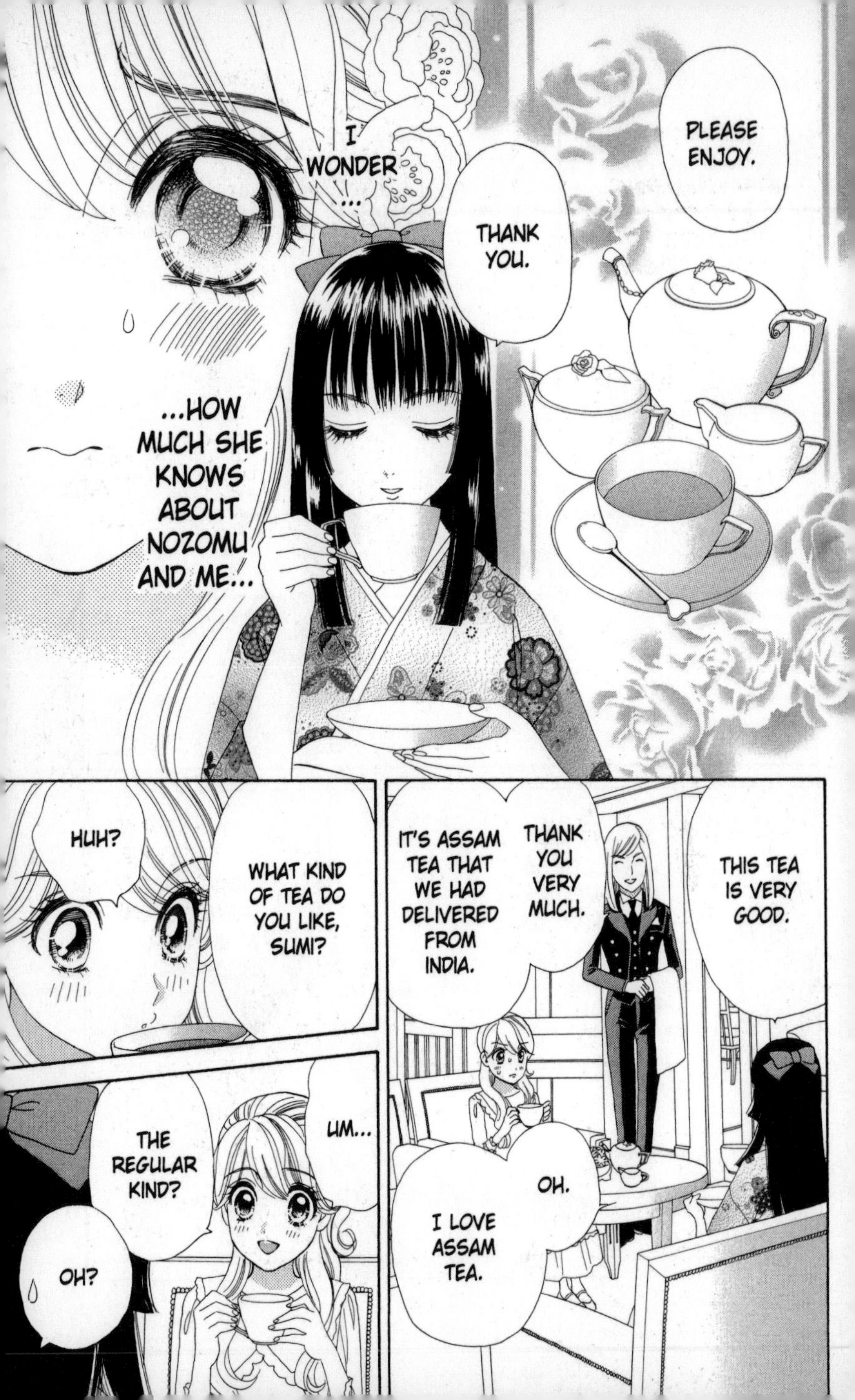
PLEASE ENJOY.
THANK YOU.
I WONDER...
...HOW MUCH SHE KNOWS ABOUT NOZOMU AND ME...
THIS TEA IS VERY GOOD.
THANK YOU VERY MUCH.
IT'S ASSAM TEA THAT WE HAD DELIVERED FROM INDIA.
OH.
I LOVE ASSAM TEA.
WHAT KIND OF TEA DO YOU LIKE, SUMI?
HUH?
UM...
THE REGULAR KIND?
OH?

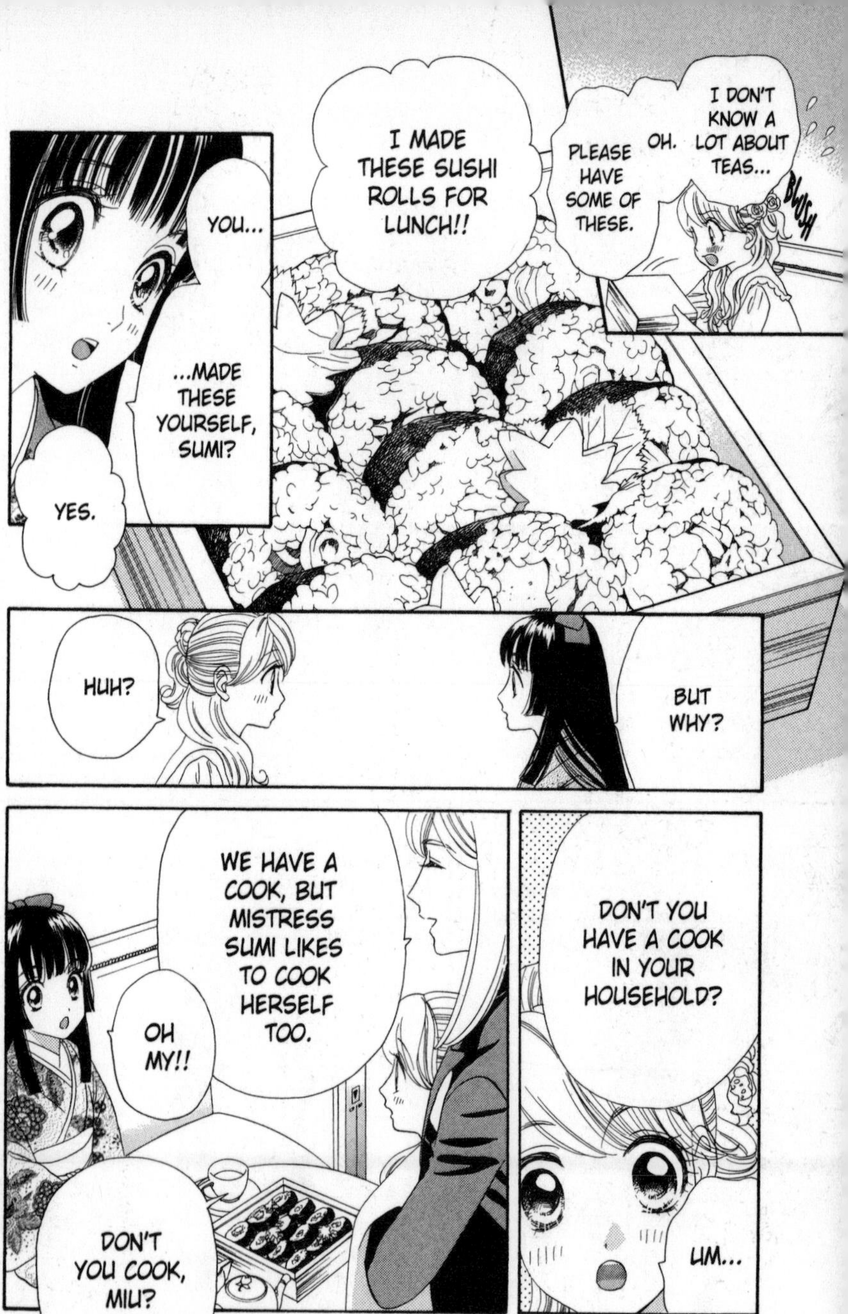
I DON'T KNOW A LOT ABOUT TEAS...
BLUSH
OH.
PLEASE HAVE SOME OF THESE.
I MADE THESE SUSHI ROLLS FOR LUNCH!!
YOU...
...MADE THESE YOURSELF, SUMI?
YES.
BUT WHY?
HUH?
DON'T YOU HAVE A COOK IN YOUR HOUSEHOLD?
UM...
WE HAVE A COOK, BUT MISTRESS SUMI LIKES TO COOK HERSELF TOO.
OH MY!!
DON'T YOU COOK, MIU?

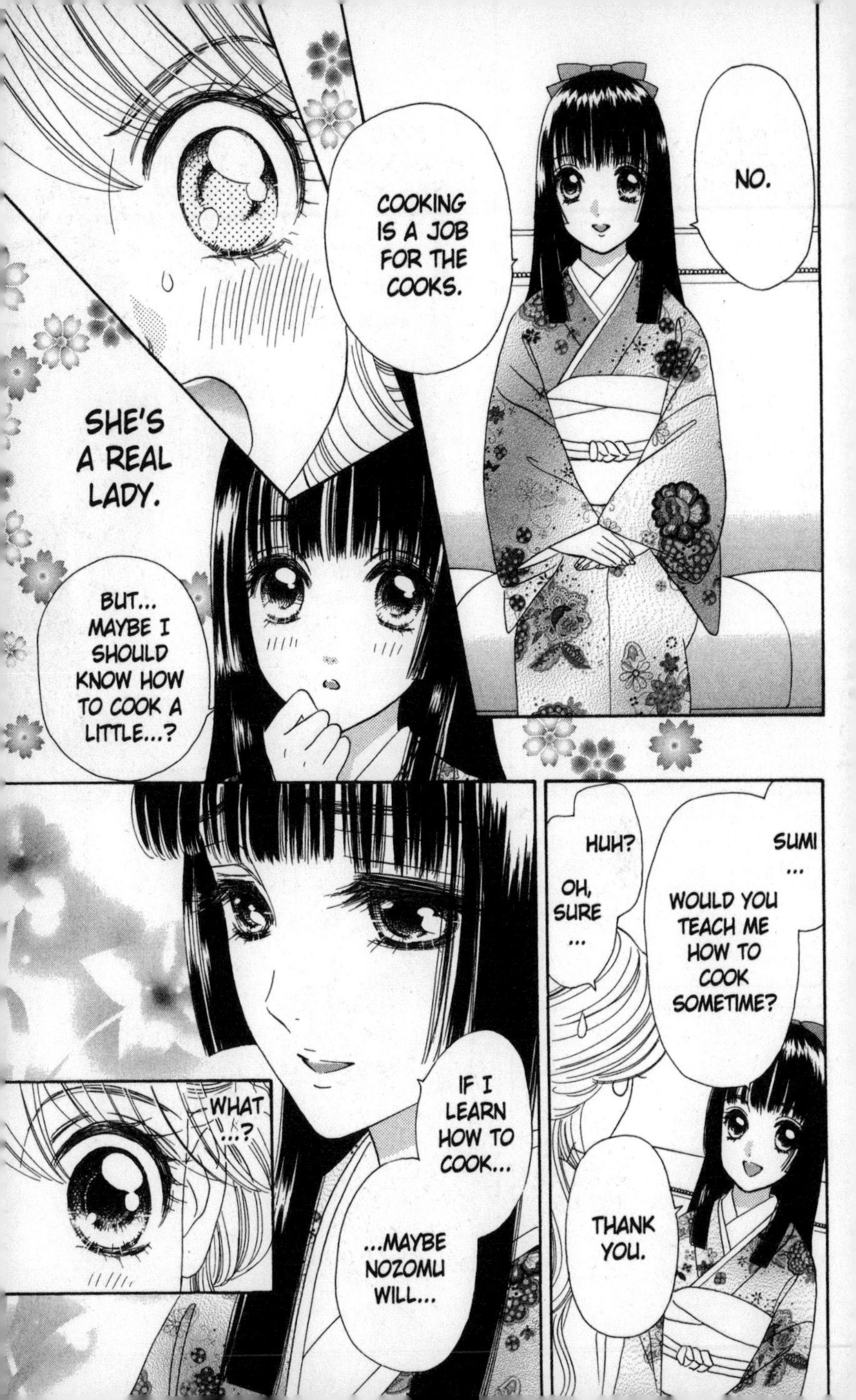
NO.
COOKING IS A JOB FOR THE COOKS.
SHE'S A REAL LADY.
BUT... MAYBE I SHOULD KNOW HOW TO COOK A LITTLE...?
SUMI ...
WOULD YOU TEACH ME HOW TO COOK SOMETIME?
HUH?
OH, SURE ...
THANK YOU.
IF I LEARN HOW TO COOK...
...MAYBE NOZOMU WILL...
WHAT ...?

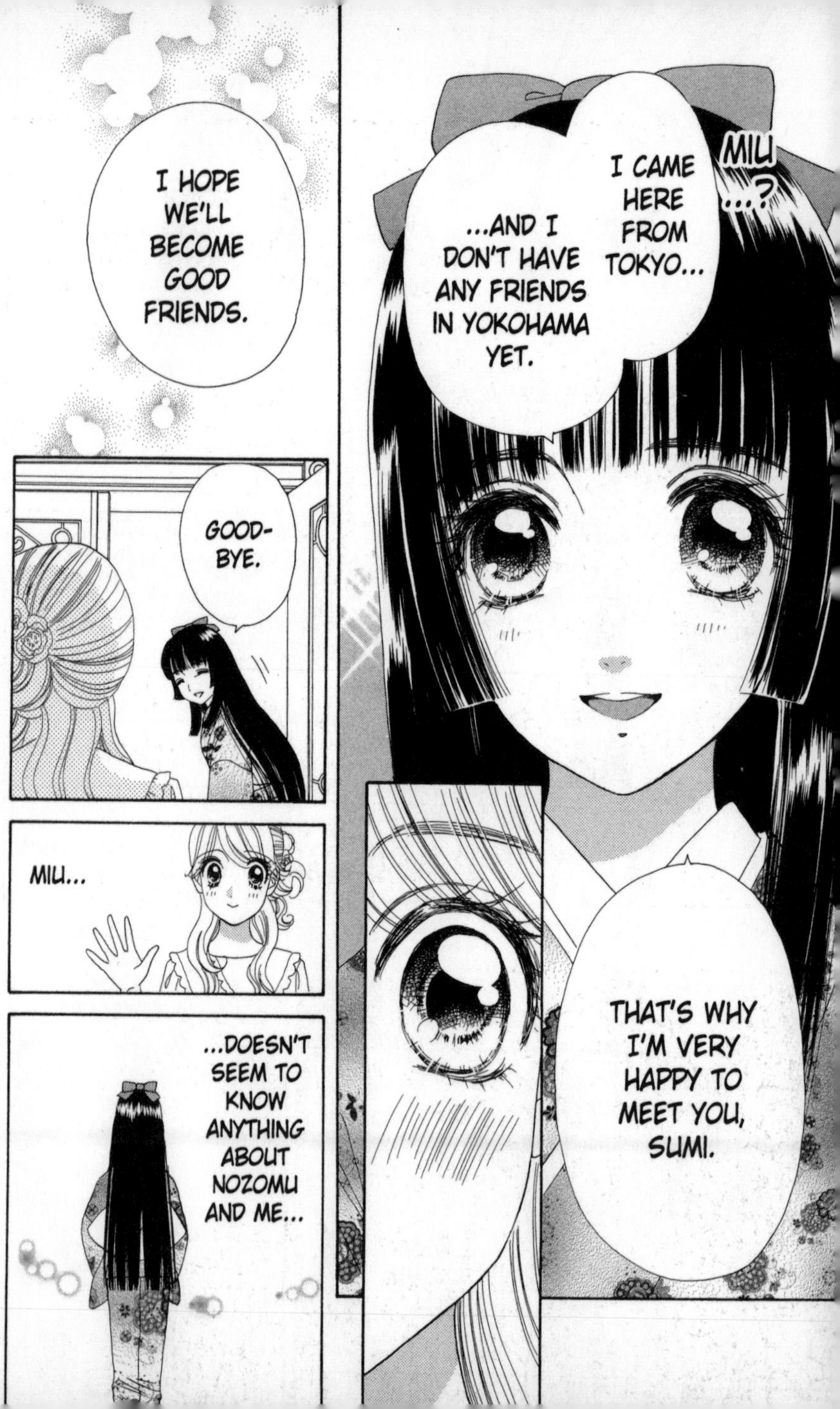

MIU ...?
I CAME HERE FROM TOKYO...
...AND I DON'T HAVE ANY FRIENDS IN YOKOHAMA YET.
THAT'S WHY I'M VERY HAPPY TO MEET YOU, SUMI.
I HOPE WE'LL BECOME GOOD FRIENDS.
GOOD-BYE.
MIU...
...DOESN'T SEEM TO KNOW ANYTHING ABOUT NOZOMU AND ME...

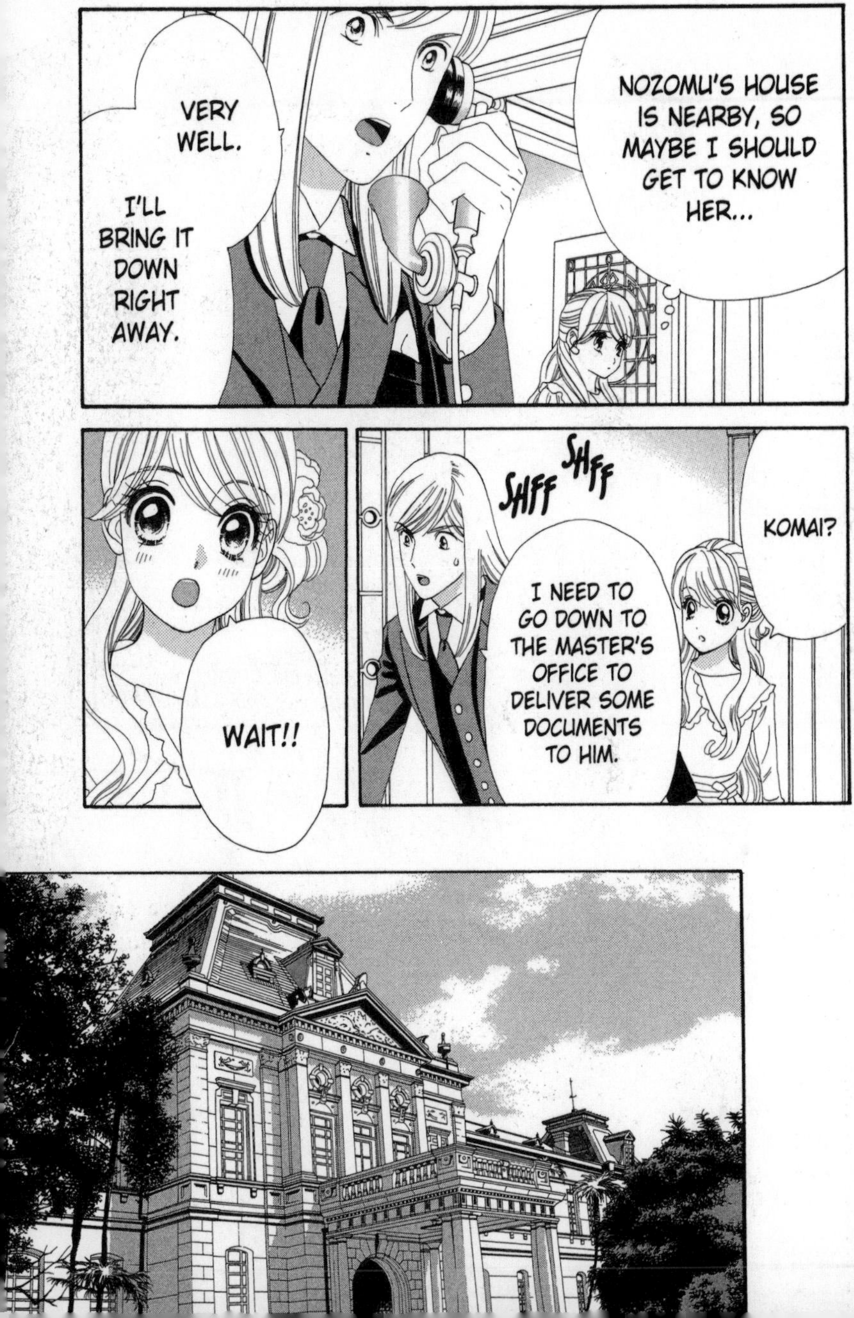
NOZOMU'S HOUSE IS NEARBY, SO MAYBE I SHOULD GET TO KNOW HER...
VERY WELL.
I'LL BRING IT DOWN RIGHT AWAY.
KOMAI?
SHFF SHFF
I NEED TO GO DOWN TO THE MASTER'S OFFICE TO DELIVER SOME DOCUMENTS TO HIM.
WAIT!!

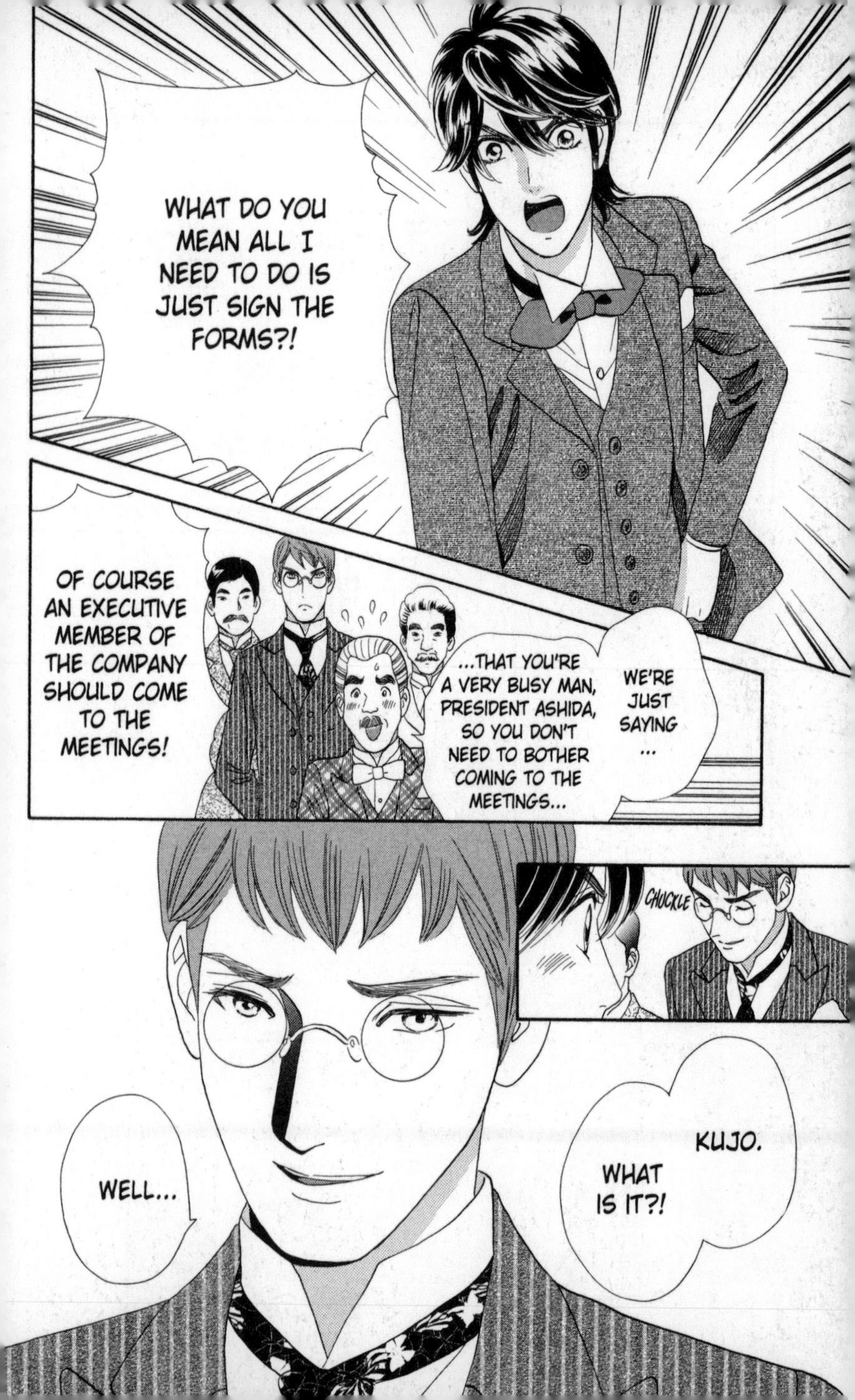
WHAT DO YOU MEAN ALL I NEED TO DO IS JUST SIGN THE FORMS?!
WE'RE JUST SAYING ...
...THAT YOU'RE A VERY BUSY MAN, PRESIDENT ASHIDA, SO YOU DON'T NEED TO BOTHER COMING TO THE MEETINGS...
OF COURSE AN EXECUTIVE MEMBER OF THE COMPANY SHOULD COME TO THE MEETINGS!
CHUCKLE
KUJO.
WHAT IS IT?!
WELL...

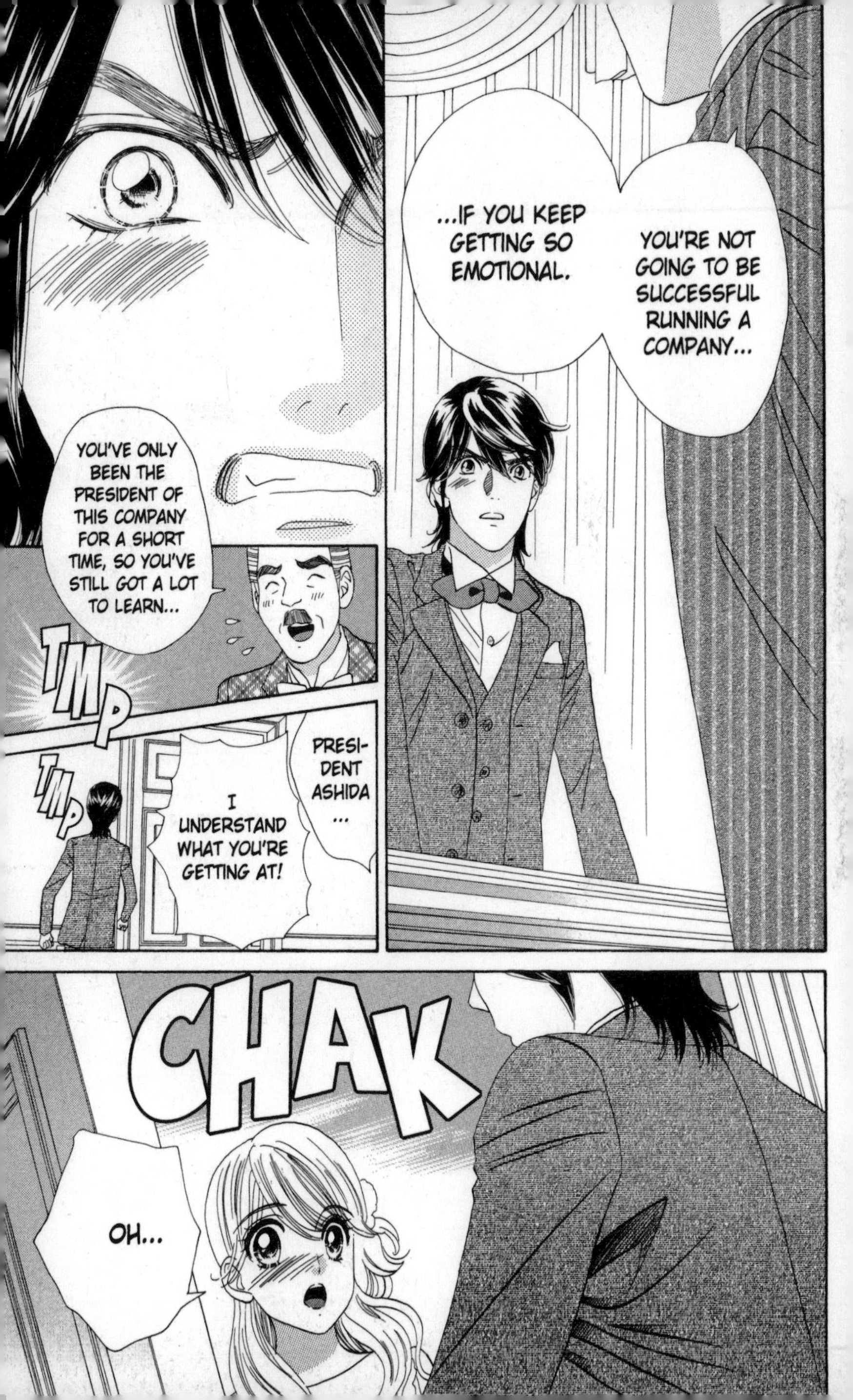
YOU'RE NOT GOING TO BE SUCCESSFUL RUNNING A COMPANY...
...IF YOU KEEP GETTING SO EMOTIONAL.
YOU'VE ONLY BEEN THE PRESIDENT OF THIS COMPANY FOR A SHORT TIME, SO YOU'VE STILL GOT A LOT TO LEARN...
TMP
TMP
PRESI-DENT ASHIDA...
I UNDERSTAND WHAT YOU'RE GETTING AT!
CHAK
OH...

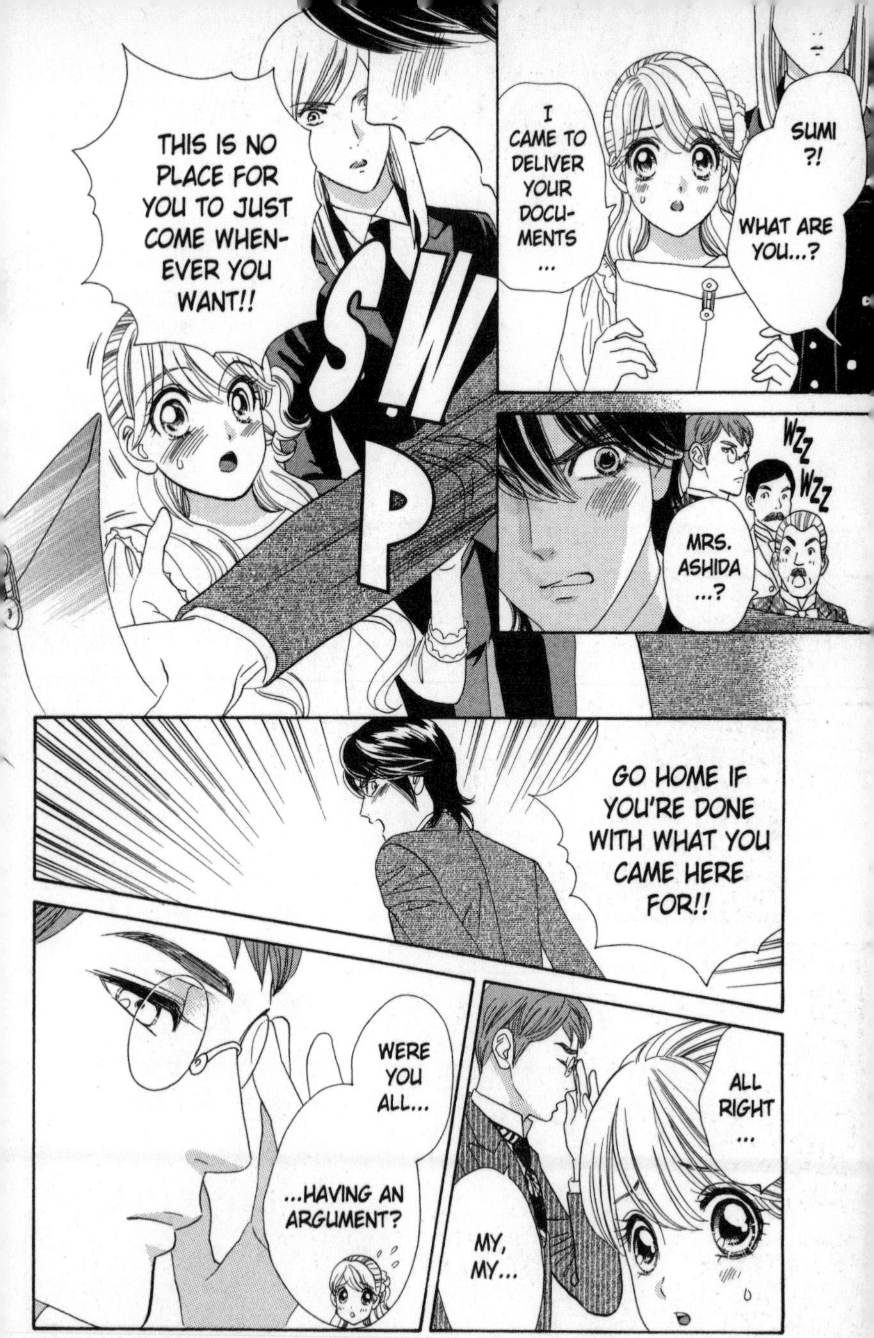
SUMI ?!
WHAT ARE YOU...?
I CAME TO DELIVER YOUR DOCU-MENTS ...
WZZ
WZZ
MRS. ASHIDA ...?
THIS IS NO PLACE FOR YOU TO JUST COME WHEN-EVER YOU WANT!!
SWP
GO HOME IF YOU'RE DONE WITH WHAT YOU CAME HERE FOR!!
ALL RIGHT ...
MY, MY...
WERE YOU ALL...
...HAVING AN ARGUMENT?

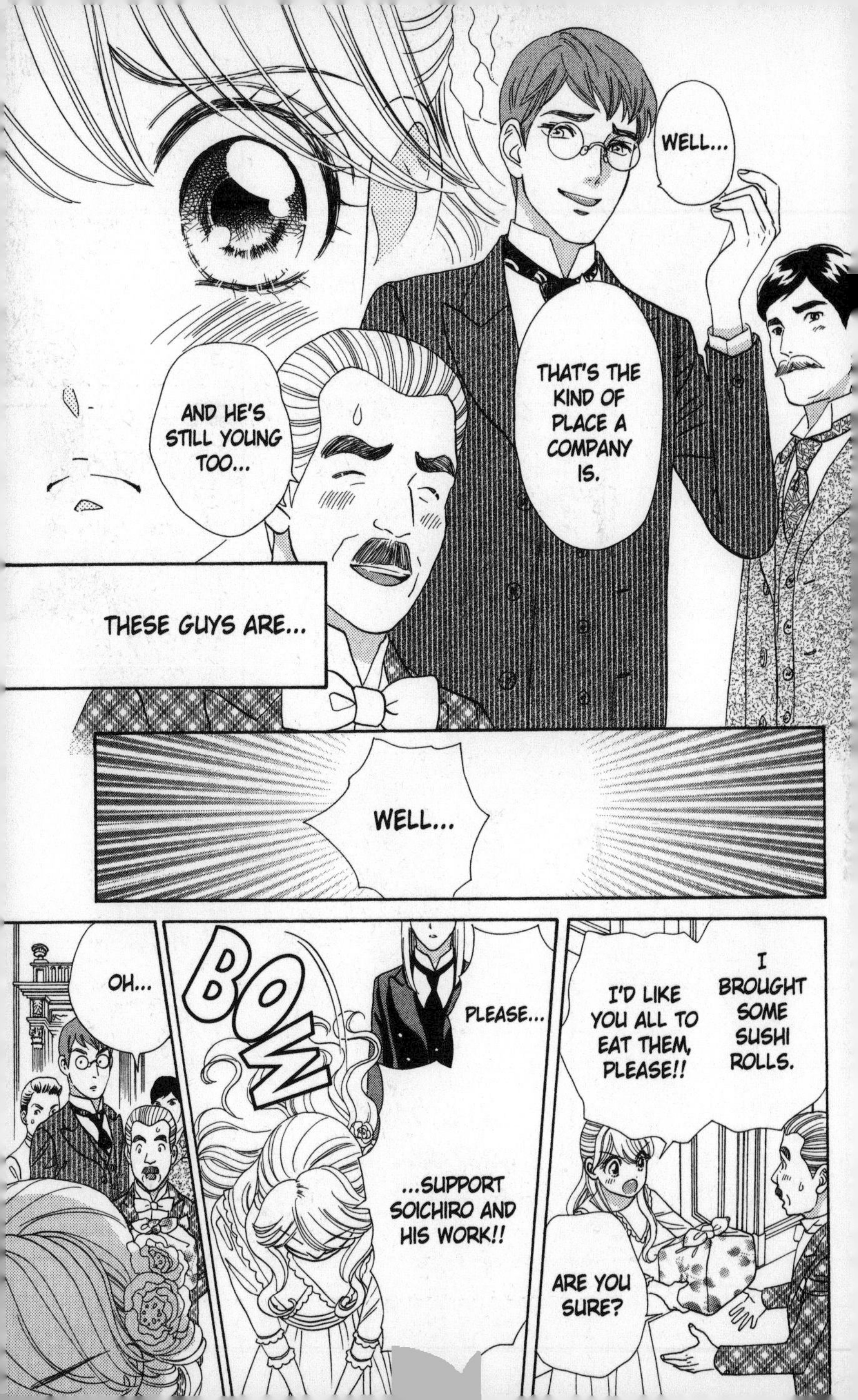
WELL...
THAT'S THE KIND OF PLACE A COMPANY IS.
AND HE'S STILL YOUNG TOO...
THESE GUYS ARE...
WELL...
I BROUGHT SOME SUSHI ROLLS.
I'D LIKE YOU ALL TO EAT THEM, PLEASE!!
ARE YOU SURE?
PLEASE...
...SUPPORT SOICHIRO AND HIS WORK!!
BOW
OH...

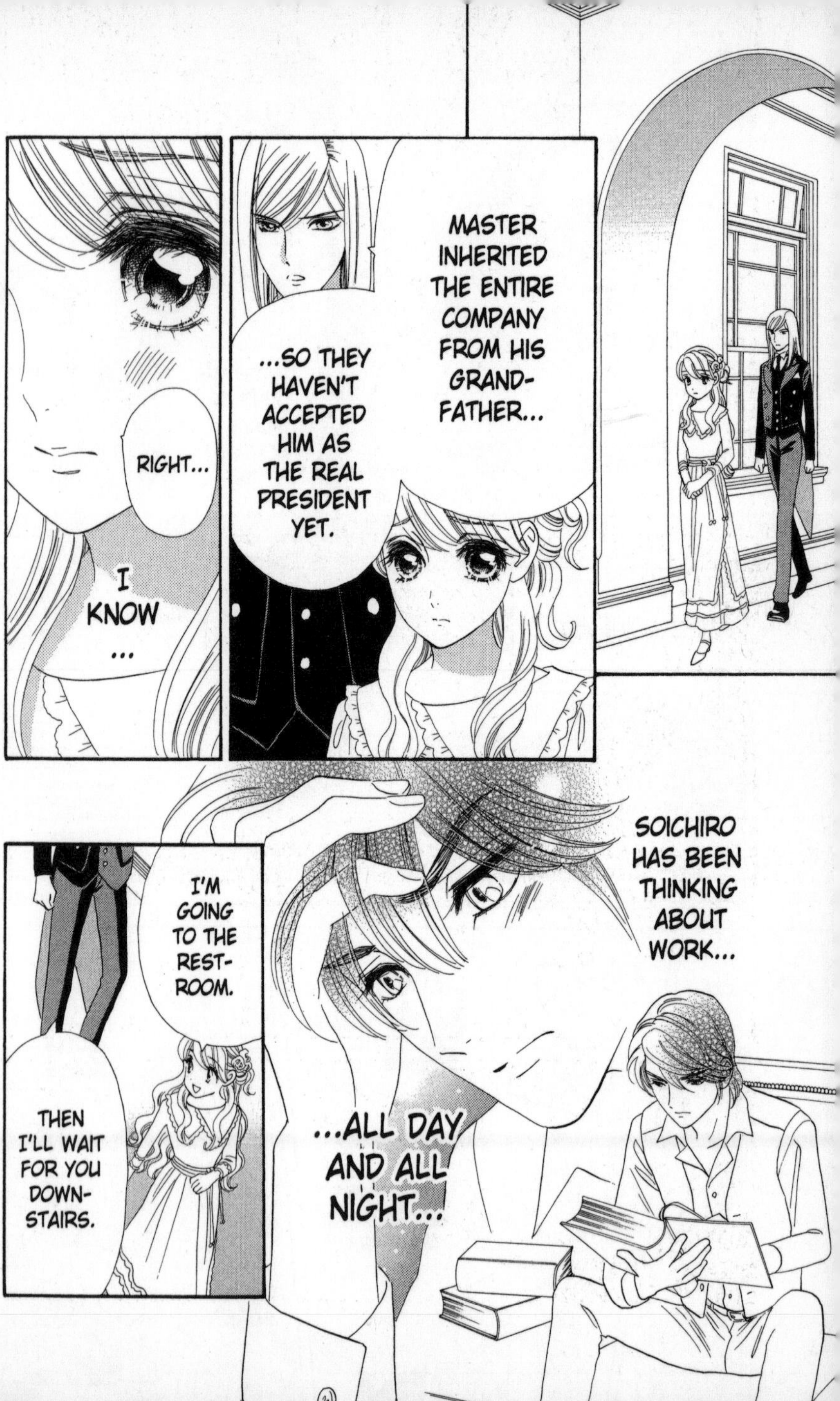
MASTER INHERITED THE ENTIRE COMPANY FROM HIS GRAND-FATHER...
...SO THEY HAVEN'T ACCEPTED HIM AS THE REAL PRESIDENT YET.
RIGHT...
I KNOW...
SOICHIRO HAS BEEN THINKING ABOUT WORK...
...ALL DAY AND ALL NIGHT...
I'M GOING TO THE REST-ROOM.
THEN I'LL WAIT FOR YOU DOWN-STAIRS.

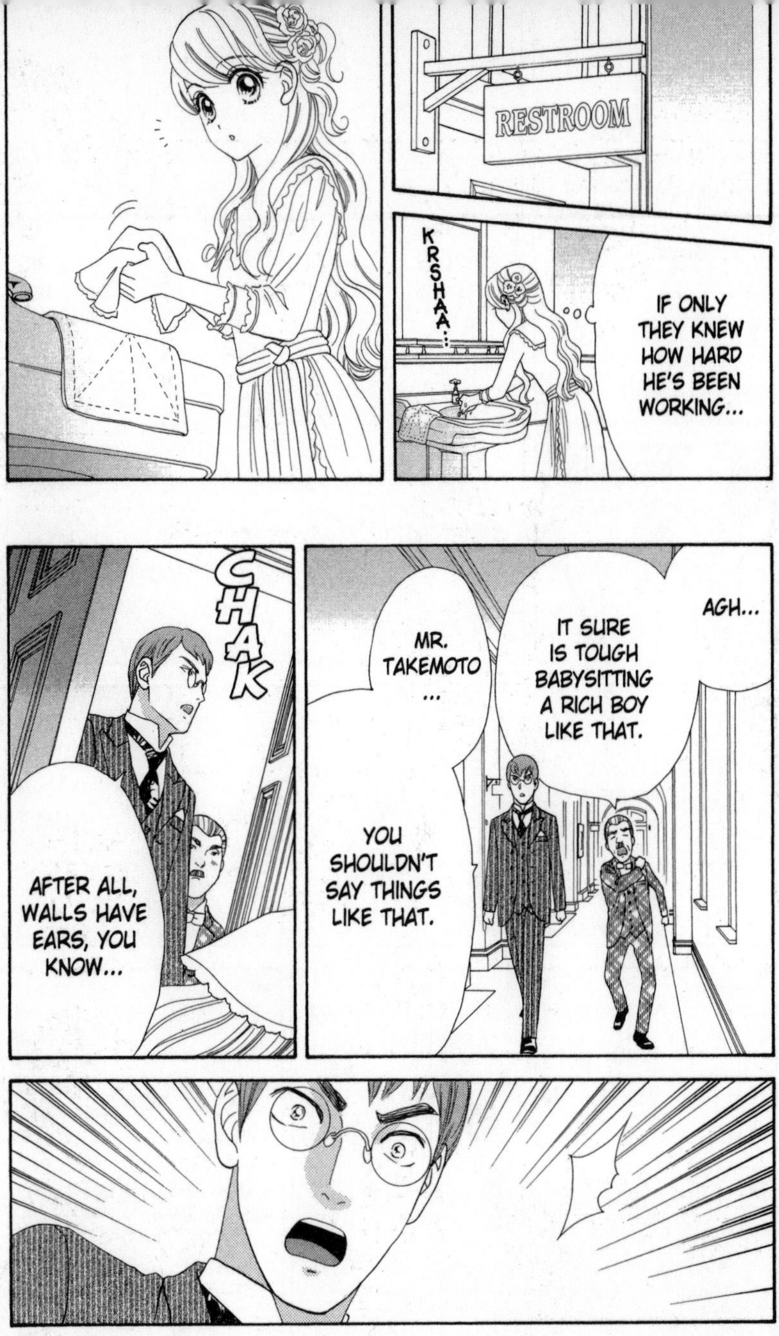
RESTROOM
KRSHAA...
IF ONLY THEY KNEW HOW HARD HE'S BEEN WORKING...
AGH...
IT SURE IS TOUGH BABYSITTING A RICH BOY LIKE THAT.
MR. TAKEMOTO...
YOU SHOULDN'T SAY THINGS LIKE THAT.
CHAK
AFTER ALL, WALLS HAVE EARS, YOU KNOW...

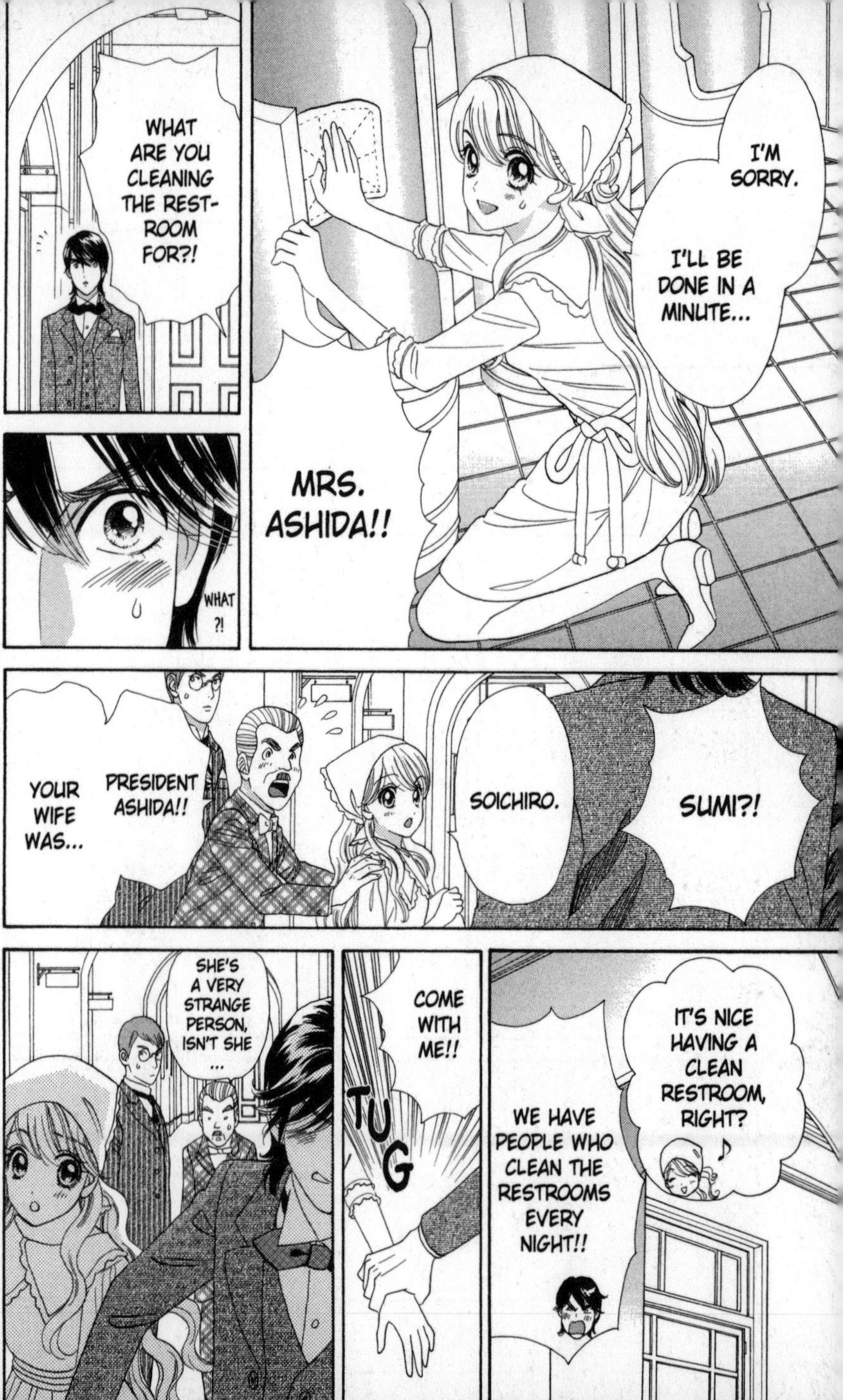
I'M SORRY.
I'LL BE DONE IN A MINUTE...
MRS. ASHIDA!!
WHAT ARE YOU CLEANING THE REST-ROOM FOR?!
WHAT?!
SUMI?!
SOICHIRO.
PRESIDENT ASHIDA!!
YOUR WIFE WAS...
IT'S NICE HAVING A CLEAN RESTROOM, RIGHT?
WE HAVE PEOPLE WHO CLEAN THE RESTROOMS EVERY NIGHT!!
COME WITH ME!!
TUG
SHE'S A VERY STRANGE PERSON, ISN'T SHE...

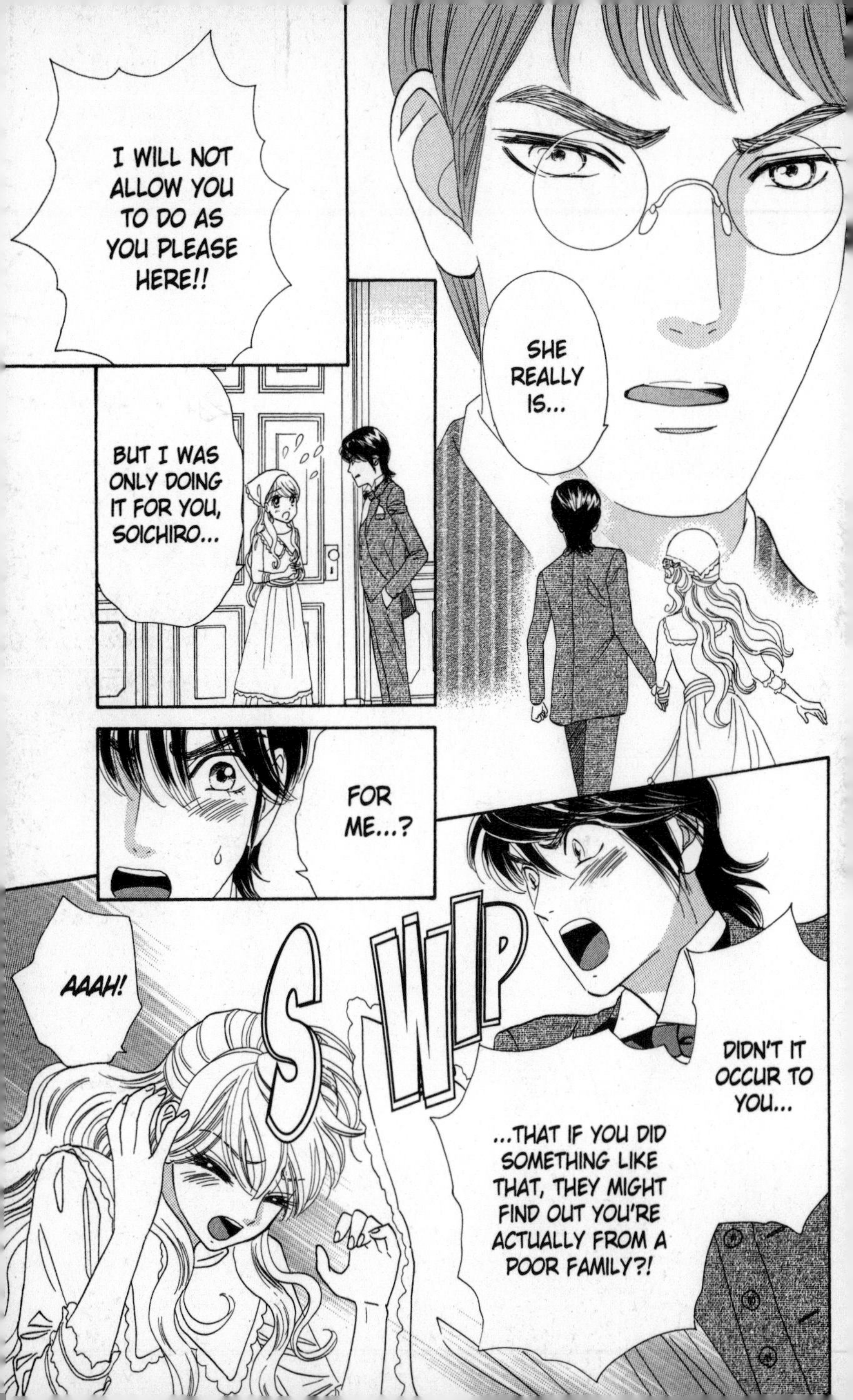
SHE REALLY IS...
I WILL NOT ALLOW YOU TO DO AS YOU PLEASE HERE!!
BUT I WAS ONLY DOING IT FOR YOU, SOICHIRO...
FOR ME...?
DIDN'T IT OCCUR TO YOU...
...THAT IF YOU DID SOMETHING LIKE THAT, THEY MIGHT FIND OUT YOU'RE ACTUALLY FROM A POOR FAMILY?!
SWIP
AAAH!

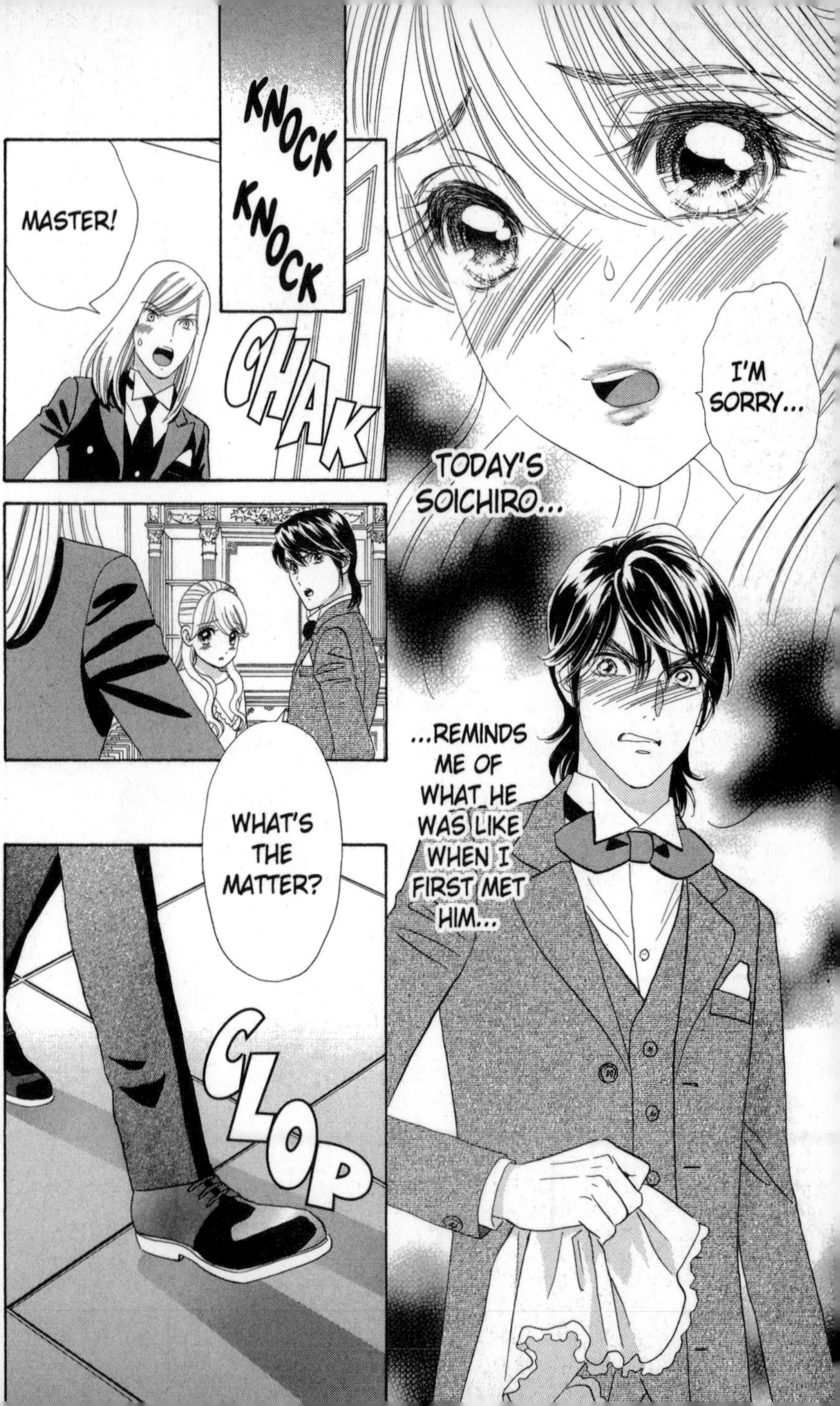
I'M SORRY...
TODAY'S SOICHIRO...
...REMINDS ME OF WHAT HE WAS LIKE WHEN I FIRST MET HIM...
KNOCK KNOCK
MASTER!
CHAK
WHAT'S THE MATTER?
CLOP

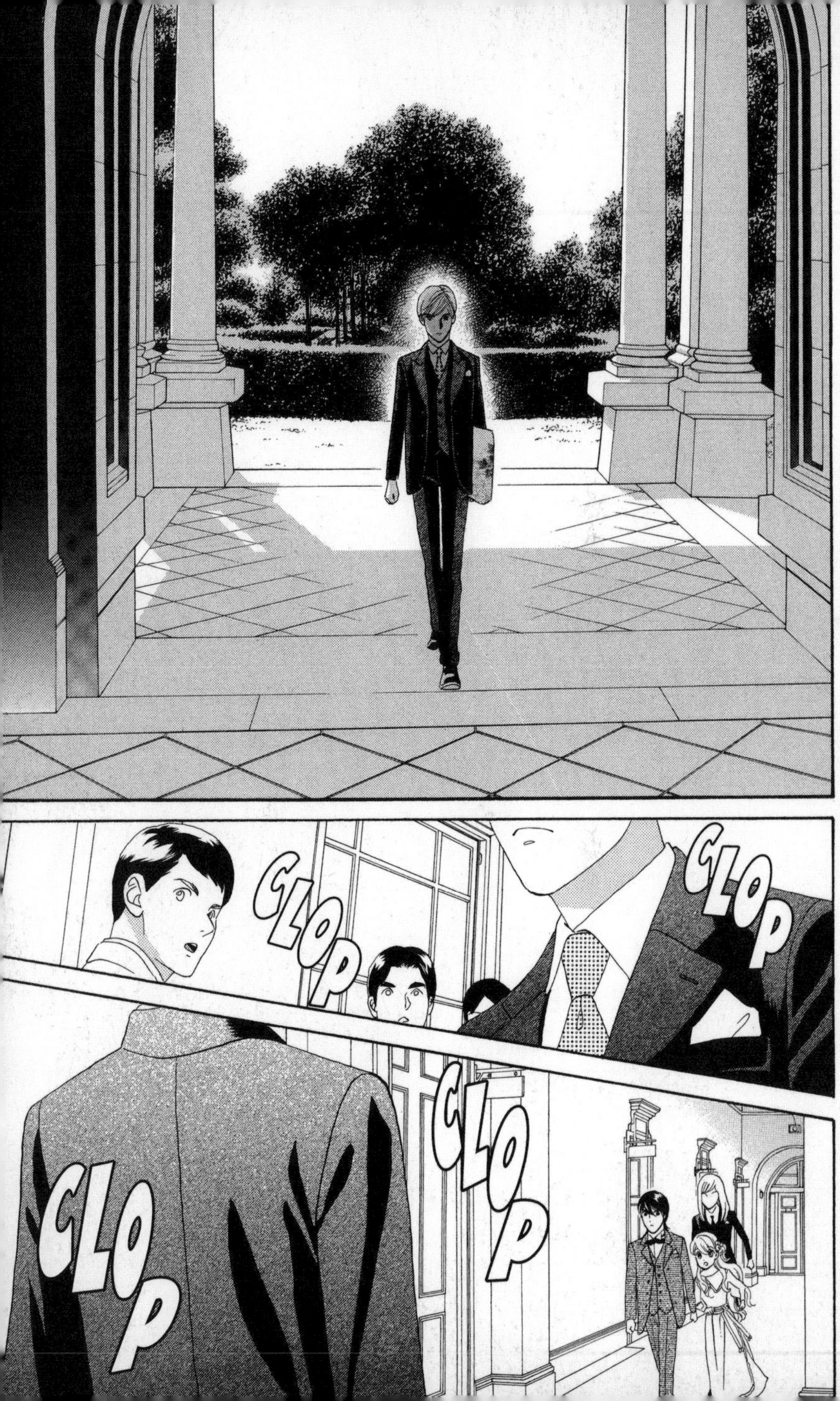
CLOP
CLOP
CLOP
CLOP

HELLO.
NOZOMU ...!
I'VE BEEN SENT BY IJUIN BANK TO WORK WITH ASHIDA PRODUCTS STARTING TODAY.

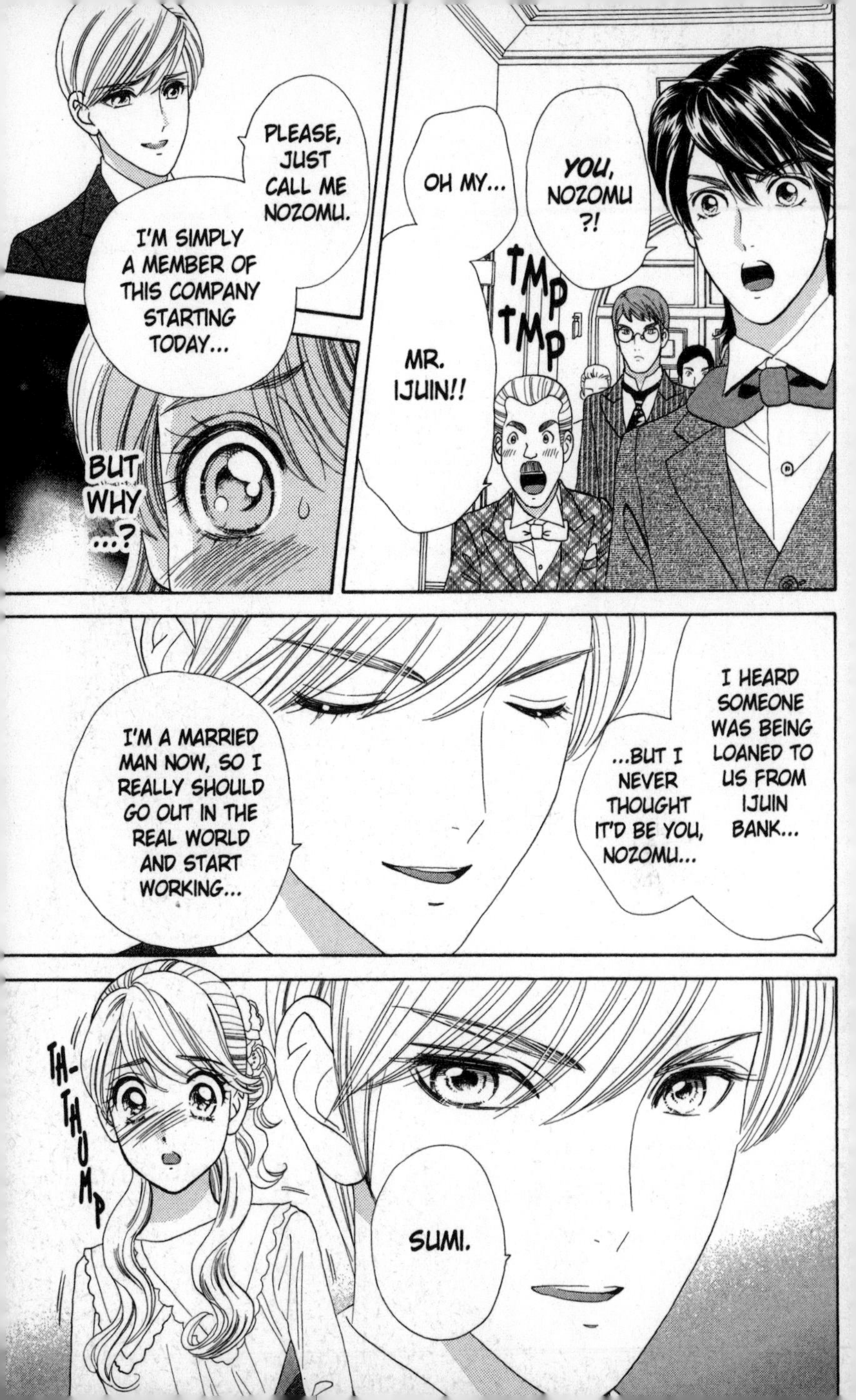
YOU, NOZOMU?!
OH MY...
TMP TMP
MR. IJUIN!!
PLEASE, JUST CALL ME NOZOMU.
I'M SIMPLY A MEMBER OF THIS COMPANY STARTING TODAY...
BUT WHY...?
I HEARD SOMEONE WAS BEING LOANED TO US FROM IJUIN BANK...
...BUT I NEVER THOUGHT IT'D BE YOU, NOZOMU...
I'M A MARRIED MAN NOW, SO I REALLY SHOULD GO OUT IN THE REAL WORLD AND START WORKING...
SUMI.
TH-THUMP

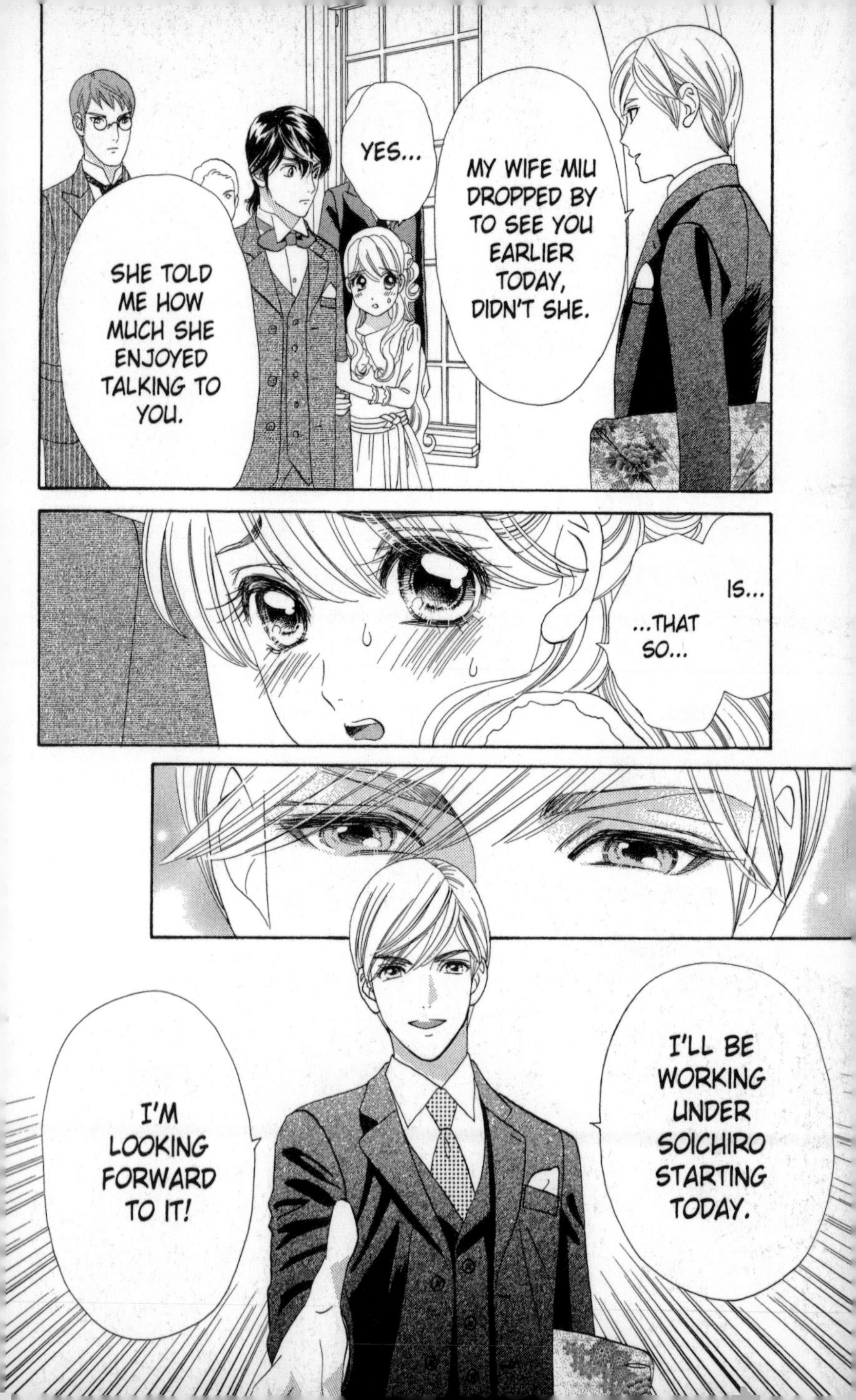
MY WIFE MIU DROPPED BY TO SEE YOU EARLIER TODAY, DIDN'T SHE.
YES...
SHE TOLD ME HOW MUCH SHE ENJOYED TALKING TO YOU.
IS...
...THAT SO...
I'LL BE WORKING UNDER SOICHIRO STARTING TODAY.
I'M LOOKING FORWARD TO IT!

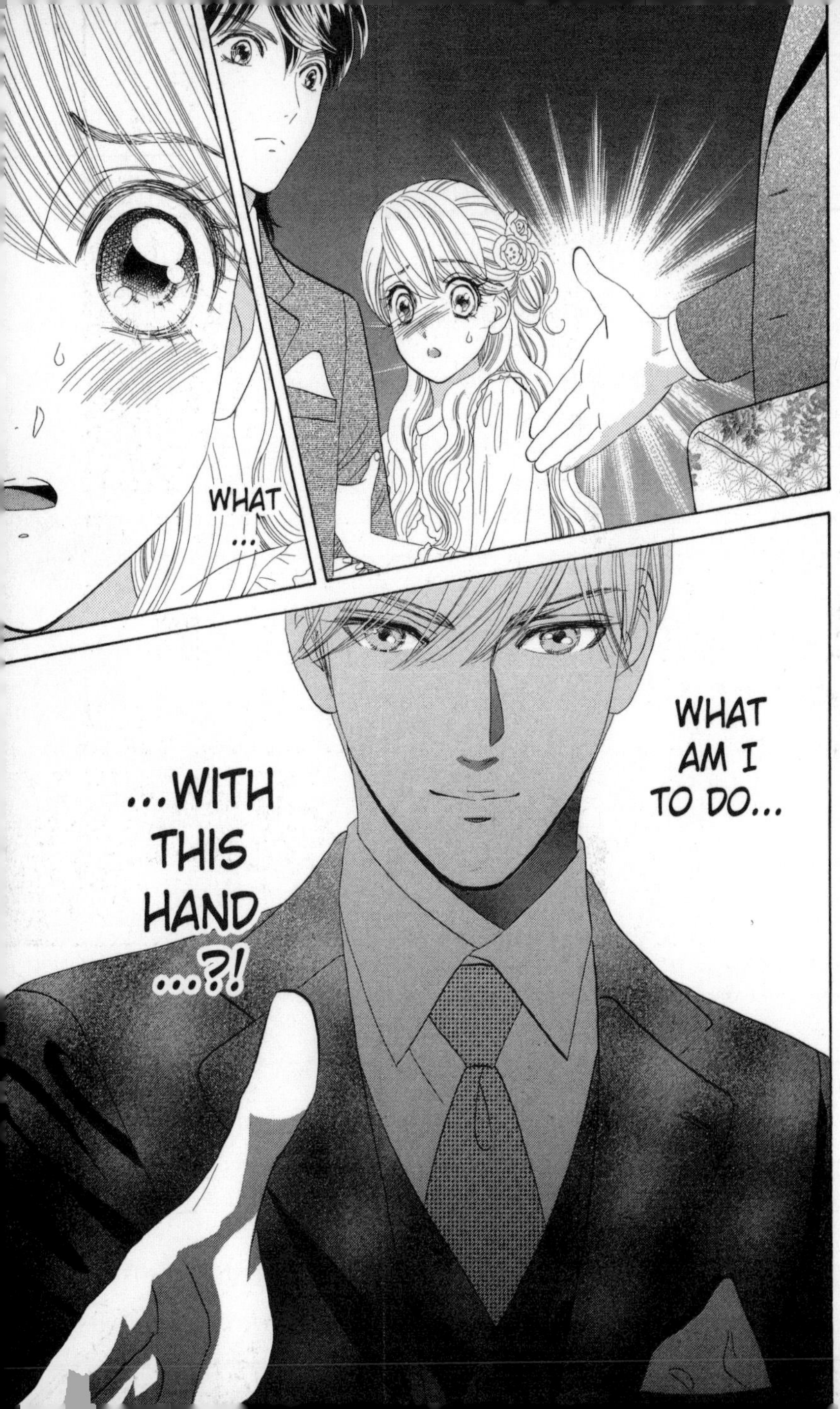
WHAT ...
WHAT AM I TO DO...
...WITH THIS HAND ...?!

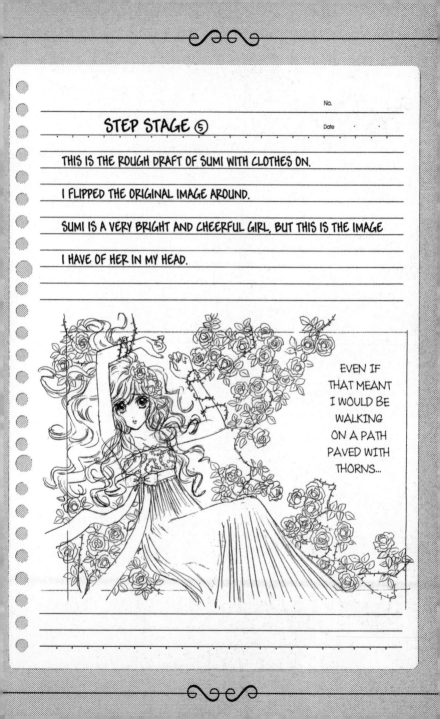

STEP STAGE ⑤

No.

Date

THIS IS THE ROUGH DRAFT OF SUMI WITH CLOTHES ON.

I FLIPPED THE ORIGINAL IMAGE AROUND.

SUMI IS A VERY BRIGHT AND CHEERFUL GIRL, BUT THIS IS THE IMAGE

I HAVE OF HER IN MY HEAD.

EVEN IF THAT MEANT I WOULD BE WALKING ON A PATH PAVED WITH THORNS...

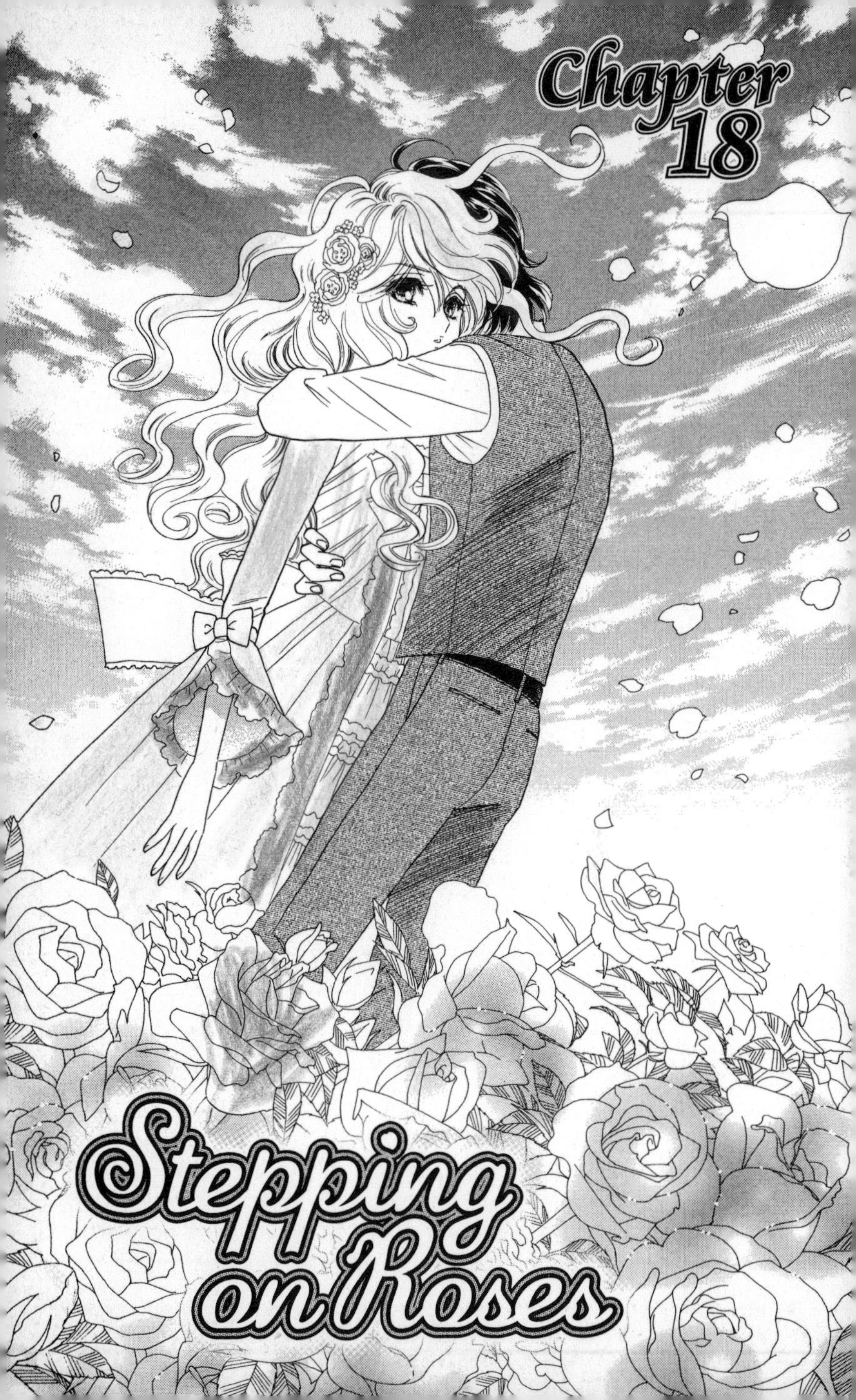
Chapter 18
Stepping on Roses

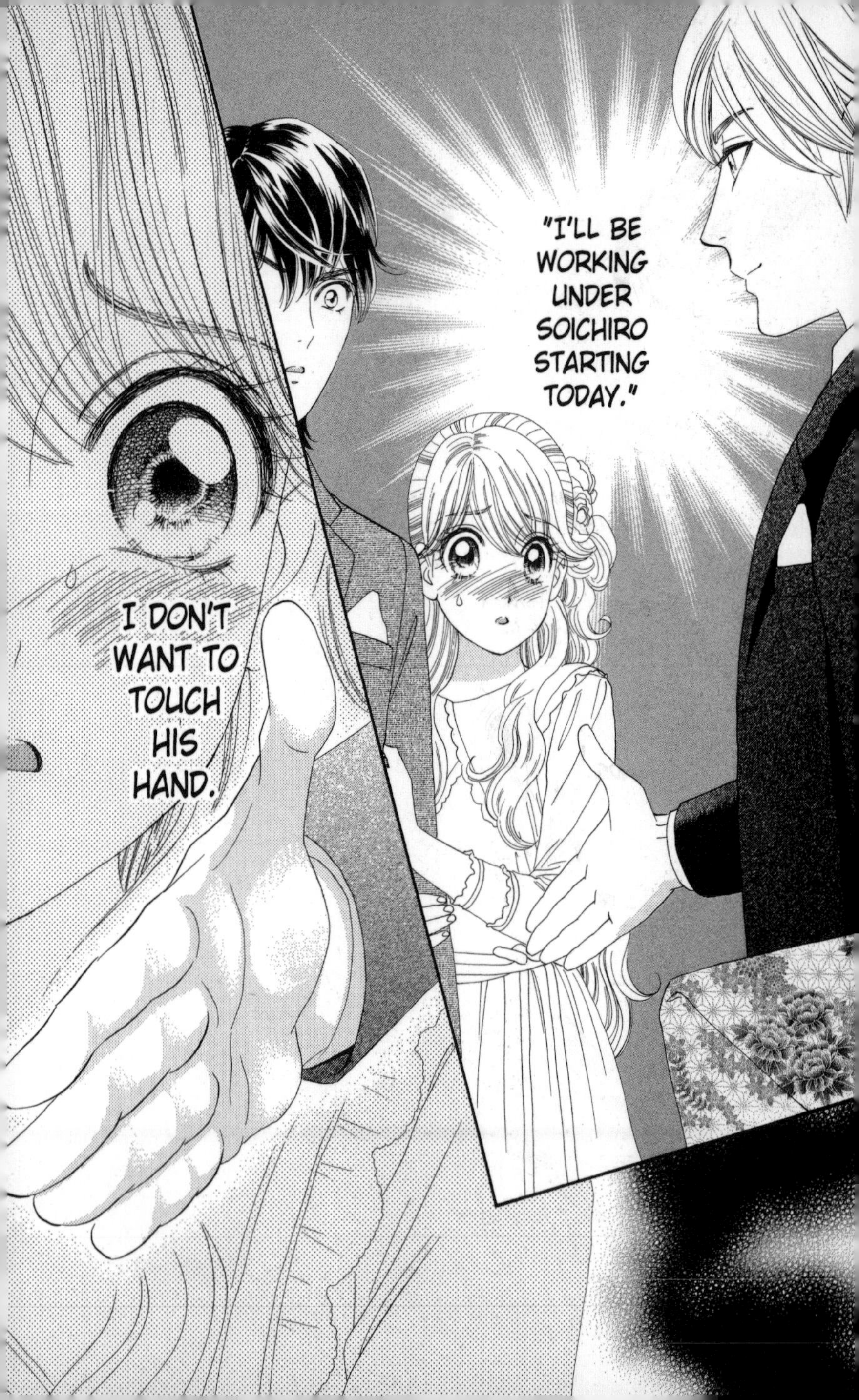
"I'LL BE WORKING UNDER SOICHIRO STARTING TODAY."
I DON'T WANT TO TOUCH HIS HAND.

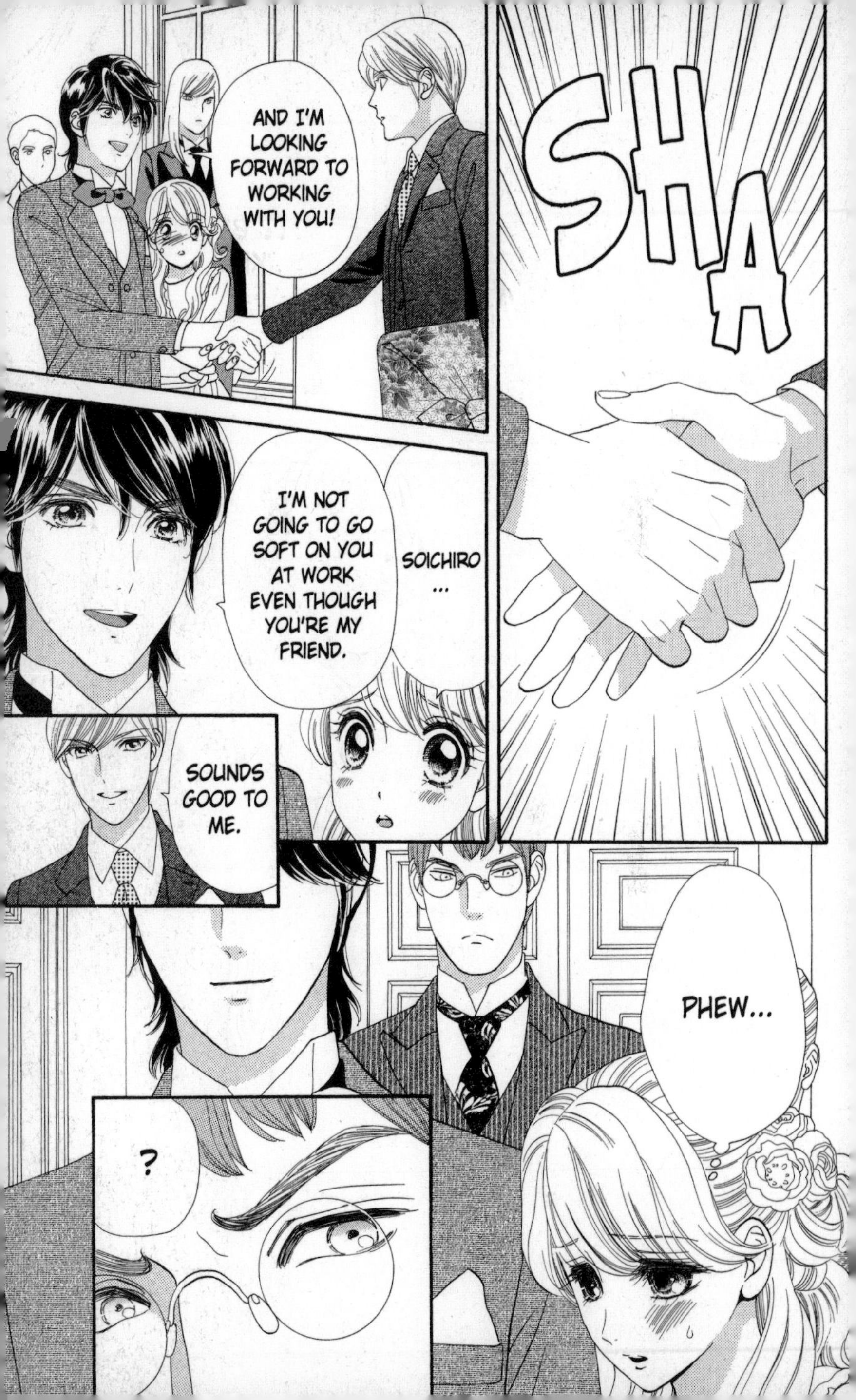
SHA
AND I'M LOOKING FORWARD TO WORKING WITH YOU!
I'M NOT GOING TO GO SOFT ON YOU AT WORK EVEN THOUGH YOU'RE MY FRIEND.
SOICHIRO ...
SOUNDS GOOD TO ME.
PHEW...
?

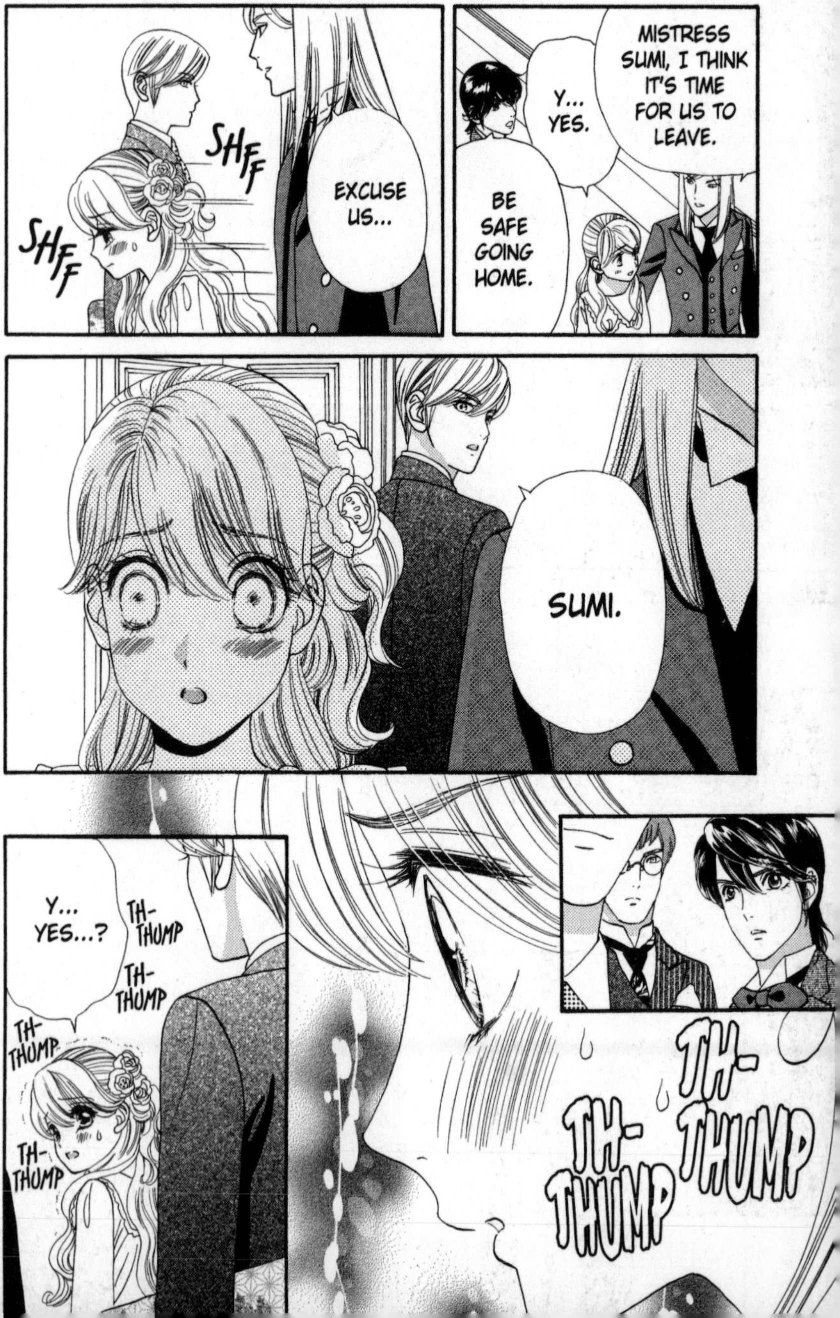
MISTRESS SUMI, I THINK IT'S TIME FOR US TO LEAVE.
Y... YES.
BE SAFE GOING HOME.
EXCUSE US...
SHFF
SHFF
SUMI.
TH-THUMP
TH-THUMP
Y... YES...?
TH-THUMP
TH-THUMP
TH-THUMP
TH-THUMP

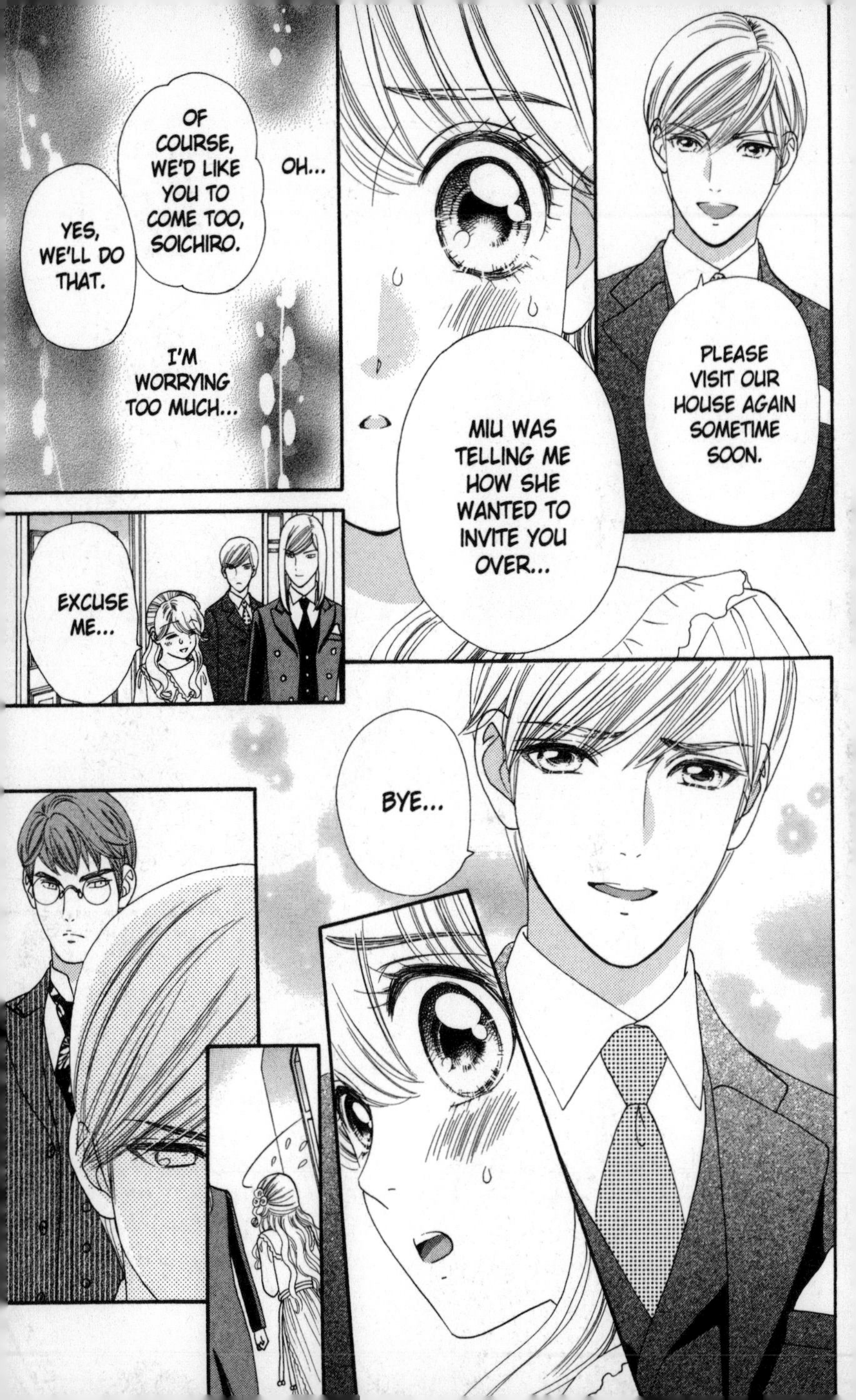
PLEASE VISIT OUR HOUSE AGAIN SOMETIME SOON.
MIU WAS TELLING ME HOW SHE WANTED TO INVITE YOU OVER...
OH...
OF COURSE, WE'D LIKE YOU TO COME TOO, SOICHIRO.
YES, WE'LL DO THAT.
I'M WORRYING TOO MUCH...
EXCUSE ME...
BYE...

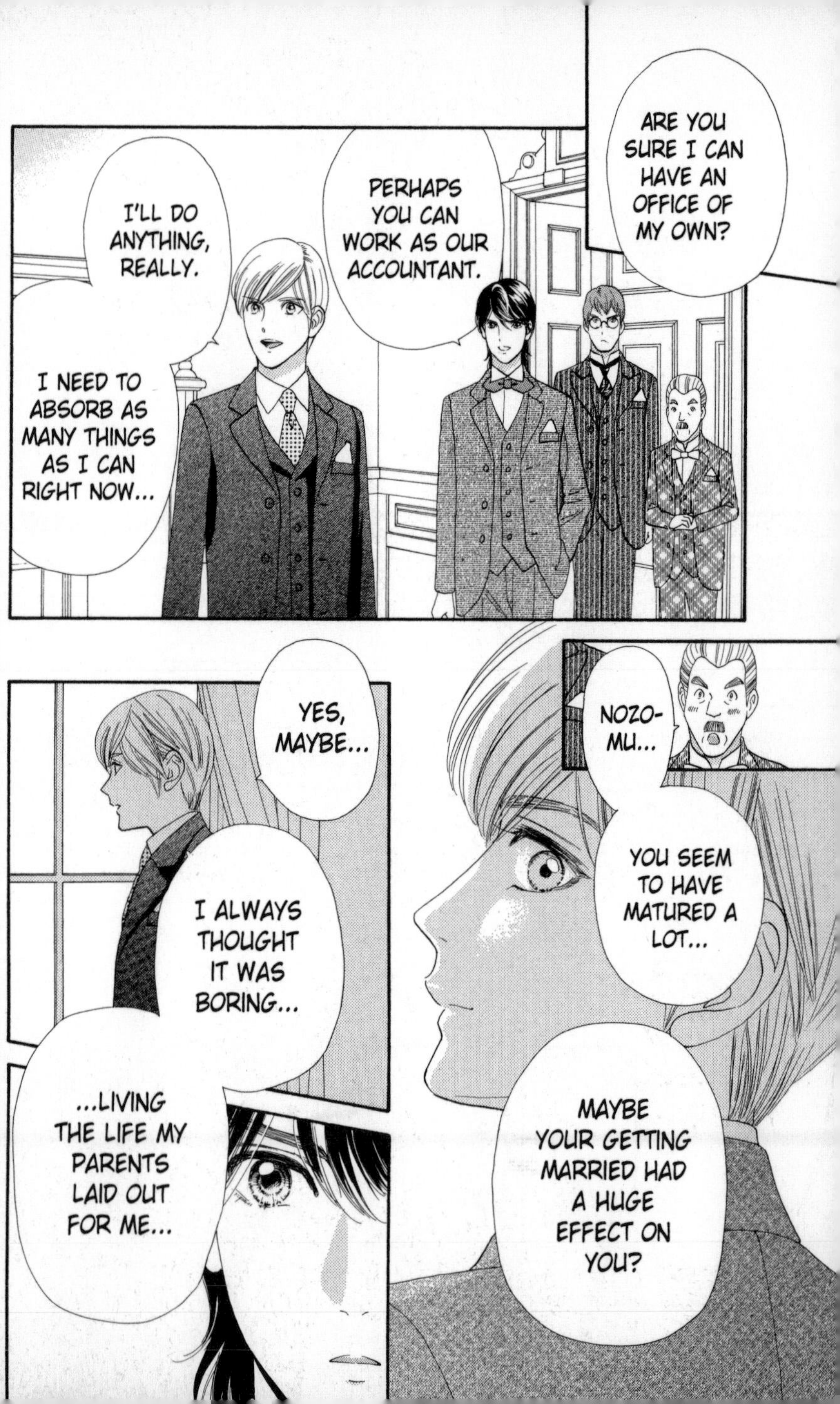
ARE YOU SURE I CAN HAVE AN OFFICE OF MY OWN?
PERHAPS YOU CAN WORK AS OUR ACCOUNTANT.
I'LL DO ANYTHING, REALLY.
I NEED TO ABSORB AS MANY THINGS AS I CAN RIGHT NOW...
NOZO-MU...
YOU SEEM TO HAVE MATURED A LOT...
MAYBE YOUR GETTING MARRIED HAD A HUGE EFFECT ON YOU?
YES, MAYBE...
I ALWAYS THOUGHT IT WAS BORING...
...LIVING THE LIFE MY PARENTS LAID OUT FOR ME...

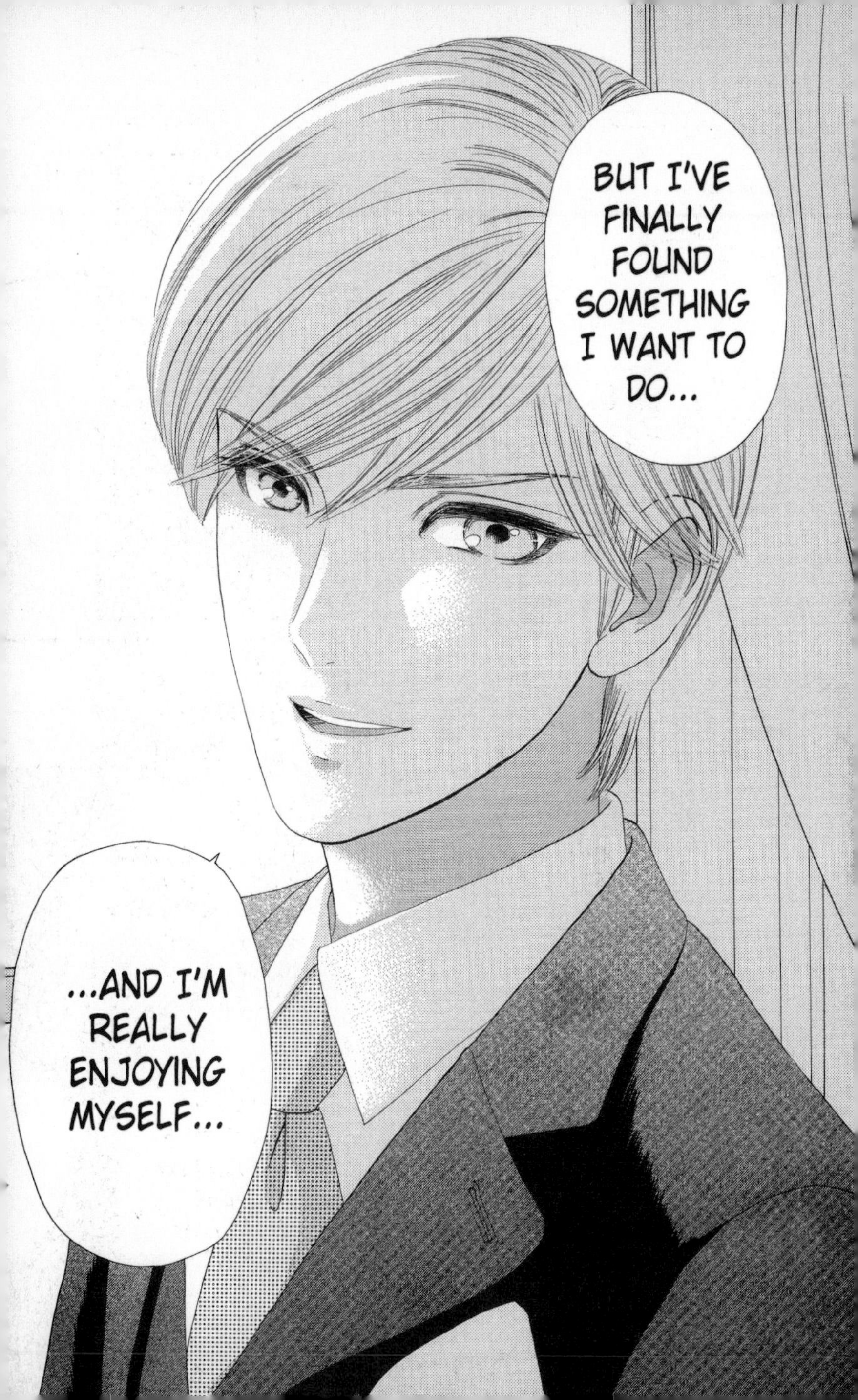
BUT I'VE FINALLY FOUND SOMETHING I WANT TO DO...
...AND I'M REALLY ENJOYING MYSELF...

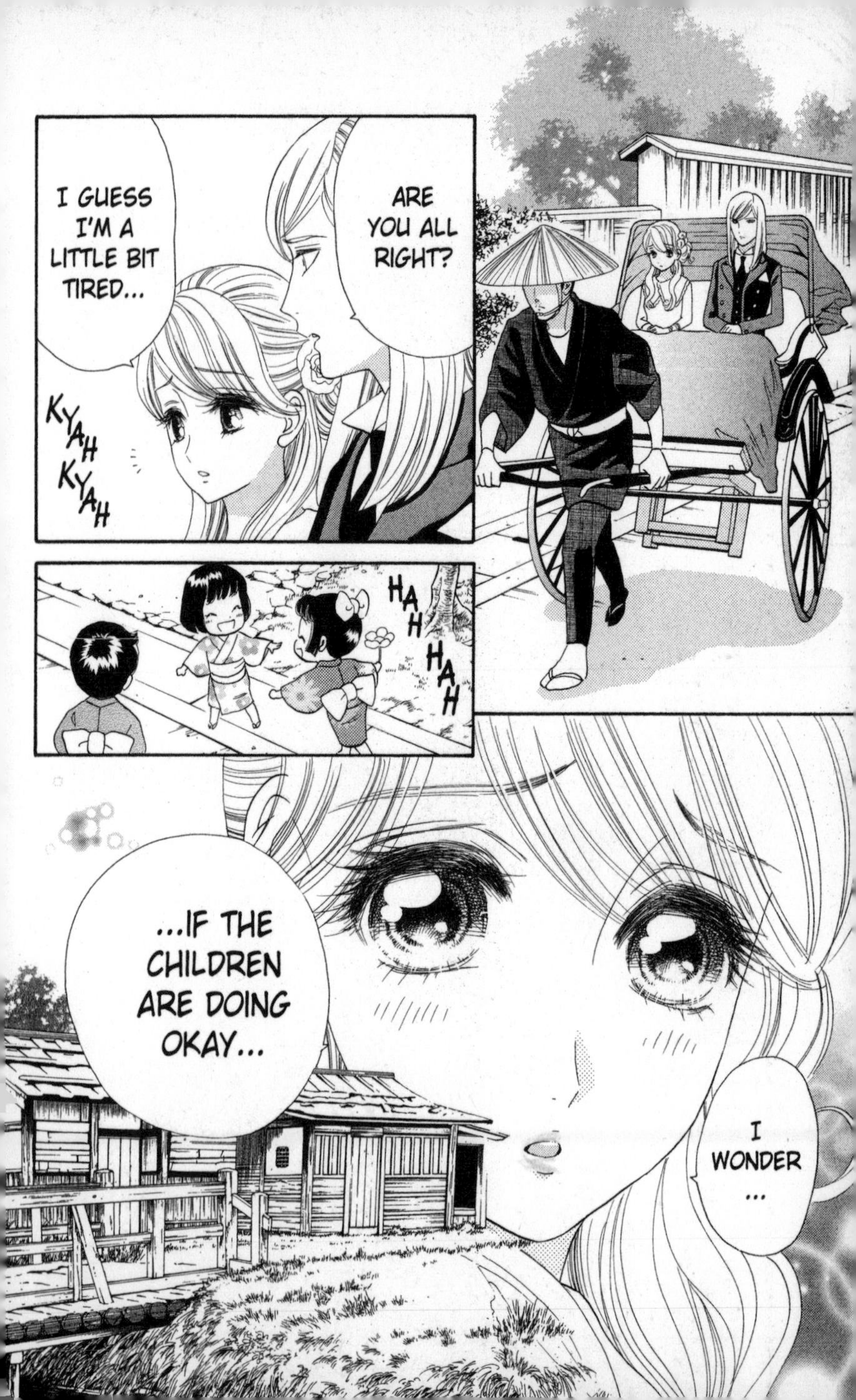
ARE YOU ALL RIGHT?
I GUESS I'M A LITTLE BIT TIRED...
KYAH KYAH
HAH HAH
I WONDER ...
...IF THE CHILDREN ARE DOING OKAY...

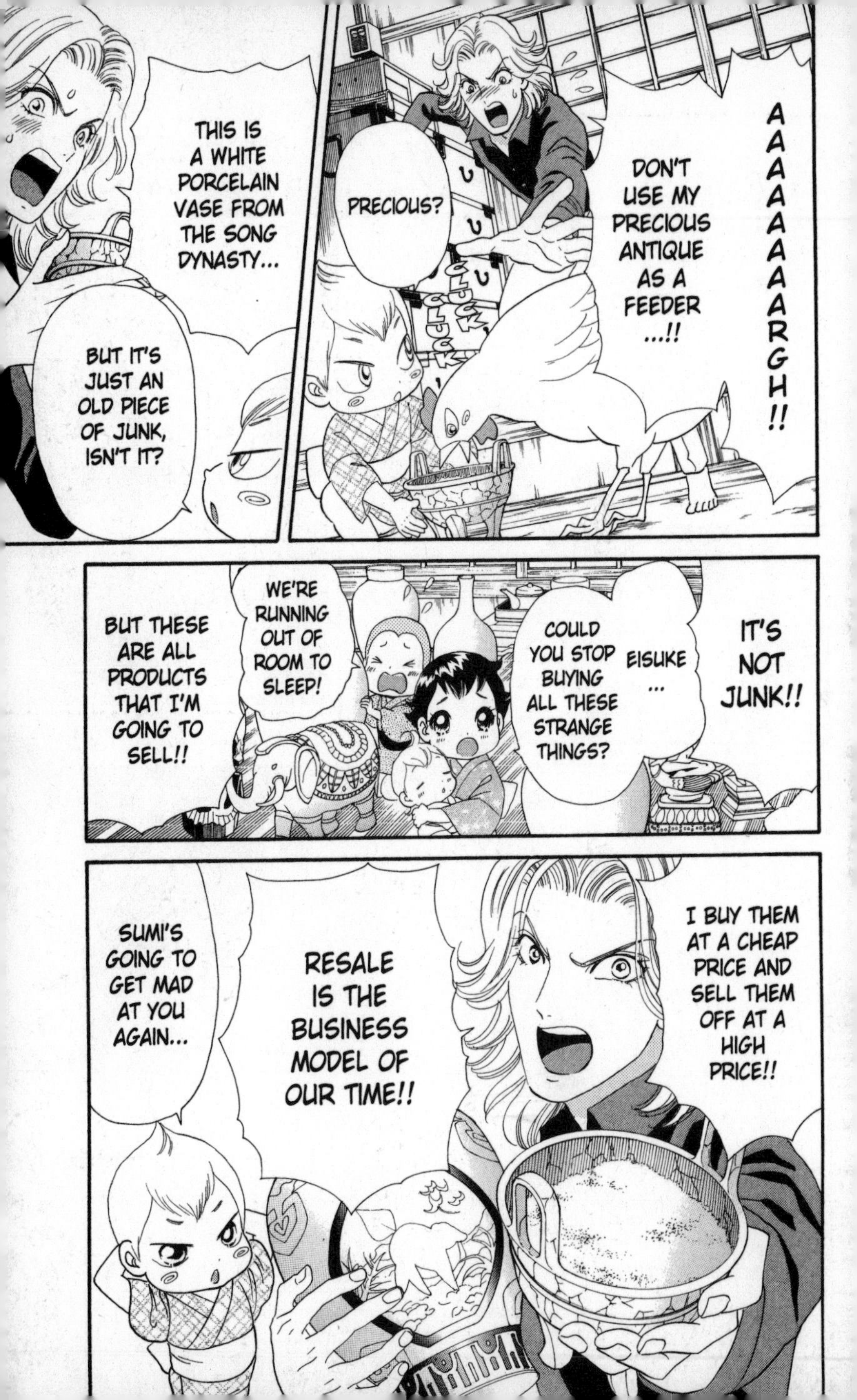
AAAAAAAAAARGH!!
DON'T USE MY PRECIOUS ANTIQUE AS A FEEDER...!!
PRECIOUS?
CLUCK CLUCK
THIS IS A WHITE PORCELAIN VASE FROM THE SONG DYNASTY...
BUT IT'S JUST AN OLD PIECE OF JUNK, ISN'T IT?
IT'S NOT JUNK!!
EISUKE...
COULD YOU STOP BUYING ALL THESE STRANGE THINGS?
WE'RE RUNNING OUT OF ROOM TO SLEEP!
BUT THESE ARE ALL PRODUCTS THAT I'M GOING TO SELL!!
I BUY THEM AT A CHEAP PRICE AND SELL THEM OFF AT A HIGH PRICE!!
RESALE IS THE BUSINESS MODEL OF OUR TIME!!
SUMI'S GOING TO GET MAD AT YOU AGAIN...

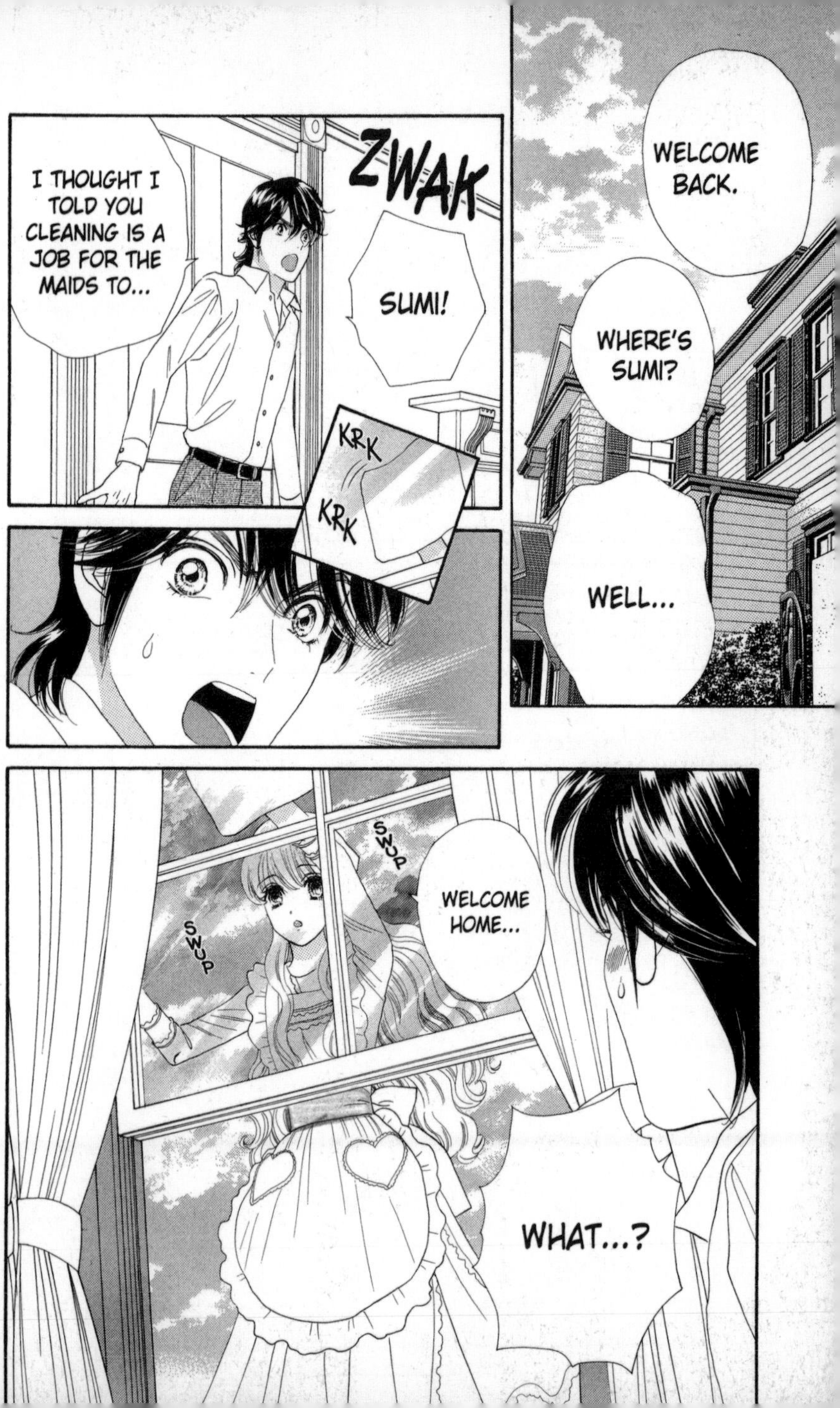
WELCOME BACK.
WHERE'S SUMI?
WELL...
ZWAK
SUMI!
I THOUGHT I TOLD YOU CLEANING IS A JOB FOR THE MAIDS TO...
KRK
KRK
SWUP
WELCOME HOME...
SWUP
WHAT...?

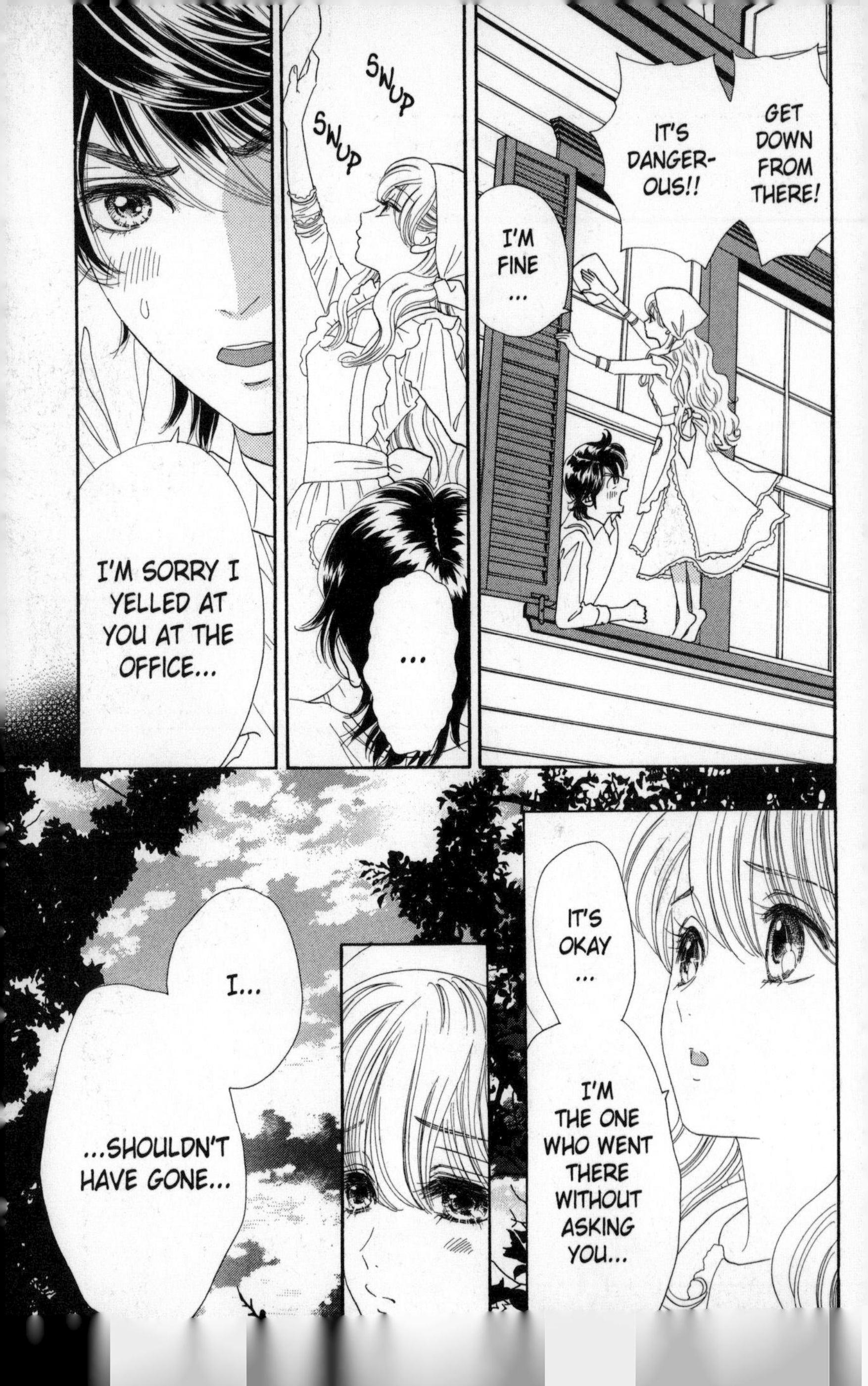
GET DOWN FROM THERE!
IT'S DANGER-OUS!!
I'M FINE ...
SWUP
SWUP
...
I'M SORRY I YELLED AT YOU AT THE OFFICE...
IT'S OKAY ...
I'M THE ONE WHO WENT THERE WITHOUT ASKING YOU...
I...
...SHOULDN'T HAVE GONE...

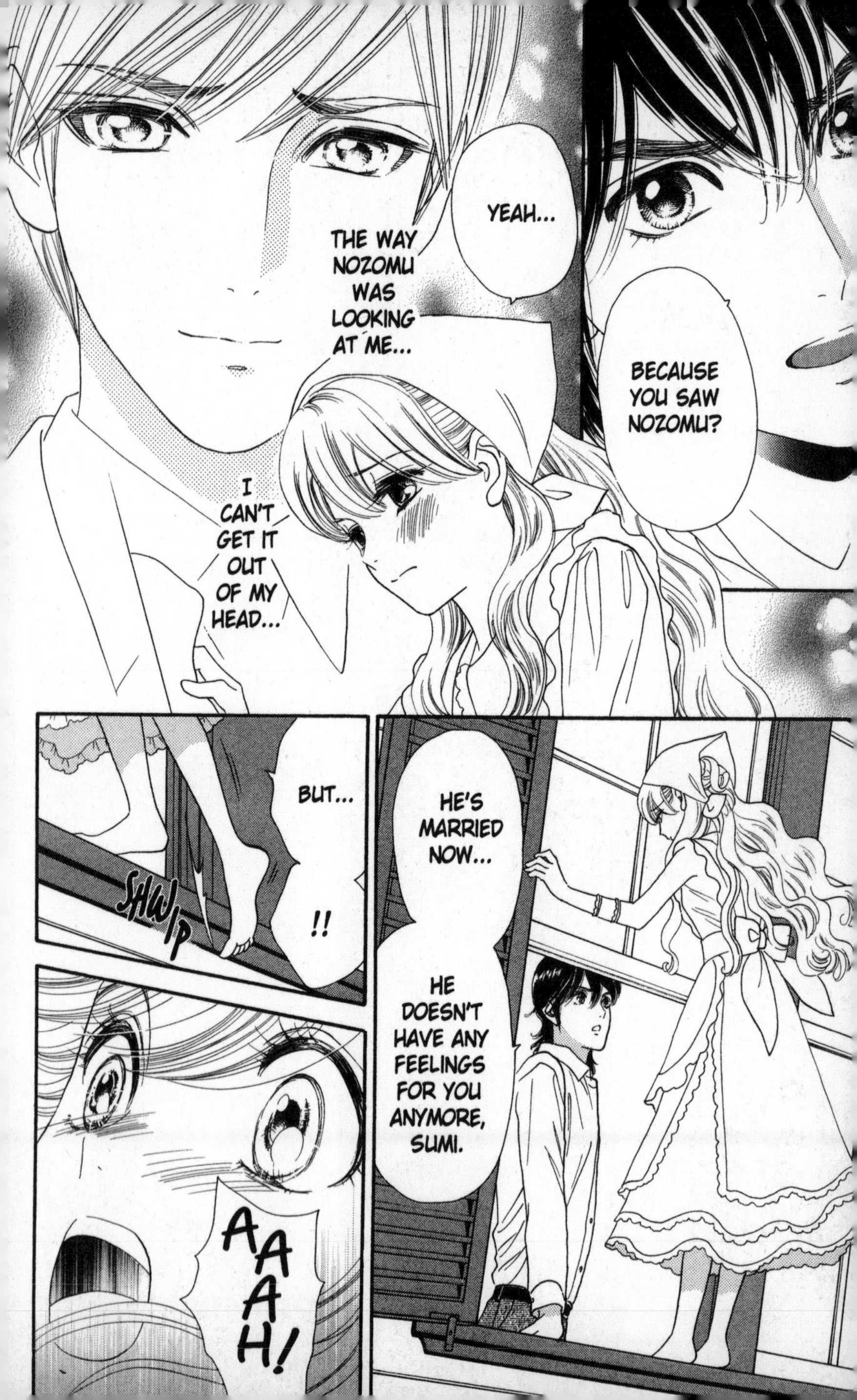
BECAUSE YOU SAW NOZOMU?
YEAH...
THE WAY NOZOMU WAS LOOKING AT ME...
I CAN'T GET IT OUT OF MY HEAD...
HE'S MARRIED NOW...
HE DOESN'T HAVE ANY FEELINGS FOR YOU ANYMORE, SUMI.
BUT...
SHWIP
!!
AAAAH!

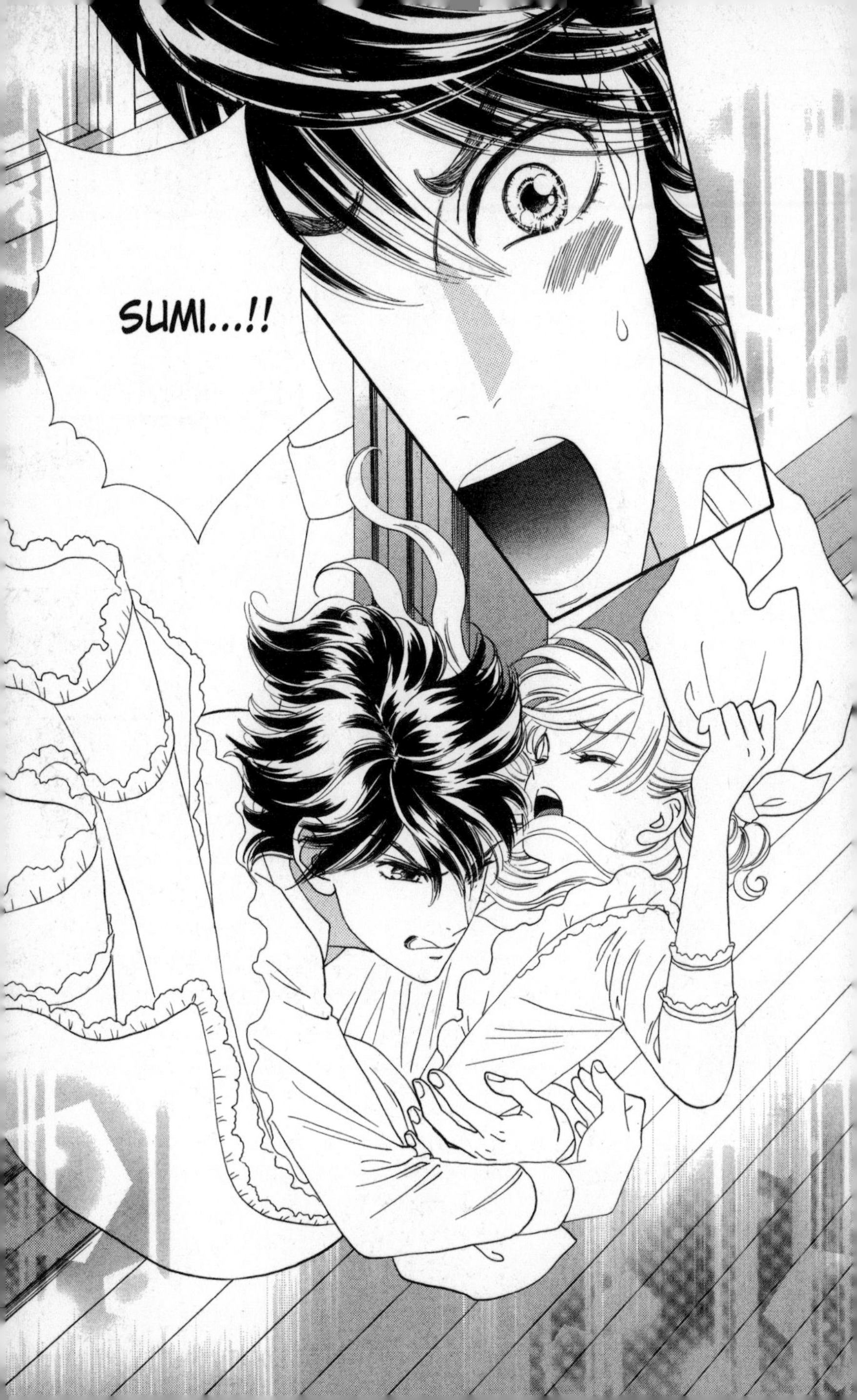
SUMI...!!

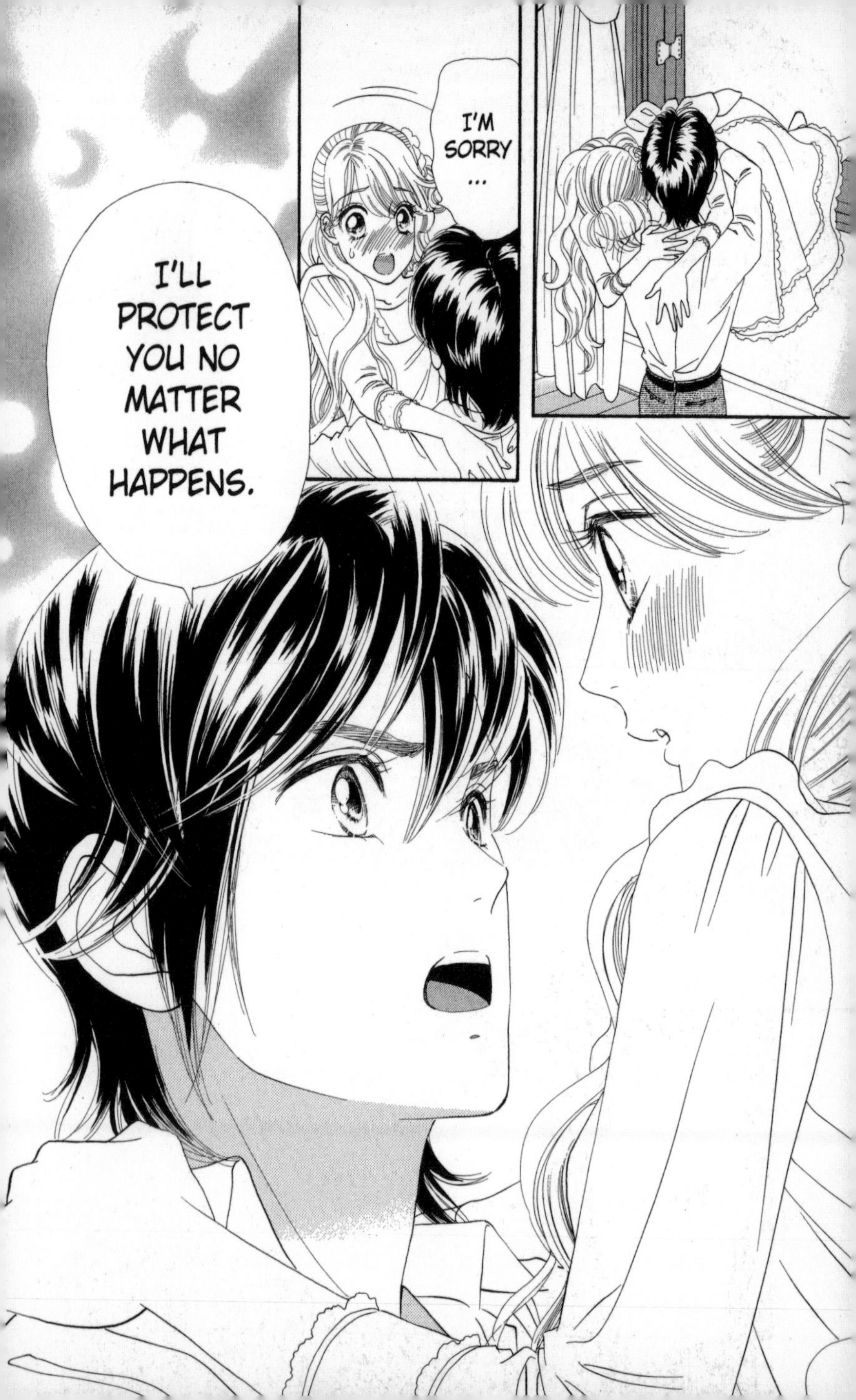
I'M SORRY ...
I'LL PROTECT YOU NO MATTER WHAT HAPPENS.

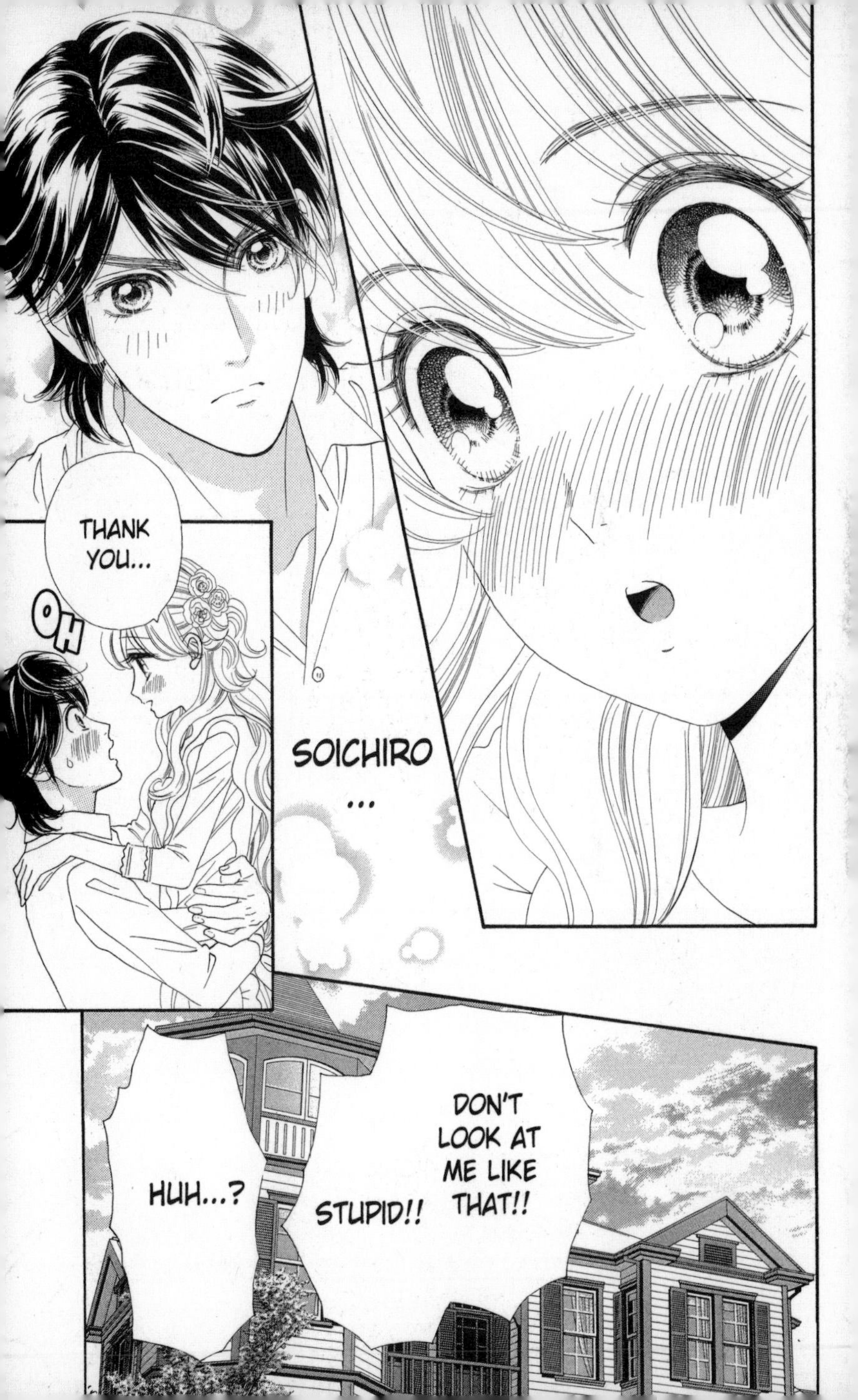
SOICHIRO ...
THANK YOU...
OH
DON'T LOOK AT ME LIKE THAT!!
STUPID!!
HUH...?

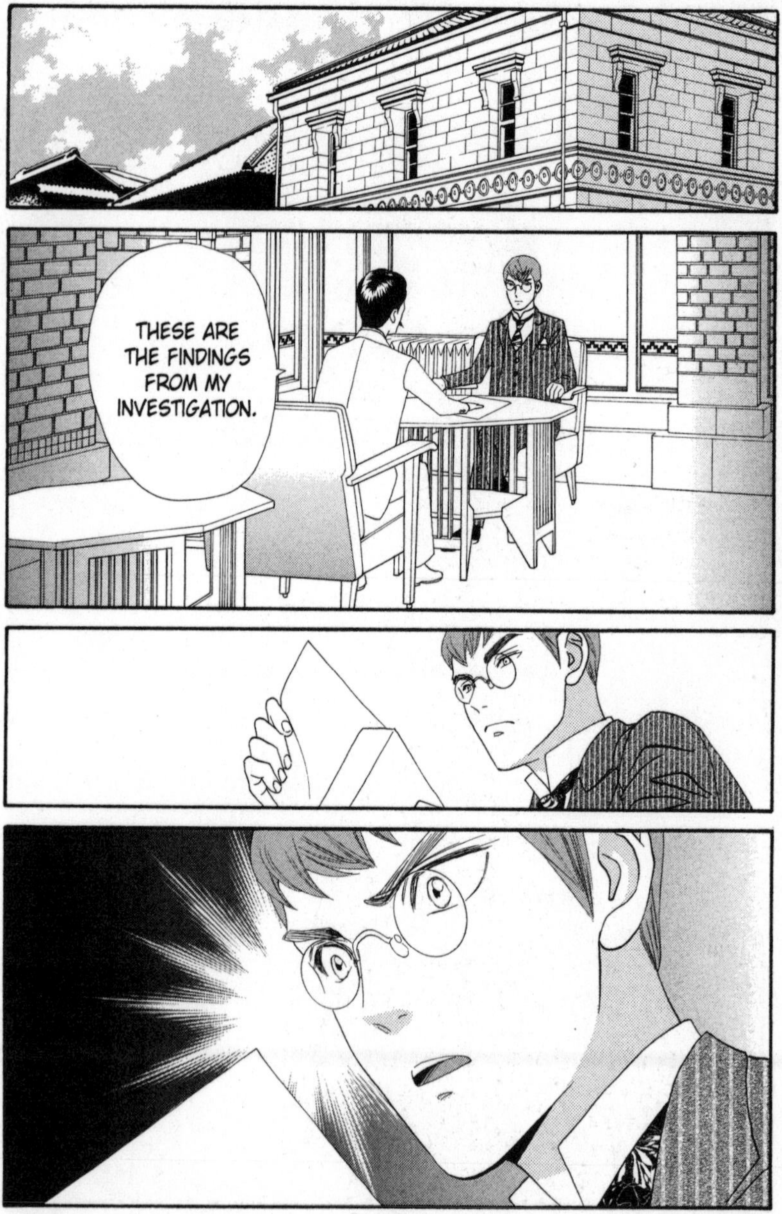
THESE ARE THE FINDINGS FROM MY INVESTIGATION.

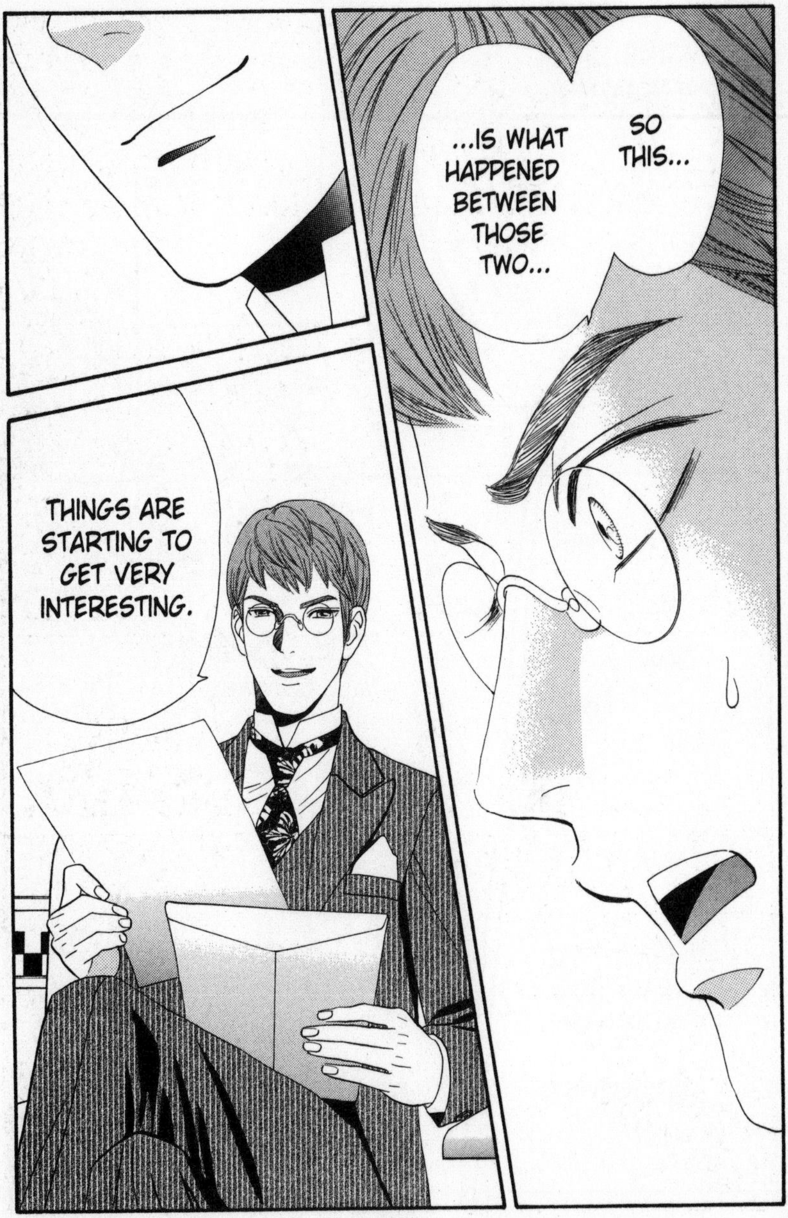
SO THIS...
...IS WHAT HAPPENED BETWEEN THOSE TWO...
THINGS ARE STARTING TO GET VERY INTERESTING.

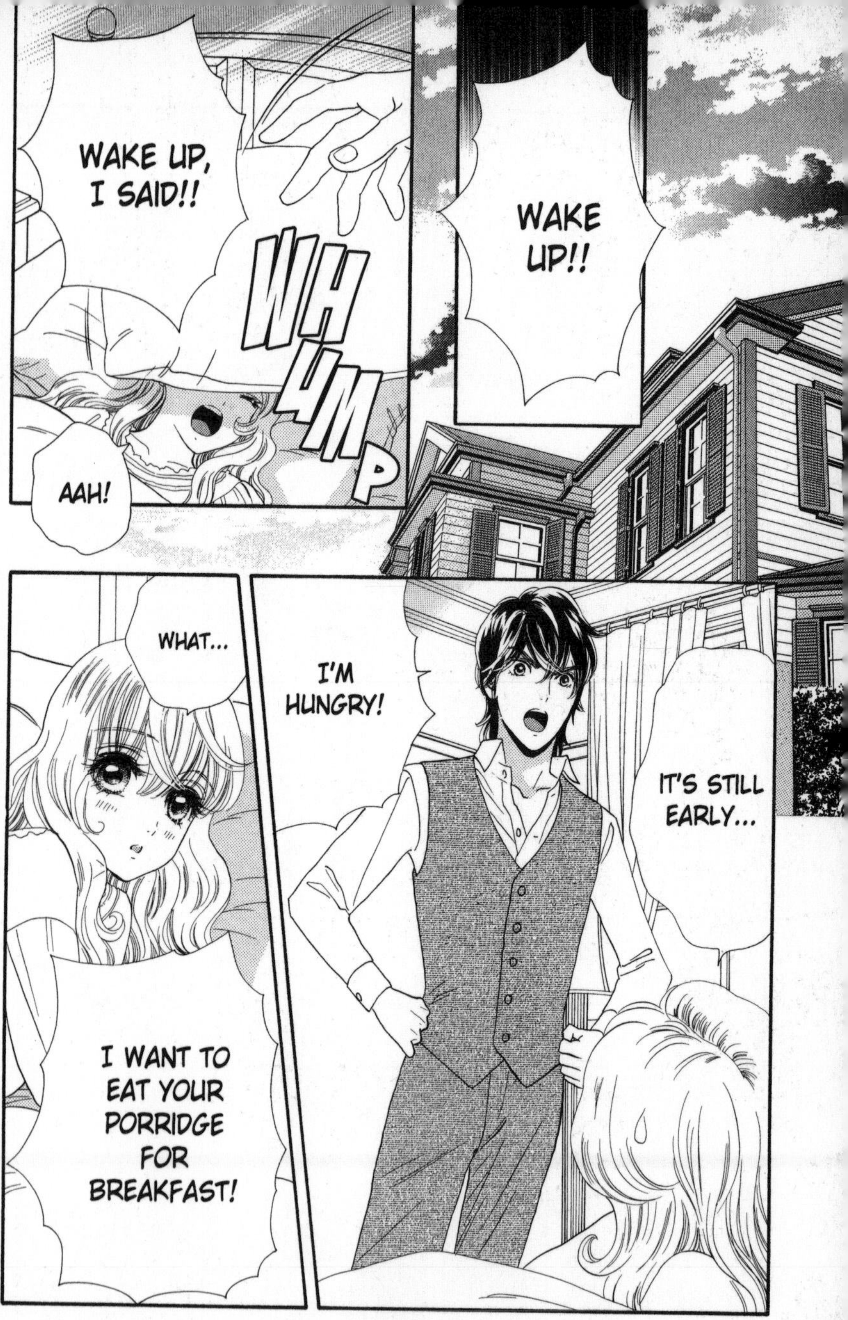
WAKE UP!!
WAKE UP, I SAID!!
WHUMP
AAH!
I'M HUNGRY!
IT'S STILL EARLY...
WHAT...
I WANT TO EAT YOUR PORRIDGE FOR BREAKFAST!

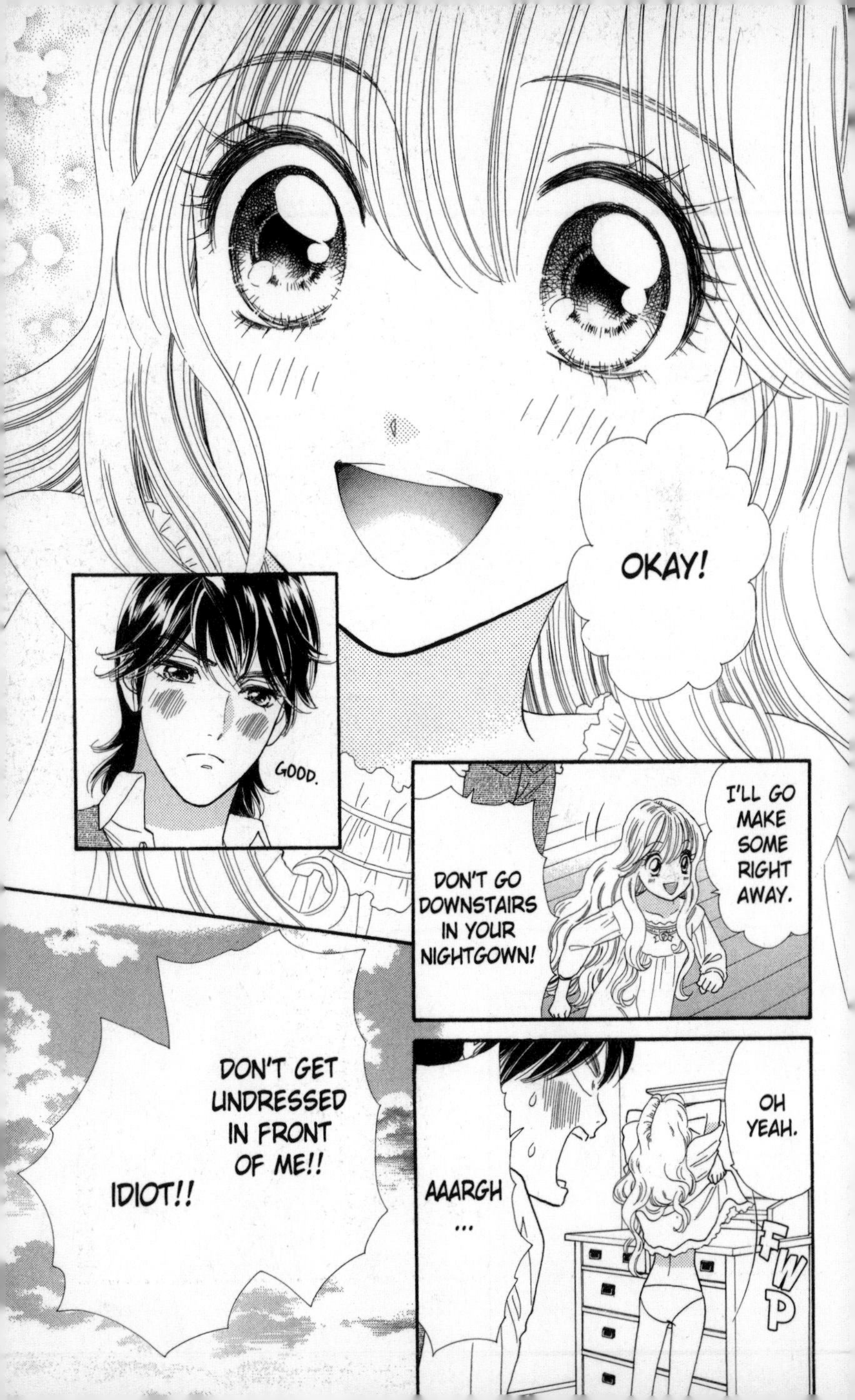
OKAY!
GOOD.
I'LL GO MAKE SOME RIGHT AWAY.
DON'T GO DOWNSTAIRS IN YOUR NIGHTGOWN!
OH YEAH.
FWP
AAARGH ...
DON'T GET UNDRESSED IN FRONT OF ME!!
IDIOT!!

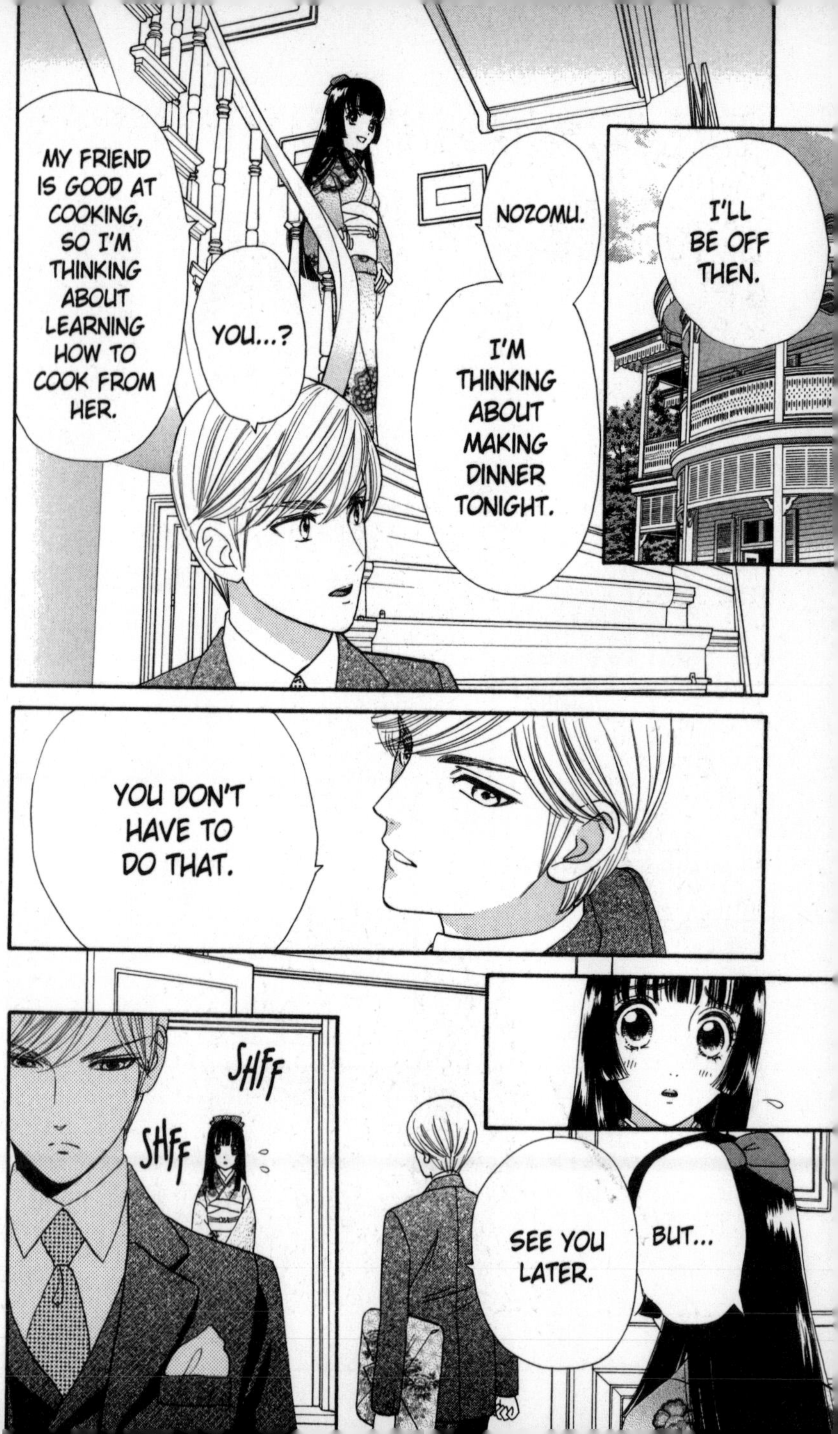
I'LL BE OFF THEN.
NOZOMU.
I'M THINKING ABOUT MAKING DINNER TONIGHT.
YOU...?
MY FRIEND IS GOOD AT COOKING, SO I'M THINKING ABOUT LEARNING HOW TO COOK FROM HER.
YOU DON'T HAVE TO DO THAT.
BUT...
SEE YOU LATER.
SHFF
SHFF

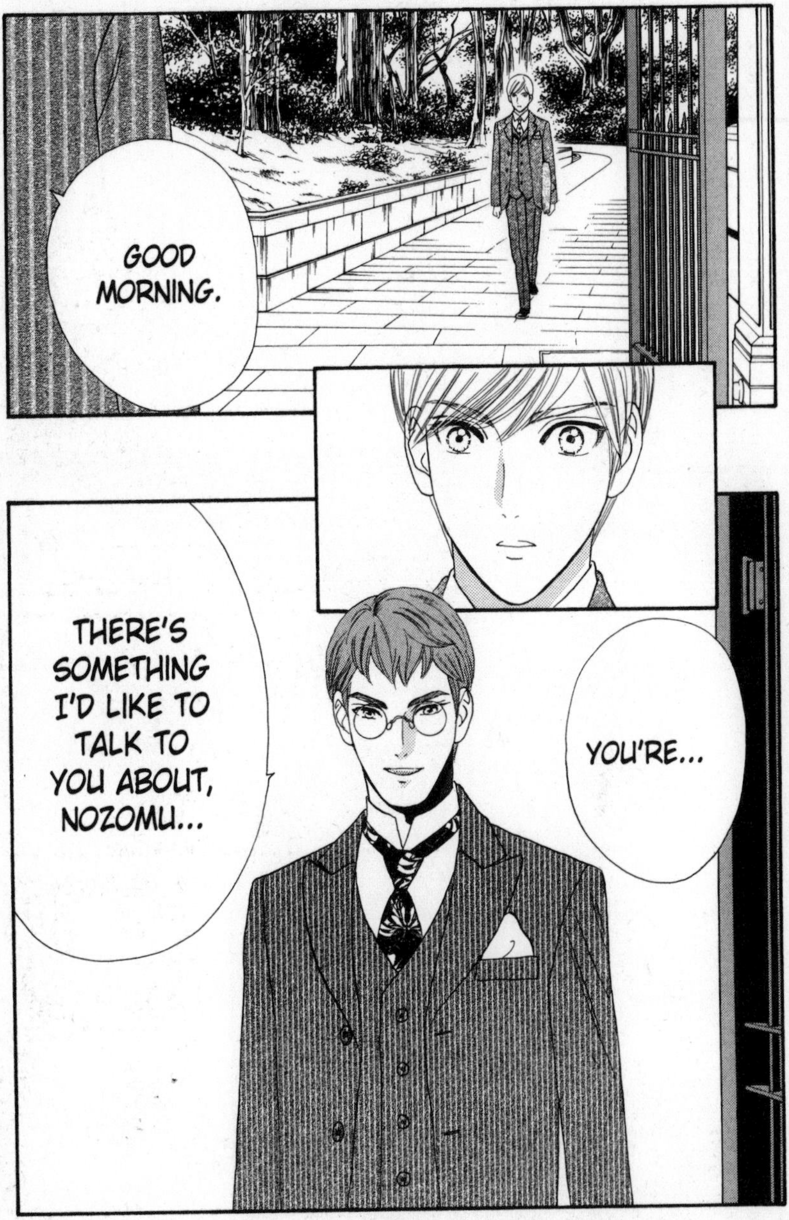
GOOD MORNING.
YOU'RE...
THERE'S SOMETHING I'D LIKE TO TALK TO YOU ABOUT, NOZOMU...

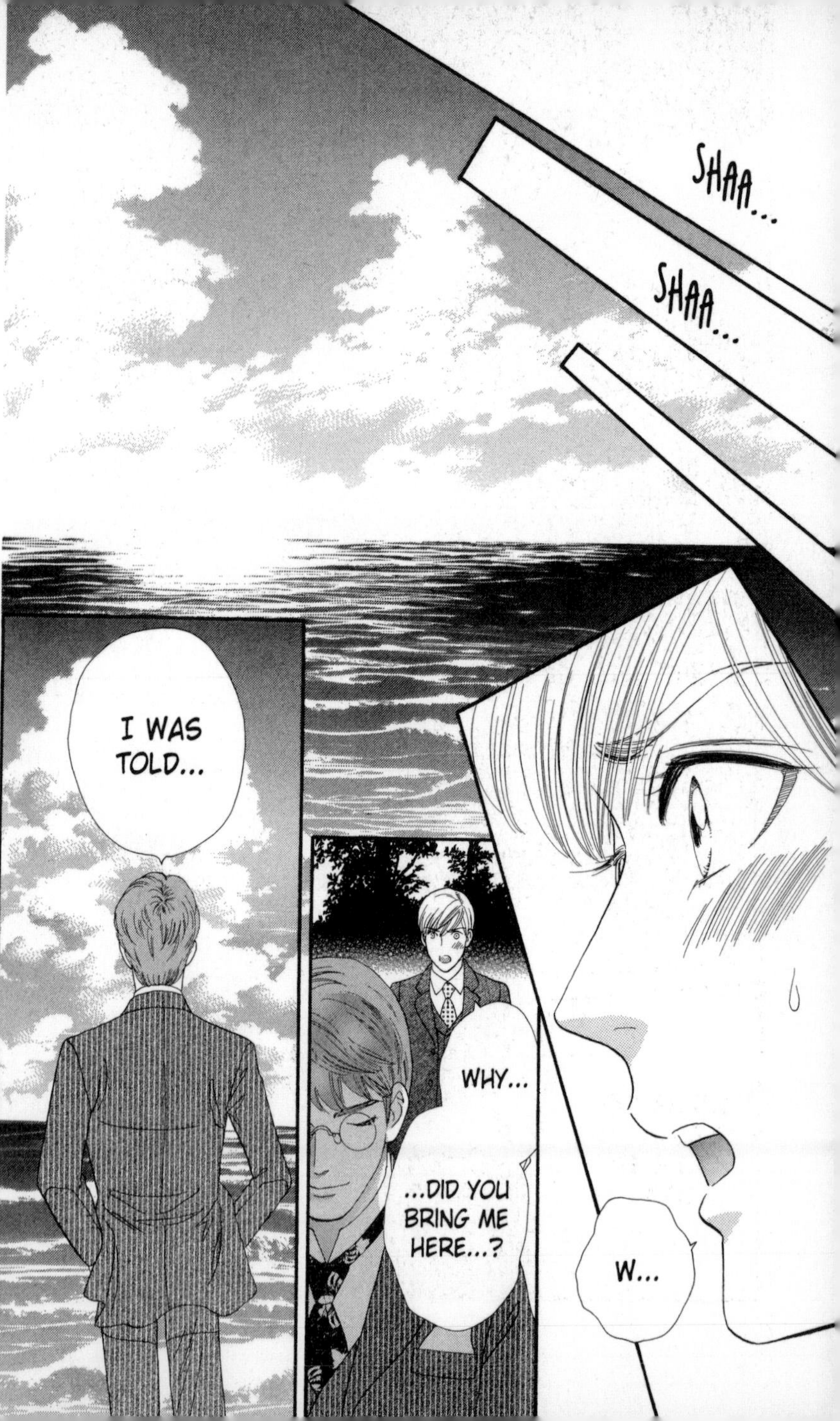
SHAA...
SHAA...
W...
WHY...
...DID YOU BRING ME HERE...?
I WAS TOLD...

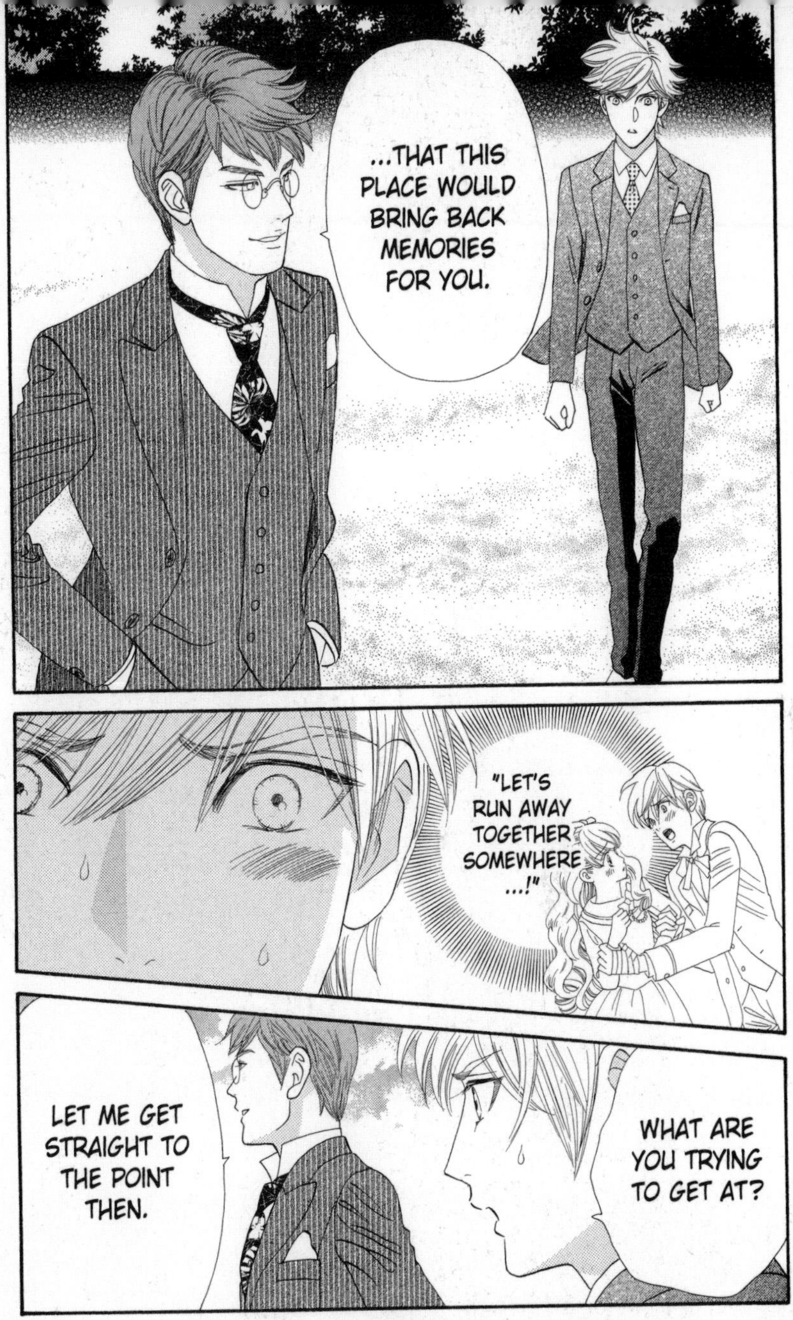
...THAT THIS PLACE WOULD BRING BACK MEMORIES FOR YOU.
"LET'S RUN AWAY TOGETHER SOMEWHERE ...!"
WHAT ARE YOU TRYING TO GET AT?
LET ME GET STRAIGHT TO THE POINT THEN.

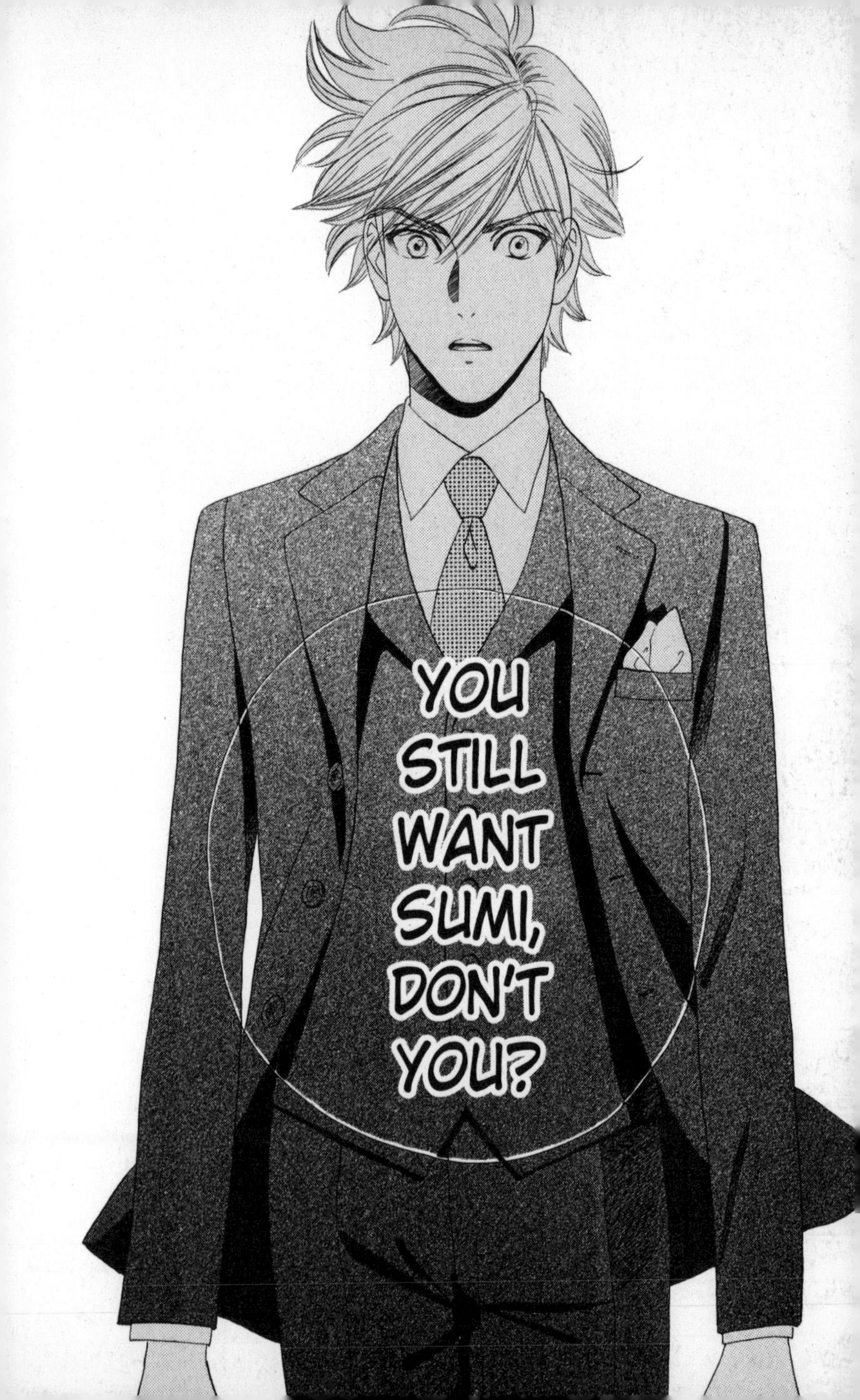
YOU STILL WANT SUMI, DON'T YOU?

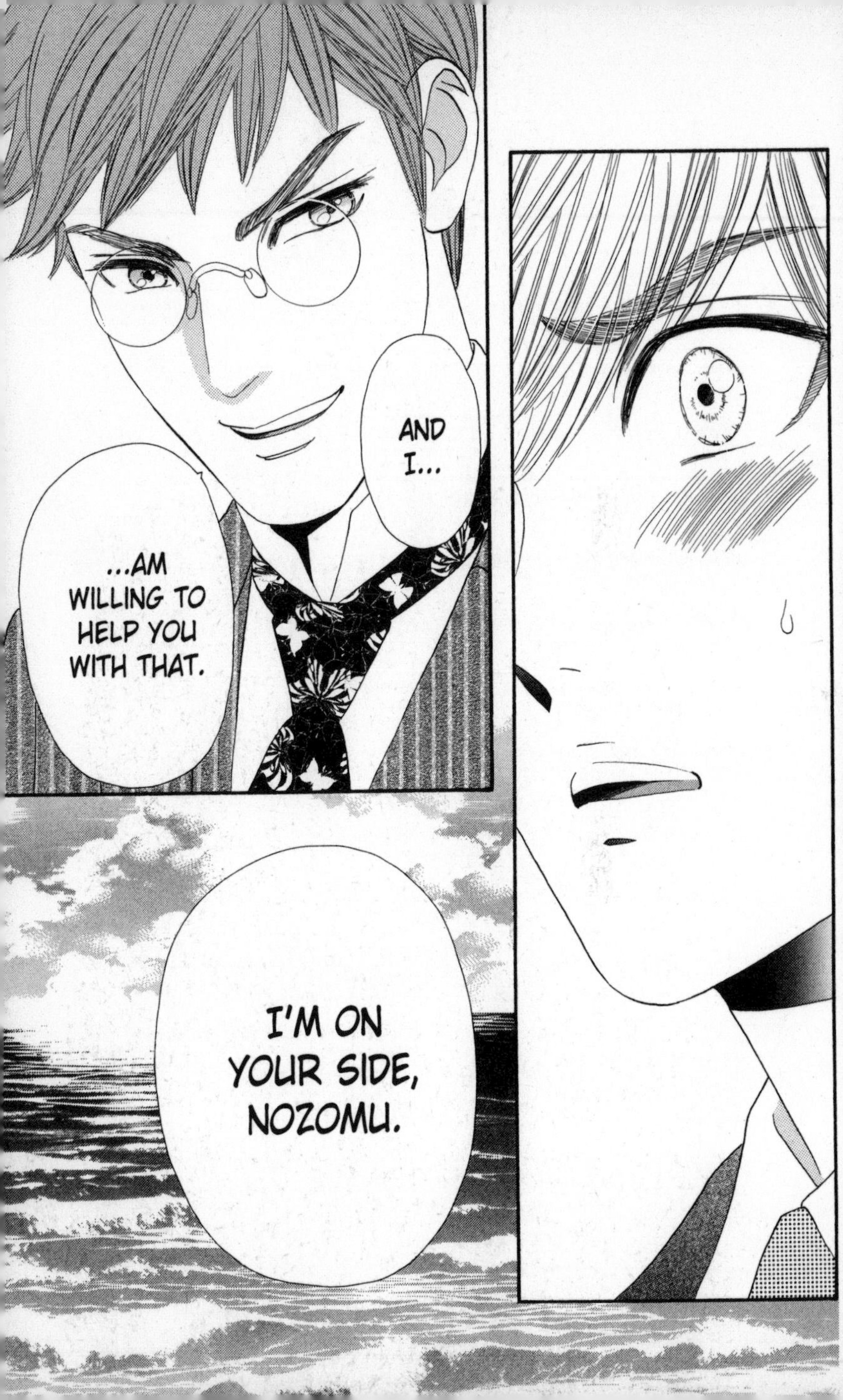
AND I...
...AM WILLING TO HELP YOU WITH THAT.
I'M ON YOUR SIDE, NOZOMU.

No.

Date .   .

�֍ IT'S BEEN A WHILE SINCE I MADE MY DEBUT AS A MANGA ARTIST, BUT EVEN NOW

WHEN I HAVE AN IMAGE INSIDE MY HEAD, ONLY 60 PERCENT OF IT COMES OUT WHEN

I DRAW IT ON PAPER. AND ONCE IT GETS PRINTED, IT GETS REDUCED TO 30 PERCENT

(SINCE THE IMAGES ARE REDUCED IN SIZE).

THERE ARE TIMES WHEN I AM SHOCKED AT NOT BEING ABLE TO EXPRESS 100 PERCENT

OF WHAT I WANT, BUT THE FAN MAIL I RECEIVE ALWAYS CHEERS ME UP. I'M GOING TO

KEEP WORKING HARD TO GET CLOSER TO THAT 100 PERCENT IMAGE INSIDE MY HEAD.

�֍ IF YOU HAVE ANY COMMENTS, PLEASE SEND THEM TO THE FOLLOWING ADDRESS:

RINKO UEDA
c/o STEPPING ON ROSES EDITOR
VIZ MEDIA
P.O. BOX 77010
SAN FRANCISCO, CA 94107

SEE YOU ALL IN VOLUME 4! ～ ♡

Rinko 😊 Ueda

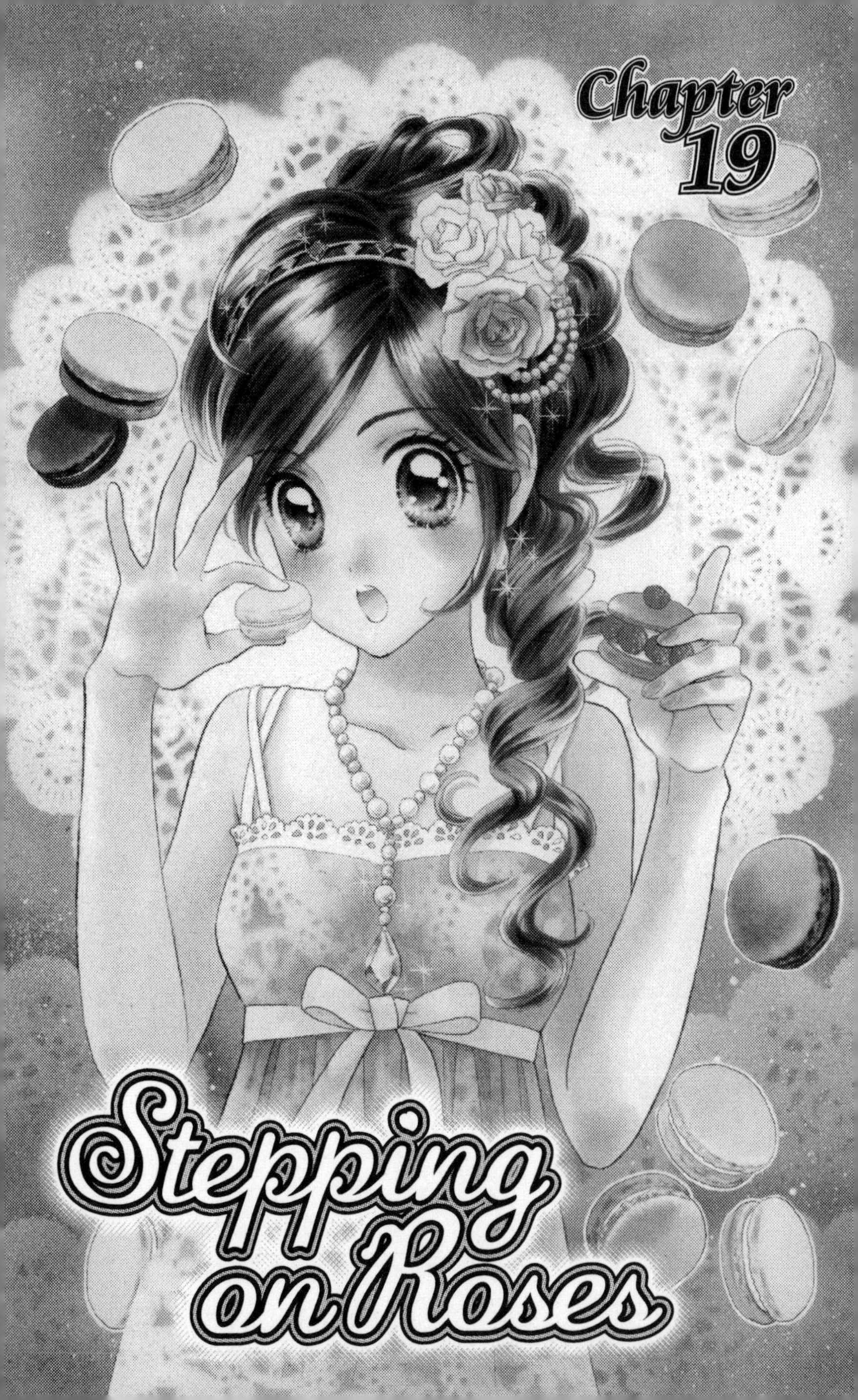
Chapter 19
Stepping on Roses

Stepping on Roses

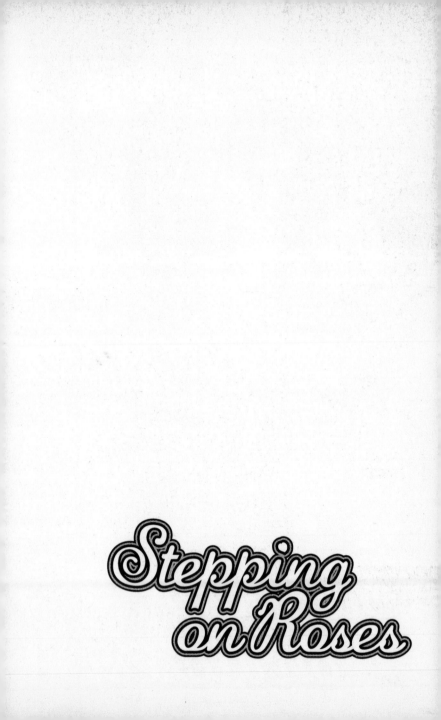

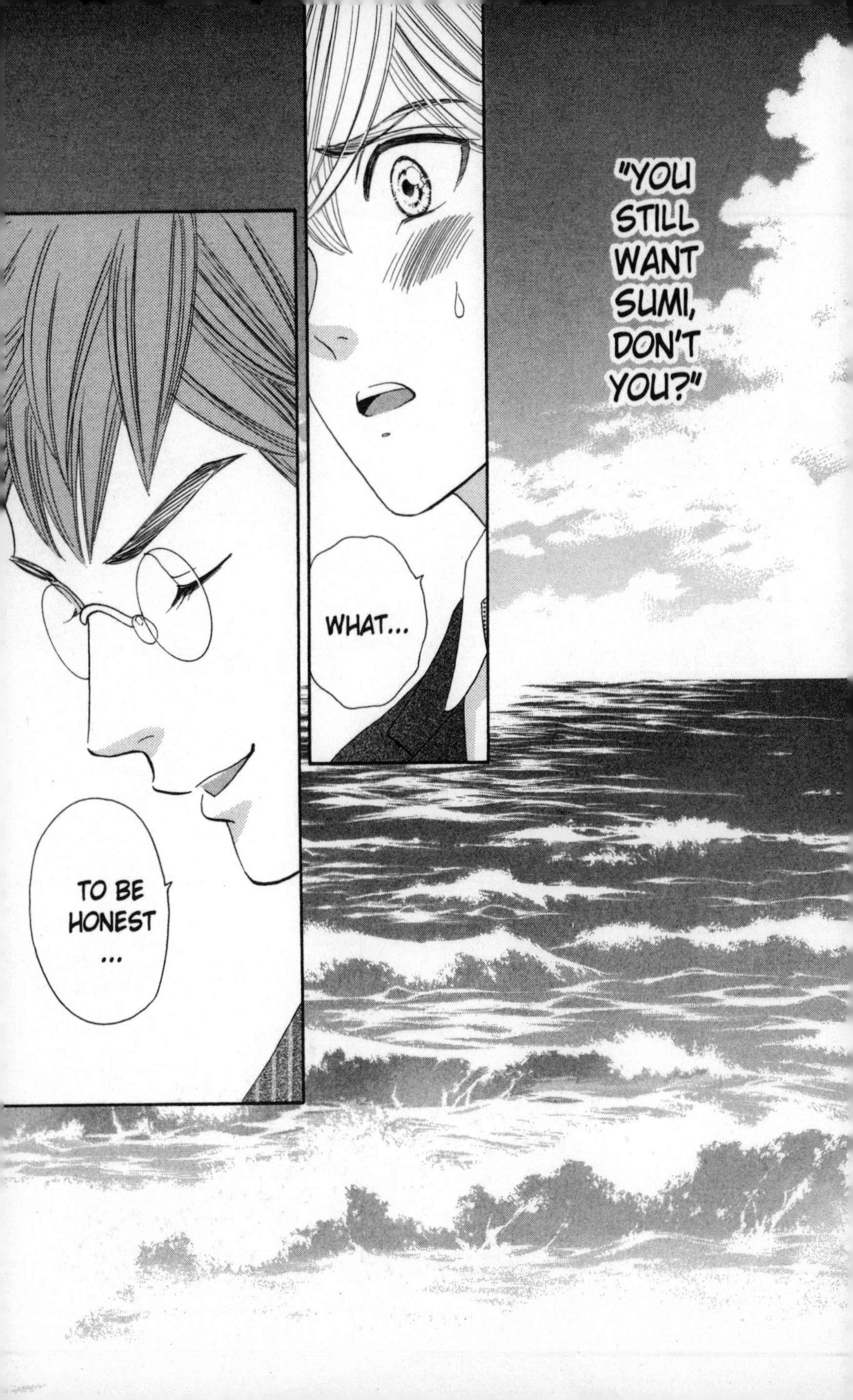
"YOU STILL WANT SUMI, DON'T YOU?"
WHAT...
TO BE HONEST ...

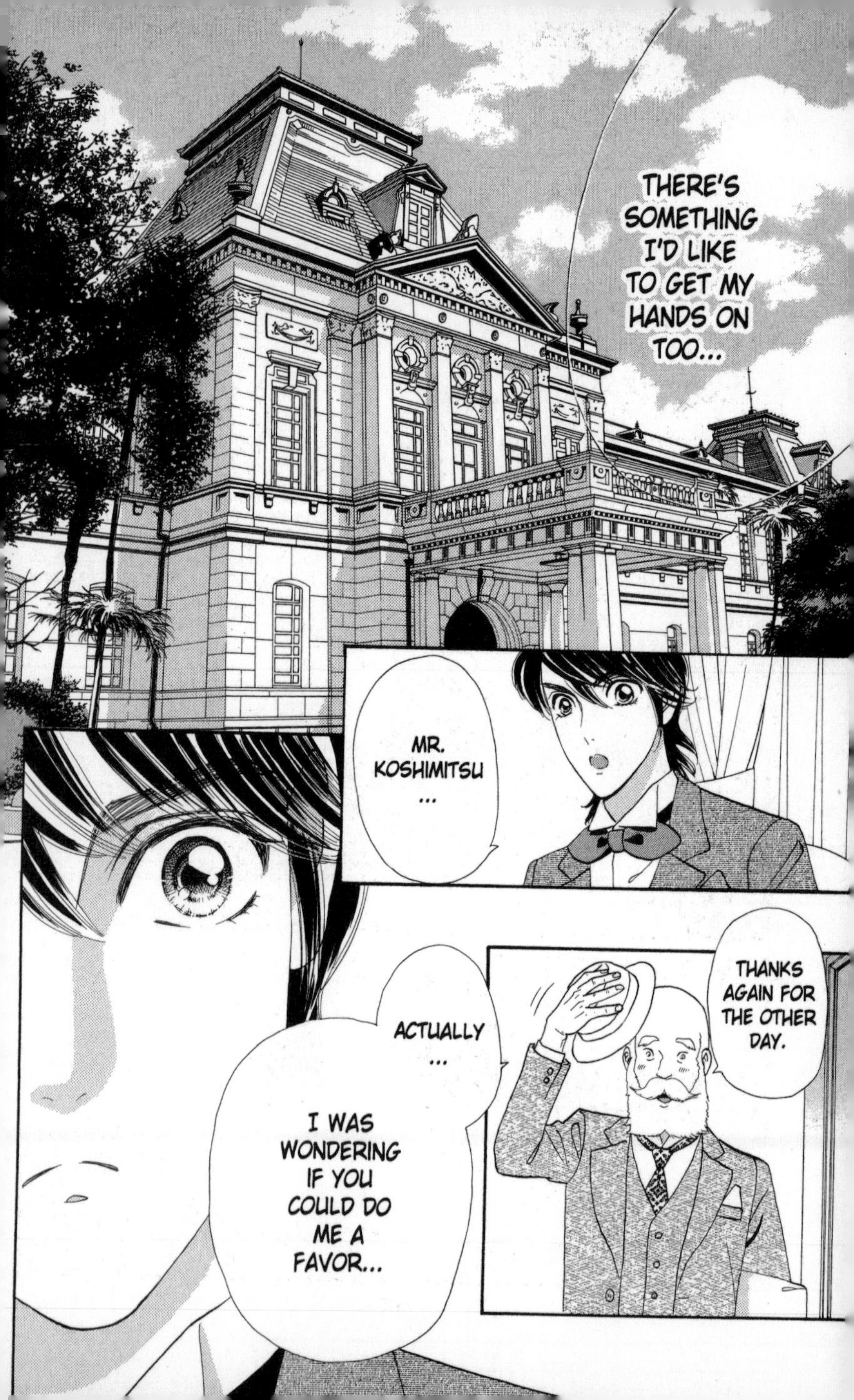
THERE'S SOMETHING I'D LIKE TO GET MY HANDS ON TOO...
MR. KOSHIMITSU ...
THANKS AGAIN FOR THE OTHER DAY.
ACTUALLY ...
I WAS WONDERING IF YOU COULD DO ME A FAVOR...

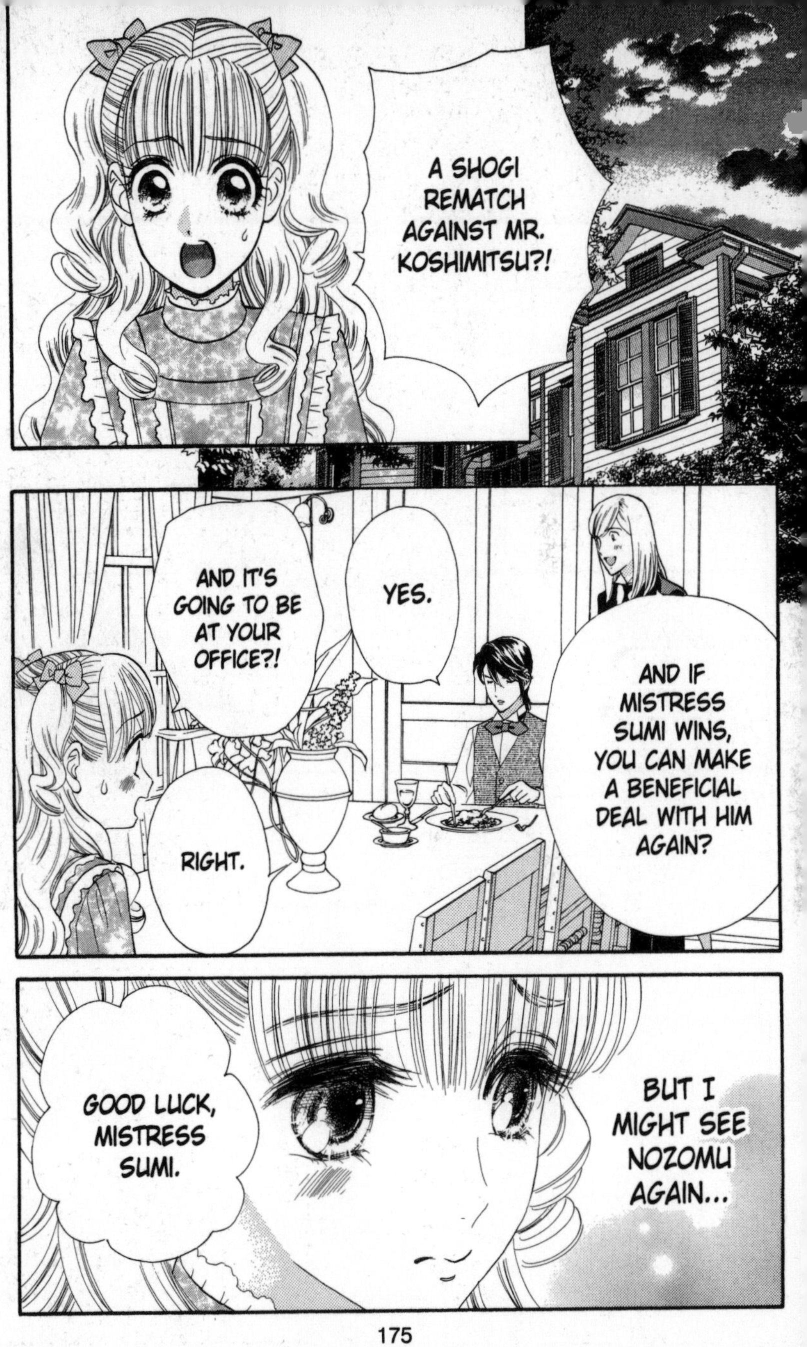
A SHOGI REMATCH AGAINST MR. KOSHIMITSU?!
AND IF MISTRESS SUMI WINS, YOU CAN MAKE A BENEFICIAL DEAL WITH HIM AGAIN?
YES.
AND IT'S GOING TO BE AT YOUR OFFICE?!
RIGHT.
BUT I MIGHT SEE NOZOMU AGAIN...
GOOD LUCK, MISTRESS SUMI.

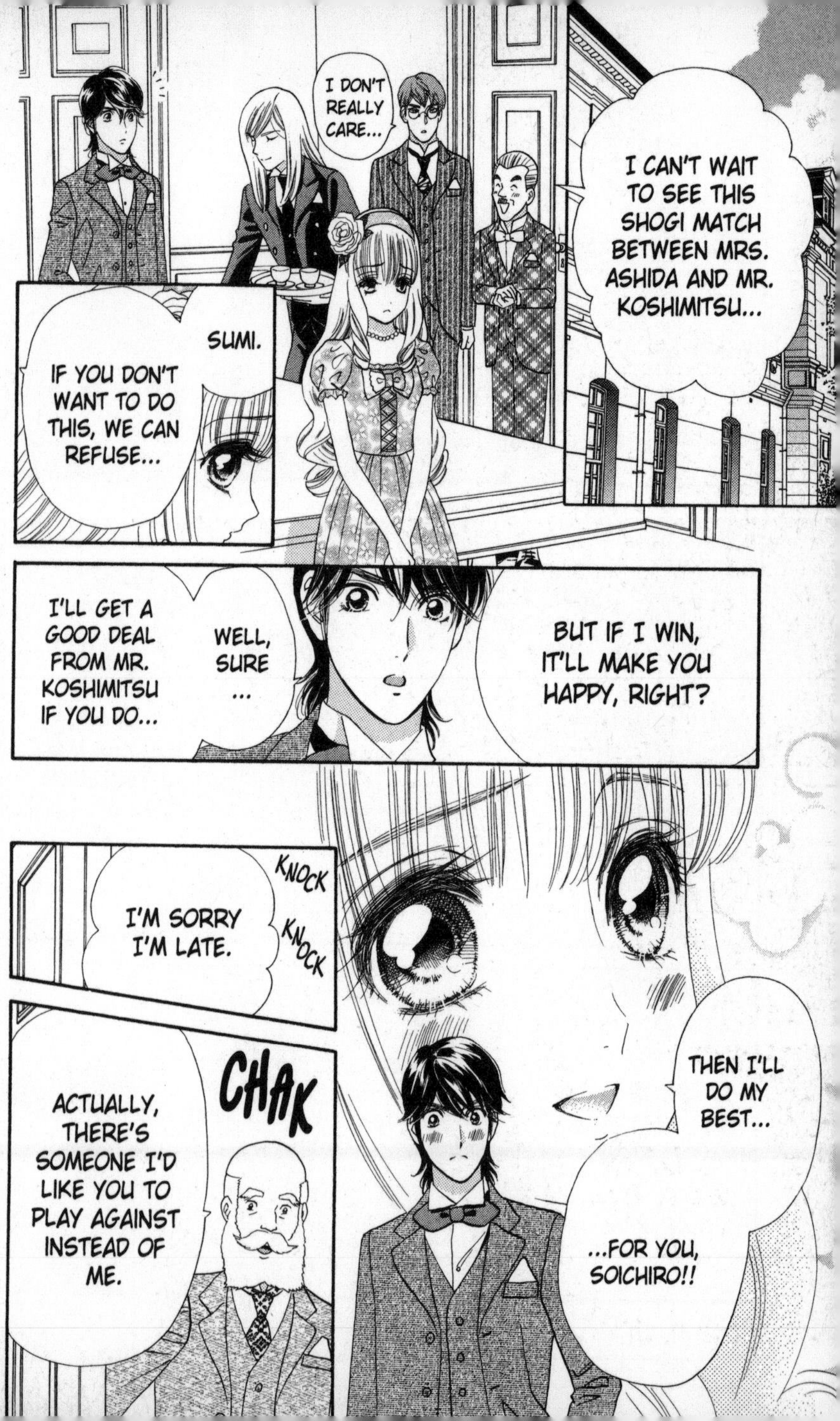
I CAN'T WAIT TO SEE THIS SHOGI MATCH BETWEEN MRS. ASHIDA AND MR. KOSHIMITSU...
I DON'T REALLY CARE...
SUMI.
IF YOU DON'T WANT TO DO THIS, WE CAN REFUSE...
BUT IF I WIN, IT'LL MAKE YOU HAPPY, RIGHT?
WELL, SURE ...
I'LL GET A GOOD DEAL FROM MR. KOSHIMITSU IF YOU DO...
THEN I'LL DO MY BEST...
...FOR YOU, SOICHIRO!!
KNOCK
KNOCK
I'M SORRY I'M LATE.
CHAK
ACTUALLY, THERE'S SOMEONE I'D LIKE YOU TO PLAY AGAINST INSTEAD OF ME.

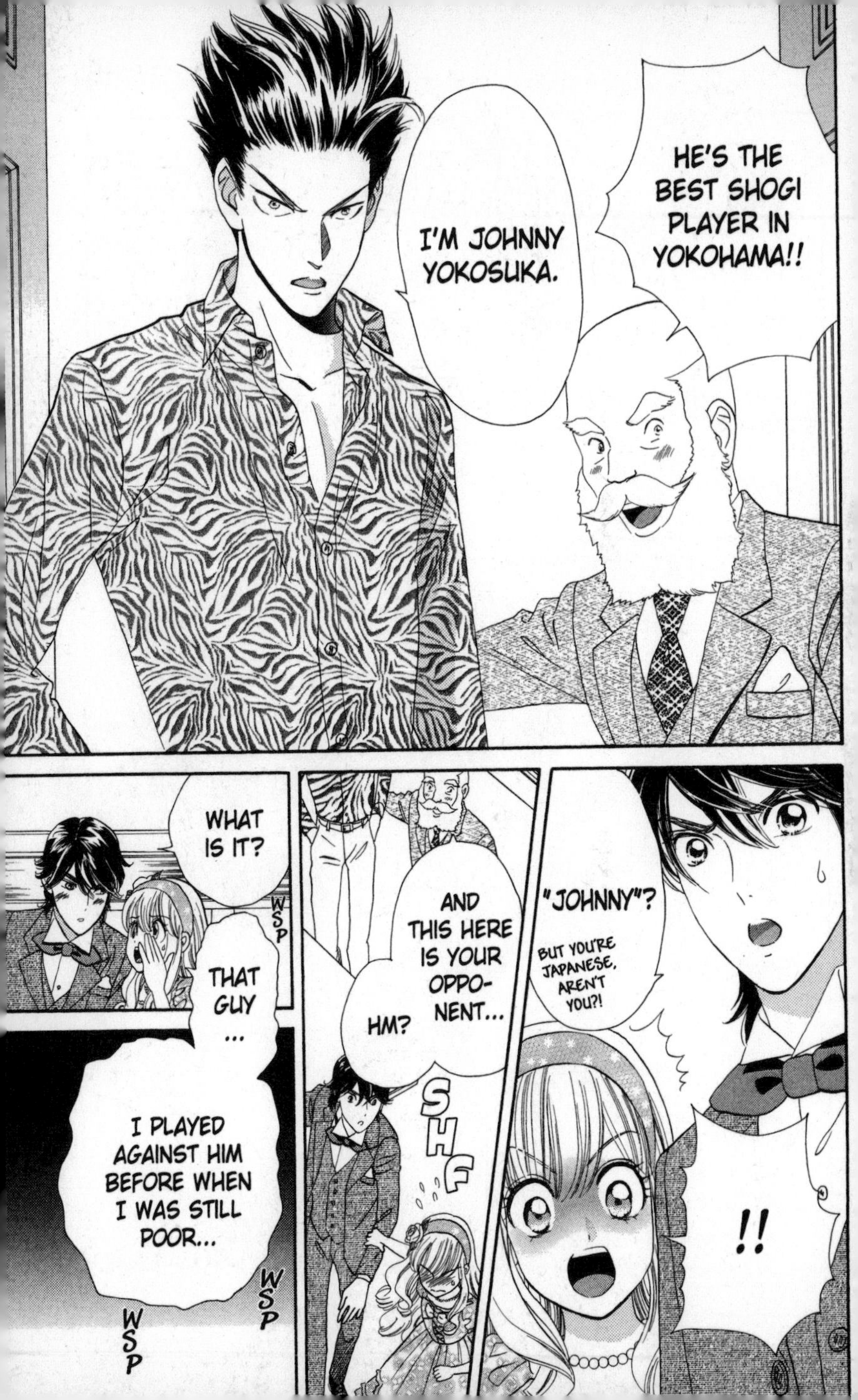
HE'S THE BEST SHOGI PLAYER IN YOKOHAMA!!
I'M JOHNNY YOKOSUKA.
"JOHNNY"?
BUT YOU'RE JAPANESE, AREN'T YOU?!
!!
AND THIS HERE IS YOUR OPPO-NENT...
HM?
SHF
WHAT IS IT?
WSP
THAT GUY...
I PLAYED AGAINST HIM BEFORE WHEN I WAS STILL POOR...
WSP
WSP

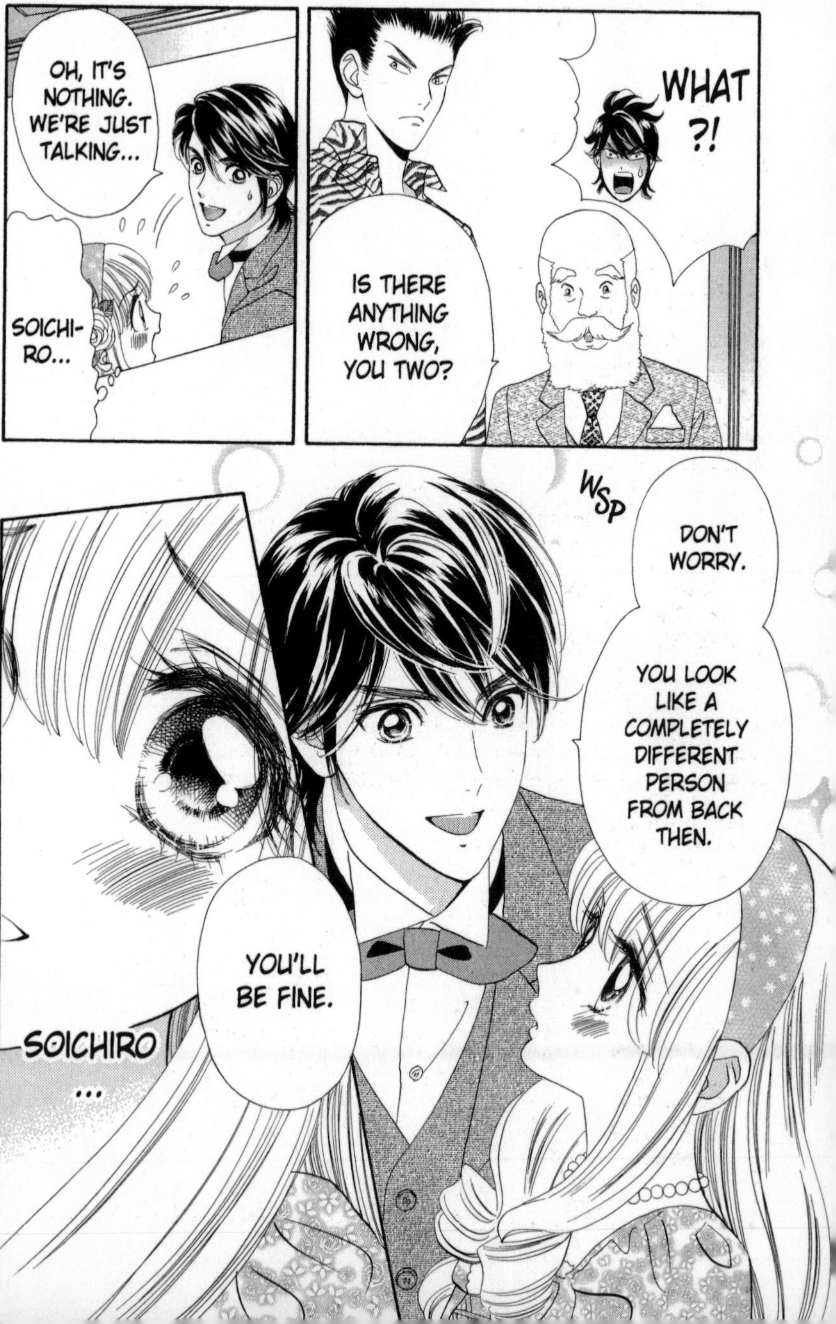
WHAT ?!
IS THERE ANYTHING WRONG, YOU TWO?
OH, IT'S NOTHING. WE'RE JUST TALKING...
SOICHI-RO...
WSP
DON'T WORRY.
YOU LOOK LIKE A COMPLETELY DIFFERENT PERSON FROM BACK THEN.
YOU'LL BE FINE.
SOICHIRO ...

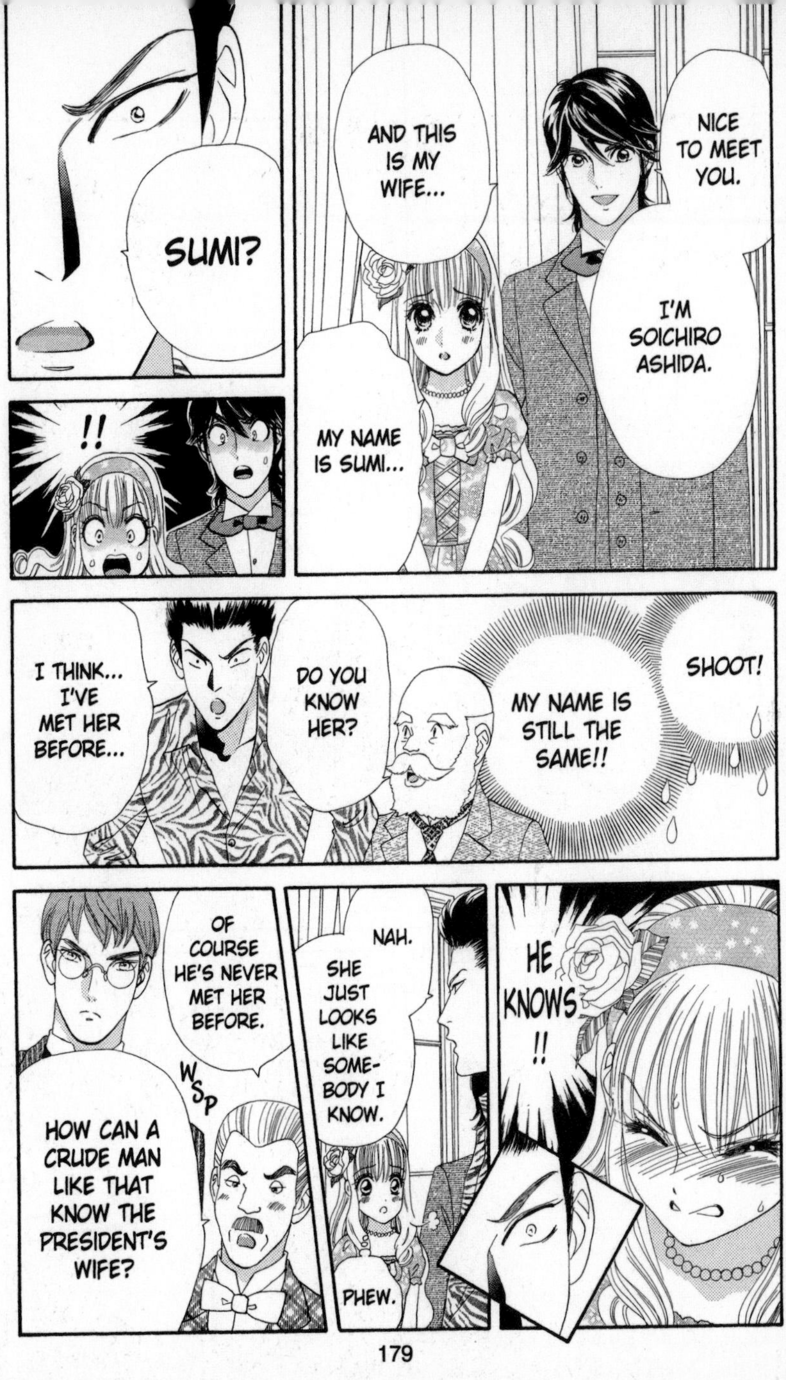
NICE TO MEET YOU.
I'M SOICHIRO ASHIDA.
AND THIS IS MY WIFE...
MY NAME IS SUMI...
SUMI?
!!
SHOOT!
MY NAME IS STILL THE SAME!!
DO YOU KNOW HER?
I THINK... I'VE MET HER BEFORE...
HE KNOWS!!
NAH.
SHE JUST LOOKS LIKE SOME-BODY I KNOW.
PHEW.
OF COURSE HE'S NEVER MET HER BEFORE.
WSP
HOW CAN A CRUDE MAN LIKE THAT KNOW THE PRESIDENT'S WIFE?

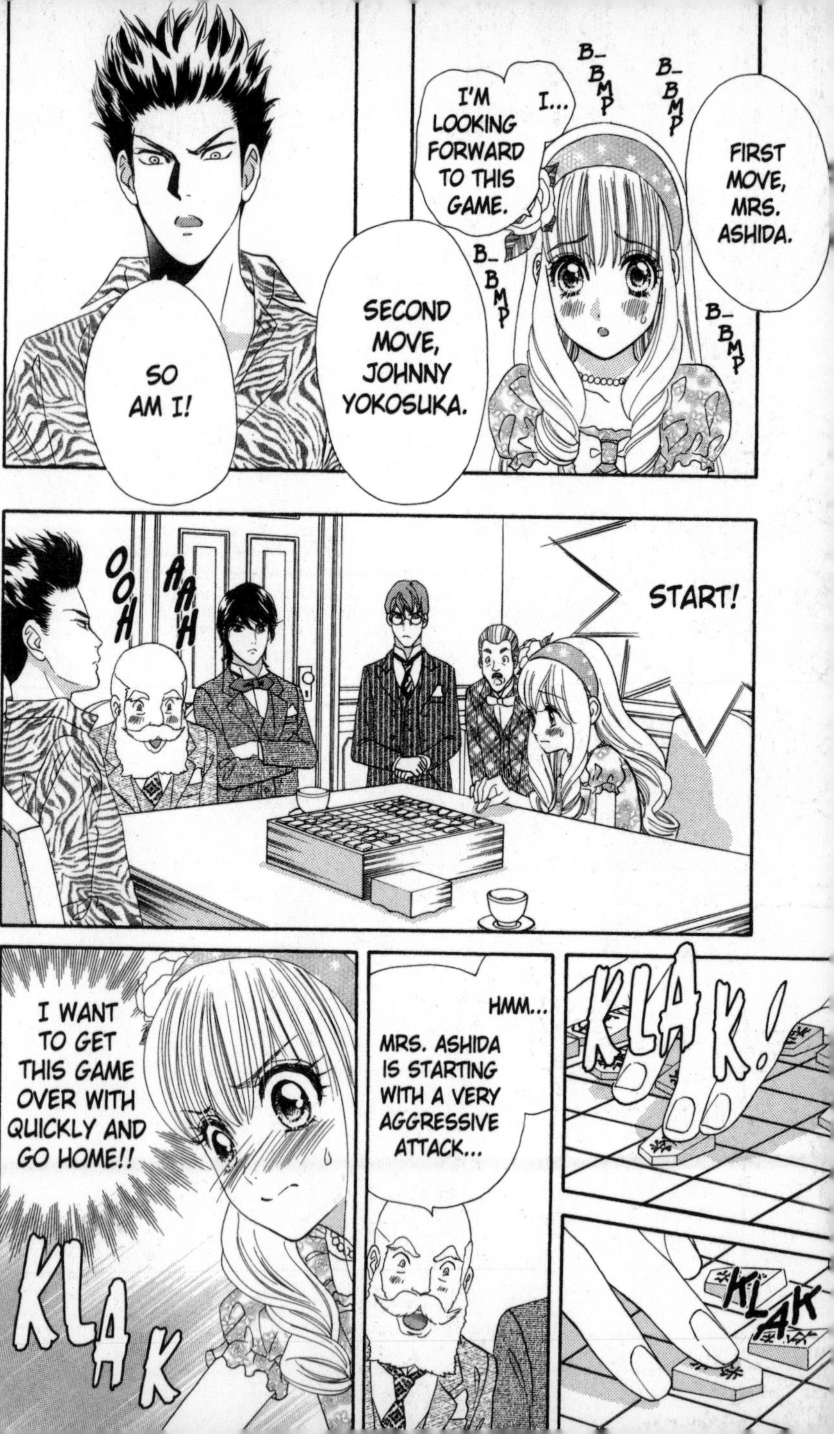
FIRST MOVE, MRS. ASHIDA.
B_BMP
B_BMP
I...
I'M LOOKING FORWARD TO THIS GAME.
B_BMP
B_BMP
SECOND MOVE, JOHNNY YOKOSUKA.
SO AM I!
START!
AAH
OOH
KLAK!
KLAK
HMM...
MRS. ASHIDA IS STARTING WITH A VERY AGGRESSIVE ATTACK...
I WANT TO GET THIS GAME OVER WITH QUICKLY AND GO HOME!!
KLAK

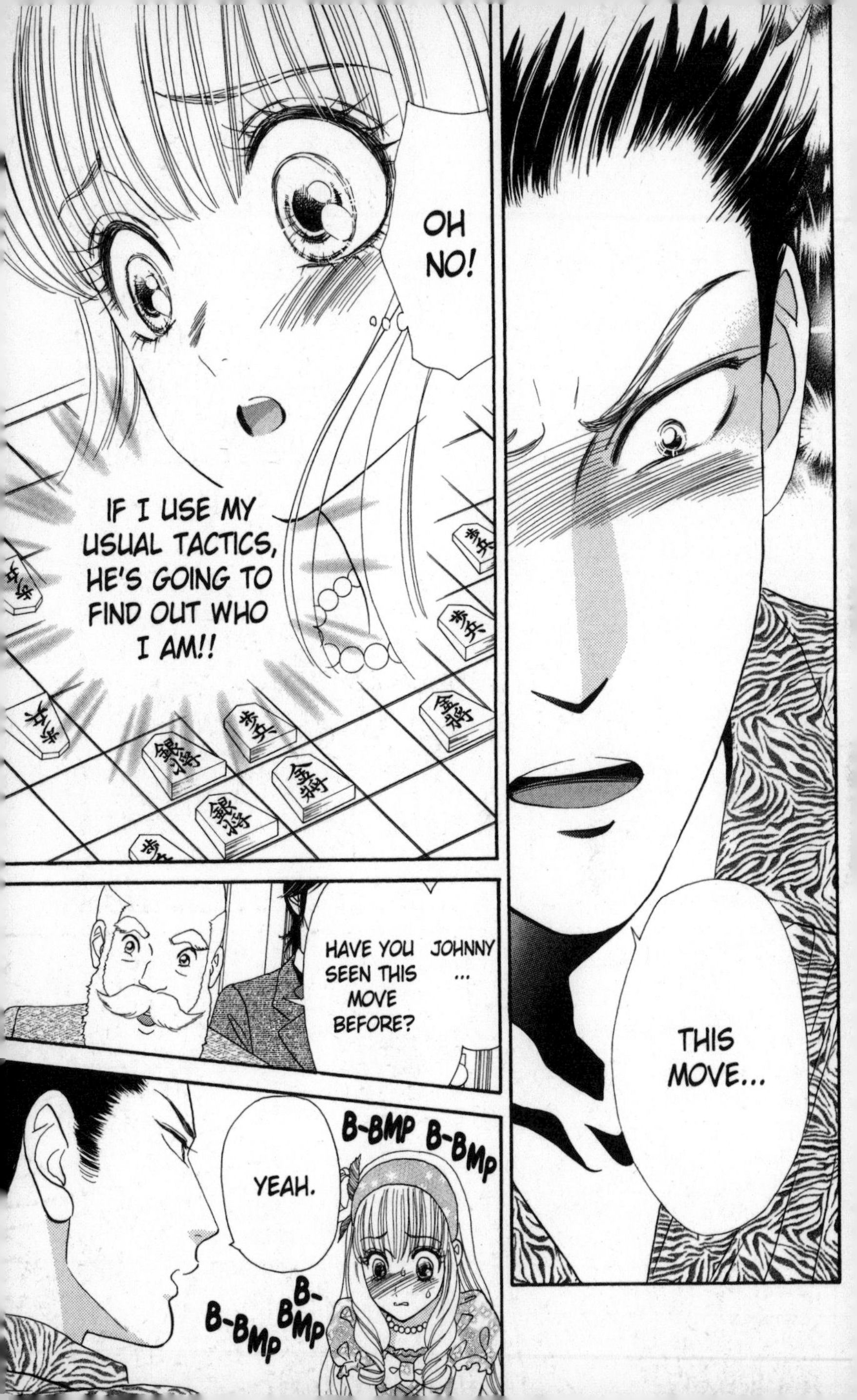

THIS MOVE...
OH NO!
IF I USE MY USUAL TACTICS, HE'S GOING TO FIND OUT WHO I AM!!
JOHNNY ...
HAVE YOU SEEN THIS MOVE BEFORE?
B-BMP B-BMP
YEAH.
B-BMP B-BMP

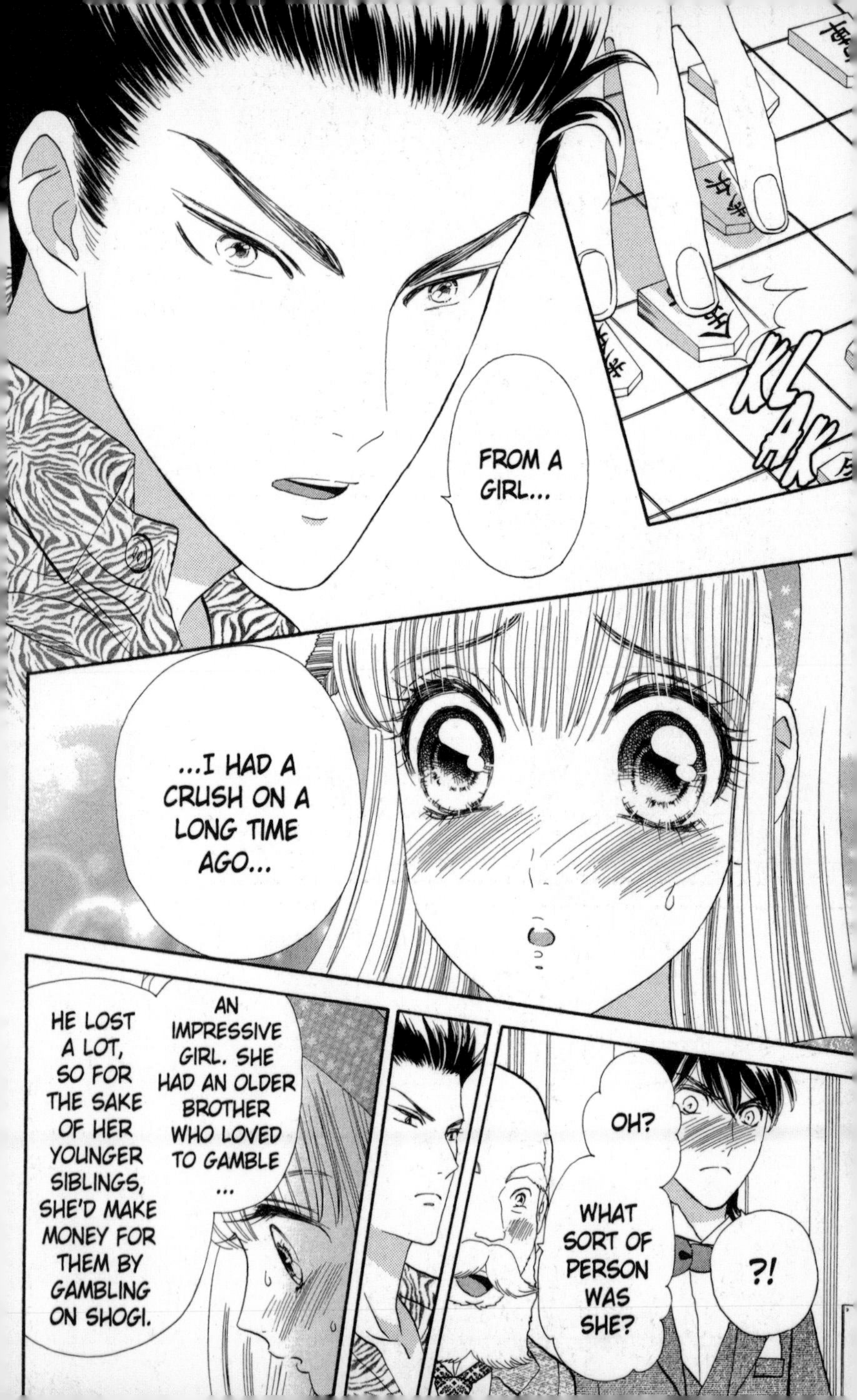
KLAK
FROM A GIRL...
...I HAD A CRUSH ON A LONG TIME AGO...
OH?
WHAT SORT OF PERSON WAS SHE?
?!
AN IMPRESSIVE GIRL. SHE HAD AN OLDER BROTHER WHO LOVED TO GAMBLE...
HE LOST A LOT, SO FOR THE SAKE OF HER YOUNGER SIBLINGS, SHE'D MAKE MONEY FOR THEM BY GAMBLING ON SHOGI.

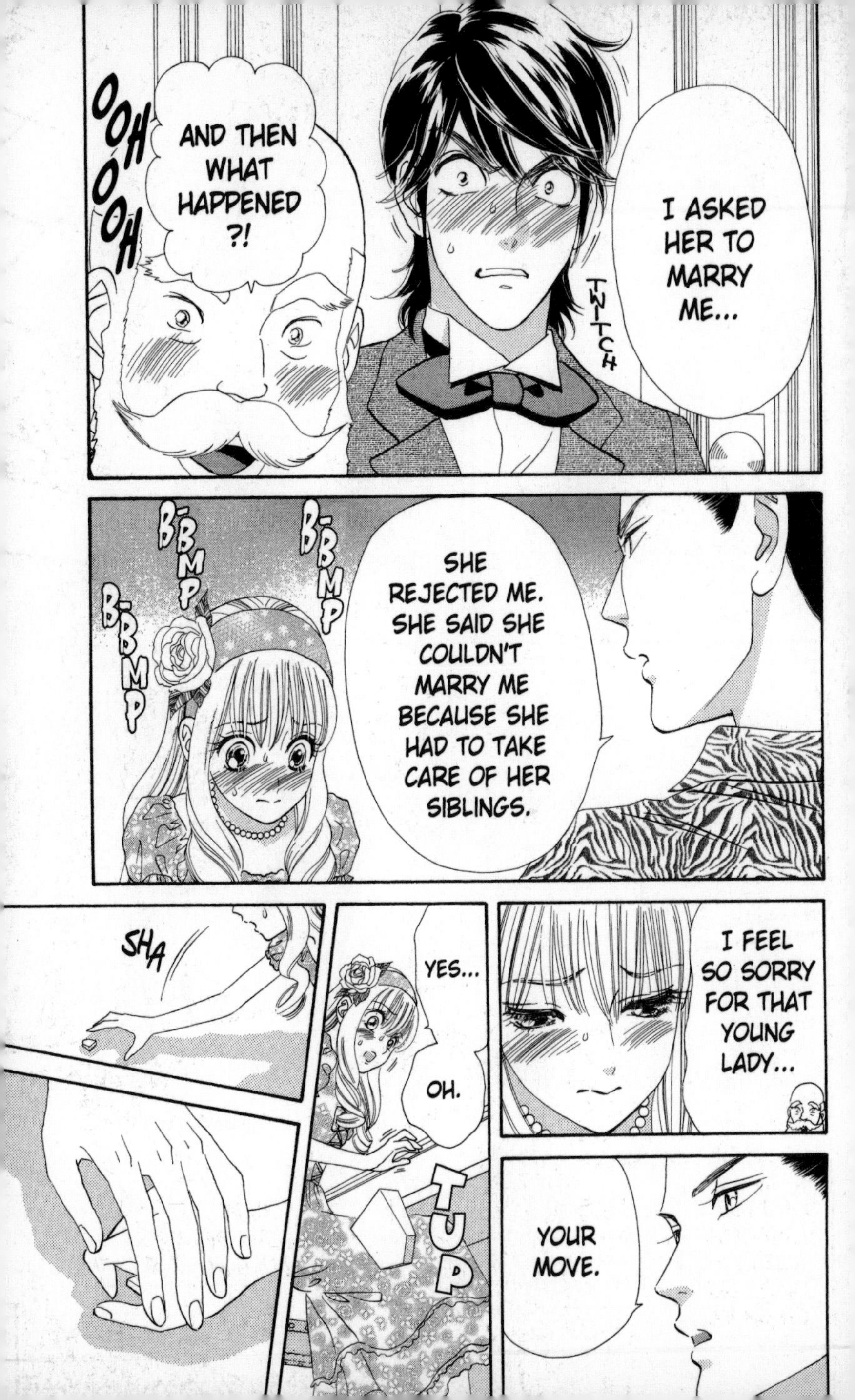
I ASKED HER TO MARRY ME...
TWITCH
AND THEN WHAT HAPPENED ?!
OOH OOH OOH
SHE REJECTED ME. SHE SAID SHE COULDN'T MARRY ME BECAUSE SHE HAD TO TAKE CARE OF HER SIBLINGS.
B-BMP
B-BMP
B-BMP
I FEEL SO SORRY FOR THAT YOUNG LADY...
YOUR MOVE.
YES...
OH.
TUP
SHA

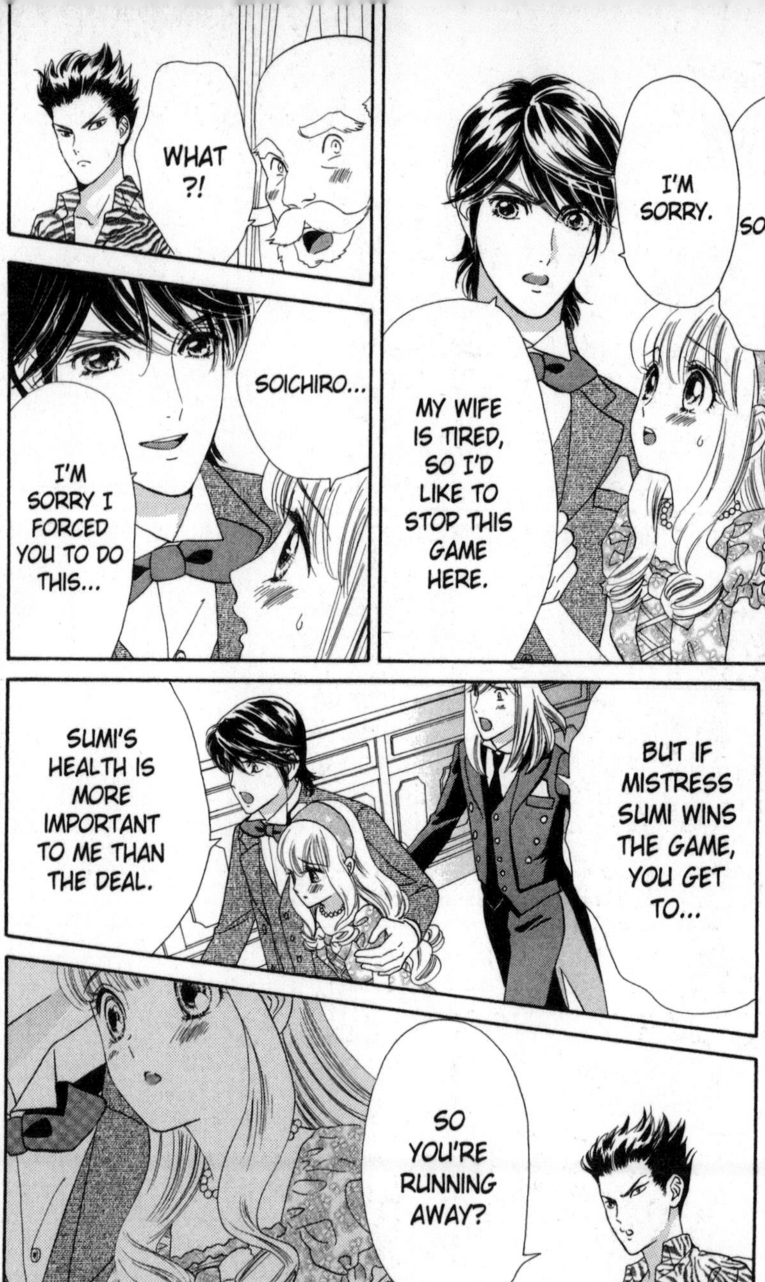
SOICHIRO ...
I'M SORRY.
MY WIFE IS TIRED, SO I'D LIKE TO STOP THIS GAME HERE.
WHAT ?!
SOICHIRO...
I'M SORRY I FORCED YOU TO DO THIS...
BUT IF MISTRESS SUMI WINS THE GAME, YOU GET TO...
SUMI'S HEALTH IS MORE IMPORTANT TO ME THAN THE DEAL.
SO YOU'RE RUNNING AWAY?

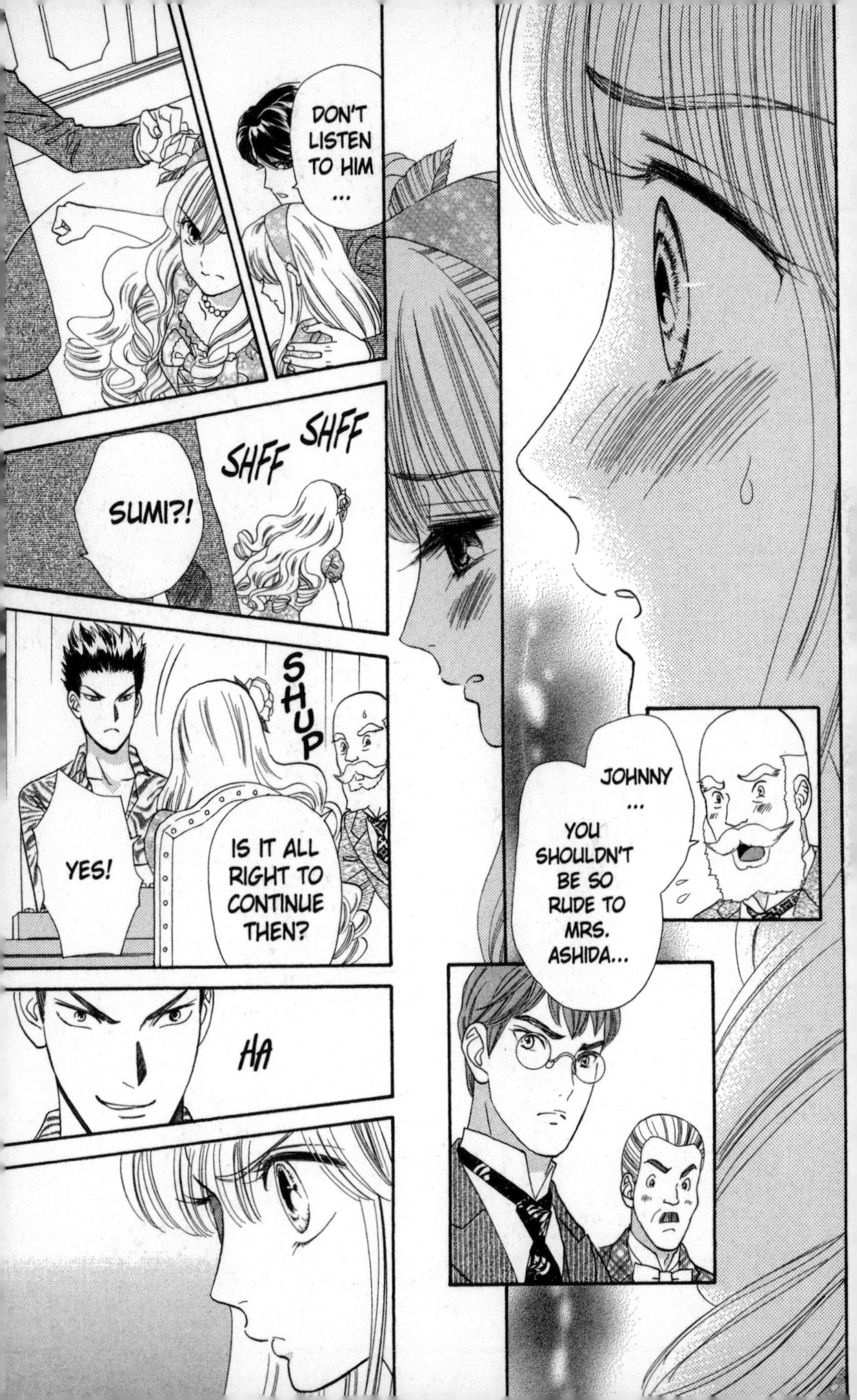
JOHNNY ... YOU SHOULDN'T BE SO RUDE TO MRS. ASHIDA...
DON'T LISTEN TO HIM ...
SHFF SHFF
SUMI?!
SHUP
IS IT ALL RIGHT TO CONTINUE THEN?
YES!
HA

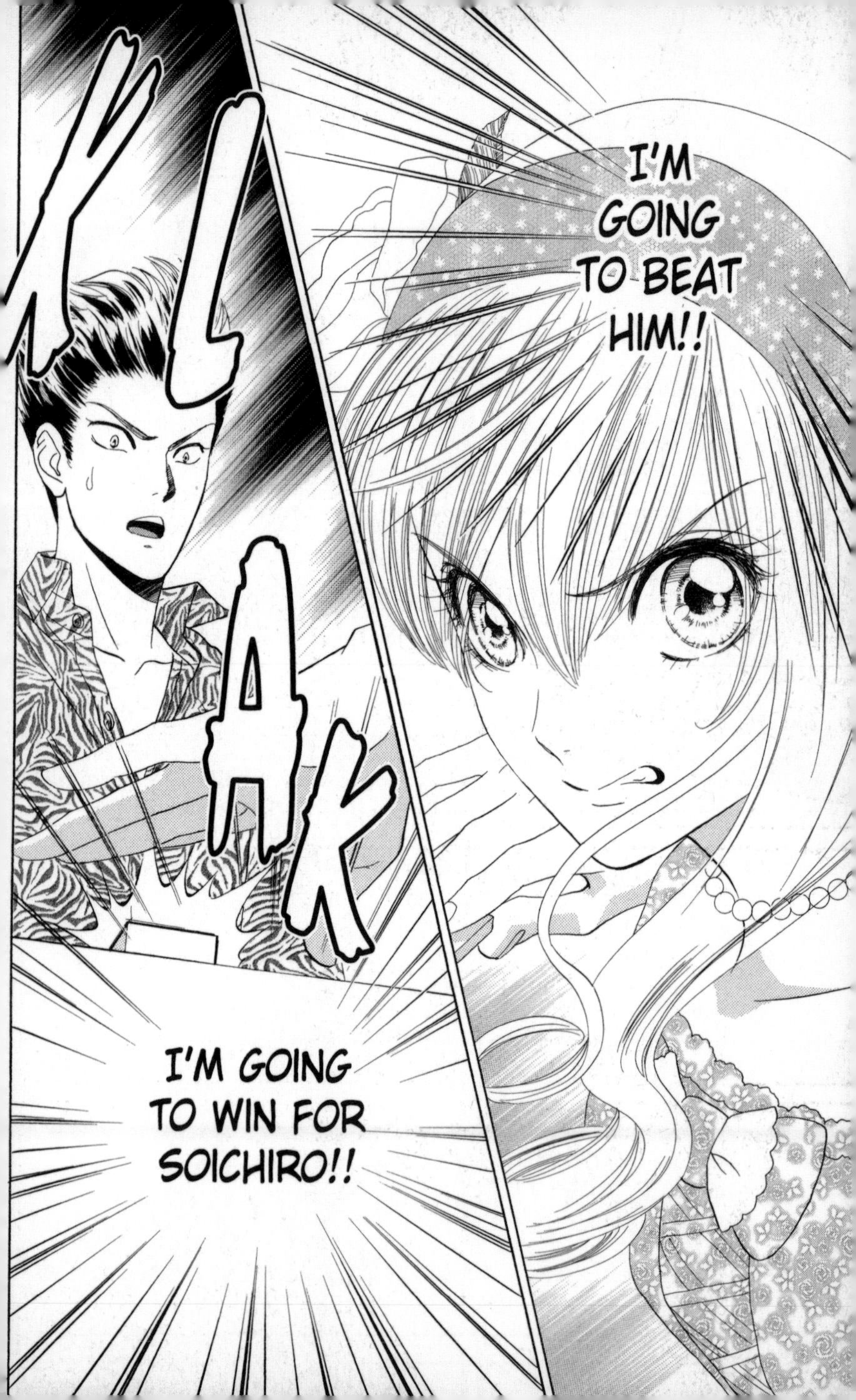
I'M GOING TO BEAT HIM!!
I'M GOING TO WIN FOR SOICHIRO!!

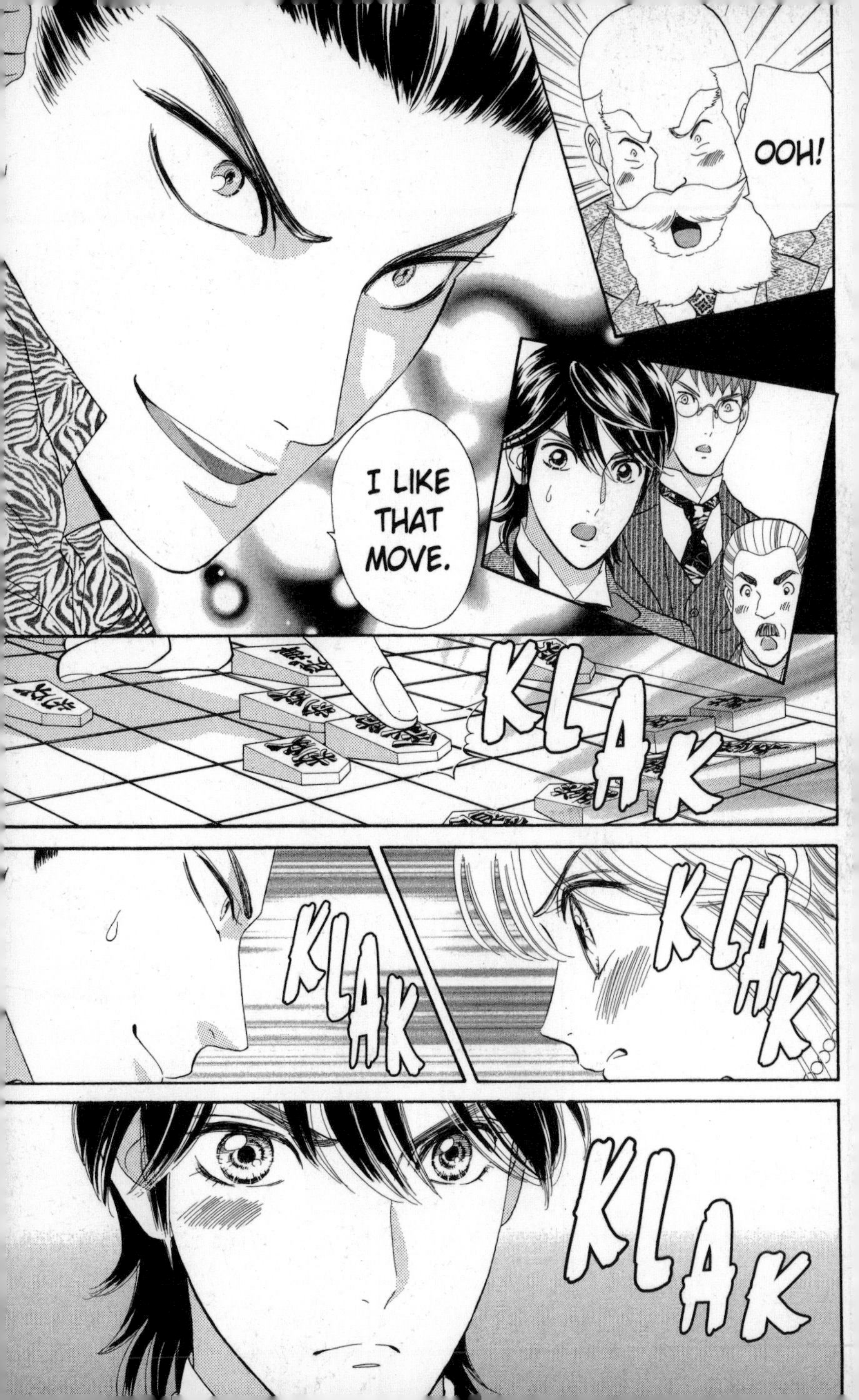
OOH!
I LIKE THAT MOVE.
KLAK
KLAK
KLAK
KLAK

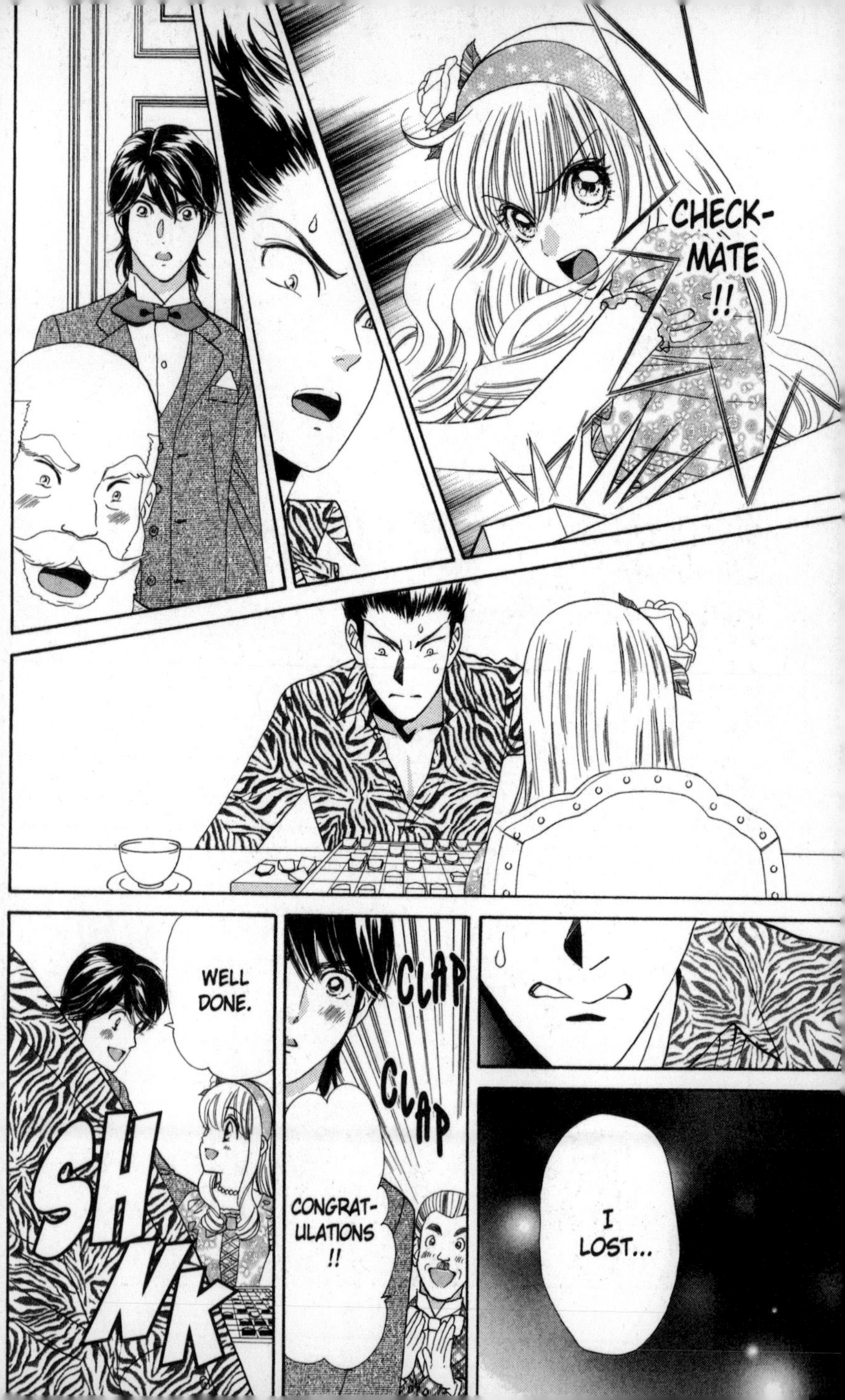
CHECK-MATE !!
I LOST...
CLAP CLAP
CONGRAT-ULATIONS !!
WELL DONE.
SHNK

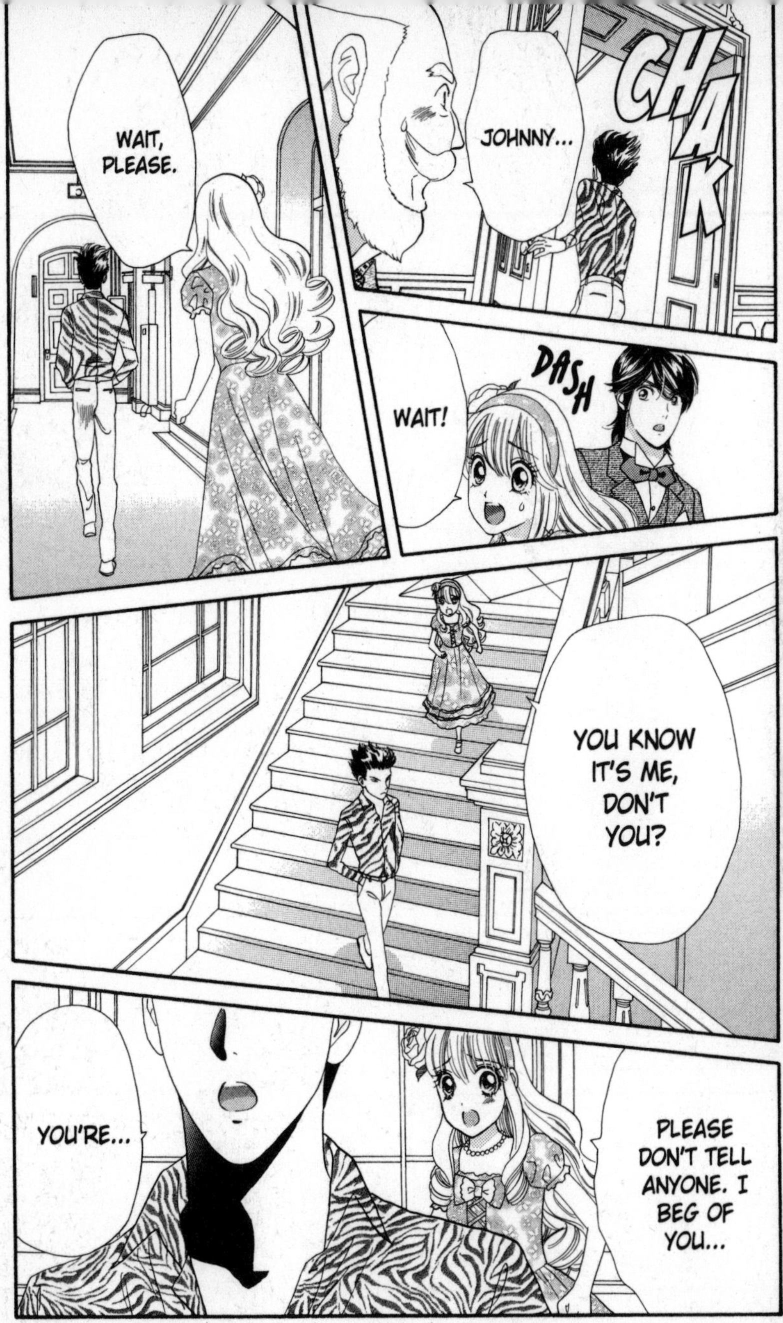
CHAK
JOHNNY...
DASH
WAIT!
WAIT, PLEASE.
YOU KNOW IT'S ME, DON'T YOU?
PLEASE DON'T TELL ANYONE. I BEG OF YOU...
YOU'RE...

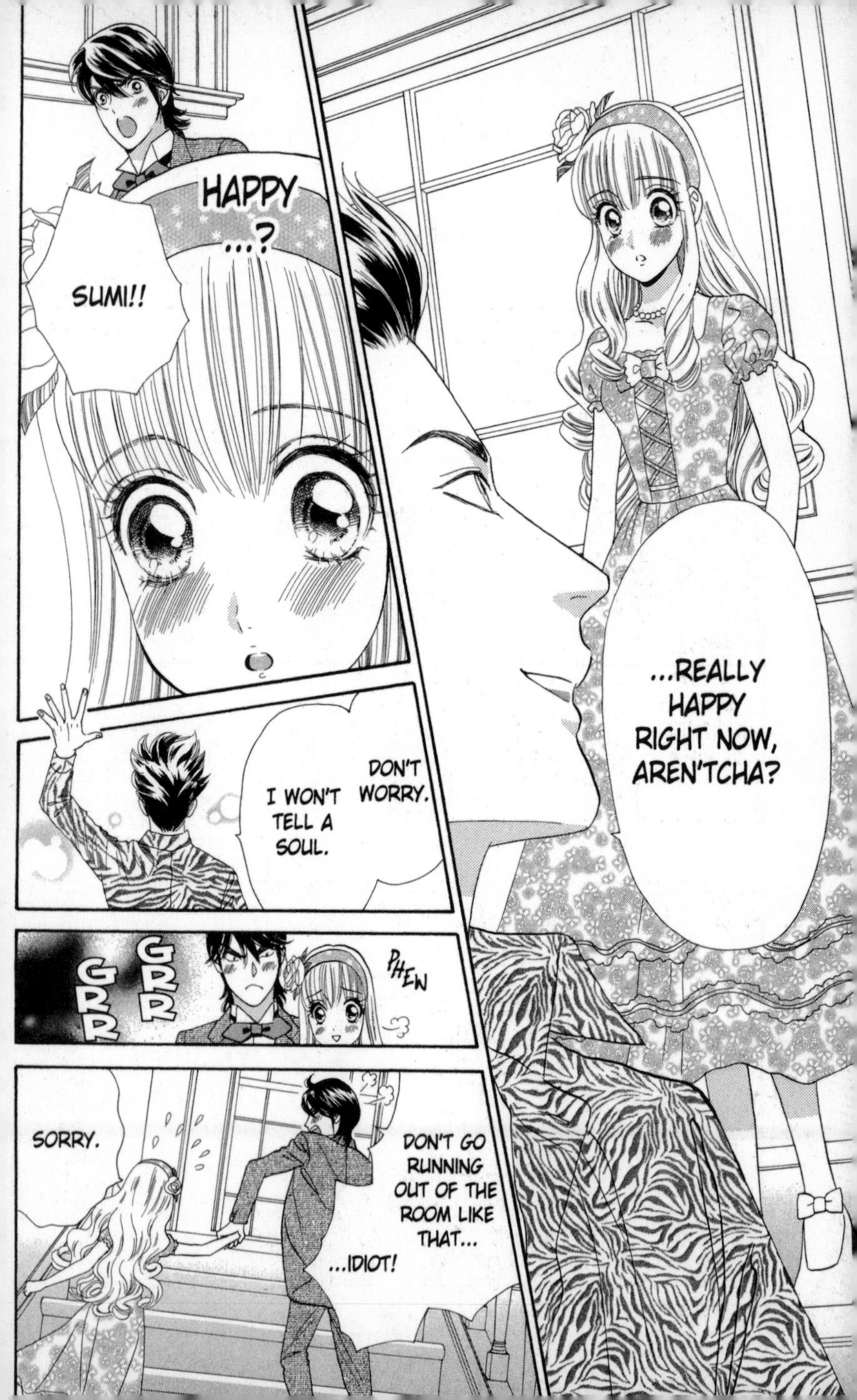
...REALLY HAPPY RIGHT NOW, AREN'TCHA?
HAPPY ...?
SUMI!!
DON'T WORRY.
I WON'T TELL A SOUL.
GRR GRR
PHEW
DON'T GO RUNNING OUT OF THE ROOM LIKE THAT...
...IDIOT!
SORRY.

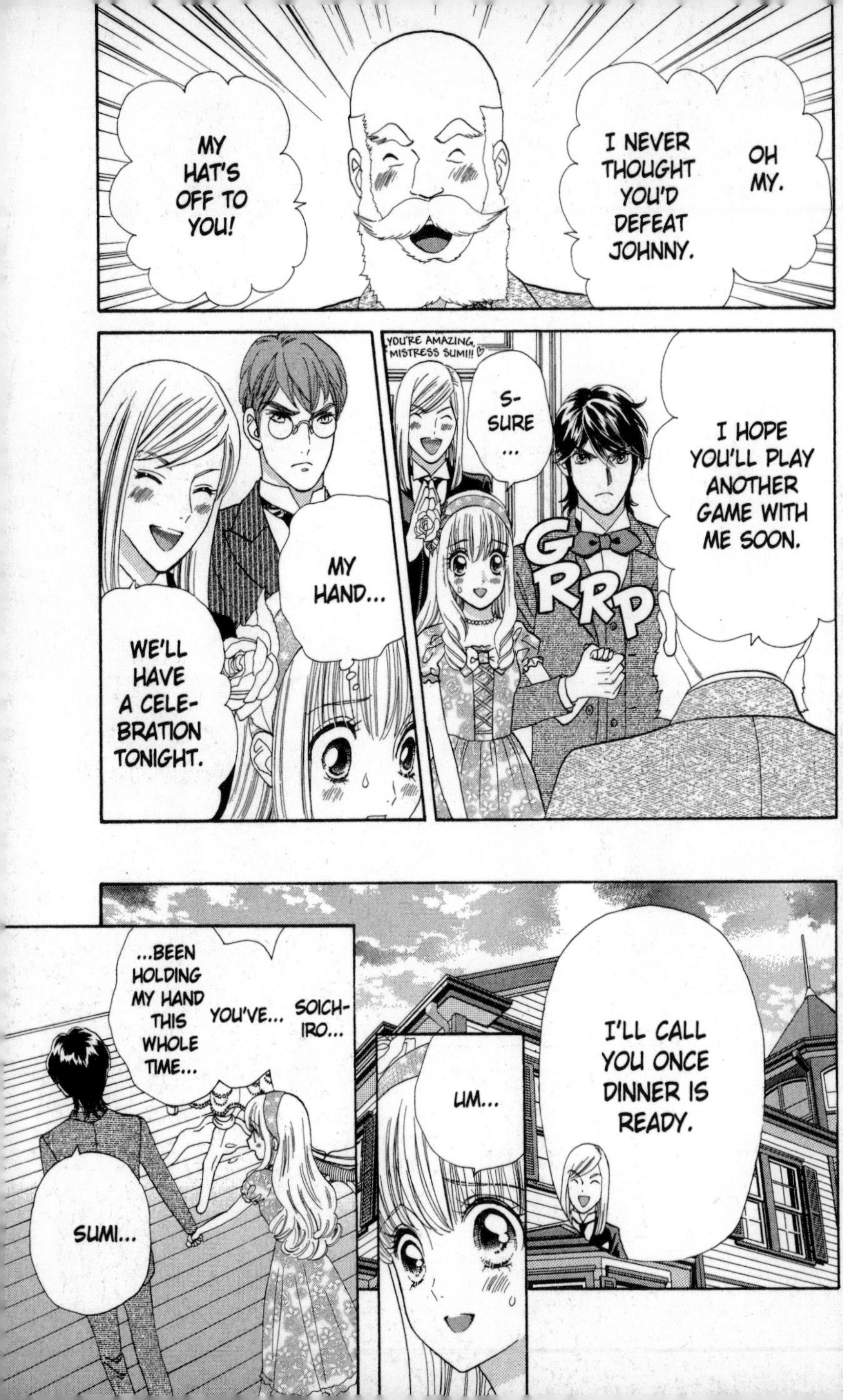
OH MY.
I NEVER THOUGHT YOU'D DEFEAT JOHNNY.
MY HAT'S OFF TO YOU!
I HOPE YOU'LL PLAY ANOTHER GAME WITH ME SOON.
S-SURE ...
YOU'RE AMAZING, MISTRESS SUMI!!
GRRP
MY HAND...
WE'LL HAVE A CELEBRATION TONIGHT.
I'LL CALL YOU ONCE DINNER IS READY.
UM...
SOICHIRO...
YOU'VE...
...BEEN HOLDING MY HAND THIS WHOLE TIME...
SUMI...

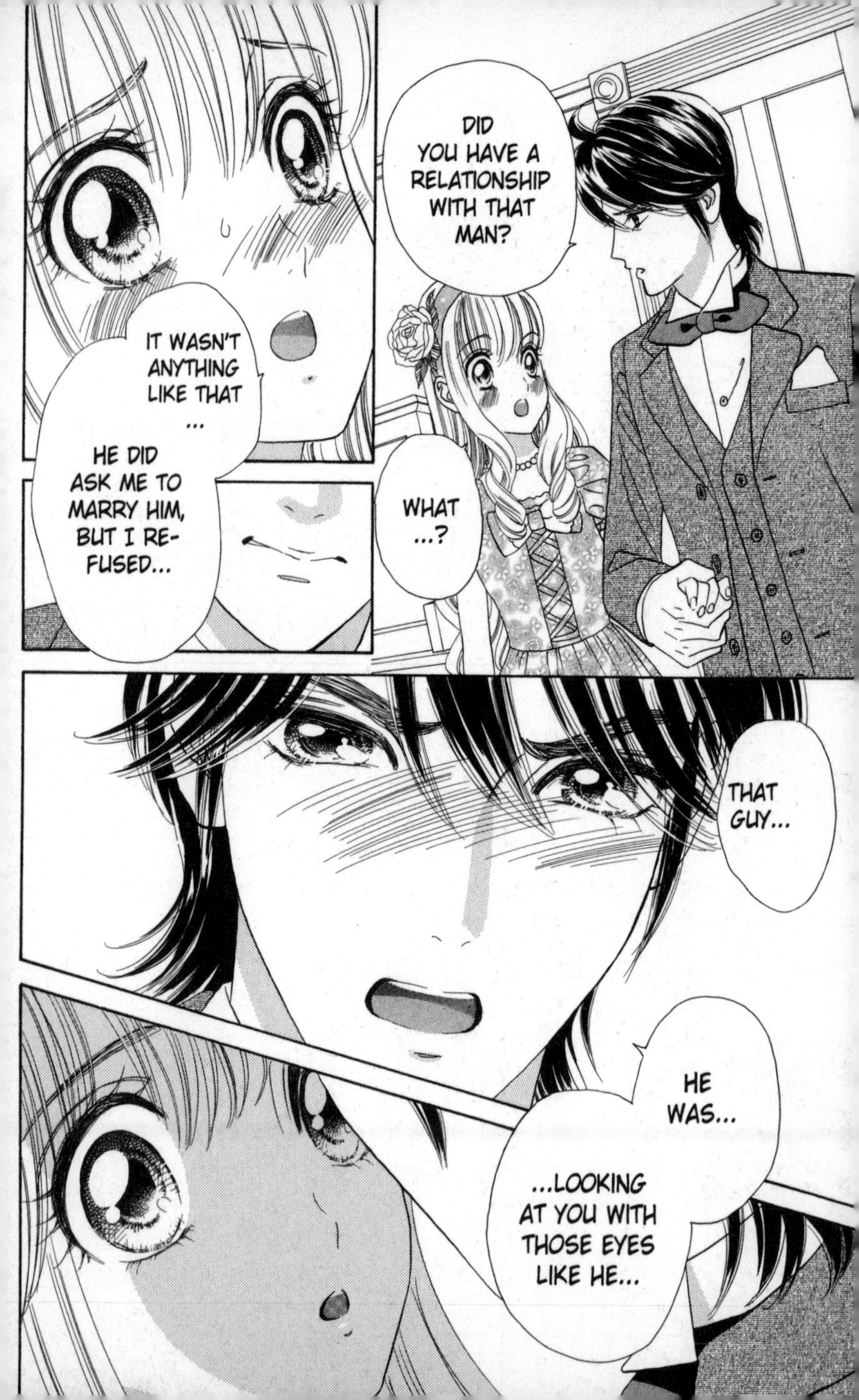
DID YOU HAVE A RELATIONSHIP WITH THAT MAN?
WHAT ...?
IT WASN'T ANYTHING LIKE THAT ...
HE DID ASK ME TO MARRY HIM, BUT I RE-FUSED...
THAT GUY...
HE WAS...
...LOOKING AT YOU WITH THOSE EYES LIKE HE...

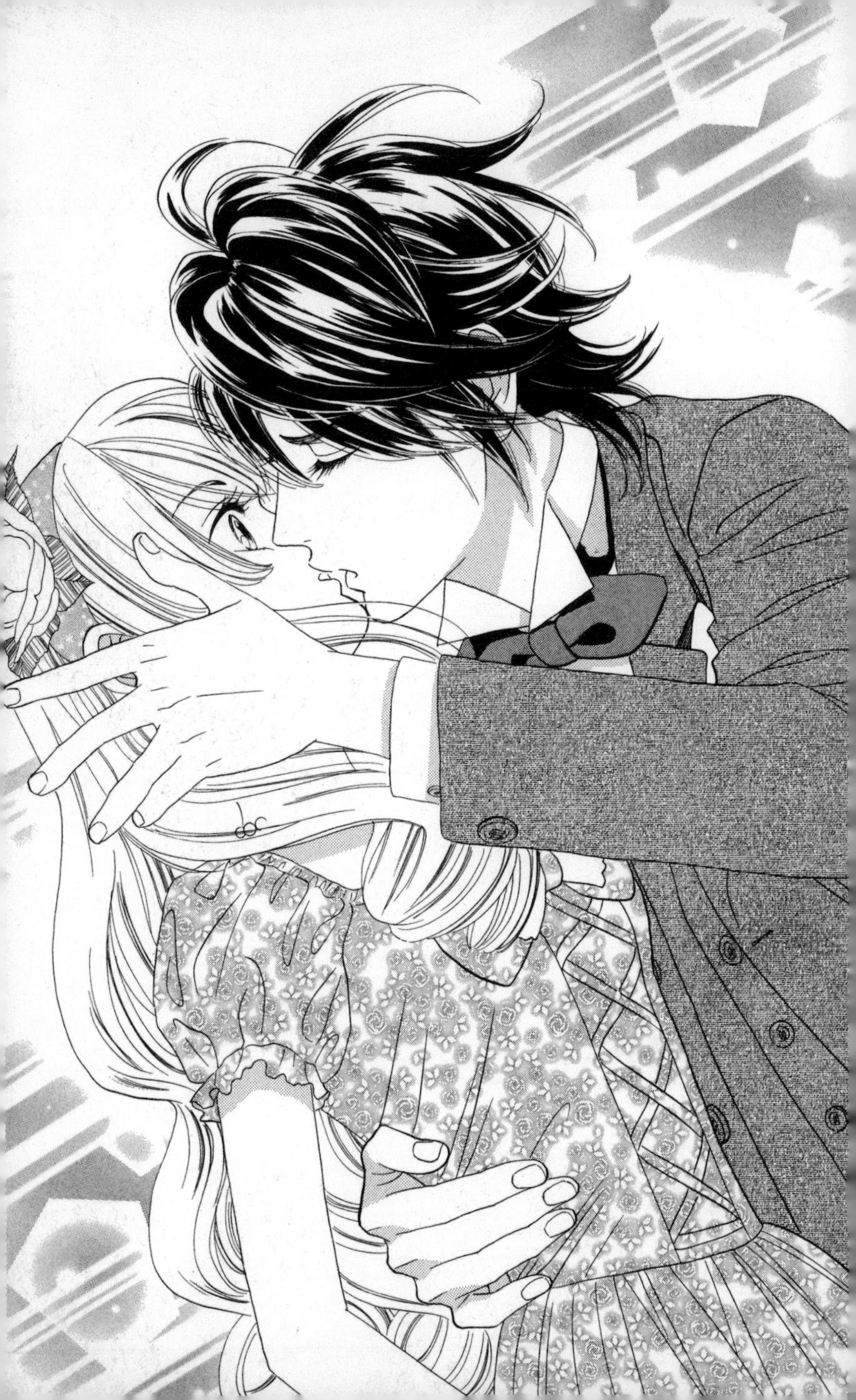

SOICHIRO...?
YOU BELONG TO ME.
THERE'S SOMETHING STRANGE GOING ON INSIDE ME...

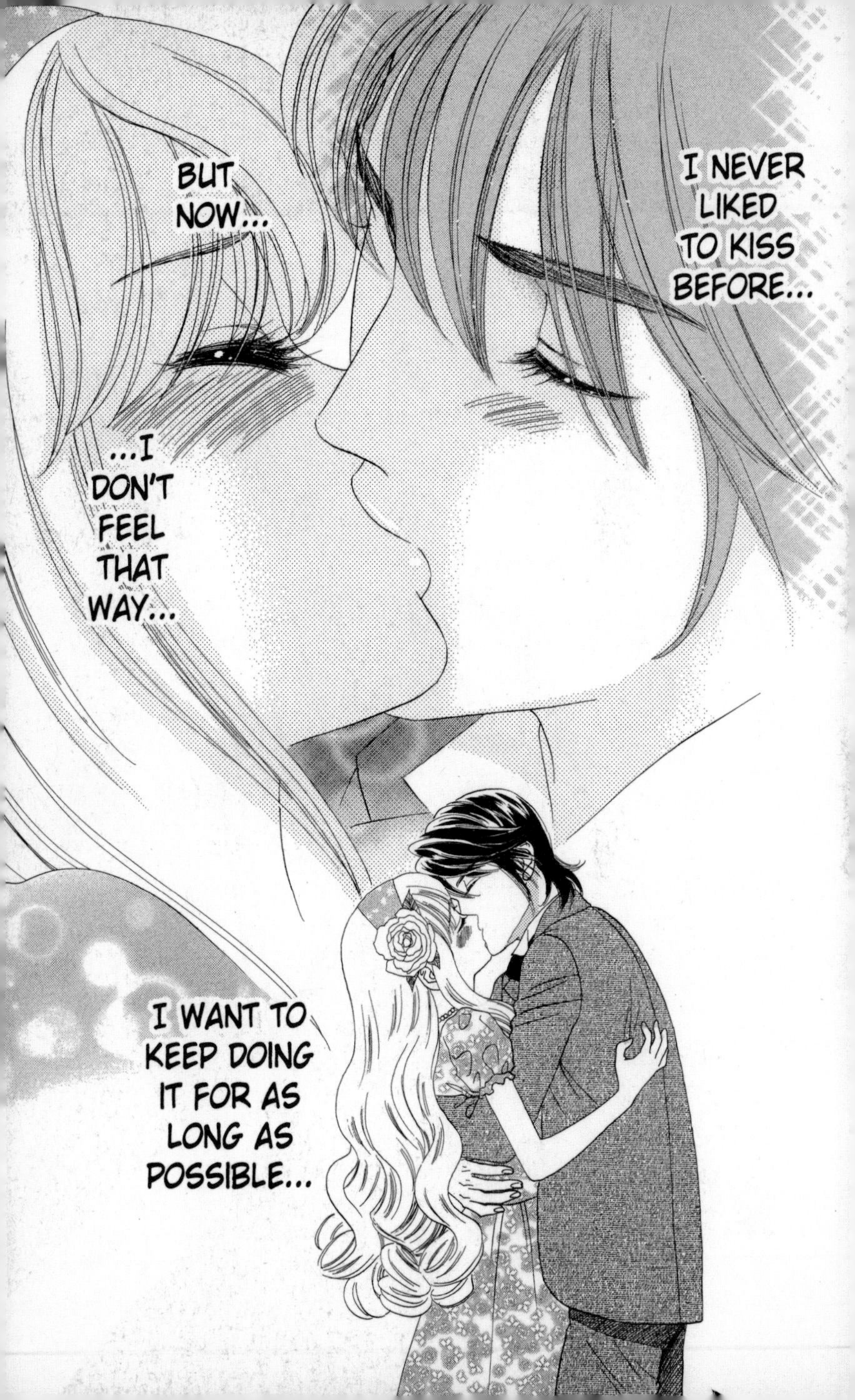
I NEVER LIKED TO KISS BEFORE...
BUT NOW...
...I DON'T FEEL THAT WAY...
I WANT TO KEEP DOING IT FOR AS LONG AS POSSIBLE...

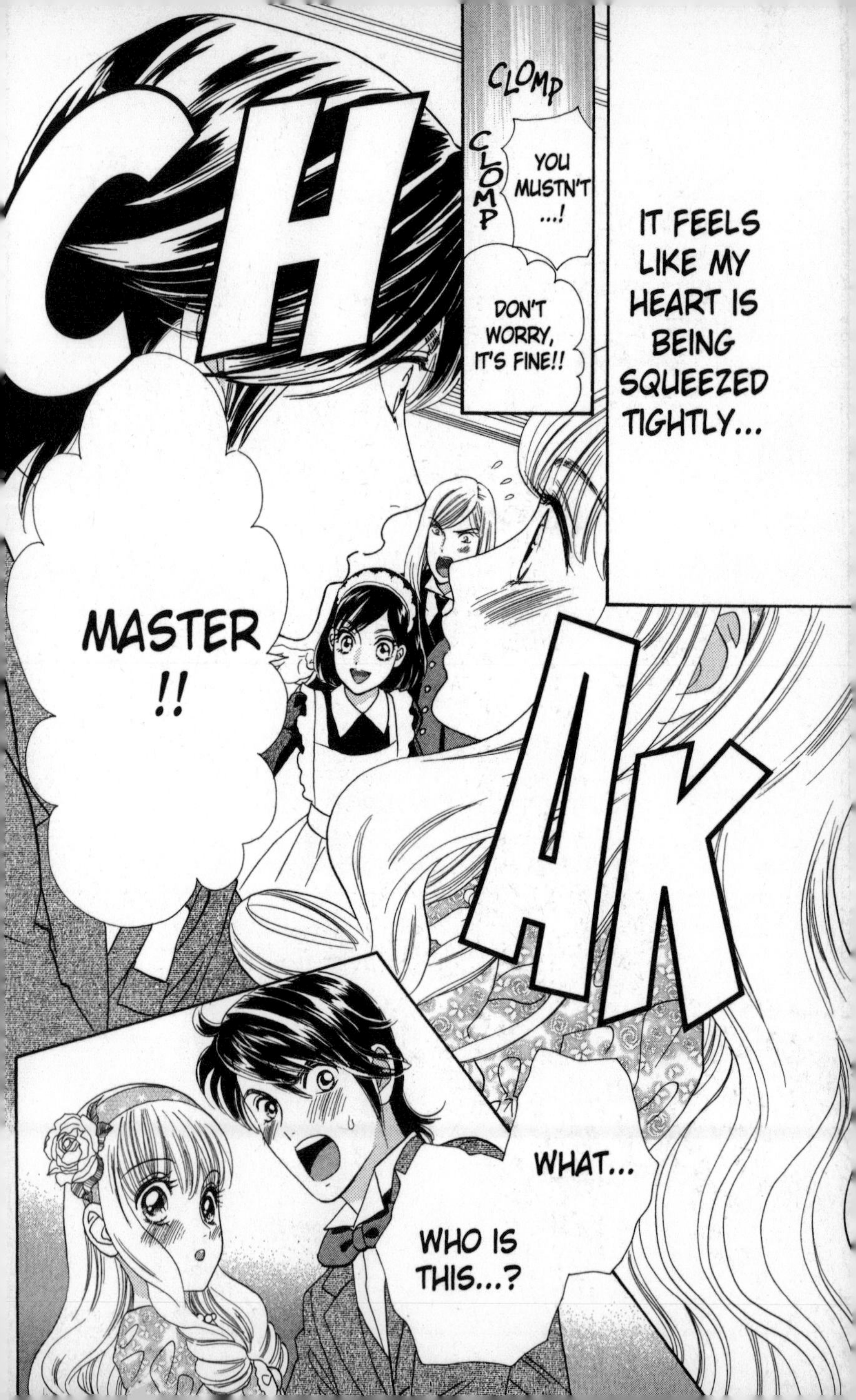
IT FEELS LIKE MY HEART IS BEING SQUEEZED TIGHTLY...
CLOMP
CLOMP
YOU MUSTN'T ...!
DON'T WORRY, IT'S FINE!!
CH
AK
MASTER !!
WHAT...
WHO IS THIS...?

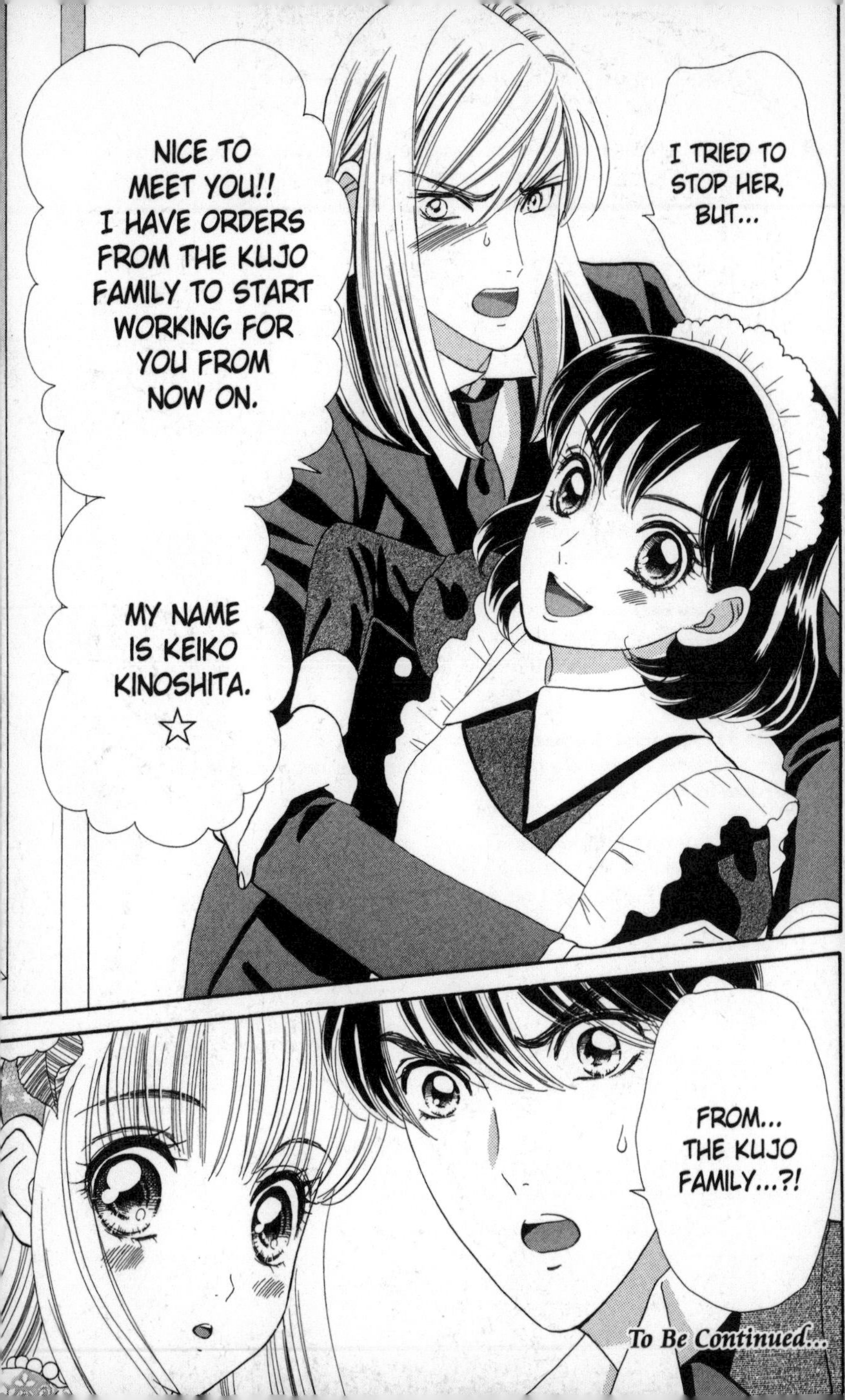
I TRIED TO STOP HER, BUT...
NICE TO MEET YOU!! I HAVE ORDERS FROM THE KUJO FAMILY TO START WORKING FOR YOU FROM NOW ON.
MY NAME IS KEIKO KINOSHITA. ☆
FROM... THE KUJO FAMILY...?!
To Be Continued...

Glossary

The setting of *Stepping on Roses* plays an important part in the story, as it showcases a unique time of change and transformation in Japan. Check out the notes below to help enrich your reading experience.

Page 36, panel 5: Mother
Soichiro says "mother" here, but the kanji meaning "stepmother" (義母) is used.

Page 67, panel 1: Arranged-marriage portraits
Nozomu's father is handing him *omiai shashin*, or formal portraits of prospective marriage partners.

Page 100, panel 5: Inari-zushi
A type of traditional sushi in which deep-fried tofu pouches are filled with vinegared rice.

Page 102, panel 2: Shogi
A Japanese board game similar to chess where the object of the game is to capture the opponent's king. Each player has twenty pieces.

Page 111, panel 3: Father
Miu addresses Nozomu's father as "father," but the kanji used is for "father-in-law" (義父).

Page 128, panel 1: Yokohama
A major port city located south of Tokyo, Yokohama is also the capital city of Kanagawa Prefecture. Yokohama's port was one of the first to be opened to foreign trade.

Since the story is a little depressing, I try to draw the illustrations and title pages as cheerful looking as possible. I'd been drawing kimono continuously until this series, so I'm having a hard time getting used to drawing Western clothes. Dresses are a lot of fun to draw, but suits are hard... I still need to practice a lot.

–Rinko Ueda

Rinko Ueda is from Nara Prefecture. She enjoys listening to the radio, drama CDs and Rakugo comedy performances. Her works include *Ryo*, a series based on the legend of Gojo Bridge; *Home*, a story about love crossing national boundaries; and *Tail of the Moon (Tsuki no Shippo)*, a romantic ninja comedy.

STEPPING ON ROSES
Vol. 3
Shojo Beat Edition

STORY AND ART BY
RINKO UEDA

Translation & Adaptation/Tetsuichiro Miyaki
Touch-up Art & Lettering/Mark McMurray
Design/Yukiko Whitley
Editor/Amy Yu

VP, Production/Alvin Lu
VP, Sales & Product Marketing/Gonzalo Ferreyra
VP, Creative/Linda Espinosa
Publisher/Hyoe Narita

Published by VIZ Media, LLC
P.O. Box 77010
San Francisco, CA 94107

10 9 8 7 6 5 4 3 2 1
First printing, October 2010

www.viz.com
www.shojobeat.com